Rational Choice and Criminal Behavior

Recent Research and Future Challenges

Current Issues in Criminal Justice

Rational Choice and Criminal Behavior

Recent Research and Future Challenges

Edited by
Alex R. Piquero
and
Stephen G. Tibbetts

Routledge
New York & London / 2002

Published in 2002 by
Routledge
29 West 35th Street
New York, NY 10001

Routledge is an imprint of the Taylor & Francis Group

10   9   8   7   6   5   4   3   2   1

Library of Congress Cataloging-in-Publication Data
Rational choice and criminal behavior : recent research and future
challenges / Alex R. Piquero and Stephen G. Tibbetts, editors.
        p. cm. — (Current issues in criminal justice)
Includes bibliographical references and index.
ISBN 0-8153-3678-0
1. Criminal psychology. 2. Criminology. 3. Decision making. 4.
Choice (Psychology) I. Piquero, Alexis Russell. II. Tibbetts, Stephen
G.
III. Current issues in criminal justice (Routledge (Firm))
HV6080.R28 2001
364—dc21   00-069039

Printed on acid-free, 250-year-life paper.
Manufactured in the United States of America.

This book is dedicated to our parents,
Jorge and Nelly Piquero
and
Stephen and Jane Tibbetts
All that is good in us comes from them.

Contents

Acknowledgments

We would like to thank Michael Blankenship who approached us with the idea of putting together a reader on rational choice theory. At Routledge, we would like to thank Amy Shipper, Stefanie Forster, and Tom Wang. We would like to extend a special thanks to the contributors to this volume. Operating under tight deadlines amid an already hectic schedule, they went beyond the call of duty and put together excellent essays. Without their efforts, there is no book. Finally, we would like to thank several colleagues who have helped us over the years, especially the faculty at the University of Maryland, where we spent our graduate careers, as well as the faculties of the University of Florida (Alex) and California State University, San Bernardino (Stephen). A special thank you goes to Raymond Paternoster who provided a spark within each of us to study the rational choice perspective. Throughout the years, he has been and continues to be a model scholar, teacher, and friend.

RATIONAL CHOICE AND CRIMINAL BEHAVIOR

Chapter 1

Individual Propensities and Rational Decision-Making: Recent Findings and Promising Approaches

Stephen G. Tibbetts and Chris L. Gibson

THE CURRENT STATUS OF RATIONAL CHOICE THEORY

A significant portion of the studies on rational choice theory in the late 1980s and early 1990s dealt with integrating perspectives that emphasize persistent individual differences with traditional decision making models that focus on hedonistic or "expected utility" factors (i.e., perceived costs and benefits). However, there has been a notable decline in the late 1990s in the amount of research and theorizing on the rational choice perspective in the criminological literature. In order to ensure that rational choice perspectives are included in future investigations, it should be emphasized that such models of behavior are valid and, furthermore, tend to complement models that highlight individual propensities in the etiology of offending. Although a great deal of progress has been made toward the integration of these two types of perspectives, future studies could be improved by utilizing more valid and delineated measures, as well as developing more fully specified theoretical models. In this chapter, we review some of the successful attempts to merge these two viewpoints, and we present a number of issues that should be addressed by future investigations.

The popularity and acceptance of rational choice theory in criminological thought, which was at least partly the consequence of a resurgence of interest in the traditional theory of deterrence in the 1970s, appears to be fading. Despite a rapid rise in research and theorizing on rational choice theory that began in the mid-1980s and continued through the mid-1990s, the number of studies examining rational choice factors has decreased substantially in the past few years. This conclusion is largely based on personal observations, and more objectively on the number of entries indexed in

3

Criminal Justice Abstracts under a "words anywhere" search for *rational choice*. The decision to use a "words anywhere" search was made because many studies do not include the words "rational choice" in their title; however, it is likely that a test of rational choice theory or some of its key variables would include such words somewhere in its abstract. Separate searches were done for each year from 1981 to 1998 (the last year for which data were complete), as well as for one group of years (1968–1980) that were not expected to have many references to "rational choice." The findings are reported in Table 1.

Table 1. Number of Items Found In Search for "Rational Choice" Words Anywhere in Criminal Justice Abstracts by Year

Year(s)	Items
1968–1980	4
1981	3
1982	2
1983	2
1984	1
1985	1
1986	18
1987	5
1988	3
1989	7
1990	7
1991	5
1992	6
1993	20
1994	14
1995	12
1996	10
1997	7
1998	3

The number of items found each year in Criminal Justice Abstracts shows that modern rational choice theory was not found much in the extant criminological literature until the mid-1980s. In 1986, largely due to the publication of Cornish and Clarke's *The Reasoning Criminal: Rational Choice Perspectives on Offending*, the theory drew a great deal of attention and established a framework for a number of subsequent studies. The late 1980s and early 1990s exhibited a relative growth in the amount of research on rational choice theory, albeit more modest than the attention given to other theories (e.g., social control, differential association/reinforcement, etc.). The peak of rational choice theory in the criminological literature took place between 1993 and 1996, in which fifty-six items were indexed. Over the past couple of years, this peak has declined dramatically to the point of only three items being indexed in 1998.

Although some may claim that this decrease is simply due to random fluctuations in the number of items, we disagree due to the fact that a similar search of the word "deterrence" as a word anywhere in Criminal Justice Abstracts showed a similar trend. Specifically, the search showed that studies on deterrence increased dramatically from the early 1970s to a peak in mid-1980s, which dropped off slightly but remained rather steady until the mid-1990s. Between 1996 and 1998, there were far fewer studies indexed under deterrence than in any other three-year period since 1972–1974. Thus, it appears that economic decision-making models of criminality are on the decline, at least to the extent that the popularity or acceptance of theories are reflected by their presence in the criminological literature indexed by Criminal Justice Abstracts.

Another, perhaps more direct, measure of the interest in and acceptance of rational choice theory is found in recent studies (Ellis & Hoffman 1988; Ellis & Walsh 1999; Walsh & Ellis 1999) that have surveyed criminologists about what they believe is most important in causing crime. The more recent of these studies (Walsh & Ellis 1999) showed that of 138 criminologists, only one respondent chose Classical theory (i.e., deterrence, free will) as their favored theory. Rational choice theory (or an equivalent) did not make the list of twenty-three theories. Furthermore, the authors reported mean responses of the criminologists regarding a variety of causal factors by separating them into two groups: important causes and unimportant causes. The causal factor most associated with rational choice theory ("punishment too lenient") was considered "unimportant" by the respondents and was near the bottom of the list.

It is interesting to note that the second most favored theory on the list of twenty-three was low self-control (Walsh & Ellis 1999), which has become the most popular of the individual propensity theories for scientific investigation and theoretical debate. Notably, the most favored theory on the list was social control, which tends to be classified as a perspective that emphasizes persistent individual differences (see Bernard & Snipes 1996). Additionally, Walsh and Ellis (1999) report that some of the most important causal factors reported by criminologists included "impulsiveness," "poor discipline practices," "lack of supervision," and "unstable family life." These are all key constructs in the *A General Theory of Crime* (Gottfredson & Hirschi 1990) that emphasizes the development of individual differences on levels of self-control, and claims that low self-control is the most significant causal factor in criminality. Given these findings, it appears that a good strategy for attempting to raise the popularity and/or acceptance of rational choice theory would be to continue to make attempts to integrate individual propensities, such as low self-control, with rational choice models of offending.

Bernard and Snipes (1996) argue that there are two categories of criminological theories: structure/process and individual difference theories. To simplify their argument to the relevant issue, these theorists claim that some perspectives, such as rational choice theory, assume criminals are "normal" in that they are comparable to noncriminals in the processes by which they interact with the immediate environment and in the motives that direct their reactions to the environment. On the other hand, individual difference theories assume that variations in characteristics of persons predict the probabilities that a particular individual will engage in criminal activity. Additional contrasting assumptions of individual difference theories are that the dispositions or characteristics of the person explain his/her behavior more so than social or other environmental/situational factors, and that criminals can be distinguished from noncriminals based on these measurable individual characteristics (Bernard & Snipes 1996).

Although many theorists suggest that these two perspectives are distinctly separate, recent studies (e.g., Nagin & Paternoster 1993, Piquero & Tibbetts 1996) have shown that these two perspectives complement one another and that measures of both must be included in estimated models of offending to attain a fully specified representation of behavior. Even Bernard and Snipes (1996) claim that these two theoretical orientations are not mutually exclusive; rather, the two perspectives maintain that, in a given situation, people with certain characteristics are more likely to engage in crime than people without such characteristics, largely due to their difference in perceptions of expected costs and benefits regarding the activity in the given circumstances. This position was supported by a recent investigation (Jeffery & Zaham 1993) that showed that rational choice theory is based upon the interaction between the mind and the environment.

Such a position is not new. In fact, the early seminal work by Walter Reckless (1961; see also, Toby 1957) noted that inner containment consisted mainly of one's disposition or level of self-control, while outer containment represents the structural buffer in the person's immediate social world (e.g., perceptions of expected sanctions, shame, etc.) that plays a significant role in holding the person within certain bounds. Such a position suggests that persistent individual differences play a significant role in offending, but just as important is the influence of more proximate factors, particularly rational choice/utility-based variables. Furthermore, several recent studies have noted the importance of integrating rational choice with other perspectives (Cornish 1993; Fattah 1993; Trasler 1993). Fortunately, there are a number of recent examples of such attempts to integrate individual propensities and rational decision making, some of which we will now review.

STUDIES INTEGRATING INDIVIDUAL PROPENSITIES AND RATIONAL CHOICE THEORY

Given the relatively short time period that rational choice models of offending have appeared in the criminological literature, there are quite a few studies that have incorporated measures of persistent individual characteristics in their frameworks. In the early 1980s, even before an emphasis on individual propensities toward deviance was established, some scholars noted that rational choice models could be improved by developing theoretical models that account for the multidimensionality of individual differences (Shapiro & Votey 1984). Still, most of the studies on rational choice factors and investigations of individual dispositions were explored separately. It was not until the publication of Wilson and Herrnstein's *Crime and Human Nature* (1985) and Gottfredson and Hirschi's *A General Theory of Crime* (1990), that rational choice and deterrence researchers began to realize the importance of incorporating time-stable individual differences in their theoretical frameworks.

As a result, the early- to mid-1990s showed a notable increase in the number of studies that examined the effects of rational choice variables on a variety of deviant behaviors while controlling for, or as a function of, individual propensities. Birkbeck and LaFree (1993) argued that theories of crime emphasizing situational circumstances, such as rational choice models, should be united with theories of criminality that emphasize time-stable individual propensities (e.g., low self-control, neuropsychological deficits, etc). For example, a study by Nagin and Paternoster (1993) demonstrated that direct effects of situational factors, such as the attractiveness and ease of the crime targets as well as perceived costs and benefits of the acts, remained significant even after controlling for self-control. Other noted studies (Gibbs & Giever 1995) have also concluded that while individual levels of self-control have consistent effects on deviant behavior, the effects of rational choice variables (e.g., perceived sanctions, perceived pleasure) have an independent direct effect on offending. In fact, most of the studies that have included both situational/utility-based measures and estimates of individual propensities (e.g., Nagin & Paternoster 1993, Piquero & Tibbetts 1996, Tibbetts 1997a) have found that variables representing both perspectives have significant influences on deviant behavior even when controlling for the effects of the other factors.

Some studies have gone beyond a simple examination of the relative direct effects of rational choice factors and individual propensities. Importantly, many of the rational choice studies of the mid-1990s have examined the conditioning or interactive effects of individual dispositions and other personal traits and characteristics. In a study of intentions to commit white-collar crime, Paternoster and Simpson (1996) found that respondents' personal moral beliefs were a very important source of inhibition: when moral inhibitions were high, considerations of the costs and benefits of corporate crime were unimportant. However, when these moral inhibitions were weak, threats of both formal and informal sanctions had much greater effects. The authors concluded that models of crime should include both instrumental components of crime (i.e., rational choice factors) as well as deontological factors (i.e., individual levels of morality). Sharpe (1994) applied corporate performance crime to rational choice theory (as well as strain and social learning theories) and found support for rational choice variables in predicting structurally coerced action as a moral concept by individuals in their decision making. Sharpe found that a vital ingredient was an encroachment on some moral right. Similar results were observed in a study that found that a rational choice model explained significantly more variation in student deviance at low levels of moral beliefs than at high levels (Tibbetts 1997b).

Thus, recent evidence has shown that individual differences on levels of moral beliefs mediate the effects of rational choice variables; specifically, individual perceptions of costs and benefits have a stronger effect at lower levels of moral beliefs than at higher levels. Such findings make sense in light of recent findings (e.g., Wright, Caspi, Moffitt, & Silva 1999) that demonstrate that the effects of more proximate variables tend to have more of an effect when the level of time-stable variables, such as self-control and/or moral beliefs, are low or weak (for further explanation, see Paternoster & Simpson 1993; Wright et al., 1999).

Piquero and Tibbetts (1996) estimated structural equation models predicting offending that supported the existence of both direct and indirect effects of situational characteristics (e.g., situational shame and perceived pleasure) and time-stable individual differences (e.g., low self-control and moral beliefs). To clarify, a significant portion of the effects of individual propensities were indirect via more situational rational choice variables. Furthermore, the effects of situational factors were affected by other rational choice factors (e.g., perceived pleasure significantly influenced perceived shame), as well as by individual propensities (e.g., levels of low self-control influenced perceptions of pleasure and shame). The authors (1996, 505) concluded that "time-stable variables . . . will always precede and influence the situational variables," and, thus, both must be included in rational choice models of offending behavior. Such an observation supports the original position of Reckless (1961) that both inner and outer containment are essential in any understanding of criminality. This conclusion is also consistent with Bernard and Snipes' (1996) claim that both process and individual propensity theories complement each other and both perspectives must be considered in order to attain a full understanding of deviant behavior.

Additionally, studies have shown that individual propensities and rational choice variables can account for the influence of demographic variables on deviant behavior. For example, Nagin and Paternoster (1993) found that the effects of demographic variables were relatively weak compared to rational choice factors and individual traits. Furthermore, some studies have shown that the effects of demographic variables are accounted for by rational choice variables. Tibbetts and Herz (1996) and Tibbetts (1997c) demonstrated that the higher likelihood of males to commit deviant acts was accounted for by gender differences in levels of perceived shame of the activity. Both of these studies included measures of individual propensities, such as low self-control and moral beliefs, as well as rational choice measures. Specifically, the well-established observation that males offend more than females can, at least to a large extent, be explained by the lower levels of perceptions of formal and informal sanctions, as well as the lower levels of self-control, among males.

Consistent with these findings, Grasmick, Blackwell, and Bursik (1993) found that threats of shame accounted for most of the reductions in self-reported drunk driving between 1982 and 1990. Also, studies (Blackwell, Grasmick, & Cochran 1994; Tittle 1980) have shown that the effects of race on criminal offending (e.g., assault, theft, drunk driving) are significantly mediated or accounted for by rational choice variables, particularly perceived formal sanctions and informal punishments (e.g., shame). Specifically, the observed over-representation of African Americans to commit acts of offending can largely be accounted for by racial differences in perceptions of rational choice variables.

Thus, a series of studies has shown that traditionally established demographic correlates of crime (e.g., gender, race, etc.) can be accounted for by variations in their perceptions of costs and benefits of crime, as well as their dispositional levels of attitudinal constructs (e.g., moral beliefs, self-control). Notably, in many of these studies the measures of demographic traits did not account for most of the individual differences in offending, whereas variations in rational choice factors (e.g., perceived shame) explained most of the variation in offending, as well as the effects of demographic or inherent traits (e.g., gender).

A good illustration of the complementary relationship between individual propensities and rational choice variables is provided by a recent study of college student deviance (Tibbetts 1997b). This study estimated the effects of thirty-six independent variables that represented six categories of factors: demographic variables, dispositional measures, personality scales, randomized situational variables, social environment/differential reinforcement measures, and rational choice variables. A model in which the separate indicators were condensed to form indexes of the six categories listed above was estimated on the students' intentions to offend. This model not only explained a majority of the variation in intentions to deviate but more importantly showed that the most influential category on intentions to offend was the rational choice variables, which was followed by disposition measures.

In congruence with other studies (e.g., Blackwell et al. 1994; Nagin & Paternoster 1993; Tibbetts & Herz 1996), the inclusion of rational choice and disposition measures in the estimated model accounted for the influence of demographic factors. Furthermore, subsequent analyses showed that the effects of the independent variables were generally diminished in a model that included only students with high moral beliefs relative to the model that included only students with low moral beliefs, which is consistent with the findings of Paternoster and Simpson (1996) that demonstrated that individuals with strong moral inhibitions were less influenced by rational choice factors than those with weak moral beliefs.

Another notable example of how individual characteristics can condition the effects of rational choice variables is provided by studies on domestic violence (Sherman 1993). Lawrence Sherman has provided a theory, based on empirical evidence, for why certain types of offenders appear to be deterred by sanctions, whereas their counterparts do not. Sherman (1993, 449) compiled evidence showing that not only do criminal sanctions have ". . . opposite or different effects in different social settings, on different kinds of offenders and offenses . . .", but that criminal sanctions also have varying effects at ". . . different levels of analysis." Sherman claimed that this pattern was found in different populations at the individual level of analysis, as well as at the macro level. Specifically, Sherman concluded that criminal sanctions (for crimes such as domestic violence) reduce recidivism among employed men, whereas it increases offending among unemployed men. He also concluded that criminal sanction threats deter older people more effectively than younger people. These observations are consistent with the extant empirical literature and show the conditional effects of traditional rational choice variables (i.e., perceived sanctions).

Finally, some studies have demonstrated that subcultural attitudes can influence the effects of rational choice variables. For example, a recent study by Marongiu and Clarke (1993) found that rational choice factors conditioned the effects of subcultural variables in predicting which individuals would be involved in crimes of ransom kidnapping. The conclusions of this study emphasized the choice-structuring properties of rational choice factors, such as the type and amount of payoff and the perceived risk of the specific episode of kidnapping, as well as the kidnapper's responsiveness to changes in the immediate environment.

In sum, rational choice variables appear to be essential in models of criminal offending. However, not only are individual trait measures equally important for inclusion, but these disposition measures tend to condition or interact with the effects of rational choice variables in individuals' decisions to engage in deviance, as well as across levels of analysis (i.e., micro versus macro measures). Although low self-control and moral beliefs are the primary attitudinal traits that have been investigated until now, it seems that other dispositional measures (e.g., narcissism, pride, neuropsychological deficits, etc.) need to be included in rational choice models of offending. Given the current state of criminological theory and research, it could only be beneficial to the advancement of rational choice theory to incorporate individual traits in utility frameworks. In the next portion of this chapter, we will provide suggestions for such endeavors.

SUGGESTIONS FOR FUTURE STUDIES OF INDIVIDUAL PROPENSITIES AND RATIONAL CHOICE THEORY

Future studies that attempt to incorporate both rational choice and individual disposition measures should focus on certain issues. A limited list of such issues include (1) the validity and/or reliability of measures of both rational choice and individual propensities, (2) the specificity of measures of rational choice measures of traits/states, (3) the statistical and methodological approach toward examining the integration of rational choice and individual propensity variables, and (4) the presentation of new theoretical perspectives that incorporate rational choice variables in frameworks that have not yet been proposed.

The first issue noted—the validity and/or reliability of measures of rational choice and individual propensity variables—can be enhanced by examining the interdisciplinary literature regarding the conceptual evidence of key constructs. For example, the definition of shame and embarrassment used by Grasmick, Bursik, and colleagues (1990, 1993) was inconsistent with the extensive work by psychologists, who have published literally hundreds of articles on the measurement and distinction of these constructs. To illustrate, Grasmick, and Bursik (1990) operationalize "shame" as: The guilt one experiences for doing something one feels is morally wrong. Specifically, Grasmick Bursik, and Arneklev (1993, 43) note that shame is considered "a self-imposed sanction," outside of external acknowledgment, which is not consistent with much of the evidence reported in the psychological literature.

Such an operationalization of shame is counter to extensive research by Tangney (the most renown researcher on shame and other self-conscious emotions) and her colleagues (Tangney 1990, 1995; Tangney, Wagner, Barlow, Marschall, & Gramsow 1996) that has shown that shame can occur in both public and private settings. Furthermore, research by Tangney and her colleagues has shown that guilt and shame are distinct emotions/dispositions (Tangney 1989, 1990; Tangney, Burggraf, & Wagner

1995), and do not necessarily correspond to the other. Thus, the commonly accepted measures of shame and/or guilt in the criminological literature
are not informed by extensive research in the psychological literature.
Therefore, the reported effects of these variables (e.g., shame vs. guilt) is in
question and should be distinguished in future studies.

One of the obvious differences between the criminological and psychological measures of shame, guilt, embarrassment, etc., is that many
criminological studies use one- or two-item measures of personality constructs (Grasmick & Bursik 1990; Nagin & Paternoster 1993; Tibbetts
1997). Multiple-item measures seem to have an advantage at determining
the best estimate of the level of a given attribute. Furthermore, multiple-
item scales of most personality/attitudinal variables that criminologists are
interested in have already been established by psychologists and can be
found in the extant literature. Thus, it follows that criminologists could be
more efficient and more accurate in their specifications of assigning scores
on personality constructs if they utilized the measures already established
by experts and found in the psychological literature. It is vitally important
that criminologists acknowledge these differences in measurement, because
recent studies (e.g., Paternoster & Simpson 1996, Wortley 1996) have
readily adopted Grasmick and Bursik's one-item measures without consideration for the more established measures found in the psychological literature.

This discussion involves a limited number of constructs that have been
misguided in definition and operationalization. Other measures of rational
choice variables (benefits [pride], sanctions, etc.) could be improved by
examining the interdisciplinary literature (psychology, neuropsychology,
economics, etc.) in determining the appropriate measures for developing
multiple-item scales to measure such constructs in rational choice models
of offending. Specifically, trait concepts (i.e., time-stable propensities) have
dominated American differential psychology for more than half a century.
Given their devotion and rigor to studying individual dispositions, the psychological literature is bound to have more established, "fine-tuned" measures of a variety of constructs in which criminologists are becoming interested (e.g., embarrassment, guilt, shame, etc.). Such understanding and
incorporation of measures found in the interdisciplinary scientific literature
regarding these constructs could only be beneficial to the advancement of
rational choice theory. This is true especially in light of recent tests that
have incorporated such established and specified measures in models of
offending, which have led to more explained variation in deviance and,
thus, more support for rational choice theories of criminality.

The next issue noted—that indicators of rational choice variables
should specify the nature of the measure (e.g., state or trait measures)—is
important in determining the situational versus time-stable nature of how

variables affect offending. For example, some factors (e.g., embarrassment, shame, narcissism, anger) may be important as situational variables, but may not be important as dispositional traits in conditioning the effects of other rational choice variables in individuals' decisions to commit crime. Furthermore, trait and state measures of the same construct can have differential effects on offending. An example of this is illustrated by a recent study that examined both state and trait levels of shame (Tibbetts 1997a). This study found that anticipated situational (i.e., state) measures of shame inhibited propensities of offending, but that dispositional (i.e., trait) measures of shame-proneness promoted inclinations to offend. The most important finding of this study for current purposes was the observation that the effects of a dispositional measure of a construct had the opposite effect on criminal offending compared to a state measure of the same construct.

Although only one study, it demonstrates the differential effects of two forms of the same construct that is entirely dependent on the state or trait nature of the measure. While there are very few examples of such distinctions between state and trait measures in the criminological literature, there has been a clear distinction drawn in the psychological literature (see Tangney 1996). Although being aware of potentially different effects of state versus trait measures is important in the advancement of our proposed integrative approach of individual differences and rational choice theories of criminality, it is equally, or more, important to be able to develop measures that accurately tap into trait versus state dimensions. In other words, researchers need to attempt to make these two types of measures as clearly specified as possible.

An example of how state versus trait dimensions can be measured is provided by the psychological testing of self-conscious emotions. Some of the measures of shame- and guilt-proneness are state based (Tangney 1991; Tibbetts 1997a), which base their measures on hypothetical scenarios. On the other hand, some measures of shame and guilt are more trait-based measures that are estimated by adjective lists (Harder & Zalma 1990). The results of empirical studies examining the effects of shame and guilt on offending vary greatly depending on the type of measure employed (see Tangney 1996). Thus, the methodological approach used by studies investigating the impact of individual propensities toward certain emotional affects are not only important, but essential in understanding the etiology of criminal behavior. In order for future studies of rational choice to be fully specified, it is essential that the researchers differentiate the nature of their measures. Specifically, researchers must distinguish between state and trait measures. Ideally, future studies on rational choice will include both state and trait measures; however, if they do not it is vital that they specify the conditions in which the measures are based.

The third major concern for future rational choice studies concerns the methods and statistical applications used for such investigations. Most recent studies of rational choice theory have used hypothetical scenarios that measure the contemporaneous intention to offend (Bachman et al. 1992; Nagin & Paternoster 1993; Piquero & Tibbetts 1996; Tibbetts & Herz 1997). The scenario method, which measures the likelihood of how a respondent would act in a specific situation, is quite distinct from traditional social control/deterrence research in that it uses third person vignettes to measure the outcome variable (i.e., offending decisions). According to Fishbein and Ajzen (1975), this technique of measurement is appropriate because a person's intention to commit an offense is associated with the probability of actually committing the act. Several researchers have shown support for Fishbein and Ajzen's statement (Green 1989; Kim & Hunter 1993).

The scenario method is subject to a few limitations. The most important point is that an expressed intention to offend is not totally synonymous with actual offending behavior. This approach of measurement could be integrated with the cognitive-script approach (Cornish 1994), which places an emphasis on the situational processes involved in decisions to commit offending. However, this method of measurement is conducive to intended behavior while accounting for several important and realistic situational factors. Given added methodological implementations, this form of measurement can control for not only realistic situations but also altered perceptions/conditions, such as being under the influence of alcohol. Being able to consider real drug and/or alcohol use in specific situations would affect how individuals respond in a given situation (i.e., rationally/irrationally), and thus would alter the effects of rational choice factors. Additionally, if multiple scenarios for each respondent are analyzed, advanced quantitative methods (e.g., generalized least squares models, random/fixed analyses) may be needed (see Paternoster & Simpson 1996; Piquero & Rengert 1999).

Such possibilities include the use of experimental settings (e.g., laboratories) that further replicate "real life" situations; however, there may be limitations due to ethical restrictions and institutional review boards. One important example is the recent research by Loewenstein, Nagin, and Paternoster (1997) that examined individuals' decisions to commit rape, in a given scenario, after being exposed to pornographic materials. Their study found that the effect of sexual arousal was not mediated by cognitive mechanisms, which has great implications regarding rational choice factors.

These types of studies are important in developing an enhanced understanding of how individuals make decisions under particular conditions or mental states. Such decisions are significantly influenced by situational/

contextual factors, as well as the mood of the individual (e.g., aroused, angry). These conditional factors are important in developing an understanding of the effects of traditional rational choice variables on offending, but have been largely unexplored.

In regard to other methodological issues, we observe that the small number of studies investigating integrative models of individual propensities and rational choice have been handicapped by their specific focus on less serious or nonviolent offenses such as shoplifting, drunk driving, general theft, and corporate crimes (Nagin & Paternoster 1993; Piquero & Tibbetts 1996; Paternoster & Simpson 1993, 1996; for exceptions, see Bachman, Paternoster, & Ward 1992; Loewenstein, Nagin, & Paternoster 1997; Mazerolle & Piquero 1998; Pallone & Hennessy 1993). Future investigations should focus on other crimes, such as acts of violence, to assess whether there is differentiation in effects across more varied types of offenses. Furthermore, most studies have typically utilized college student samples. As suggested by Hagan and McCarthy (1997), these types of samples have several advantages for criminology. College students are renown for their offending behavior, whether it be nonviolent (e.g., drunk driving, shoplifting, etc.) or violent (e.g., date rape), however, they are not representative of the population of offenders that criminologists often want to make generalizations about, such as serious, recidivistic offenders. Thus, the next step for improved rational choice frameworks may be to target certain populations and/or develop different sampling frames that would be considered more at risk for higher frequencies of serious, violent offending.

Another concern for future rational choice investigations is the statistical modeling techniques that have yet to be employed. Many in the criminological discipline have grown tired with the inclusion of cost and benefit indicators in ordinary least squares (OLS) regression, along with the incorporation of numerous control variables. Future statistical models should attempt to employ structural equation models in order to diagnose what cost/benefit indicators are influential relative to other variables (particularly individual differences), and to estimate the direct and indirect effects of all constructs on offending. A notable example is provided in a study by Piquero and Tibbetts (1996) that found that individual propensities (i.e., low self-control and moral beliefs) exerted both direct effects and indirect effects on offending via perceptions of shame and perceived benefits. Future studies should expand our understanding of such findings, and further specify the causal processes that are involved in decisions to commit deviant activity at varying levels of personality traits.

Beyond structural equation models, investigators should continue to make advanced attempts to examine interaction models, which go beyond the traditional linear framework of rational choice theory. Specifically, researchers should investigate the combined effects of time-stable individual differences with rational choice variables on criminal behavior. This type of analysis will allow researchers to assess whether there are differences in the effects of rational choice variables at varying levels of disposition measures (e.g., IQ). It is likely, for example, that anticipated actions (or non-action) are conditioned by the individuals' levels of certain personality/attitudinal measures.

Future examinations of conditional and interactive effects of rational choice and disposition variables could be complemented by other empirical studies that explore micro-macro level integration within a hierarchal linear model (HLM) structure. One advantage of HLM is the ability to estimate the influence of variables measured at one level (e.g., aggregate level) on the effects of variables measured at another level (e.g., individual level)(Bryk & Raudenbush 1992; Simpson, Paternoster, & Piquero 1998). Although both rational choice theory and disposition perspectives focus on the individual level of analysis, it is possible that macro-level variables (e.g., neighborhood crime rate) may have a significant impact on both the direct and indirect (or even interactive) effects of the micro-level variables. Recent studies (Sherman 1993, Van-Dijk 1994) have revealed the importance of separating the micro and macro effects of rational choice variables.

Furthermore, interactional/conditional effects among different types of rational choice factors should be examined. One example of such conditional effects among rational choice variables is provided by a study of 604 college students' reports of drunk driving and shoplifting (Tibbetts 1994). For both offenses, students who reported low levels of expected pleasure or "fun" in committing drunk driving and shoplifting were more inhibited in their choices to offend by their perceptions of anticipated shame states than those who perceived higher pleasure in offending. Interestingly, the group of students who reported low pleasure in committing drunk driving and shoplifting were also significantly more inhibited by perceived external sanctions (Tibbetts 1994). On the other hand, the subsample of students who reported a higher pleasure in performing the acts specified in the given drunk driving and shoplifting scenarios were not as influenced by perceived external sanctions or anticipated shame (but this group was significantly more affected by their level of low self-control). Thus, it appears that the effects of rational choice variables of cost and benefit have conditional effects in light of the individual levels of other "economic" variables, even while controlling for measures of individual differences (i.e., low self-control). Furthermore, it also seems that the influence of individual dispositions (in this case low self-control) depends on levels of individual perceptions of the costs/benefits of the activity.

Another aspect of individual propensities that rational choice theorists may want to incorporate in tests of rational choice models is an individual's neuropsychological/cognitive functioning, such as differential verbal abilities. For example, Wilson and Herrnstein (1985) concluded that low verbal intelligence contributes to a present-oriented mental style that may foster careless and exploitative behavior. In addition, ample research has shown that the link between verbal intelligence and criminality is one of the most substantial and robust effects in studying criminal behavior (see Hirschi & Hindelang 1977; Moffitt 1990; Moffitt & Henry 1991). According to Moffitt (1997), verbal deficits of antisocial individuals are ubiquitous, in turn, affecting their ability to solve problems in a given situation, retain verbal material, listen and read, and speak and write. Thus, research on neuropsychological deficits does suggest that individuals possessing low verbal intelligence may have difficulty in weighting costs and benefits of committing a criminal act.

Typically, measurement of cognitive deficits (e.g., neuropsychological deficits) has been based on standardized tests which have been criticized for socio-cultural biases. Although these types of tests (e.g., Wechsler Intelligent Score for Children) have been found to be reliable measures, other measures may be more accurate in measuring verbal deficits. For example Adrian Raine (1993) has recently used Positron Emission Tomography (PET) scans to assess neurological deficiencies in violent offenders. Although this method is quite expensive, it would provide a more direct measure of neuropsychological deficiencies.

Given the evidence on verbal deficits, rational choice researchers should see the importance of how this and other neuropsychological/cognitive factors may fit into rational choice models of offending. As mentioned previously, individuals with verbal or other intelligence deficits (see Pallone & Hennessy 1993) may find it difficult to solve problems. For example, individuals with verbal deficits may react differentially when faced with a confrontation that has the potential of escalating into an act of violence. Due to a lack of verbal and problem solving skills, an individual possessing a low (verbal) intelligence could be increasingly more likely to resort to physical means to try to handle a situation, as opposed to verbally working through the stressful episode. Recent evidence (Pallone & Hennessy 1993) shows that neurogenic impulsivity and risk-taking among certain individuals create a "tinderbox" of violence that arises among people who know each other. Pallone and Hennessy claim that this "tinderbox" is explained by individuals self-selecting their environments that contain similar others (i.e., aggressive peers), thereby creating a proximate opportunity for criminal violence. Additionally, individuals possessing neuropsychological/cognitive deficits may lack the ability to consider both long term and short term consequences, as well as the ability to accurately determine the likely costs and/or benefits of their actions.

CONCLUSION

We have shown that the survival of rational choice theory largely depends on its integration with frameworks that emphasize individual propensities, which has been shown to complement both perspectives. We have also demonstrated that although rational choice studies have decreased in number in recent years, it is quite defensible as a theory of behavior and it is critically essential that other criminologists incorporate cost/benefit factors in their models of offending.

A recent perspective proposed by a well-respected criminologist (Raine 1993) made a strong theoretical and empirical argument that criminality is largely a "psychopathological disorder." While we agree with Raine (1993) that many of the relatively few chronic, violent offenders do fit the stereo-typical profile of having psychopathological tendencies that predispose them to commit serious crimes, most typical (i.e., marginal) offenders do not fit into this paradigm. In fact, most people do offend while they are in their mid- to late-teenage years, as well as into their early twenties (Moffitt, 1993). Although the idea of rational choice theory appears counter to Raine's theory, it is our argument that rational choices made in situations of offending are conditional and/or interact with individual propensities. Thus, the two approaches to criminality—individual propensities and rational choice—complement each other and establish a strong symbiotic dependency between these two types of predictors of offending.

In his recent Presidential address in Toronto, David Farrington (2000) stated that the approach to investigating various factors of criminal behavior should include estimation of the "independent, additive, interactive, and sequential effects of risk factors. . . ." We wholeheartedly agree with this statement, and propose that the best way to advance rational choice theory is to examine the effects of perceptions of costs and benefits in relation to other types of predictors, especially individual propensities. Furthermore, a recent article (Jones & Jones 2000) has proposed the contagious nature of antisocial behavior, meaning that people in the immediate social environment contribute to the criminality of individuals' offending behavior. We believe that rational choice models should not only include the time-stable propensities of respondents, but should also seek to incorporate measures of their significant others' propensities. Other recent studies of rational choice theory have emphasized the need to examine the effect of co-offenders (e.g., Pallone & Hennessy 1993, Tremblay 1993). These approaches are unexplored, but provide examples of the key element for what is needed in future rational choice investigations: creativity. Regardless of the given theoretical or methodological approaches taken in advancing our knowledge on rational choice theory, it is imperative that researchers use innovation and originality in their formulations of how perceived utility factors influence human behavior.

One way of expanding rational choice theory is to expand our investigations into ethnographic studies. A recent example of this was provided by a study that applied rational choice principles to the decision-making processes of male street prostitutes (Calhoun & Weaver 1997). A further example of the application of ethnography in the study of rational choice theory was provided by a study of high-rate property offenders (Johnson, Natarajan & Sanabria 1993), which found that such a perspective was "well-suited" for addressing such behavior. Another illustration of new applications to investigating rational choice theory is the incorporation of cognitive scripts for committing offenses (Cornish 1994) that provide more details of the crime-commission process. These scripts provide more attention to the way events and episodes unfold while offering a useful analytical tool for looking at behavioral routines and outcomes for rational, goal-oriented action. The survival of rational choice theory, as well as the advancement of our understanding of the etiology of criminal offending depends on the creativity and persistence of our fellow criminologists in examining individual perceptions of the costs and benefits of criminal activity, as well as the discovery and emphasis of the role of such factors and measurement strategies in various perspectives of criminality.

REFERENCES

Akers, R. 1997. *Criminological Theories: Introduction and Evaluation*, Second Edition. Los Angeles: Roxbury.

Bachman, R., Paternoster, R., & Ward, S. 1992. "The Rationality of Sexual Offending: Testing a Deterrence/Rational Choice Conception of Sexual Assault." *Law and Society Review*, 26, 343–372.

Bernard, T., & Snipes, J. 1996. "Theoretical Integration in Criminology." In Tonry, M. (Ed.), *Crime and Justice: An Annual Review of Research*. Chicago: University of Chicago Press.

Birkbeck, C., & LaFree, G. 1993. "The Situational Analysis of Crime and Deviance." *Annual Review of Sociology*, 19, 113–137.

Blackwell, B., Grasmick, H., & Cochran, J. 1994. "Racial Differences in Perceived Sanction Threat: Static and Dynamic Hypotheses." *Journal of Research in Crime and Delinquency*, 31, 210–224.

Bryk, A., & Raudenbush, S. 1992. "The Dangerous Morality of Managing Earnings." *Management Accounting,* 72, 22–41.

Calhoun, T., & Weaver, G. 1997. "Rational Decision-Making among Male Street Prostitutes." *Deviant Behavior*, 17, 209–227.

Clarke, R. (1995). "Situational Crime Prevention." In Tonry, M., & Farrington, D. (Eds.), *Building a safer society: Strategic approaches to crime prevention*. Chicago: University of Chicago Press.

Cornish, D. 1993. "Theories of Action in Criminology: Learning Theory and Rational Choice Approaches." In Clarke, R., & Felson, M. (Eds.), *Advances in Criminological Theory*, Volume 5 (pp. 351–382). New Brunswick, NJ: Transaction Press.

Cornish, D. 1994. "The Procedural Analysis of Offending and its Relevance for Situational Prevention." In Clarke, R. (Ed.), *Crime Prevention Studies* (pp. 151–196). New York: Criminal Justice Press.

Cornish, D., & Clarke, R. 1986. *The reasoning criminal: Rational choice perspectives on offending*. New York: Springer-Verlag.

Ellis, L., & Hoffman, H. 1990. "Views of Contemporary Criminologists on Causes and Theories of Crime." In Ellis, L., & Hoffman, H. (Eds.), *Crime in biological, social and moral contexts*. Westport, CT: Praeger.

Ellis, L., & Walsh, A. 1999. "Criminologists' Opinions about Causes and Theories of Crime and Delinquency." *The Criminologist*, 24, 1–4.

Farrington, D. 1999. "Explaining and Preventing Crime: The Globalization of Knowledge–The American Society of Criminology 1999 Presidential Address." *Criminology*, 38, 1–24.

Fattah, E. 1993. "The Rational Choice/Opportunity Perspectives as a Vehicle for Integrating Criminological and Victimological Theories." In Clarke, R., & Felson, M. (Eds.), *Advances in Criminological Theory*, Volume 5 (pp. 225–258). New Brunswick, NJ: Transaction Press.

Fishbein, M., & Ajzen, I. 1975. *Belief, attitudes, intention, and behavior*. Reading, MA: Addison-Wesley.

Gibbs, J., & Giever, D. 1995. "Self-Control and its Manifestations among University Students: An Empirical Test of Gottfredson and Hirschi's General Theory." *Justice Quarterly*, 12, 231–255.

Gottfredson, M., & Hirschi, T. 1990. *A General Theory of Crime*. Stanford: Stanford University Press.

Grasmick, H., & Bursik, R. 1990. "Conscience, Significant Others, and Rational Choice: Extending the Deterrence Model." *Law and Society Review*, 24, 837–861.

Grasmick, H., Blackwell, B., & Bursik, R. 1993. "Changes over Time in Gender Differences in Perceived Risk of Sanctions." *Law and Society Review*, 27, 679–705.

Grasmick, H., Bursik, R., & Arneklev, B. 1993. "Reduction in Drunk Driving as a Response to Increased Threats of Shame, Embarrassment, and Legal Sanctions." *Criminology*, 31, 41–67.

Green, D. 1989. "Measures of Illegal Behavior in Individual-Level Deterrence Research." *Journal of Research in Crime and Delinquency*, 26, 253–275.

Hagan, J., & McCarthy, B. 1997. *Mean streets: Youth crime and home-lessness*. New York: Cambridge University Press.

Harder, D. W., & Zalma, A. 1990. "Two Promising Shame and Guilt Scales: A Construct Validity Comparison." *Journal of Personality Assessment*, 55, 729–745.

Hirschi, T., & Hindelang, M. 1977. "Intelligence and Delinquency." *American Sociological Review*, 42, 571–587.

Jeffery, C., & Zahm, D. 1993. "Crime Prevention through Environmental Designs, Opportunity Theory, and Rational Choice Models." In Clarke, R., & Felson, M. (Eds.), *Advances in Criminological Theory*, Volume 5 (pp. 323–350). New Brunswick, NJ: Transaction Press.

Johnson, B., Natarajan, M., & Sanabria, H. 1993. "'Successful' Criminal Careers: Toward an Ethnography within the Rational Choice Perspective." In Clarke, R., and Felson, M. (Eds.), *Advances in Criminological Theory*, Volume 5 (pp. 201–224). New Brunswick, NJ: Transaction Press.

Jones, M., & Jones, D. 2000. "The Contagious Nature of Antisocial Behavior." *Criminology*, 38, 25–46.

Kim, M., & Hunter, J. 1993. "Relationships among Attitudes, Behavioral Intentions, and Behavior: A Meta-analysis of Past Research." *Communications Research*, 20, 331–364.

Loewenstein, G., Nagin, D., & Paternoster, R. 1997. "The Effect of Sexual Arousal on Expectations of Sexual Forcefulness." *Journal of Research in Crime and Delinquency*, 34, 443–473.

Marongiu, P., & Clarke, R. 1993. "Ransom Kidnapping in Sardinia: Subcultural Theory and Rational Choice." In Clarke, R., & Felson, M. (Eds.), *Advances in Criminological Theory*, Volume 5 (pp. 179–200). New Brunswick, NJ: Transaction Press.

Mazerolle, P., & Piquero, A. 1998. "Linking Exposure to Strain with Anger: An Investigation of Deviant Adaptions." *Journal of Criminal Justice,* 26, 195–213.

Moffitt, T. 1990. "The Neuropsychology of Delinquency: A Critical Review of Theory and Research." In Morris, N., & Tonry, M. (Eds.), *Crime and justice: An Annual review of research*. Chicago: University of Chicago Press.

Moffitt, T. 1993. "Adolescence-limited and Life-course Persistent Antisocial Behavior: A Developmental Taxonomy." *Psychological Review,* 100, 674–701.

Moffitt, T. 1997. "Neuropsychology, Antisocial Behavior, and Neighborhood Context." In McCord, J. (Ed.), *Violence and childhood in the inner-city*. New York: Cambridge University Press.

Moffitt, T., & Henry, B. 1991. "Neuropsychological Studies of Juvenile Delinquency and Juvenile Violence." In Milner, S. (Ed.), *The Neuropsychology of Aggression*. Boston: Kluwer Academic Publisher.

Nagin, D., & Paternoster, R. 1993. "Enduring Individual Differences and Rational Choice Theories of Crime." *Law and Society Review*, 27, 467–496.

Niggli, M. 1994. "Rational Choice Theory and Crime Prevention." *Studies on Crime and Crime Prevention*, 3, 83–103.

Pallone, N., & Hennessy, J. 1993. "Tinderbox Criminal Violence." In Clarke, R., & Felson, M. (Eds.), *Advances in Criminological Theory*, Volume 5 (pp. 127–158). New Brunswick, NJ: Transaction Press.

Paternoster, R., & Simpson, S. 1993. "A Rational Choice Theory of Corporate Crime." In Clarke, R., & Felson, M. (Eds.), *Advances in Criminological Theory*, Volume 5 (pp. 37–58). New Brunswick, NJ: Transaction Press.

Paternoster, R., & Simpson, S. 1996. "Sanction Threats and Appeals to Morality: Testing a Rational Choice Model of Corporate Crime." *Law and Society Review*, 30, 378–399.

Piquero, A., & Rengert, G. 1999. "Studying Deterrence with Active Residential Burglars: A Research Note." *Justice Quarterly*, 16, 451–472.

Piquero, A., & Tibbetts, S. 1996. "Specifying the Direct and Indirect Effects of Low Self-control and Situational Factors in Offenders' Decision Making: Toward a More Complete Model of Rational Offending." *Justice Quarterly*, 13, 481–510.

Raine, A. 1993. *The psychopathology of crime: Criminal behavior as a clinical diagnosis*. San Diego, CA: Academic Press.

Reckless, W. 1961. "A New Theory of Delinquency and Crime." *Federal Probation*, 25, 42–46.

Shapiro, P., & Votey, H. 1984. "Deterrence and Subjective Probabilities of Arrest: Modeling Individual Decisions to Drink and Drive in Sweden." *Law and Society Review*, 18, 583–604.

Sharpe, A. 1994. "Corporate Performance Crime as Structurally Coerced Action." *Australian and New Zealand Journal of Criminology*, 28, 73–92.

Sherman, L. 1993. "Defiance, Deterrence, and Irrelevance: A Theory of the Criminal Sanction." *Journal of Research in Crime and Delinquency*, 30, 445–473.

Simpson, S., Paternoster, R., & Leeper Piquero, N. 1998. "Exploring the Micro-Macro Link in Corporate Crime Research." *Research in the Sociology of Organizations*, 15, 35–68.

Tangney, J. 1989. "A Qualitative Assessment of Phenomenological Differences between Shame and Guilt." Poster presented at the meetings of the American Psychological Association, New Orleans, August 1989.

Tangney, J. 1990. "Assessing Individual Differences in Proneness to Shame and Guilt: Development of the Self-Conscious Affect and Attribution Inventory." *Journal of Personality and Social Psychology*, 59, 102–111.

Tangney, J. 1995. "Shame and Guilt in Interpersonal Relationships." In Tangney, J., & Fischer, K. (Eds.), *Self-conscious emotions: Shame, guilt, embarrassment, and pride* (Pp. 114–139). New York: Guilford Press.

Tangney, J. 1996. "Conceptual and Methodological Issues in the Assessment of Shame and Guilt." *Behavioral Research Therapy*, 34, 741–754.

Tangney, J., Burggraf, S., & Wagner, P. 1995. "Shame-proneness, Guilt-proneness, and Psychological Symptoms." In Tangney, J., & Fischer, K. (Eds.), *Self-conscious emotions: Shame, guilt, embarrassment, and pride*. New York: Guilford Press.

Tangney, J., Wagner, P., Barlow, D., Marschall, D., & Gramsow, R. 1996. "The Relation between Shame and Guilt to Constructive vs. Destructive Responses to Anger across the Lifespan." *Journal of Personality and Social Psychology*, 70, 797–809.

Tangney, J., Wagner, P., Gavlas, J., & Gramzow, R. 1991. The Test of Self-Conscious Affect for Adolescents (TOSCA-A). Fairfax, VA: George Mason University.

Tibbetts, S. 1994. "The Effects of Shame on Intentions to Offend: A Theoretical Revision and Test." Unpublished masters thesis, University of Maryland, College Park.

Tibbetts, S. 1997a. "Shame and Rational Choice in Offending Decisions." *Criminal Justice and Behavior*, 24, 234–255.

Tibbetts, S. 1997b. "College Student Perceptions of Utility and Intentions of Test Cheating." Unpublished doctoral dissertation, University of Maryland, College Park.

Tibbetts, S. 1997c. "Gender Differences in Students' Rational Decisions to Cheat." *Deviant Behavior*, 18, 393–414.

Tibbetts, S., & Herz, D. 1996. "Gender Differences in Factors of Social Control and Rational Choice." *Deviant Behavior*, 17, 183–208.

Tittle, C. 1980. *Sanctions and social deviance*. New York: Praeger.

Toby, J. 1957. "Social Disorganization and Stake in Conformity: Complimentary Factors in the Predatory Behavior of Hoodlums." *Journal of Criminal Law, Criminology, and Police Science*, 48, 12–17.

Trasler, G. 1993. "Conscience, Opportunity, Rational Choice, and Crime." In Clarke, R., & Felson, M. (Eds.), *Advances in Criminological Theory*, Volume 5 (pp. 305–322). New Brunswick, NJ: Transaction Press.

Tremblay, P. 1993. "Routine Acts and Rational Choice." In Clarke, R., & Felson, M. (Eds.), *Advances in Criminological Theory*, Volume 5 (pp. 17–36). New Brunswick, NJ: Transaction Press.

Van-Dijk, J. 1994. "Understanding Crime Rates: On the Interactions between the Rational Choice of Victims and Offenders." *British Journal of Criminology*, 34, 105–121.

Walsh, A., and Ellis, L. 1999. "Political Ideology and American Criminologists' Explanations for Criminal Behavior." *The Criminologist*, 24, 1 & 14.

Wilson, J., & Herrnstein, R. 1985. *Crime and human nature*. New York: Simon and Schuster.

Wortley, R. 1996. "Guilt, Shame and Situational Crime Prevention." In Homel, R. (Ed.), *The politics and practice of situational crime prevention* (pp. 115–132). New York: Criminal Justice Press.

Wright, B., Caspi, A., Moffitt, T., & Silva, P. 1999. "Low Self-control, Social Bonds, and Crime: Social Causation, Social Selection, or Both?" *Criminology*, 37, 479–514.

Chapter 2

Rationality and Corporate Offending Decisions

Sally S. Simpson, Nicole Leeper Piquero,
and Raymond Paternoster

INTRODUCTION

Based upon the same utilitarian philosophy as the deterrence doctrine, rational choice theory was introduced into the field of criminology by economists (Becker 1968). The underlying foundation of the theory is based upon the expected utility model found in economic theory which contends that people will make rational decisions based upon the extent to which they expect that choice to maximize their profits or benefits and to minimize their costs or losses (Akers 2000). Therefore, rational choice theory builds on the traditional deterrence model by coupling the perceived rewards or benefits of the act along with its perceived costs (see Pilivian et al. 1986; Grasmick and Bursik 1990; Nagin and Paternoster 1993; Piquero and Tibbetts 1996). *Ceteris paribus*, the theory predicts that offending will occur when the perceived benefits of offending outweigh its perceived costs. Because persons actions are based on their subjective expectations of gain and loss, the rational choice model is a subjective expected utility model of crime (Tuck and Riley 1986).

Three common elements run throughout the many variations of rational choice theory. First, the decision to commit a crime is (at least minimally) rational. Second, because decisions to engage in behavior are believed to be informed decisions, the information needed to make these decisions will vary by specific crime types (Cornish and Clarke 1986). Finally, the decision to offend will be affected by the immediate contextual characteristics of the crime (Cornish and Clarke 1987).

The purpose of this chapter is to review and assess rational choice theory as it applies to corporate crime. Two main questions will guide us in this task: (1) how is our understanding of corporate offending enhanced

25

through the rational choice model and (2) what are the unique challenges to this model posed by the organizational (or corporate) context? In order to pursue these questions, we must first define corporate crime.

DEFINITIONS AND APPLICATIONS

Though varying definitions of corporate crime exist, we favor a parsimonious one. Corporate crime is the conduct of a corporation (or of employees acting on its behalf) which is proscribed and punishable by civil, administrative, or criminal statutes (Sutherland 1949; Clinard and Yeager 1980; Braithwaite 1984:6; Cohen and Simpson 1997). Descriptions of offender and victim characteristics and/or offender motivations that are common to other definitions are purposively excluded because they may unnecessarily restrict the scope of the phenomenon (see research by Calavita and Pontell 1990 and Paternoster and Simpson 1996).[1]

There are many reasons to believe that corporate crime and corporate offending can be understood within a cost-benefit framework (Chambliss 1967; Braithwaite and Geis 1982; Paternoster and Simpson 1993, 1996). First, most corporate executives and managers are not committed to crime as a way of life (Chambliss 1967). They are well-bonded to conventional society (to family, work, and community), generally tending toward conformity in both behaviors and attitudes. Because of these pro-social ties to society, corporate decision-makers have much to lose if they get involved in illegal behavior and/or are apprehended for it. Second, corporate crimes are rarely spontaneous events or driven by emotion (Braithwaite and Geis 1982). Rather, crimes by corporations are seen as calculated and instrumental (Braithwaite and Geis 1982:302) and, as such, require some degree of planning and foresight on the part of the would-be offender (Cornish and Clarke 1986; Wright and Decker 1994). Given these characteristics, the rational actor model can be useful for understanding the situations and conditions under which corporate offending occurs (Lofquist, Cohen, and Rabe 1997). This model also can help to pinpoint the kinds of crime control strategies that should maximize corporate compliance.

RATIONAL CHOICE THEORY OF CORPORATE CRIME

The rational choice perspective assumes that, under conditions of uncertainty, the decision to engage in corporate crime is a function of the perceived costs and benefits of crime relative to the perceived costs and benefits associated with noncrime. Individuals, therefore, are assumed to be sensitive to the consequences of their actions and thus make reasoned judgments after considering the costs and benefits of legal and illegal solutions to problems (Finney and Lesieur 1982; Cohen and Simpson 1997). From this perspective, it is well understood that rationality is bounded by a variety of individual and situational factors that affect how information is comprehended and processed (Simon 1957).

Utility is typically conceptualized by economists as "the personal satisfaction one receives from various pecuniary and nonpecuniary pleasures in life" (Cohen and Simpson 1997:35). Satisfaction can be achieved from an almost endless array of possibilities, but economists emphasize three main sources: (1) monetary income, (2) "quality of life" activities (leisure time, enjoyable activities), and (3) one's reputation and stature among significant others and in the community as a whole (Cohen and Simpson 1997:35). Critics have suggested that the economists' view of utility is overly narrow and, in an attempt to broaden the parameters of the theory, Paternoster and Simpson (1993) developed a rational choice theory of corporate crime that incorporates other factors, such as a "moral dimension" (see, e.g., Etzioni 1988).

In their theory, Paternoster and Simpson (1993:47) present a subjective expected utility model that privileges individuals over organizations as actors and decision-makers yet recognizes that the cost/benefit assessments will incorporate both individual and organizational factors. For instance, influential factors can include: 1) the perceived certainty/severity of formal legal sanctions (for the firm and individual actor), 2) perceived certainty/severity of informal sanctions (stigmatic, attachment, and commitment costs), 3) perceived certainty/severity of loss of self-respect (feel bad or guilty if the illegal act is committed), 4) perceived cost of rule compliance (what will I and/or the company lose if we follow the law), 5) perceived benefits of noncompliance (what will I and/or the company gain if we break the law), 6) moral inhibitions (how wrong is this behavior generally, for me, and for the company), 7) perceived sense of legitimacy/fairness (is the law legitimate; is it fairly applied; is it overly punitive; does it hurt companies like mine), 8) characteristics of the criminal event (crime opportunities, cultural conduciveness, environmental pressures), and 9) the prior offending history of the individual.

EMPIRICAL EVIDENCE

Despite the belief that corporate crime is amenable to deterrence strategies and that both individual and organizational factors influence the etiology of corporate offending, relatively little empirical research has directly tested this presumption. There have been some studies that explore "objective" deterrence—assessing how punishment risks affect offending levels generally (for all market participants) and/or more specifically for prior offenders (e.g., Block, Nold, and Sidek's [1981] study of price-fixing in the white pan bread industry or Simpson and Koper's [1992] research on antitrust recidivism). These studies and others that are comparable (see, Stotland,

Brintnall, L'Heureux, and Ashmore 1980; Lewis-Beck and Alford 1980; Weisburd, Waring, and Cyat 1995) report mixed support for a deterrence model.

In one of the first tests of perceptual deterrence for corporate offenders, Braithwaite and Makkai (1991) interviewed top managers of Australian nursing homes to ascertain whether firm compliance correlated with estimated punishment risks. Using both self-report and official data, additive and multiplicative models of sanction certainty and severity generally were unrelated to regulatory compliance. Based on this application, the authors concluded that the subjective utility model was a "stark failure" (Braithwaite and Makkai 1991: 29). A more rigorous test of the model was conducted three years later using panel data (Makkai and Braitwaite 1994). This study also failed to link compliance with deterrence.

As the above deterrence studies suggest, the traditional deterrence model of corporate offending lacks strong and consistent empirical support.[2] Paternoster and Simpson (1993: 40) suggest that the empirical deficiencies of mere deterrence could stem from model specification problems. Specifically, since both organizations and individual managers may be sanction targets, a better test of deterrence should include the perceived threat of legal actions against each. Moreover, a better rational choice model of corporate offending would include not only formal sanction threats directed toward responsible managers and firms, but a variety of individual and organizational level factors that could promote or inhibit offending. Indeed, much of the theorizing in the corporate crime area assumes that individual and organizational level factors interact to affect the decision-making process, but few have empirically explored these linkages (Sutherland 1949; Aubert 1952; Quinney 1963; Schrager and Short 1978; Gross 1980; Finney and Lesieur 1982; for an exception see Vaughan 1996).

In order to fill this void, Paternoster and Simpson (1996) used a vignette design to assess whether managers' offending intentions (price fixing, bribery, manipulation of sales data, and violation of EPA standards) were affected by individual and firm-level sanction threats (both formal and informal), moral evaluations of the act, and organizational factors. They found that moral considerations were a powerful source of social control, so much so that they condition the effects of more rational factors. Only when moral obligations were weakened was compliance based upon the perceived incentives and costs of the crime. Paternoster and Simpson interpreted their findings to mean that some behaviors are "non-market areas" where moral inhibitions are so predominate that instrumental considerations are simply not salient. Other behaviors are market areas wherein the decision to commit them are influenced by considerations of cost and benefit.

Simpson and her colleagues (1998) further explore the micro-macro link by focusing on individuals' intentions to engage in corporate crimes. Using the same factorial survey described above, the authors found that intentions to offend were predicted by an interplay of individual and organizational factors (Simpson et al. 1998). Two firm-level factors, a criminogenic firm culture (where illegality is commonplace in the firm or where supervisors condone crime by ordering their managers to break the law) along with environmental pressures and pulls toward crime (market and legal constraints on the firm or direct benefits to the company) were found to consistently influence intentions to offend. Most of these factors acted independently on offending decisions, however, there was a significant interaction between corporate culture (the act is common practice in the firm) and one of the firm-level benefits (increased firm revenues). Finally, offending decisions were predicted by how managers thought their career would be affected (positively or negatively), whether it would be fun to commit the crime, and if they believed that significant relationships such as those with family and friends would be negatively impacted.

Overall, tests of Paternoster and Simpson's theory demonstrate that a rational choice model that is broadly conceived—one that includes normative restraints along with individual and firm level costs/benefits—enhances our understanding of how corporate offending decisions may occur. That said, however, there are important challenges to the rational choice model. Among these is the implicit assumption that crime is the intended outcome of some kind of cost-benefit calculus. Vaughan (1996, 1998) points out this flaw when describing the intra- and inter-organizational conditions and circumstances that gave rise to the disastrous *Challenger* launch decision. She contends that not all organizational deviance involves intentional acts of misconduct. Instead, a configuration of professional, occupational, and organizational factors may produce a decision framework in which "risky" decisions fall within the parameters of acceptable and normative behavior. In this situation, crime is not intentional. In fact, illegality (the thought that what one is doing is breaking the law) is not even on the radar screen.

Below, Vaughan's arguments will be discussed in greater detail along with several other challenges to the rational choice model that relate to her work. Specifically, some critics have suggested that varying characteristics and situations (context) of corporations (e.g., size, stability, and executive-team tenure) can affect rationality in strategic decision processes (Fredrickson and Iaquinto 1989; Goll and Rasheed 1997) and that rational choice assumptions are violated when the model is applied to corporate entities instead of individual decision-makers (Metzger and Schwenk 1990). After taking these problems into consideration and in keeping within the tradition of the perspective, we will assess whether the positives gained from this application outweigh the negatives.

CHALLENGES TO THE RATIONAL CHOICE MODEL
Intentionality

In a series of articles, Diane Vaughan (1998, 1999a, 1999b) discusses how organizations, acting in a reasonable and non-deviant manner, can produce sub-optimal results. Essentially, she asserts that "aspects of social organizations typically associated with the bright side also are implicated in the dark side" (Vaughan 1999b:274). In her careful review of the 1986 *Challenger* Launch, Vaughan reconstructs the situated context in which the decision to launch the space shuttle was made. She concludes that decision-makers were not amoral calculators. They were under no economic or political pressure to launch that day (there was no risk in delaying that shuttle—hence there was no "strain"). Instead, she suggests that as problems associated with the launch arose, each was defined and evaluated within work groups who compared it to other problems, one at a time, and against pre-existing definitions of the situation (1998:38). These micro-level decision-making processes were buttressed by structural secrecy (which kept others from successfully challenging the workgroup's definition of the situation) and bureaucratic accountability (going by the book, which didn't leave room for challenging definitions of acceptable risk). As a consequence of this confluence of micro and macro level factors, decision-makers descended into poor judgment while adhering to every rule and procedure.

Vaughan's point is that unintended consequences can emerge from ostensibly rational processes. If outcomes are unintended and unpredictable, what are the implications for the rational actor model? Her position is that rational choice theory falls short. It falls short because organizational decision-making cannot be divorced from its organizational context and the organizational environment (1998:47). The decision process is heavily affected by precedent (organizational culture, history, and structure) and less so by "forward-looking" benefit seeking. Consequently, decisions and outcomes tend to be loosely-coupled, not tightly linked (as rational choice would predict).

The view that the organizational situation and context can affect corporate decision-making is shared by other critics of rational choice. In management theory, for instance, scholars have debated the link between decision rationality and firm performance—with a focus on the mediating effect of the environmental context (see the review by Goll and Rasheed 1997) or on organizational characteristics that can affect decision-making comprehensiveness (Fredrickson and Iaquinto 1989). These arguments are highlighted below.

Organizational Situations/Contexts

There is no doubt that decision-making in corporations is a complex affair. Some decisions, like strategic ones, center around a firm's future direction. Such decisions, most typically, involve multiple actors, extensive information and analyses, along with a formal planning process (although, as noted below, the level of comprehensiveness is apt to vary by organizational and/or market characteristics). Others relate to the day-to-day tasks and problems that arise in the course of doing business. While day-to-day problem solving may not foster the same degree of information collection and assessment as strategic decisions do, some of these problems may be "hot," requiring immediate attention and action. Finally, some organizational decisions are so routinized that little thought is given to them. These decision types are guided formally by standard operating procedures (SOPs) or by intuition (defined by Isenberg as "automatic performance of learned behavior sequences" [1988:530]). In either case, little reflection or assessment of the situation is required of decision-makers unless nonstandard problems arise; even then, managers will search through existing SOPs to try to solve the problem (recall Vaughan's discussion of the *Challenge* launch). As critics point out, SOPs may be a poor fit to the new problem and economically irrational behavior may result (Metzer and Schwenk 1990:352).

Of the above decision types, strategic decisions are the ones most closely associated with rational assessment processes. Yet, studies of organizational decision-making suggest that organizational and environmental factors can affect the degree of comprehensiveness employed in strategic decisions (and thus the amount and quality of information brought to bear in the decision process). Moreover, managers "seldom think in ways that one might simplistically view as 'rational'"—especially when problems are intractable, novel, or complex (Isenberg 1988:526). The longer that managers have been at a company (their tenure) and the more stable the membership on the leadership team, the more likely that habit will guide decision-making (Tushman and Romanelli 1985) and management will be isolated from critical information sources (Fredrickson and Iaquinto 1989). Interaction between team members is also likely to decline as role definitions emerge and stabilize over time.

Organizational and environmental features that affect rationality in strategic decision-making include firm growth and market uncertainty (or dynamism), complexity, and munificence. As firms grow, they shift into a planning mode which requires a more detailed strategic process—more data, analysis, and strategizing. Similarly, as firms stop growing, comprehensiveness decreases (Fredrickson and Iaquinto 1989). Comprehensiveness works against the company in a dynamic environment (decreasing performance) since "data are unavailable, relationships are not obvious, and the future is unpredictable" (Goll and Rasheed 1997:584). On the other hand, comprehensiveness works well in stable environments because the environment is more amenable to predictability. However, studies suggest that once a comprehensive model is in place, it may be slow to change, even as environmental conditions change ("creeping rationality"). This situation appears to be more likely under conditions of firm growth and when executive teams are stable (Fredrickson and Iaquino 1989:536).

One conclusion that can be drawn from these studies is that "rationality" within organizations is a social phenomenon that varies. It varies across decision types, by managerial characteristics, as organizations grow or decline, as markets stabilize or shift, across firms and over time. Decision-making processes—even those that are ostensibly most rational (or comprehensive)—can slip into habit or inertia. "Creeping rationality" can negatively affect the development of new strategies that would enhance firm performance (an optimal outcome). Another conclusion that seems reasonable here is that the rational actor model, which is based on the assumption of individual agency, does not adequately account for collective actors (Shoch 1989). This problem with rational choice is discussed in greater detail below.

Individual versus Corporate Level Analysis

The "collectivity problem" with rational choice theory alludes to the difficulties associated with applying the rational actor model to corporate aggregates (Metzger and Schwenk 1990). Organizational sociologists, specifically, have criticized the model's assumption that the corporation behaves like an individual (French 1984; Laufer 1994; Vaughan 1996; Ermann and Rabe 1997). Instead, critics note, modern corporations are characterized by hierarchy and subdivision (Chandler 1962). As corporations grow, they are apt to suffer from internal communication problems (Downs 1967). Depending on the structural form they assume, large firms typically experience information loss as commands and data are communicated up and down the hierarchy (functional forms) or the isolation of the central decision authority from divisions, divisional competition for resources, and the development of discretionary objectives (multidivisional form). Both forms are vulnerable to intra-organizational parochialism (a situation in which smaller subunits are delegated a narrow set of problems and tasks). All of these factors are linked to nonoptimal decision processes and outcomes (Metzger and Schwenk 1990:346–350).

Within corporations, subgroups compete for scarce organizational resources and the power to define firm direction (Pfeffer 1981; Fligstein 1987; Simpson and Koper 1997). While top management (the subunit that "wins" the intra-corporate battle for dominance) generally provides a worldview from which managers define how organizational problems are understood and solved (Fligstein and Brantley 1992), there are still multiple actors, subunits, and tasks within any corporation which contribute to the multiple goals, perceptions, and values at work at any given time. Thus, corporate decisions are best understood as an amalgamation of individual input, corporate culture, constrained by organizational structures, and communicated via corporate policy (Laufer 1994:668).

The question of interest, then, is whether these decisions are rational or optimal. One body of research suggests that individuals working in groups are more risk tolerant than they are individually (Insko and Shopler 1972). This phenomenon, called "groupthink" by Irving Janis (1972), emphasizes the pressures placed on individuals to reach accordance at the expense of realistic assessments of alternative courses of action (Metzger and Schwenk 1990:339). Rather than producing higher levels of rationality, such processes demonstrate the power of groups to stifle dissent and to limit information brought to bear on the question at hand.

In sum, the complexities of organizational life seriously challenge the simple assumptions of the rational actor model. What, then, are the merits of this approach? What can be learned from a rational choice model of corporate offending?

CONCLUSIONS

Many of the challenges to rational choice posed by organizations are not unique to this venue. Critics of rational choice have noted that individual decisions are often made without relevant information, absent careful consideration of evidence, out of habit, or under pressure from others. There are situations in which the theory does not make unique predictions (choices are equally attractive or no option that is at least as good as any other) and, conversely, situations in which the theory fails to predict behavior, i.e., people behave irrationally (Elster 1986).

Our purpose here is not to resolve these problems, but to evaluate whether rational choice theory provides something useful to say about corporate offending decisions. We agree with Isenberg (1988:536) that there are intra-organizational systems and processes (like strategic planning, budgeting, human resource planning, market assessment) that improve on individual judgments because they are systematic, time sequenced, and linear. Decisions that emerge from such systems and processes should conform to a rational actor model.

Additionally, we believe that the challenges to rational choice models discussed above emphasize situations and conditions under which rationality may be compromised. But, our position is that these pose challenges to a rational choice model of corporate offending rather than invalidate it. Furthermore, it is equally clear that there are conditions and situations under which rational choice assumptions are not violated. Corporations, by their very nature, are goal-oriented. Firm survival depends on staying in business. Thus, firms are apt to have primary goals (profitability, market share expansion) that co-exist alongside secondary goals. Firm and environmental characteristics will affect which goals are privileged at any given time. Metzger and Schwenk (1990:360–362), for instance, assert that small firms (generally) and large firms facing competitive product markets are most likely to conform to the rational actor model. They specify further that among large firms in less competitive environments, multi-divisional firms will exhibit greater long-term rationality than their functionally structured counterparts. Conversely, organizational complexity and formalization should be negatively correlated with rationality due to multiple goals and perspectives (in the former case) and the development of standard operating procedures (in the latter).

Individual managers are also goal-oriented (whether the goal is personal, organizational, or both) and many of the decisions they make on behalf of the organization are affected by these goals. Their decision processes reflect a combination of prior experience, gut instinct, and in-depth thinking with action (Simpson 2001). Where rational choice theory gets it wrong is the assumption that A (thinking) produces B (action). Instead, research indicates that action can occur absent thinking (SOPs or habit) and that thinking and action are linked in a nonrecursive loop. "Analysis is not a passive process but a dynamic, interactive series of activity and reflection" (Isenberg 1988:537). Rational choice theory can inform us about linear decision processes (given goal G, A produces B), but it is less successful in accounting for dynamic ones.

So, where does this leave us? Even with its deficiencies, we believe that a rational choice perspective illuminates how illegal decisions can occur in some corporate settings within particular decision types. It is not necessary to assume that organizations act like individuals, just that organizations have some of the capabilities as individuals—like sensitivity to costs and benefits and that individual agents can factor organizational concerns into choices. As Cohen and Lofquist (1997:212) point out, rational choice theory can consider how "rational agents are affected by organizational and environmental factors" and theories of structure "allow for rational actors within the organization who affect outcomes." Both levels of the theory grant some degree of rationality to corporate actors. Empirically specifying the parameters of rationality within organizational decision-making will inform rational choice theory development and improve predictability.

Some of the challenges to rational choice theory have already led to modifications of the theory—like Paternoster and Simpson's incorporation of habit, organizational context and culture (1993, 1996) or Alexander and Cohen's principal agent theory (1995; see also, Cohen and Simpson 1997). Neither of these modified theories, however, have received the kind of empirical attention necessary to confirm or reject the modified theory. Until this occurs, we think that the rational choice paradigm provides a useful way of thinking about corporate offending decisions.

NOTES

1. Conversely, we exclude from our definition corporate behaviors that are harmful but not legally proscribed (Brown and Chiang 1993; Simon 1999) because such a broad scope obscures the bounds of the phenomenon. Although it is likely that a rational choice framework could explain these behaviors, along with those delineated above, what sets the legally proscribed behaviors apart is the fact that legal sanctions are a cost consideration that should (according to the theory) factor into offending decisions.

2. For a more detailed coverage of corporate deterrence and its problems, see Simpson (2001).

REFERENCES

Akers, Ronald. 2000. *Criminological Theories: Introduction and Evaluation*. Third Edition. Los Angeles: Roxbury Publishing Company.

Alexander, Cindy R. and Mark A. Cohen. 1996. "Why do Corporations Become Criminals?" Unpublished manuscript.

Aubert, Vilhelm. 1952. "White Collar Crime and Social Structure." *American Journal of Sociology* 58: 263–271.

Becker, Gary S. 1968. "Crime and Punishment: An Economic Approach." *Journal of Political Economy* 76:169–217.

Block, Michael Kent, Frederick Carl Nold, and Joseph Gregory Sidak. 1981. "The Deterrent Effects of Antitrust Enforcement." *Journal of Political Economy* 89:201–229.

Braithwaite, John. 1984. *Corporate Crime in the Pharmaceutical Industry*. London: Routledge & Paul Kegan.

Braithwaite, John, and Gilbert Geis. 1982. "On Theory and Action for Corporate Crime Control." *Crime and Delinquency* 28: 292–314.

Braithwaite, John, and Toni Makkai. 1991. "Testing an Expected Utility Model of Corporate Deterrence." *Law and Society Review* 25:7–39.

Brown, Stephen E., and Chau-Pu Chiang. 1993. "Defining Corporate Crime: A Critique of Traditional Parameters." In *Understanding Corporate Criminality*, edited by Michael B. Blankenship. New York: Garland Publishing, Inc.

Calvita, Kitty and Henry N. Pontell. 1990. "'Heads I Win, Tails You Lose': Deregulation, Crime, and Crisis in the Savings and Loan Industry." *Crime and Delinquency* 36:309–341.

Chandler, Alfred D., Jr. 1962. *Strategy and Structure: Chapters in the History of the American Industrial Enterprise.* Boston: MIT Press.

Chambliss, William J. 1967. "Types of Deviance and the Effectiveness of Legal Sanctions." *Wisconsin Law Review,* (Summer): 705–719.

Clinard, Marshall B., and Peter C. Yeager. 1980. *Corporate Crime.* New York: Free Press.

Cohen, Mark A. and Sally S. Simpson. 1997. "The Origins of Corporate Criminality: Rational Individual and Organizational Actors." In *Debating Corporate Crime,* edited by William S. Lofquist, Mark A. Cohen, and Gary A. Rabe. Cincinnati, OH.: Anderson Publishing.

Cornish, Derek B., and Ronald V. Clarke. 1986. *The Reasoning Criminal.* New York: Springer-Verlag.

Cornish, Derek B., and Ronald V. Clarke. 1987. "Understanding Crime Displacement: An Application of Rational Choice Theory." *Criminology,* 25(4): 933–947.

Downs, Anthony. 1967. *Inside Bureaucracy.* Boston: Little, Brown.

Elster, Jon. 1986. *Rational Choice.* New York: New York University Press.

Ermann, M. David and Gary A. Rabe. 1997. "Organizational Processes (not rational choices) Produce most Corporate Crimes." In *Debating Corporate Crime,* edited by William S. Lofquist, Mark A. Cohen, and Gary A. Rabe. Cincinnati, OH: Anderson Publishing.

Etzioni, Amitai. 1988. *The Moral Dimension.* New York: The Free Press.

Finney, Henry C., and Henry R. Lesieur. 1982. "A Contingency Theory of Organizational Crime." In *Research in the Sociology of Organizations, Volume 1,* edited by Samuel B. Bacharach. Greenwich, CT: JAI Press.

Fligstein, Neil. 1987. "The Intraorganizational Power Struggle." *American Sociological Review* 52:44–58.

Fligstein, Neil and Peter Brantley. 1992. "Bank Control, Owner Control, or Organizational Dynamics: Who Controls the Large Modern Corporation?" *American Journal of Sociology* 98: 280–307.

Frederickson, James W. and Anthony L. Iaquinto. 1989. "Inertia and Creeping Rationality in Strategic Decision Processes." *Academy of Management Journal,* 32:516–542.

French, Peter. 1984. *Collective and Corporate Responsibility.* New York: Columbia University.

Goll, Irene and Abdul M. A. Rasheed. 1997. "Rational Decision-Making and Firm Performance: The Moderating Role of Environment." *Strategic Management Journal* 18:583–591.

Grasmick, Harold G. and Robert J. Bursik, Jr. 1990. "Conscience, Significant Others, and Rational Choice: Extending the Deterrence Model." *Law and Society Review* 24:837–861.

Gross, Edward. 1980. "Organizational Structure and Organizational Crime." In *White Collar Crime: Theory and Research*, edited by Gilbert Geis and Ezra Stotland. Beverly Hills, CA: Sage.

Insko, Chester and John Shopler. 1972. *Experimental Social Psychology*. New York: Academic Press.

Isenberg, Daniel J. 1988. "How Senior Managers Think." In *Decision Making*, edited by David E. Bell, Howard Raiffa, and Amos Tversky. Cambridge: Cambridge University Press.

Janis, Irving.L. 1972. *Victims of Groupthink*. Boston: Houghton-Mifflin.

Laufer, William S. 1994. "Corporate Bodies and Guilty Minds." *Emory Law Journal* 43:647–730.

Lewis-Beck, Michael S. and John R. Alford. 1980. "Can Government Regulate Safety? The Coal Mine Example." *The American Political Science Review* 74:745–756.

Lofquist, William S., Mark A. Cohen, and Gary A. Rabe. 1997. *Debating Corporate Crime*. Cincinnati, OH: Anderson Publishing.

Makkai, Toni, and John Braithwaite. 1994. "The Dialectics of Corporate Deterrence." *Journal of Research in Crime and Delinquency*, 31(4): 347–373.

Metzger, Michael B. and Charles R. Schwenk. 1990. "Decision Making Models, Devil's Advocacy, and the Control of Corporate Crime." *American Business Law Journal* 28: 323–377.

Nagin, Daniel S., and Raymond Paternoster. 1993. "Enduring Individual Differences and Rational Choice Theories of Crime." *Law and Society Review*, 27: 467–496.

Paternoster, Raymond, and Sally Simpson. 1993. "A Rational Choice Theory of Corporate Crime." In *Routine Activities and Rational Choice: Advances in Criminological Theory, Volume 5*, edited by Ronald V. Clarke and Marcus Felson. New Brunswick, NJ: Transaction Publishers.

Paternoster, Raymond, and Sally Simpson. 1996. "Sanction Threats and Appeals to Morality: Testing a Rational Choice Model of Corporate Crime." *Law and Society Review*, 30(3): 549–583.

Pfeffer, Jeffrey. 1981. *Power in Organizations*. Marshfield, MA: Pitman.

Piliavin, Irving, Rosemary Gartner, Craig Thornton, and Ross Matsueda. 1986. "Crime, Deterrence, and Rational Choice." *American Sociological Review*, 51: 101–119.

Piquero, Alex R., and Stephen Tibbetts. 1996. "Specifying the Direct and Indirect Effects of Low Self-Control and Situational Factors in

Offending Decision Making: Toward a More Complete Model of Rational Offending." *Justice Quarterly*, 13: 481–510.

Quinney, Earl R. 1963. "Occupational Structure and Criminal Behavior: Prescriptions Violations by Retail Pharmacists." *Social Problems*, 11: 179–185.

Schrager, Laura S., and James F. Short. 1978. "Toward a Sociology of Organizational Crime." *Social Problems*, 25: 407–419.

Shoch, Jim. 1989. "Rational Choice Explanation: A 'Sociological' Critique." Unpublished Manuscript.

Simon, Herbert. 1957. *Models of Man*. New York: John Wiley.

Simon, David R. 1999. *Elite Deviance*, 6th edition. Boston, MA: Allyn and Bacon.

Simpson, Sally S. 2001. *Why Corporations Obey the Law*. New York: Cambridge University Press.

Simpson, Sally S., and Christopher S. Koper. 1992. "Deterring Corporate Crime." *Criminology*, 30(3): 347–376.

Simpson, Sally S. and Christopher S. Koper. 1997. "The Changing of the Guard: Top Management Characteristics, Organizational Strain, and Antitrust Offending." *Journal of Quantitative Criminology* 13:373–404.

Simpson, Sally S., Raymond Paternoster, and Nicole Leeper Piquero. 1998. "Exploring the Micro Macro Link in Corporate Crime Research." In *Research in the Sociology of Organizations, Volume 15*, edited by Peter A. Bamberger and William J. Sonnenstuhl. Greenwich, CT: JAI Press.

Stotland, Ezra, Michael Brintnall, Andre L'Heureux, and Eva Ashmore. 1980. "Do Convictions Deter Home Repair Fraud?" In *White Collar Crime: Theory and Research*, edited by Gilbert Geis and Ezra Stotland. Beverly Hills, CA: Sage.

Sutherland, Edwin. 1949. *White Collar Crime*. New York: Dryden Press.

Tuck, Mary and David Riley. 1986. "The Theory of Reasoned Action: A Decision Theory of Crime." In *The Reasoning Criminal: Rational Choice Perspectives on Offending*, edited by Derek B. Cornish and Ronald V. Clarke. New York: Springer-Verlag.

Tushman, Michael and E. Romanelli. 1985. "Organizational Evolution: A Metamorphosis Model of Convergence and Reorientation." In *Research in Organizational Behavior, Volume 7*, edited by Larry L. Cummings and Barry M. Staw. Greenwich, CT: JAI Press.

Vaughan, Diane. 1996. *The Challenger Launch Decision*. Chicago: University of Chicago Press.

Vaughan, Diane. 1998. "Rational Choice, Situated Action, and the Social Control of Organizations." *Law and Society Review* 32: 23–102.

Vaughan, Diane. 1999a. "Boundary Work: Levels of Analysis, the Macro-Micro Link, and the Social Control of Organizations." In *Social Science,*

Social Policy, and the Law, edited by Patricia Ewick, Robert Kagan, and Austin Sarat. New York: Russell Sage.

Vaughan, Diane. 1999b. "The Dark Side of Organizations: Mistake, Misconduct, and Disaster." *Annual Review of Sociology* 271–305.

Weisburd, David, Elin Waring, and Ellen Cyat. 1995. "Specific Deterrence in a Sample of Offenders Convicted on White-Collar Crimes." *Criminology* 33:587–607.

Wright, Richard and Scott Decker. 1994. *Burglars on the Job*. Boston: Northeastern University Press.

Chapter 3

Analyzing Organized Crimes

Derek B. Cornish and Ronald V. Clarke

INTRODUCTION

The rational choice approach to offending assumes that when criminals offend they do so because crime provides the most effective means of achieving desired benefits (Clarke and Cornish 1985, 2000; Cornish and Clarke 1986). Similarly, the choice of methods for carrying out the crime, and the decision-making involved, are also best regarded as instrumental behaviors in the service of offenders' goals. Not surprisingly, the usual criticism of this perspective is precisely that, in general, it imputes too much deliberation, forethought, and planning and too little pathology and impulsivity to offenders' behaviors; and that, in particular, it provides little help in understanding or preventing the so-called "expressive" crimes of sex and violence.

Whatever the merits of these criticisms for other offenses (see, for example, Tedeschi and Felson 1994, in relation to violent crime) they carry little weight in respect of organized crime. This is rational crime par excellence: it is highly planned and organized, directed and committed by older, more determined offenders, usually with strong economic motivations. But although the impetus behind organized crime is an economic one, the principal contribution of the rational choice perspective is not so much to provide an answer to the question of "why" such criminal activities occur, but rather to address the question of "how" they are carried out. It is only by being in a position to answer questions about the process of crime commission that policy responses, particularly preventive ones, can be developed.

This chapter outlines a conceptual framework and some associated research strategies designed to develop better ways of addressing such "how" questions for policy purposes. In particular, it proposes that detailed descriptions, or "crime scripts," of the modi operandi of organized crimes need to be developed at an appropriately crime-specific level of analysis. It goes on to suggest how such an approach might contribute to the theory and practice of preventing organized crimes.

CHARACTERISTICS OF ORGANIZED CRIMES

For the purposes of this discussion we use the term "organized crimes" to refer to offenses with the following features:

- They are complex: that is, their commission involves a complex interplay of criminal actors, equipment, locations, and activities.
- They are often serial: that is, the offenses in question tend to be repeated, routinized, and linked by a particular modus operandi.
- They are committed by organized groups of offenders who provide the infrastructure, resources, skills, and experience necessary to plan and carry out the crimes concerned.
- These organized groups vary in terms of their longevity, continuity, and complexity from very temporary associations created for the purposes of a particular project (McIntosh 1975), through those established to carry out a time-limited series of offenses (Cressey's (1972) "working groups"), to more permanent organizations, or businesses, with a long-term investment in one or more on-going criminal activities.
- Such organized groups may exist at various levels—transnational, national, regional and local (Hobbs 1998)—but these will be dictated in part by the nature and scope of the organized crimes in which they are involved (Stelfox 1998), and the way in which they have evolved or are evolving.

Our starting-point, however, will be the characteristics of specific organized crimes, and the requirements for their commission. By focusing on specific crimes rather than on the nature of criminal organizations (a distinction also made by Stelfox 1998, 394), we are reversing the focus of much traditional academic interest. We aim in this way to avoid two potential pitfalls: (1) that of paying more attention to the characteristics of criminal organizations than to those of organized crimes; and (2) that of treating "organized crime" as a blanket term without paying due attention to the varied phenomena that it covers. Furthermore, since the primary function of criminal organization is to facilitate the commission of complex crimes, we will suggest that studying the latter in greater detail may throw new light on the characteristics of the former. We hope that this will address some of the inadequacies of current thinking about "organized crime" (see Levi 1998a, for a discussion of the issues) and, more importantly, will improve the policy relevance of research in this area.

RATIONAL CHOICE AND ORGANIZED CRIMES

In general terms, the rational choice perspective asserts that crime is chosen because of the benefits it brings to the offender. On this analysis, the reasoning criminal, like other rational economic decision-makers (Becker 1968), considers the risks, effort, and rewards associated with alternative courses of action and selects the one which maximizes, or at least gives a reasonable return on, his or her investment of time and energy. It uses this general assumption both to explain why people become involved in particular forms of crime, and the conditions needed for specific crimes to take place (Clarke and Cornish 2000).

There are a number of reasons for suggesting that the rational choice perspective might be particularly well suited to the analysis of organized crimes.

The Purposive Nature of Organized Crimes
Organized crimes are, of all offenses, the most readily seen as purposeful and instrumental—not least because their benefits are the obvious ones of money or material goods, achieved through the careful and deliberate exploitation of opportunities for gain. In this sense, they come closest to representing the ideal type of crime for analysis in rational choice terms, and least like those sorts of crimes—spontaneous, ill-considered, "senseless"—which, it is often claimed, the perspective cannot handle.

Organized Crimes as Business
Of all forms of crime, organized crimes most closely mirror the purposive economic activity of the non-criminal marketplace. Although there are limits to its applicability, the analogy of crime as work (Lektemann 1973) captures the instrumental nature of organized crimes. The rational choice approach sensitizes the researcher to examine organized crimes as the products of criminal business enterprises. If, as Levi comments, ". . . we need to examine crime as a business process, requiring funding, technical skills, distribution mechanisms, and money-handling facilities" (Levi 1998a, 343), then we need a suitable discourse within which to pursue our analysis.

Organization and Planning
The emphasis of the rational choice perspective on strategic thinking, planning and sequential decision making may capture important aspects of the successful undertaking of organized crimes. Such complex crimes involve the assembling of resources, the coordination of efforts among self-interested and untrustworthy collaborators, the orderly and timely completion of contributory tasks, and the routinization of methods through constant refinement and repetition (see also Cusson 1993). Although such crimes are inevitably the product of imperfect rather than perfect rationality, they are—given the uncertain conditions under which they operate—among the best examples of planned offending.

The Diverse Nature of Organized Crimes
As mentioned earlier, one of the limitations of the existing literature is its preoccupation with the social organization of offending, as evidenced in discussions of how organized crime should be defined and described (Reuter 1983). This debate often takes place at the expense of paying due attention to the range of phenomena that the term encompasses. The rational choice perspective, on the other hand, starts from the position that organized crime may be better understood—and certainly better controlled—through the undertaking of crime-specific studies into its constituent phenomena and the determinants (including organizational ones) of their successful undertaking.

While the rational choice approach may be generally useful in understanding and explaining organized crimes, its most important contribution may flow directly from its focus on how particular crimes are committed. Those who design situational crime measures try to understand offenders' crime-commission strategies with a view to preventing or disrupting them. They have proceeded on the basis of a combination of expert knowledge, studies of offender decision-making and crime-scene analyses of modi operandi in relation to specific crimes. The rational choice perspective has assisted this process in several ways. In particular, it has:

1. emphasized the need for crime-specific analyses of crime commission;
2. made an early attempt to model some of the decision processes (the "event" model: Clarke and Cornish 1985);
3. developed a rational choice analysis of crime displacement that stresses the unique "choice-structuring properties" of

different forms of crime (Cornish and Clarke 1987, 1989); and

4. elaborated a classification of situational crime prevention strategies based on the rational choice principles of increasing risk, increasing effort, reducing rewards and removing excuses (Clarke 1997).

CRIME SCRIPTS

Committing a specific crime involves a sequence of choices and decisions made at each stage of the criminal act: preparation, target selection, commission of the act, escape, and aftermath. Some of these stages were referred to in our original "event" model, and others are captured by the notions of modus operandi, or "criminal tactics" (Cusson 1993). Recently the concept of the crime script (Cornish 1994a, 1994b) has been developed as a way of enlarging and systematizing knowledge of what is required in the way of criminal actors, equipment, locations and activities to complete each stage of this process successfully.

In cognitive science, the script is generally viewed as being a special type of hypothesized knowledge structure, known as an "event" schema, which organizes our knowledge about how to understand and carry out commonplace behavioral processes or routines (for a more detailed review, see Cornish 1994a). A favorite example of one such sequence is the "restaurant script," discussed by Schank and Abelson (1977). This script organizes our knowledge about what to do in a restaurant into a sequence of skilled actions: enter, wait to be seated, get the menu, order, eat, get the check, pay, and exit. The script concept's potential for use as a way of analyzing the routine performance of skilled tasks quickly attracted the attention of applied researchers. Script analyses were undertaken in marketing, management, and consumer research as a way of studying, and utilizing information on professional skills, such as buying and selling, for training purposes.

Since the rational choice perspective represents offending as relatively skilled instrumental action guided by choices and decisions made in the light of situational circumstances, the script concept offers a way of developing step-by-step accounts of the procedures used by offenders to commit crimes. Scripts have much in common with the "choice-structuring properties" of crimes (Cornish and Clarke 1987, 1989). These list the properties of particular offenses, or of methods of committing offenses, that distinguish one type of criminal activity from another, make them differentially attractive to offenders and, hence, place rational limits to the likelihood of displacement. They include, for example, issues of access, skills required, resources, effort, moral scruples, emotional capacity and other personal preferences—any feature that serves to structure the choices of those contemplating the type of crime or method in question. In short, just as scripts list the procedural requirements for crimes, so choice-structuring properties list their casting requirements in terms of willing and able offenders.

Some rudimentary scripts have been developed by Cornish (1994a, 1994b, 1999) for professional auto theft, subway mugging, auto theft for temporary transport (or "joy-riding"), "tag-writing" (graffiti), child sexual abuse by a stranger, and child sexual abuse in institutions. Figure 1 uses auto theft data from Light et al. (1993) to illustrate some features of this approach. Committing a crime can be broken down into a progressive sequence of conditions and actions with the help of a general framework[1] developed by Leddo and Abelson (1986) for analyzing instrumental action into stages (see left-hand side of figure). The opening stages are concerned with the conditions under which various preparatory actions can take place. These are followed by stages that select and work upon the target or victim selected. They culminate in "doing" the defining action of the crime concerned—taking, raping, hitting, breaking, ingesting, etc. Further stages designed to secure the offender from capture—by allowing escape from the setting and disposal of evidence—may then follow. These wind down the action and complete the script.

Fig. 1: A Simple Crime Script—Auto Theft for Temporary Use

Stages	Script Action
Preparation	Get screwdriver
	Get short length of steel tubing
	Select co-offender
Entry to Setting	Enter public parking lot
Enabling Conditions	Loiter unobtrusively
Target Selection	Reject alarmed cars
	Choose older vehicle
Initiation of Action	Force lock with screwdriver
	Enter vehicle
Completion of Action	Break off lock surround
	Use tubing to break ignition barrel
	Remove ignition and steering lock
	Activate starter switch
Doing	Drive vehicle away
Exit from Setting	Leave parking lot
Aftermath	Abandon by next day

(Adapted from Cornish, 1994b)

Analyzing crime commission in this way identifies a wide range of possible intervention points both for specific crimes, and for crime in general. This allows situational prevention strategies (Clarke 1997) to be mapped onto stages in the crime-commission process (see Cornish 1994b for an example in relation to "tag-writing"). In relation to Figure 1, remedies at each step might take the following form:

- Preparation: control over the sales of special equipment such as hand scanners and duplicate keys;
- Entry to setting: parking lot barriers; attendants; few entrances;
- Enabling conditions: CCTV and/or regular patrols to deter loiterers;
- Target selection: labeling or visible protection of tempting vehicles;
- Initiation: CCTV to monitor suspicious behavior;
- Completion: vehicle alarm to alert security;
- Doing: vehicle immobilizer;
- Exit from scene: exit screening to prevent removal;
- Aftermath: vehicle-tracking system activated.

THE VALUE OF THE SCRIPT APPROACH

As routinizations of criminal decision making, scripts represent offenders' standing solutions to the issues of risk, effort, and reward in connection with particular crimes in particular settings. Thinking of crime commission as a routinized procedure gives a more realistic view of what it is to act rationally. This is because it suggests that rational choice may be evidenced as much by the utilization of successful instrumental routines developed by others as by evidence of planning activities, or innovative decision making on the job.

The script concept further emphasizes the potential value of studying crime commission as a decision-making process. Script analyses encourage researchers to model the crime-commission process from start to finish, without confining attention only to selected aspects of the process, such as target selection. The story that scripts tell about crime commission extends the process backward and forward from the act itself, and indicates how crime-commission processes—and the potential for disrupting them—reach beyond the immediate situation of offending.

Script analysis clarifies important, but often neglected aspects of crimes. Although crimes are often treated as outcomes or "events," defined by some culminating instrumental or expressive act (stealing, raping), they can also be viewed as the complete sequence of instrumental actions preceding, including, and following the defining act. All crimes, even the simplest, involve such chains of decisions and actions, separable into interdependent stages, involving the attainment of sub-goals that serve to further the overall goals of the crime. These separable stages may be carried out in different settings, utilizing a variety of props, and requiring the assistance at some points of co-offenders and others.

Even simple crimes, viewed this way, involve multiple steps for their commission, some of which become readily identifiable only when the process has been properly described and understood. Incomprehension or disgust in the face of the culminating act itself—or how it was committed—can often interfere with consideration of the crime-commission process as a whole. Just as apparently "senseless" crimes can seem more rational once their purposes have been properly identified, so apparently "impulsive" or "unplanned" offenses may be revealed as more deliberate once their stages and objectives have been described. Steps in the crime-commission process are hardest to unscramble where the offending is more-or-less seamlessly integrated within the daily routines of a deviant lifestyle. It can be difficult to distinguish criminal from other background activities, where multi-tasking is occurring, time-scales are fluid, and momentary situational circumstances regulate actions. In such cases, knowledge of the procedural steps involved in a particular crime can alert the analyst to behaviors that may be part of a crime script.

On the practical side, the script concept offers a useful way of developing better accounts of crime commission. By "better" is meant fuller, more systematic, appropriately crime-specific, and helpful for crime prevention purposes. Scripts act as a device to tie people, places, props, and procedures into detailed accounts of purposeful and routinized activities at the right (micro-social) level for situational interventions. More generally, script analyses may be helpful in two further ways: in elaborating and choosing between the range of possible "context-mechanism-outcome" configurations (Pawson and Tilley 1994) which may be offered as rationales for particular situational crime prevention projects; and in stimulating thinking about new ways of tackling crime.

SCRIPTS AND COMPLEX CRIMES

Complexity in crime commission arises from a number of inter-related sources: the number, duration and location of stages; the role of contributory crimes; the logistics of crime commission; and the compound nature of some crimes.

Number, Duration, and Location of Stages

Although the script concept provides a universal template for analyzing crimes, some crimes seem inherently simpler than others do in terms of the number and duration of stages they involve. Few preparations are required for purse snatching: presence in streets or shops needs little explanation; victim selection is straightforward; taking is simple; and escape is dependent merely upon some knowledge of the locality and a reasonable turn of speed. Some other crimes, such as burglary for cash on public housing estates, increase complexity somewhat through the additional time and activity involved in searching out and selecting targets, approaching, and breaking-into properties.

Major increases in complexity, however, tend to relate to the density and value of the victims or targets sought. Burglary of valuable works of art from wealthy gated communities, for example, will require more preparation (e.g., acquiring information about security precautions and the location of targets), more careful plans for entering the setting and leaving again, and more elaborate methods of removing and transporting the spoils. In the same way, victim-rich but protected environments such as residential homes for children may require potential abusers to spend considerable amounts of time and effort assuming the roles that enable them to gain and maintain legitimate access (Cornish 1999).

Crimes also vary in terms of the variety of locations required by the nature of the action. Preparatory planning and assembly of tools and co-offenders may take place in one location, the search for and selection of targets or victims in another, and completion of the remaining elements of the crime elsewhere. Such shifting between locations can occur at the local, regional, national, and transnational levels. In summary, the greater the number of stages to a script, the longer it takes for individual stages of the script to be completed, and the greater the number of locations involved, the more complex the script will be to perform.

The Role of Contributory Crimes

In crimes like vandalism, theft of cash, rape, and violent assault where the offender makes direct use of targets and victims, the action may be relatively self-limiting; once the defining action has been completed little other than escape is necessary, and the script is completed. But most crimes are not so clearly circumscribed; they involve further transactions. Dud checks and counterfeit money have to be passed, stolen credit cards used to obtain goods or cash, and stolen or illegal goods have to be converted into cash. As Sutton (1998) points out, markets of one sort or another—from friendship networks and hawking, to commercial fences—operate to handle stolen goods. Indeed, so important are some of these markets as purveyors of illegal goods and services that associated activities (supplying, receiving, trafficking) to support them are defined as important crimes in their own right.

For many crimes, too, preparation may involve the offender in preliminary offenses or criminalizable actions: guns may have to be obtained, cars stolen, tools or equipment assembled and conveyed to the place of the main crime. This is to say that the crime of interest—even the so-called "craft" crime (McIntosh 1975) committed by the individual offender—is generally embedded within a range of contributory criminal activities with which it may have contingent or necessary relationships. By encouraging the development of more complete knowledge about the crime-commission process, a script analysis can provide a more definitive description of these activities.

Logistics of Crime Commission

The performance of some crimes will require more resources at some or all of their stages than others, whether in terms of information, finance, facilitators (tools, transport, weapons, communications), locations, or technical expertise (Ekblom and Tilley 2000). Where these requirements cannot be met from within the offender's own resources, he or she will be obliged to turn to others for help. The more demanding the crime script, then, the more likely it will need to involve co-offenders, some of whom will provide the necessary resources and bring their own skills to bear at particular stages in the offense.

The Compound Nature of Some Crimes

The sources of complexity discussed above (number, duration and location of stages; the role of contributory crimes; and the logistics of crime commission) all suggest that complex offenses may be best viewed as a series of simpler scripts strung together to form a higher-order compound entity. Such complex crimes may usefully be treated as having the following features:

1. a string of interlinked offense scripts, each component script having its own stages, casts, locations and activities;
2. an extended plan (a "master-script") that guides or, at least, makes sense of the whole process by nesting individual scripts within a larger purpose;
3. ownership of the plan or its component parts by one or more members of the cast;
4. division of labor so that commission of each of the component offenses is carried out by subsets of the total cast; and
5. an organizational structure appropriate to the nature of the specific crime under analysis.

Professional car theft (or "ringing") provides one such example of a complex crime (Hinchliffe 1994; Cornish 1994a). In this crime, the different stages—steal, conceal, disguise, market, dispose—themselves constitute separable offenses with their own crime-commission scripts, carried out as required by subsets of the cast with special expertise and resources (See Figure 2). Such crimes are even more complex when they involve trafficking across national borders (Mack and Kerner 1975; Clarke 1999; Tremblay et al. In Press). In such cases a further series of "scenes" and their associated offenses (preparation of export and import documents for customs, conveyance to country of destination, delivery to local contact, registration, and sale) must be added to the master-script.

Fig. 2: A Complex Crime—Professional Auto Theft ("Ringing")

MASTER-SCRIPT				
STEAL	CONCEAL	DISGUISE	MARKET	DISPOSE
SCRIPT	SCRIPT	SCRIPT	SCRIPT	SCRIPT
"stealing from street"	"acquire-disused-premises"	"obtain-false-documents	"put-advert-in-paper"	"sell-to-greedy-punter"
STAGES	STAGES	STAGES	STAGES	STAGES
select target	locate premises	obtain crashed auto	arrange safe phone #	take to buyer
break-in	do deal			offer big discount for cash
		transfer documents	place ad	
deliver to premises	deliver any equipment	get false plates	wait for calls	exit
CAST	CAST	CAST	CAST	CAST
Andy	Chas Bill	Chas Bill	Chas Di	Eddie Chas

(Adapted from Cornish, 1994a)

ORGANIZED CRIMES AND CRIMINAL ORGANIZATION
Studying Organized Crimes

We have seen how adopting a script approach can improve our understanding of the crime-commission process, especially where the crimes are complex ones. But there is something of a paradox here: in so doing, it also suggests that individual crimes, as conventionally understood, may be only analytically separable from the general flow of offending. It is, of course, helpful for many practical purposes of criminal justice to divide up this flow into criminalizable "chunks" of actions and events. But if, in reality, criminal activities tend to grow opportunistically into longer "chains"— and if these chains in turn often come to form elements in higher-order chains, or even webs, of interconnected offending—then techniques of analysis are needed that are true to these phenomena.

The idea of linkages is crucial to the script approach, which is built upon web-like concepts (nodes, connections, interfaces, intersections, and networks) and analogies of opportunistic organic growth (stages, extensions, variations, elaborations, innovations, and concatenations: see Cornish 1994b). The crime script concept, therefore, may not only clarify the nature of the actions involved in simple and complex crimes; it may also help in the broader task of portraying the web of criminal activities to be found within and across particular geographical areas.

A script approach to the study of organized crimes might usefully begin with the following issues:

- the evolution over time of complex, organized crimes from simpler crimes;
- the emergence of progressively more organized forms of crimes in particular sectors (e.g., vehicle theft) in response to changing opportunity structures and resources; and
- the conditions which promote the growth of links between both similar and different forms of crime (perhaps including the mutually beneficial links that may develop between traditional craft crimes and more organized ones, or between different types of organized crimes).

Studying Criminal Organization

We have argued that the initial focus of research on organized crimes, and its starting point, should be that of exploring particular types of criminal activity, and linkages among them, rather than particular types of criminal organization per se. Organizational structures, in other words, would be treated as emergent properties of crime scripts, to be studied once the demands of the scripts themselves were better known. Since the two are likely to be functionally related, however, some discussion of the issues is required.

As Levi comments, in relation to credit and debit card frauds, ". . . different forms of crime *require* different levels of organisation . . ." (Levi 1998b, 456). In the case of simple crimes, organization is largely imposed by the purposes of the individual offender. Compound crimes, however, need organization not only in relation to their constituent offenses, but also to keep the component parts in synchronization and on course; and this usually requires the coordinated activities of more than one offender.

Tremblay et al.'s (In Press) study of co-offender networks in the stolen vehicle business looked at sets of offenders involved in three script variants, or "tracks," of increasing complexity. These were the theft of vehicles for sale of parts ("chopping"); the local resale of stolen vehicles; and theft of vehicles for export and resale. Since there were relatively few stages in the "chopping" script, division of labor, although present, was not strictly necessary (car thieves could dismantle vehicles and mechanics could steal cars), and co-offender groups tended to be small and cohesive. In the case of vehicle theft for local resale, however, a different pattern of involvement tended to emerge over time. Some division of labor resulted from the replacement of relatively simple forms of disguising the vehicle's original identity with more elaborate makeovers involving "body switching"—the switching of VINs (vehicle identification numbers) from crashed but legitimate vehicles to the bodies of stolen ones. This required more specialized resources, locations and know-how, and had the effect of creating a division of labor between those stealing the vehicles, those storing and disguising them, and those finally selling them. (Figure 2 provides a somewhat similar hypothetical example.) In the third script—the export resale of stolen vehicles—a variety of transportation and export-import requirements are added to the basic resale script. This had the effect of adding further stages, more cast, and increased complexity.

Script elaboration tends therefore to require multiple casts, an increasing division of labor, and corresponding shifts in the sources of control. The relationship between degree of complexity and style of organization has been captured in the early work of writers on organized crime. McIntosh (1971, 1975), for example, makes a distinction between "craft" crimes and "projects." Craft crimes are routinized offenses such as thieving, burglary, and vehicle theft that provide a consistent livelihood for individual offenders. "Project" crimes, on the other hand, involve the ad hoc assembling of offenders with special skills to play their parts—often exploiting expertise gained from craft crimes—in complex crimes such as bank robberies or commercial burglaries. In a similar vein, Cressey (1972) makes a distinction between the multiple skills of the professional thief, and the organization of working groups of professional thieves, which relies upon "assembling and co-ordinating these skills and methods" (Cressey 1972, 61).

These suggestions help to clarify the circumstances under which routinized craft crimes may be displaced by one-off project crimes, or those that determine the routinization of project crimes as ongoing "businesses"—becoming "craft" crimes again in many respects, but at a different level of organizational complexity. These accounts, however, need to be carefully grounded in the specifics of criminal activity. The advantage of the script approach is that by proceeding from an analysis of the nature of the offending process itself and its instrumental requirements, it allows the shape of criminal organization to emerge from the requirements of crime commission. As McIntosh comments, this involves "[t]reating the organization of professional crime as rationally geared to handling the technical problems of crime . . ." (McIntosh 1975, 73).

While increasing complexity requires increasing organization, some caveats seem appropriate. First, it seems clear that once a particular level of complexity has been reached changes occur in the *way* that offenses are organized. More implicit and diffuse forms of organization tend to be replaced by more explicit ones, which locate responsibility for planning and organization at one or more stages in the script where crucial resources are located and where important transformations and transactions have to be performed. An example would be where vehicles need to be more elaborately disguised, or arrangements made to export them (see Tremblay et al. In Press).

Second, the use of master-scripts as devices to unpack the procedural stages of complex crimes therefore has no necessary implications for how they are organized: master plans do not imply master planners. A more likely model than that of the overarching criminal organization is one in which local centers for operations naturally evolve (Reuter 1983) from the practical script requirements at different stages (such as the need to direct the work of subcontractors, receive, store and dispatch goods, or negotiate as sellers with buyers) and the ability of particular individuals or groups to supply the necessary resources and skills.

Lastly, the script approach tends to emphasize the influence of crime-commission requirements on the emergence of specific organizational structures. But, once established, these organizational structures may themselves begin to exert an influence upon future criminal activity. Thus, the existence of organized crime groups may well have important implications for the future elaboration and concatenation of complex crimes, such as the horizontal and vertical integration of criminal activities, and the development of crime conglomerates. Once the constituent crime scripts are better understood, the possibility of such developments, too, will ultimately have to be investigated.

Organizational Structures

We mentioned above that considered in terms of its organizational structure, the mature master-script of a complex crime may more often resemble a chain of reciprocal relationships, each link developed and sustained by the self-interest of groups of offenders at neighboring stages, than a wheel at the hub of which sits a single organizer who oversees activity at the periphery. Certainly, the metaphor of links and chains seems true to the opportunistic nature of criminal behaviors and their evolution over time within and across particular settings (see, for example, Tremblay, Cusson and Morselli's (1998) discussion of chain networks in relation to international drugs markets). At this stage, however, more empirical data are needed on the form(s) of organization favored by particular types of crimes. Once this is better understood, it may be possible, using concepts drawn from the early research on communication networks (Bavelas 1950; Leavitt

1951; Shaw 1954), to relate the specific communication structures they discuss (the wheel, chain, circle, and others), more closely to the logistical demands of particular organized crimes.[2]

In practical terms this might provide helpful pointers to investigators when trying to match likely suspects to particular crimes. Knowing about complex crime scripts and their organizational requirements might also assist in preventing and predicting the future activities of particular known offenders. At the local level, the availability of experienced and well-resourced individuals to act as potential "patrons," "link-men" (Mack and Kerner 1975), or "hubs" (Hobbs 1998) for future criminal activity may well influence the types of organized crime groups that subsequently develop. This, in turn, will influence the types of crime that can be undertaken or may become established.

IMPLICATIONS FOR A POLICY-RELEVANT RESEARCH STRATEGY
Problems of Traditional Research Techniques

The above analysis suggests the need for detailed studies of the crime-commission procedures of complex organized crimes. But without disputing this need, some caveats must be made about the ability of traditional programs and methods of research to deliver the necessary information for guiding successful policy interventions. The main difficulties are those of resources, access, timeliness, and fidelity to the nature of the phenomena under investigation.

The most obvious problem is that of resources. There are simply too many crimes to study and not enough resources available to mount wide-scale studies using traditional methods. Access, too, presents a problem. While it may be possible to undertake traditional ethnographic studies on craft and project crimes, getting fieldwork access to study complex organized crimes, which depend upon concealment for their continuing success, is likely to be much more difficult to achieve. On the issue of timeliness, it is increasingly the case that, in an age of ever-shrinking policy "windows," many traditional research techniques simply take too long to complete.

The question of fidelity to the nature of the phenomena being investigated is a corollary of timeliness. There is the danger—given the time-scale required by detailed studies—of providing yesterday's answers to the questions of today. Organized crimes are dynamic activities characterized by contingency and innovation, and these sources of instability and change apply even more to the fluid relationships and temporary dependencies that may exist among complex crimes. While research is being conducted, permutations and innovations are constantly occurring as opportunities and technologies change, and as crime-control agencies stimulate further change and complexity (Ekblom 1997). Thus, even though the complexities of criminal activity at one point in time might well be best described by lengthy and rigorous research, they might still shed little light on the complexities of ongoing forms of organized crimes at another point. Indeed, the results of such research may be counterproductive insofar as they misdirect policy makers as to the nature of the phenomena in question, and the properties—dynamic rather than static—of the underlying processes involved.

These sorts of methodological problems are, of course, not unique to the study of organized crime. Similar questions have been raised about the ability of prospective longitudinal studies of birth cohorts—which are also rigorous and detailed, but lengthy and expensive — to provide timely, relevant and theoretically appropriate input to contemporary policy debates.

The Importance of Analytic Frameworks

We believe that the development and refinement of analytic frameworks such as the script approach are themselves important theoretical tasks for criminologists to undertake. It is essential to provide the police, other criminal justice officials, legislators, and policy makers with conceptual tools that enable them to anticipate and respond to complexity, change, and innovation in organized crime. This capability helps, in turn, to direct intelligence-gathering efforts, guide detection and investigation, develop expertise and, more generally, design interventions that prevent and disrupt criminal activity more successfully.

The script approach is essentially a distillation and systemization of much practical wisdom about the importance of modi operandi (see, for example, Hinchliffe 1994). This gives it some advantage in the marketplace of ideas. Not only is it implicit in strategies of policing and situational crime prevention, but also in the development of criminal law, which has long recognized the need to address separate elements of crime commission for the purposes of punishment and deterrence by seeking to criminalize as many of them as possible. Offenses such as solicitation, conspiracy, going equipped, behaving suspiciously, aiding and abetting, attempting, being an accessory after the fact, deliberate concealment or compounding of a felony, all represent attempts to address offending as a process as well as an event. As new communication media are exploited for the commission of crimes (as in the case of the Internet for the distribution of pornography) then their misuse can also be quickly criminalized.

A Prescription for Policy-Relevant Research

Given the importance of developing and refining analytic frameworks, there may be a place for the undertaking of a few detailed studies using traditional methods of research, even though these may have little direct policy relevance. For policy purposes, however, the objective of gaining a well-grounded understanding of fashions and methods of contemporary organized crimes should be tackled using a mix of speedier research strategies. "Quick-and-dirty" studies can outline the contours of organized crimes in enough detail for the purpose of guiding preventive approaches and interventions. Intelligence-gathering exercises can be undertaken, where required, in relation to particular crime-commission issues: e.g., procedures for the re-registration of cars in different jurisdictions, novel methods for distributing pornography, changes in script elements in response to police activity or as the result of innovation.

The focus of any such research should follow the general prescriptions of the rational choice perspective discussed above. In the present instance this would involve using the script analytic approach to unpack the procedural steps, together with their logistical requirements, involved in committing particular organized crimes. A number of methods may provide relatively speedy and policy-relevant information:

- analyzing published studies from a script perspective;
- studying the police and prosecution case papers of known crimes (Natarajan and Belanger 1999; Natarajan 2000);
- interviewing experts and offenders in depth about script elements and linkages;
- studying the reports of undercover operations;
- interviewing those involved in the legal analogues of crime, such as the export of used cars or the running of legal internet video sites, in order to understand the means by which legal business is transacted and the loopholes available to offenders;
- undertaking ethnographic research, where this can be done (see below), and done quickly.

All these methods use the script approach to guide the gathering of either existing or easily obtainable information. Many of them also avoid the problems of access faced by ethnographic fieldwork. Mack put it well when he commented that "Successful criminals are by definition inaccessible. The major skill they have in common, over and above their special expertise, is that of keeping out of sight" (Mack 1972, 50). For all these reasons, the above methods offer the best chance of enabling policy makers and practitioners to respond quickly to change and innovation in an area where illegal entrepreneurial expertise, opportunism and responsiveness to changing market conditions combine to set the pace.

CONCLUSIONS

If researchers want to find ways of tackling organized crime, rather than merely "appreciating" it, then they must ask different questions, develop different concepts, and be prepared to employ alternative, sometimes rough-and-ready, methods of investigation. As a start, we have argued for the need to develop more detailed descriptions, or "crime scripts," of specific organized crimes. We end this chapter by summarizing what is distinctive about the script approach and why it is useful.

Like other concepts associated with rational choice theory, the crime script is designed to enhance understanding of offending as instrumental behavior, undertaken with the intention of benefiting the criminal. It provides a framework for organizing and exploring the moment-to-moment decisions and actions involved in the process of committing the crime itself. In doing so it moves beyond the conventional notion of the modus operandi in two important ways.

First, as its origins in cognitive science suggest, the script concept draws attention to the structure of purposive action, showing how it is organized to unfold through time to achieve its objectives. It suggests that criminal action proceeds in an orderly often routinized fashion, guided by implicit or explicit plans. These plans break down the ongoing action into separate stages, each with its distinctive part to play in furthering the progress of the overall project. Within each of these stages, specific situational requirements have to be met if actions to further the crime are to be successful. Examples of such demands include being able to get information, tools, or co-offenders; being able to enter a setting; being able to remain there without challenge; being able to select victims/targets. Thus, the use of scripts permits much more detailed accounts of crime commission to be developed from available data, and identifies where gaps in information exist.

The script concept also draws its terminology and ideas from the theatre, which has its own specialist discourse and techniques for presenting lengthy sequences of action in a meaningful way. Scripts deal with the mechanics of breaking down plots into acts and scenes so that the overall storyline is made more readily understandable to the audience, and so that the drama of unfolding action can be systematically conveyed. But the script also has a logistical function: it provides a detailed ongoing account of plot requirements in terms of cast, props, locations, and actions at successive points in the plot. In the context of criminal activity, these translate into the practical requirements of successful crime commission: a cast of experienced criminal actors and suitable victims or targets, tools and facilitators, and settings that permit the necessary criminal actions to be prepared, initiated and carried through to completion.

By drawing attention to the structure of purposive action and to its logistic requirements, the script concept provides a much fuller and more systematic treatment of crime commission than descriptions of the modus operandi. In addition, the crime script draws attention to the range of requirements for criminal activities to succeed and to the resulting implications for the growth and the prevention of particular forms of crime. We end with the following list of uses to which script analysis might be put:

- By treating crimes, even complex ones, as aggregations of simpler elements, it enables organized crimes to be analyzed into their constituent parts, so that the requirements for the success of all their aspects can be more closely identified.

- By providing a fuller and more systematic understanding of all the relevant stages involved in committing specific organized crimes, it extends the options of the situational crime prevention strategist by offering a wider range of possible intervention points at which situational techniques can be applied.

- By illustrating how opportunity structures (Clarke 1997) for particular crimes—for example, those favoring trafficking in stolen cars (Clarke 1999)—get translated into particular crime-commission techniques, it suggests how changes in opportunities may lead to changes in methods.

- It provides a means of exploring and anticipating the likely impact of changes in legislation, technology, and commercial practices on opportunity structures for crimes and, hence, on the emergence of new forms of crime or methods of crime commission (Jackson et al., 1999).

- It offers a conceptual framework for exploring how elaboration in criminal methods takes place, and how relationships among different forms of crime emerge and develop. For example, it may help to identify likely points of convergence between different crimes—as when the same safe routes and carriers for one form of trafficking are adopted for others (Mack and Kerner 1975).

- It provides pointers to the likely nature of the organizational structures required to service complex organized crimes. As Mack and Kerner (1975) point out, while the activities of frontline operatives, such as burglars, robbers, and thieves tend to receive much attention from criminologists, the actions of organizers often go unnoticed. Yet key background operatives (strategic planners, bankrollers, service providers, and receivers) and key locations (vehicle repair shops, scrap metal merchants, markets for stolen goods) may play a crucial role in the long-term resourcing and sustaining of serious criminal activity (Cressey 1972; McIntosh 1975; Mack and Kerner 1975; Sutton 1998; and Tremblay et al. 1999). As more information emerges to identify these criminal actors and locations, situational prevention strategies can be complemented by other strategies that target offenders and crime settings directly.

All these considerations suggest that access to detailed and up-to-date intelligence about the nature of criminal activity at each stage of crime commission is essential if the growth of organized crimes is to be contained (Stelfox 1998). Such knowledge enhances the expertise of those trying to prevent the occurrence of organized crimes. Indeed, the very complexity of these crimes, and the resources, coordination, and routinization that they require will render them particularly susceptible to disruption by those with an intimate knowledge of how they are accomplished.

NOTES

1. Leddo and Abelson's (1986) concept of the "universal script" provides guidelines for breaking down any sequence of goal-oriented activity into generic stages that further the action: e.g., preparation, entry (into setting), preconditions (for the action in question), instrumental preconditions, instrumental initiation, instrumental actualization, doing, exit (from setting), postconditions. In practice, the order of the later stages may vary, and repetitions of one or more stages often occur.

2. These patterns of communication have also been used by the criminal law as ways of conceptualizing distinctions between different types of conspiracy (e.g., "wheels" from "chains": see LaFave and Scott 1986) characteristic of particular forms of complex crime. We are grateful to Marti Smith for bringing this to our attention.

REFERENCES

Bavelas, A. 1950. "Communication Patterns in Task-Oriented Groups." *Journal of the Acoustical Society of America* 22: 725–730.

Becker, Gary S. 1968. "Crime and Punishment: An Economic Approach." *Journal of Political Economy* 76: 169–217.

Clarke, Ronald V., ed. 1997. *Situational Crime Prevention: Successful Case Studies (2nd ed.).* Albany, NY: Harrow and Heston.

Clarke, Ronald V. 1999. "International Trafficking in Stolen Vehicles: A Policy-Oriented Research Agenda." (mimeo).

Clarke, Ronald V. and Derek B. Cornish. 1985. "Modeling Offenders' Decisions: A Framework for Research and Policy." In *Crime and Justice: An Annual Review of Research, Volume 6*, edited by Michael Tonry and Norval Morris, 147–185. Chicago: University of Chicago Press.

Clarke, Ronald V. and Derek B. Cornish. 2000. "Rational Choice." In *Explaining Crimes and Criminals: Essays in Contemporary Criminological Theory*, edited by Raymond Paternoster and Ronet Bachman. CA: Roxbury.

Cornish, Derek B. 1994a. "Crimes as Scripts." In *Proceedings of the International Seminar on Environmental Criminology and Crime Analysis, University of Miami, Coral Gables, Florida, 1993*, edited by Diane Zahm and Paul Cromwell, 30–45. Tallahassee, FL: Florida Statistical Analysis Center, Florida Criminal Justice Executive Institute, Florida Department of Law Enforcement.

Cornish, Derek B. 1994b. "The Procedural Analysis of Offending, and Its Relevance for Situational Prevention." In *Crime Prevention Studies, Vol. 3*, edited by Ronald V. Clarke, 151–196. Monsey, NY: Criminal Justice Press.

Cornish, Derek B. 1999. "Regulating Lifestyles: A Rational Choice Approach." In *Environmental Criminology and Crime Analysis: Papers of the Seventh International Seminar. Barcelona, June 1998*, edited by Manuel Martin, 165–176. Barcelona, Spain: University of Barcelona.

Cornish, Derek B. and Ronald V. Clarke, eds. 1986. *The Reasoning Criminal: Rational Choice Perspectives on Offending*. New York: Springer-Verlag.

Cornish, Derek B. and Ronald V. Clarke. 1987. "Understanding Crime Displacement: An Application of Rational Choice Theory." *Criminology* 25 (4): 901–916.

Cornish, Derek B. and Clarke, Ronald V. 1989. "Crime Specialisation, Crime Displacement and Rational Choice Theory." In *Criminal Behavior and the Justice System: Psychological Perspectives*, edited by H. Wegener, F. Lösel and J. Haisch, 102–117. New York, NY: Springer-Verlag.

Cressey, Donald H. 1972. *Criminal Organisation: Its Elementary Forms*. London: Heinemann.

Cusson, Maurice. 1993. "A Strategic Analysis of Crime: Criminal Tactics as Responses to Precriminal Situations." In *Routine Activity and Rational Choice. Advances in Criminological Theory, Vol.5*, edited by Ronald V. Clarke and Marcus Felson, 295–304. New Brunswick, NJ: Transaction Publishers.

Ekblom, Paul. 1997. "Gearing up against Crime: A Dynamic Framework to Help Designers Keep up with the Adaptive Criminal in a Changing

World." *International Journal of Risk, Security and Crime Prevention* 2 (4): 249–265.

Ekblom, Paul and Nick Tilley. 2000. "Going Equipped: Criminology, Situational Crime Prevention and the Resourceful Offender." *British Journal of Criminology* 40 (3): 376–398.

Hinchliffe, Michael. 1994. *Professional Car Thieves, Their Knowledge and Social Structure*. A Police Award Scheme Project. Police Research Group. London: Home Office.

Hobbs, Dick. 1998. "Going Down the Local: The Local Context of Organised Crime." *The Howard Journal* 37 (4): 407–422.

Jackson, Janet, Robert W. Jasen, Arwen Pieterse, and John A. Michon. 1999. "Strategies for Profiling Economic Criminals". In *Environmental Criminology and Crime Analysis: Papers of the Seventh International Seminar. Barcelona, June 1998*, edited by Manuel Martin, 55–70. Barcelona, Spain: University of Barcelona.

LaFave, Wayne R. and Austin W. Scott, Jr. 1986. *Criminal Law (2nd ed.)*. St Paul, MN: West Publishing Co.

Leavitt, H.J. 1951. "Some Effects of Certain Communication Patterns on Group Performance." *Journal of Abnormal and Social Psychology* 46: 38–50.

Leddo, John and Robert P. Abelson. 1986. "The Nature of Explanations." In *Knowledge Structures*, edited by James A. Galambos, Robert P. Abelson and John B. Black, 103–122. Hillsdale, NJ: Erlbaum.

Letkemann, P. 1973. *Crime as Work*. Englewood Cliffs, NJ: Prentice-Hall.

Levi, Michael. 1998a. "Perspectives on "Organised Crime": An Overview." *The Howard Journal* 37 (4): 335–345.

Levi, Michael. 1998b. "Organizing Plastic Fraud: Enterprise Criminals and the Side-Stepping of Fraud Prevention." *The Howard Journal* 37 (4): 423–438.

Light, Roy, Claire Nee, and Helen Ingham. 1993. *Car Theft: The Offender's Perspective*. Home Office Research Study No.130. London, UK: HMSO.

McIntosh, Mary. 1971. "Changes in the Organization of Thieving." In *Images of Deviance*, edited by Stanley Cohen, 98–133. Harmondsworth, Middlesex: Penguin.

McIntosh, Mary. 1975. *The Organisation of Crime*. London: Macmillan.

Mack, John A. 1972. "The Able Criminal." *British Journal of Criminology* 12 (1): 44–54.

Mack, John A. with the collaboration of Hans-Jurgen Kerner. 1975. *The Crime Industry*. Farnborough, Hants: Saxon House.

Natarajan, Mangai. 2000. "Understanding the Structure of a Drug Trafficking Organization: A Conversational Analysis." In *Illegal Drug Markets: From Research to Prevention Policy*. Crime Prevention Studies

Volume 11, edited by Mangai Natarajan and Michael Hough. Monsey, NY: Criminal Justice Press.

Natarajan, Mangai and Mathieu Belanger. 1998. "Varieties of Upper-Level Drug Dealing Organizations: A Typology of Cases Prosecuted in New York City." *Journal of Drug Issues* 28 (4): 1005–1026.

Pawson, Ray and Nick Tilley. 1994. "What Works in Evaluation Research?" *British Journal of Criminology* 34 (3): 291–306.

Reuter, Peter. 1983. *Disorganized Crime: Illegal Markets and the Mafia.* Cambridge, MA: M.I.T. Press.

Schank, Roger C. and Robert P. Abelson. 1977. *Scripts, Plans, Goals and Understanding: An Inquiry into Human Knowledge.* Hillsdale, NJ: Erlbaum.

Shaw, Marvin E. 1954. "Some Effects of Unequal Distribution of Information upon Group Performance in Various Communication Nets." *Journal of Abnormal and Social Psychology* 49: 547–553.

Stelfox, Peter. 1998. "Policing Lower Levels of Organised Crime in England and Wales." *The Howard Journal* 37 (4): 393–406.

Sutton, Mike. 1998. *Handling Stolen Goods and Theft: A Market Reduction Approach.* Home Office Research Study 178. A Research and Statistics Directorate Report. London: Home Office.

Tedeschi, James T. and Richard B. Felson. 1994. *Violence, Aggression, and Coercive Actions.* Washington, DC: American Psychological Association.

Tremblay, Pierre, Maurice Cusson, and Carlo Morselli. 1998. "Market Offenses and Limits to Growth." *Crime, Law and Social Change* 29: 311–330.

Tremblay, Pierre, Bernard Talon, and Douglas Hurley. In Press. "Body Switching and Related Adaptations in the Resale of Stolen Vehicles: Script Elaborations and Aggregate Crime Learning Curves," *British Journal of Criminology.*

Chapter 4

Understanding Intoxicated Violence from a Rational Choice Perspective

Jean-Marc Assaad and M. Lyn Exum

INTRODUCTION

In the tradition of the rational choice perspective, researchers have invoked an expected utility model in order to explain crime in terms of its probabilistic costs and benefits to the offender (Bachman, Paternoster, and Ward 1992; Nagin and Paternoster 1991; Piliavan et al. 1986). However, while emphasizing the importance of the thought processes that underlie criminal decision making, rational choice theorists have largely ignored the role of psychopharmacological agents that may attenuate cognitive ability. Particularly striking is the lack of study on alcohol. Of the estimated 5.3 million offenders under criminal justice supervision in the United States in 1996, approximately 40 percent were under the influence of alcohol *at the time* they committed their crimes (Greenfeld 1998). Furthermore, many of these crimes were likely to have been serious, violent offenses. Indeed, alcohol is more closely linked to violent crime than property crime (Center on Addiction and Substance Abuse 1997), and more commonly associated with acts of violence than all other drugs combined (Miczek, Weerts, and DeBold 1993).

Several studies have examined the prevalence of alcohol intoxication[1] during the commission of a violent criminal act. In general, the findings from this research indicate that an intoxicated offender is the norm rather than the exception. For example, Wolfgang and Strohm (1956) found that 54 percent of the homicides committed in Philadelphia were committed by offenders who were drinking just prior to their crimes, while Gerson (1978) reported that approximately 66 percent of the rapes and 87 percent of the marital assaults in Ontario were committed by intoxicated offenders. More globally, epidemiological reviews of intoxicated violence suggest that as many as 85 percent of murderers, 60 percent of sexual offenders, 72 percent of robbers, and 57 percent of assailants consume alcohol prior to their criminal acts (Roizen 1997). Still other reviews report the prevalence of intoxicated assaults to be as high as 82 percent (Murdoch, Pihl, and Ross 1990).

Though striking, these findings do not offer a theoretical basis for the link between alcohol intoxication and violence. The relationship may be artifactual (spurious), such that situational or personality factors act as a common cause for both alcohol consumption and violent behavior (Pernanen 1981). Alternatively, the relationship between alcohol and violence may be causal, such that alcohol directly, indirectly, or interactionally causes aggression.

In the following pages, a review of the experimental literature on alcohol and aggression will indicate that alcohol is in fact causally linked to aggressive behavior. We then discuss three theoretical models that attempt to explain this alcohol/aggression relationship, focusing most heavily on the "indirect causal models" that suggest alcohol disrupts higher-order cognitive functioning and emotions associated with decision-making. Finally, and consistent with the rational choice perspective of criminal behavior, we will argue that through this disruption of processes related to decision-making, alcohol intoxication makes aggression a more likely behavioral outcome.

EXPERIMENTAL STUDIES OF ALCOHOL AND AGGRESSION

In an attempt to examine the multifaceted alcohol/aggression relationship, many researchers have championed the use of randomized experiments. Experimental studies allow researchers to systematically manipulate the occurrence of key events (alcohol consumption) and record subsequent changes in various outcomes (violent behavior), while at the same time controlling for other rival explanations (situational and individual factors). In this way, experimental studies allow causal inferences regarding the effect of alcohol on violence to be drawn with greater ease and confidence. More importantly for this review, these experimental studies can also shed light on how alcohol might affect the perceived costs and benefits of aggression that are thought to underlie the "rational choice" of violent, criminal behavior.

Contemporary scholars generally define "aggression" as a type of behavior intended to inflict unwanted harm on another person (e.g., Baron and Richardson 1994). Though aggressive behavior can manifest itself in a host of forms (see Buss 1961), the type most commonly studied by alcohol researchers is "physical-direct-active" aggression (Bushman 1997). That is, alcohol/aggression researchers generally seek to study acts that inflict bodily harm (physical), that are overt (direct), and that involve some instrumental response on the part of the aggressor (active). In the real world, assaulting another person with fists or weapons would constitute an act of physical-direct-active aggression. In the laboratory, however, physical-direct-active aggression must be measured in another, safer, manner. In doing so, many researchers rely on the Taylor Aggression Paradigm (TAP; Taylor 1967), or a modification thereof.

Researchers using the TAP to study intoxicated aggression inform subjects that the purpose of the study is to examine the effects of alcohol on some (bogus) performance measure such as reaction time (Jeavons and Taylor 1985; Leonard 1989; Taylor and Gammon 1975, 1976). After consuming either an alcoholic or non-alcoholic beverage,[2] subjects are pitted against a fictitious opponent who is supposedly playing from an adjoining room in a reaction time task. Subjects are told that winning a reaction time trial allows them to deliver a noxious stimulus (such as an electric shock) of the intensity and duration of their choice to their opponent. However, if the subject loses the trial, he receives the noxious stimuli set by his opponent. As the "opponent" in the study is bogus, the order of the wins and losses as well as the intensity of the noxious stimuli administered to the subjects is predetermined by the experimenter. Shock intensity and shock duration selected by the subjects, however, serve as dependent measures of physical-direct-active aggression.[3]

Currently, the TAP and its modified versions are the most widely used and accepted techniques for the measurement of aggression in a laboratory setting (Giancola and Chermack 1998). However, the paradigm is not without its critics (Tedeschi and Quigley 1996). The most common concern is how well this seemingly "artificial" measure of aggression corresponds to real-world behaviors. Though such a discussion is beyond the scope of this chapter, we should note that many studies have provided both direct and indirect support for the validity of laboratory aggression-machine paradigms. For further discussion of this debate, see Giancola and Chermack (1998).

To date, more than sixty experimental studies of alcohol and aggression have been conducted using the aggression-machine paradigms. In general, these studies report a main effect of drink condition such that those subjects who consume an alcoholic beverage administer more intense shocks than those consuming an inert beverage (Chermack and Giancola 1997). Given these positive findings within the context of randomized experimental designs, some scholars have subsequently concluded that ". . . a moderate dose of alcohol *definitely does facilitate* aggressive responding" (Gustafson 1993:27, emphasis added), and that ". . . alcohol *does indeed cause* aggressive behavior" (Bushman and Cooper 1990:48, emphasis added). Additionally, meta-analytic reviews of these experimental studies have typically found the mean effect size for alcohol to be approximately 0.50 standard deviations, an impressive value consistent with Cohen's (1988) benchmark for a moderate effect (Bushman 1997; Ito et al. 1996; Lipsey et al. 1997). Under conditions of high provocation (i.e., when subjects receive intensive electric shocks), the effect size for alcohol is 0.72 standard deviations—a value approaching Cohen's criteria for a large effect (0.80: Lipsey et al. 1997).

Furthermore, the effect of alcohol appears to be (to a degree) directly related to the dosage of alcohol and whether the blood alcohol content (BAC) is rising or falling. That is, subjects who consume moderately potent drinks administer shocks of greater intensity than those consuming "weak" drinks (Taylor and Leonard 1983). Similarly, subjects who consume high potency drinks are more aggressive than those consuming the moderately potent beverages (Gustafson, 1985; Taylor and Gammon 1975; Taylor et al. 1976). Thus, these findings would suggest that—within the limited range of doses examined—aggression is a positive linear function of alcohol consumption.

However, alcohol may only impact aggression while the subject's BAC is rising. In a study by Giancola and Zeichner (1997), sober and intoxicated subjects (BAC=0.08 percent) participated in the TAP. Half of the intoxicated subjects participated while on the ascending limb of the BAC curve (that is, when their BACs were rising), while the remaining half participated while on the descending limb of the curve. Results indicated that subjects in the ascending group were more aggressive than those in the descending group, who—despite their 0.08 percent BAC—administered shocks at intensities that were indistinguishable from those of the sober subjects. Thus, these findings would suggest that alcohol has a biphasic effect such that intoxicated-aggression is more likely to occur while the subject is in the process of "becoming intoxicated" rather than when he is "sobering up."

ALCOHOL AND AGGRESSION: EXPLANATORY MODELS

The above research indicates that a relatively high dose of alcohol (producing ascending BACs of approximately 0.08 percent-0.10 percent) can lead to aggressive behavior, especially under conditions of provocation. But exactly how does alcohol exert its effect? Several theoretical interpretations have been offered (e.g., see Chermack and Giancola 1997), but most can be classified into one of three theoretical perspectives: the expectancy model, the disinhibition model, and the indirect causal model (Bushman, 1997).

The expectancy model states that the effect of alcohol is the result of the individual's learned beliefs about intoxicated behavior. That is, aggression occurs after alcohol consumption not because of the psychopharmacological properties of the drink, but because the person simply believes or "expects" that alcohol makes him behave aggressively. Though expectancy effects have been documented, they are generally found to have weak explanatory power and are not currently favored among alcohol/aggression researchers (Hull and Bond 1986; Lipsey et al. 1997).

The disinhibition model has been the traditional explanation for intoxicated aggression. The model has three central propositions: (1) human beings are innately aggressive, (2) this innate aggression is kept in check by certain cortical functions, and (3) alcohol directly and invariantly alters this cortical inhibitory process. Thus, drinking leads to a psuedostimulation of Man's innate aggressivity, unleashing his violent nature (Taylor and Leonard, 1983). As can be seen, the disinhibition model is inherently deterministic; yet, research has shown intoxicated aggression to be moderated by a number of individual and situational factors (see Chermack and Giancola 1997). As a result, the disinhibition model has fallen out of favor with many contemporary scholars.

More popular (and supported) is the indirect causal model, which states ". . . alcohol increases aggression by causing certain cognitive, emotional, and physiological changes that increase the probability of aggression" (Bushman 1997:234). Much like the disinhibition model, the indirect causal model regards the pharmacological properties of alcohol as the primary agent in the production of intoxicated aggression. However, as the name suggests, this view considers the effect of alcohol to be "indirect" and also more probabilistic than disinhibitory models will allow. Here, alcohol is not seen as a psuedostimulator of Man's innate aggression, but is instead thought to produce certain physiological and/or psychological changes that interact with environmental cues (such as provocation) thereby making aggression a more likely outcome. In this manner, Pihl and colleagues (1993) proposed a model describing how alcohol's dose and rate-dependent pharmacological properties (affecting pain sensitivity, disrupting higher order cognitive functions, producing anxiolysis and psychomotor stimulation) may increase the likelihood of physical aggression. Particularly relevant to decision-making, alcohol appears to attenuate higher-order cognitive functioning and alters mood. As we will discuss, these effects can then impact the decision to engage in a violent manner.

ALCOHOL INTOXICATION AND EXECUTIVE COGNITIVE FUNCTIONS

The manifestation of aggression in response to provocation is thought to be mediated by cognitive processes associated with the executive cognitive functions (ECF). Although this construct is yet to be unequivocally defined

(Benton 1994; Block 1995), the ECF is thought to be comprised of abilities involved in the initiation and maintenance of goal-directed activity (Damasio 1979; Giancola 1995; Lezak 1985; Luria 1980). These include "higher-order" mental abilities such as abstract reasoning, conditional learning, attention, problem solving, the organization and planning of behavior, and the modulation of behavior in light of expected future consequences (Damasio 1979; Fuster 1989; Lezak 1985; Luria 1980; Welsh and Pennington 1988). These capacities require active monitoring of ongoing behavior, and operate within working memory (Petrides et al. 1993). A large body of literature from different fields of study identifies the prefrontal cortex as one of the key neural structures subserving these abilities as well as the process of decision making and reasoning (Damasio 1996; Giancola 1995; Séguin et al. 1995; Shallice 1988).

It is important to make a distinction between intelligence (IQ) and ECF, as they are not synonymous. Despite the nature of the abilities associated with the prefrontal cortex, it is generally accepted that the latter is not particularly involved with conventional intelligence, as defined psychometrically (Teuber, 1972). To exemplify this distinction, we can turn to several studies of patients with major lesions of the prefrontal cortex and related deficiencies in their abilities reflecting the executive cognitive functions, but who nevertheless preserve good scores on traditional measures of intelligence (Duncan, 1995; Eslinger and Damasio 1985; Shallice and Gurgess 1991, Warrington, James and Maciejewski 1986; Weinstein and Teuber 1957).

The executive cognitive functions are therefore comprised of abilities related to the process of decision making and to aggressive behaviors, and thus the prefrontal cortex is thought to be essential in the formulation of strategies—either verbal or behavioral—aimed at dealing with issues of threat or novelty (Luria 1980; Peterson and Pihl 1990). Thus, ECF may be involved in our perceptions of threat and our decisions regarding how to respond to such threats. A growing body of evidence suggests that individuals with impaired ECF might demonstrate increased aggression when the salient cue is provocation and when the cues that inhibit aggression, such as fear of violence-related consequences, are reduced (Lau, Pihl, and Peterson 1995). Likewise, a growing body of evidence indicates that alcohol disrupts ECF, impairing the drinker's ability to plan, reason, self-monitor, and utilize feedback to govern behavior (Hoaken, Giancola, and Pihl 1998). Such findings have given rise to "cognitive disruption theories" of intoxicated aggression.

Cognitive disruption theories posit that alcohol diminishes the drinker's capacity to attend to multiple situational cues equally while also minimizing the perceived consequences of one's actions (Chermack and Giancola 1997). Thus, when faced with a potentially violent encounter, the intoxicated person will heavily attend to the more salient cues (which are also generally the more provocative cues) while blissfully ignoring the distal consequences of aggression. Few studies have attempted to examine cognitive disruption theories directly as they relate to aggressive behavior; however, indirect evidence supports their point-of-view (Chermack and Giancola 1997; Hoaken et al. 1998).

For example, after providing them with either a low, moderate, or high potency drink, Peterson and his colleagues (1990) administered a battery of neuropsychological tests to their subjects. Results indicate that alcohol significantly diminished certain cognitive abilities, especially those associated with complex motor behavior, abstract conceptualization, goal directed planning and foresight, assessment, organization of behavior, and memory transfer of information—all abilities associated with ECF. In fact, the performance of highly intoxicated subjects was likened to that of patients suffering from prefrontal damage, though the authors note the two conditions are clearly distinct. Furthermore, alcohol seems to have little effect on performance on standard IQ tests, and these results do not seem to be accounted for by expectancy effects (Peterson et al. 1990).

In a subsequent study, Hoaken and his colleagues (1998) administered a series of neuropsychological tests measuring abilities usually associated with frontal lobe functioning to sober and intoxicated subjects. Before any drinks were consumed, baseline functioning scores were recorded and no significant differences were found across groups. Yet, post-consumption functioning scores revealed significant impairment among intoxicated subjects. Despite the learning effect that typically occurs across the pre- and post-administrations, intoxicated subjects' post-test measures nevertheless contained more errors than their pre-test measures, further suggestive of an effect of alcohol on cognitive functioning.

Several other examples can be drawn from the literature in support of the notion that alcohol has the ability to affect cognitive processes related to decision making. Illustratively, alcohol intoxication reduces simple decision-making speed in subjects required to give motor responses (Maylor and Rabbitt 1993). Alcohol intoxication also impairs performance on divided attention tasks, which consist of the simultaneous performance of a decision-making and a motor task (Zacchia et al. 1991). Lastly, in electroencephalogram studies aimed at exploring the effects on the electrical activity of the brain by alcohol intoxication at rest and during task performance, alcohol intoxication has also been shown to decrease response amplitude as well as increase event-related potential latency, findings that suggest delayed and impaired responding (Krull et al. 1993; Lukas et al. 1990).

The above research provides evidence for a link between alcohol consumption and diminished cognitive (prefrontal) performance. Further research has linked this type of diminished cognitive performance to aggressive behavior. For example, Lau and his colleagues (1995) recruited subjects with high and low prefrontal functioning to participate in the TAP. Results revealed that those with lower cognitive functioning were more aggressive than "high functioners," especially under highly provocative conditions. These findings were later replicated in a subsequent study (Lau and Pihl 1996).

ALCOHOL INTOXICATION AND THE RELATIONSHIP BETWEEN EMOTION AND DECISION-MAKING

Visceral influences such as moods and emotions may have an impact on decision-making (Loewenstein 1996; Vogel 1997). Thus, decisions are not solely based on the information received from the outside world. Such information is assessed against an internal reference composed of the present internal state and relevant memories of past experience (Altman, 1995). It is thought that the prefrontal cortex is where all this information converges.

A positive relationship exists between physiological arousal and aggressive behavior (Tannenbaum and Zillmann 1975; Rule and Nesdale 1976). In addition, increases in heart rate, blood pressure and skin conductance have been observed prior to, and/or during, aggressive behaviors (Dengerink 1971; Donnerstein 1980; Edguer and Janisse 1994). Alcohol intoxication is able to affect mood and emotions, such as increasing stimulation (Connors and Maisto 1979), excitement (Hartocollis 1962), elation (Babor et al. 1983), and vigor (Moss, Yao and Maddock 1989). In addition, alcohol consumption is associated with physiological arousal as indicated by increases in heart rate, blood pressure, digital blood flow and skin conductance (Levenson, et al. 1980; Stewart and Pihl 1994; Turkkan, Stitzer and McCaul 1988).

Thus, it is not unreasonable to hypothesize that alcohol may indirectly increase the likelihood of aggressive behaviors by inducing an arousing state similar to the one experienced prior to and/or during an aggressive encounter (Giancola and Zeichner 1997). Conforming to this hypothesis is the theory proposed by Berkowitz (1989, 1990) suggesting that experiencing cues associated with aggression may increase the likelihood of aggressive responding.

The reduction of threat can also increase aggressive responding. Fear has the ability to inhibit the expression of aggressive behaviors, specifically when the expression of a violent act would expose the aggressor to punishment or threat in the form of interpersonal retaliation or societal revenge. In this manner, fear produced in response to threat encourages individuals to avoid harm. It therefore follows that if a substance is consumed with the ability to reduce the anxiety (the behavioral inhibition) produced by threatening cues, then the probability for aggression may increase (Pihl, Peterson and Lau 1993). Alcohol is such a substance (Josephs and Steele 1990; Sayette 1993; Sayette, Wilson, and Carpenter 1989).

The anxiolytic effects of alcohol may therefore be responsible for the attenuation of the inhibitory effects of fear that usually accompany the expression of behaviors such as aggression, a dangerous behavior associated with the receipt of punishment or threat (Gray, 1982, 1987). Thus, alcohol may increase the propensity of aggressive responding when the expression of such a behavior is under the inhibitory control of fear (Pihl, Peterson and Lau 1993), an effect that conforms to the cognitive disruption model.

Further confirming the association between alcohol intoxication and emotions are the findings that alcohol produces changes in mood associated with changes in glucose metabolism in the frontal and temporal areas of the brain (de Wit et al. 1990). Additionally, alcohol intoxication is also related to blood flow alterations in the brain, particularly in the frontal and temporal lobes (Schwartz et al. 1993; Sano et al. 1993). It has been found that different doses produce different patterns of blood flow alterations, possibly related to the biphasic arousal-sedation effects, and mood effects, of alcohol (Sano et al. 1993). Lastly, other related experimental studies support the notion of a disruption of emotion recognition following alcohol intoxication, such that alcohol has been found to impair the judgment of facial expressions of some emotions, such as anger and disgust/contempt, but not necessarily for all facial emotions (e.g. sadness, surprise, happiness, fear: Borrill, Rosen, and Summerfield 1987).

We have therefore reviewed evidence suggesting that alcohol may increase the propensity of violent behaviors by either increasing arousal or decreasing anxiety. It is interesting to note that the grouping of aggressive individuals in terms of anxious and nonanxious has already received preliminary empirical support (Harden et al. 1995). Anxious-aggressive boys reflected significant increases in responsivity to a stressor, while the nonanxious aggressives did not. This finding conforms to both the under-arousal theory of psychopathy—the nonanxious aggressives (Raine 1993), as well as to the notion of visceral influences on behavior—the anxious aggressives (Loewenstein 1996). As mentioned above, the underarousal theory implicates the roles of decreased anxiety or sensitivity to cues of punishment (Quay 1988) in increasing the likelihood of aggressive responding, while the notion of visceral influences on behavior would implicate the role of arousal in interfering with the cognitive processes that normally inhibit reactive aggression (Tyson 1998).

INDIRECT CAUSAL MODELS AND THE RATIONAL CHOICE PERSPECTIVE

The above research suggests that alcohol may indirectly lead to aggression by disrupting cognitive functioning and/or altering emotional states associated with decision-making. Thus, under the influence of alcohol individuals (1) may not attend to non-provocative cues but instead focus on the provocative cues, (2) may not recognize the risk associated with acting on those provocative cues, (3) may experience increases in arousal interfering with cognitive processes which normally inhibit aggression and (4) may not experience the anxiety (or fear) that would normally inhibit the confrontation of a situation. When these effects are considered within an expected utility model of behavior, aggression may be viewed by the intoxicated individual as logical or rational. Research using the TAP indirectly substantiates this point-of-view.

ALCOHOL INTOXICATION AND CUE RESPONSIVITY

Recall that cognitive disruption theories contend that, under the influence of alcohol, the brain cannot attend to multiple cues equally. As a result, intoxicated individuals will respond to the most salient cues, which are typically the most provocative. Research by Taylor and his colleagues (1979) offers support for this claim. Here, sober and intoxicated subjects participated in the TAP with either normally provocative or highly provocative cues. In the latter condition, the fictitious opponent occasionally attempted to shock the subject at twice his maximum pain threshold. Results revealed that intoxicated subjects exposed to the highly provocative conditions were more aggressive than sober subjects in either cue condition.

Similarly, Taylor and Sears (1988) allowed subjects to participate in the TAP in the presence of two observers (research confederates). Throughout the trials, the observers used peer-pressure to encourage subjects to deliver highly intensive shocks. Results again revealed that intoxicated subjects were more aggressive in the presence of these instigatory cues than their sober counterparts. Also using the TAP, Leonard (1989) allowed half of his subjects to "overhear" the opponent say he intended to deliver the maximum shock intensity for every trial (an explicit, aggressive cue). Once the game began, however, the opponent always delivered the minimum shock intensity (an implicit, nonaggressive cue). Results from this study revealed that while sober subjects decreased their shock intensities when exposed to the nonaggressive cue, intoxicated subjects continued to deliver high-level shocks. Consistent with a cognitive disruption theory of intoxicated aggression, these studies suggest that intoxicated subjects are indeed more responsive to salient, aggressive cues than sober subjects.

ALCOHOL INTOXICATION AND THE RISKS/CONSEQUENCES OF AGGRESSION

Recall that cognitive disruption theories also suggest that aggression is more likely to occur under the influence of alcohol because the intoxicated person is less likely to understand the risks and consequences of aggression. Research by Weisman and Taylor (1994) offers support for this claim. In this study of risk perception, subjects participated in a modified version of the TAP in which they had complete control over the shock intensity levels to be administered. If the subject won the trial, the shock he selected would be delivered to his opponent. However, if the subject lost the trial, the shock he selected would be administered to himself. Generally speaking, then, it was in the subject's best interest to administer low-level shocks.

Prior to the task, subjects were allowed several practice trials (without the shock) so that they could evaluate their opponent's ability. The number of practice trials subjects won was manipulated so that the fictitious opponent would be viewed as either equally competent or highly superior to the subject. Following this practice period, subjects completed the reaction-time task with the use of shocks. Results revealed that sober subjects selected low-intensity shocks regardless of their opponent's skill-level. This is consistent with previous research indicating that sober subjects are not terribly aggressive and also suggests that these subjects recognized that selecting low-level shocks was self-serving and advantageous. Intoxicated subjects who saw their opponent as their competitive equal selected shocks of greater intensity than sober subjects. This is consistent with prior research indicating that alcohol increases aggressive responding. Most interesting, however, is the finding that intoxicated subjects competing against a *superior* opponent responded similarly to intoxicated subjects playing against an opponent who was equally skilled. In other words, despite being at great risk of receiving the shock they selected, intoxicated subjects nevertheless chose highly aggressive responses. This apparent inability to attend to risky situations is consistent with a cognitive disruption theory of intoxicated aggression.

Zeichner and Pihl (1979) examined the effect of alcohol on subjects' perceived consequences of their actions using a modified version of the TAP. After each trial in which the subject shocked his partner, the partner responded by administering an electronic tone through the subject's headphones. These "contingency tones" were played at intensities that were either randomly determined or perfectly correlated with the shock the subject administered. In this latter condition, subjects who administered high-level shocks would receive in return high-volume contingency tones making aggression more "costly" to them. Results revealed that—as expected—sober subjects who heard correlated tones were less aggressive than those who heard random tones. Among intoxicated subjects, however, contingency was irrelevant. Intoxicated subjects delivered high-level shocks, seemingly overlooking the consequences of their aggressive behavior.

Similarly, Schmutte and Taylor (1980) examined the effect of victim-feedback on intoxicated aggression. During the reaction-time task, subjects were allowed to "overhear" their opponent vocalize either low- or high-level groans whenever the subjects administered shocks. Among sober subjects, high victim-feedback curbed aggressive responding. However, intoxicated subjects were equally aggressive regardless of the victim's cries. Moreover, this aggression in the presence of intense victim-feedback was driven by those subjects who had the highest BACs. Whereas "intoxicated but low BAC" subjects appeared to lower their shocks in response to the opponent's cries of pain, intoxicated subjects with high BACs actually *increased* their aggressivity, apparently finding their aggressive behavior rewarding. In sum and consistent with a cognitive disruption theory of intoxicated aggression, these findings suggest that alcohol can diminish subjects' perceptions of the costs associated with aggression.

However, not all research has found intoxicated subjects to be so short-sighted and insensitive. Using the Taylor paradigm, Hoaken, Assaad, and Pihl (1998) provided half of their subjects with incentives for nonaggressive responses. Each shock intensity level was assigned a monetary value, with the low-intensity shocks worth more money. Thus, it was in the subject's best interest to select low-level shocks. Results indicate that when aggression is costly, sober subjects will be less aggressive than when there is no monetary incentive. This is not surprising, as it indicates that sober subjects recognized the consequences of their actions and responded accordingly. Interestingly, the same pattern of results was found among intoxicated subjects. When aggressive responding was costly, intoxicated subjects were also more pacifistic. These findings were counter to the authors' predictions. However, they note that all subjects were selected for participation in the study based on their above-average cognitive abilities. The authors therefore suggest that this sample of subjects may ". . . retain sufficient residual functioning, even when acutely intoxicated, to inhibit aggressive responding when in the presence of appropriate cues . . ." (Hoaken, Assaad, and Pihl 1998, 606). In other words, subjects with higher baseline prefrontal abilities may be more insulated from the cognitive disruption associated with alcohol intoxication. Such an interpretation would be consistent with a cognitive disruption theory of intoxicated-aggression, though future research is needed in order to examine the authors' hypotheses.

CONCLUSION

The rational choice perspective seeks to explain the occurrence of crime in terms of its perceived costs and benefits. Criminal acts that are thought to offer great rewards and few costs are viewed as attractive opportunities to would-be offenders. In the "real world," violent crimes such as murder, rape, and physical assault are often committed under the influence of alcohol. Can these seemingly irrational drunken acts also be explained within the rational choice perspective? We believe that they can.

Although several different models can be proposed to explain the multifaceted relationship between alcohol and aggression (Pihl et al., 1993), the research reviewed in this chapter suggests that alcohol (under the proper conditions) *can facilitate* aggressive behavior by altering aspects of executive cognitive functioning, especially those associated with attention, reasoning, and risk assessment and by affecting emotions, especially decreasing anxiety/fear, or by increasing arousal. Under the influence of alcohol, individuals are more likely to attend to salient, provocative cues in the environment. Under the influence of alcohol, individuals may not experience anxiety or fear that inhibits risky behavior. Under the influence of alcohol, individuals are less likely to recognize the costs associated with their own aggressive behavior. Under the influence of alcohol, individuals may experience increases in arousal that in turn interferes with the cognitive processes that normally inhibit aggression. Therefore, with apparently little perceived risk or fear of punishment, physical aggression can in fact be seen as a "rational" and opportune choice to the intoxicated offender.

NOTES

1. Methodological problems prevent the precise measurement of an offender's level of intoxication at the moment a violent incident occurs. Thus, the term "intoxication" is broadly defined here to denote (1) reports of the offender drinking alcohol (any amount) immediately prior to the crime, and/or (2) the presence of alcohol (any level) in the offender's system shortly after the crime.

2. The type and dose of alcohol administered varies across alcohol/aggression studies. Generally speaking, researchers provide subjects with enough alcohol to elevate their blood-alcohol content (BAC) within the range of 0.08 percent-0.10 percent. Though higher BACs are of theoretical and practical interest, ethical considerations largely forbid their study (Gustafson 1994).

3. Modified versions of the TAP include, for example, the Point Subtraction Aggression Paradigm (PSAP; Kelly and Cherek, 1993) in which subjects remove "points" that are worth monetary value from one another. For a more thorough description of these tasks and also of the origin of

the aggression paradigms, see Giancola and Chermack (1998) and Buss (1961).

REFERENCES

Altman, Jennifer. 1995. "Deciding What to do Next." *Trends in Neurosciences* 18: 117–118.

Babor, Thomas F., Steven Berglas, Jack H. Mendelson, James E. Ellingboe, and Kristin Miller. 1983. "Alcohol, affect, and the disinhibition of verbal behavior."
Psychopharmacology 80: 53–60.

Bachman, Ronet, Raymond Paternoster, and Sally Ward. 1992. "The Rationality of Sexual Offending: Testing a Deterrence/Rational Choice Conception of Sexual Assault." *Law & Society Review* 26(2): 343–372.

Baron, Robert A., and Deborah R. Richardson. 1994. *Human Aggression, Second Edition.* New York: Plenum Press.

Benton, Arthur L. 1994. "Neuropsychological Assessment." *Annual Review of Psychology* 45: 1–23.

Berkowitz, Leonard. 1989. "Frustration-Aggression Hypothesis: Examination and Reformulation." *Psychological Bulletin* 106: 59–73.

Berkowitz, Leonard. 1990. "On the Formation and Regulation of Anger and Aggression." *American Psychologist* 45: 494–503.

Block, Jack. 1995. "On the Relation Between IQ, Impulsivity, and Delinquency: Remarks on Lynam, Moffitt, and Stouthamer-Loeber (1993) Interpretation." *Journal of Abnormal Psychology* 104: 395–398.

Borrill, Josephine A., Bernard K. Rosen, and Angela B. Summerfield. 1987. "The Influence of Alcohol on Judgement of Facial Expressions of Emotion." *British Journal of Medical Psychology* 60: 71-77.

Bushman, Brad J. 1997. "Effects of Alcohol on Human Aggression: Validity of Proposed Explanations." In *Recent Developments in Alcoholism, Volume13: Alcohol and Violence*, edited by Marc Galanter, 227–243. New York: Plenum Press.

Bushman, Brad J. and Harris M. Cooper. 1990. "Effects of Alcohol on Human Aggression: An Integrative Research Review." *Psychological Bulletin* 107(3): 341–354.

Buss, Arnold H. 1961. *The Psychology of Aggression.* New York: John Wiley & Sons, Inc.

Center on Addiction and Substance Abuse. 1998. *Behind Bars: Substance Abuse and America's Prison Population.* National Center on Addiction and Substance Abuse at Columbia University.

Chermack, Stephen T. and Peter R. Giancola. 1997. "The Relation Between Alcohol and Aggression: An Integrated Biopsychosocial Conceptualization." *Clinical Psychology Review* 17(6): 621–649.

Cohen, Jacob. 1998. *Statistical Power Analysis for the Behavioral Sciences, Second Edition*. Hillsdale, NJ: Lawrence Erlbaum Associates.

Connors, Gerald, and Stephen A. Maisto. 1979. "Effects of Alcohol, Instructions, and Consumption Rate on Affect and Physiological Sensations." *Psychopharmacology* 62: 261–266.

Damasio, Antonio. 1979. "The Frontal Lobes." In *Clinical Neuropsychology*, edited by Kenneth M. Heilman and Edward Valenstein, 360–412. New York: Oxford University Press.

Damasio, Antonio R. 1996. "The Somatic Marker Hypothesis and the Possible Functions of the Prefrontal Cortex." *Philosophical Transactions of the Royal Society - Ser B - Biological Sciences* 351: 1413–1420.

de Wit, H., J. Metz, N. Wagner, and M. Cooper. 1990. "Behavioral and Subjective Effects of Ethanol: Relationship to Cerebral Metabolism using PET." *Alcoholism: Clinical and Experimental Research* 14: 482-489.

Dengerink, H. 1971. "Anxiety, Aggression, and Physiological Arousal." *Journal of Experimental Research in Personality* 5(3): 223–232.

Donnerstein, Edward. 1980. "Aggressive Erotica and Violence Against Women." *Journal of Personality and Social Psychology* 39: 269–277.

Duncan, John, Paul Burgess, and Hazel Emslie. 1995. "Fluid Intelligence after Frontal Lobe Lesions." *Neuropsychologia* 33: 261–268.

Edguer, Nukte and Michael Janisse. 1994. "Type A Behaviour and Aggression: Provocation, Conflict and Cardiovascular Responsivity in the Buss Teacher-Learner Paradigm." *Personality and Individual Differences* 17: 377–393.

Eslinger, Paul J., and Antonio R. Damasio. 1985. "Severe Disturbance of Higher Cognition after Bilateral Frontal Lobe Ablation: Patient EVR." *Neurology* 35:1731–1741.

Fuster, Joaquin M. 1989. *The Prefrontal Cortex: Anatomy, Physiology, and Neuropsychology of the Frontal Lobe*. New York: Raven Press.

Gerson, Lowell W. 1978. "Alcohol-Related Acts of Violence: Who was Drinking and Where the Acts Occurred." *Journal of Studies on Alcohol* 39(7): 1294–1296.

Giancola, Peter R. 1995. "Evidence of Dorsolateral and Orbital Prefrontal Involvement in the Expression of Aggressive Behaviour." *Aggressive Behavior* 21: 431–450.

Giancola, Peter R., and Stephen T. Chermack. 1998. "Construct Validity of Laboratory Aggression Paradigms: A Response to Tedeschi and Quigley (1996)." *Aggression and Violent Behavior* 3: 237–253.

Giancola, Peter R., and Amos Zeichner. 1997. "The Biphasic Effects of Alcohol on Human Physical Aggression." *Journal of Abnormal Psychology* 106(4): 598–607.

Gray, Jeffrey A. 1982. *The Neuropsychology of Anxiety: An Enquiry into the Function of the Septo-Hippocampal System.* New York: Oxford University Press.

Gray, Jeffrey A. 1987. *The Psychology of Fear and Stress, Second Edition.* New York: Cambridge University Press.

Greenfeld, Lawrence A. 1998. *Alcohol and Crime.* Washington, DC:USDOJ/BCJ NCJ 168632.

Gustafson, Roland. 1985. "Frustration as an Important Determinant of Alcohol-Related Aggression." *Psychological Reports* 57: 3–14.

Gustafson, Roland. 1993. "What Do Experimental Paradigms Tell Us About Alcohol-Related Aggressive Responding?" *Journal of Studies on Alcohol* Suppl. 11: 20–29.

Gustafson, Roland. 1994. "Alcohol and Aggression." *Journal of Offender Rehabilitation* 21(3–4): 41–80.

Harden, Philip W., Robert O. Pihl, Frank Vitaro, Paul L. Gendreau, et al. 1995. "Stress Response in Anxious and Nonanxious Disruptive Boys." *Journal of Emotional & Behavioral Disorders* 3(3): 183–190.

Hartocollis, Peter. 1962. "Drunkenness and Suggestion: An Experiment with Intravenous Alcohol." *Quarterly Journal of Studies on Alcohol* 28: 376–389.

Hoaken, Peter N.S., Jean-Marc Assaad, and Robert O. Pihl. 1998. "Cognitive Functioning and the Inhibition of Alcohol-Induced Aggression." *Journal of Studies on Alcohol* 59: 599–607.

Hoaken, Peter N.S., Peter R. Giancola, and Robert O. Pihl. 1998. "Executive Cognitive Functions as Mediators of Alcohol-Related Aggression." *Alcohol & Alcoholism* 33(1): 47–54.

Hull, Jay G., and Charles F. Bond. 1986. "Social and Behavioral Consequences of Alcohol Consumption and Expectancy: A Meta-Analysis." *Psychological Bulletin* 99(3): 347–360.

Josephs, Robert A. and Claude M. Steele. 1990. "The Two Faces of Alcohol Myopia: Attentional Mediation of Psychological Stress." *Journal of Abnormal Psychology* 99: 115-126.

Kelly, Thomas H., and Don R. Cherek. 1993. "The Effects of Alcohol on Free-Operant Aggressive Behavior." *Journal of Studies on Alcohol* 11: 40–52.

Ito, Tiffany A., Norman Miller, and Vicki E. Pollock. 1996. "Alcohol and Aggression: A Meta-Analysis on the Moderating Effects of Inhibitory Cues, Triggering Events, and Self-Focused Attention." *Psychological Bulletin* 120(1): 60–82.

Jeavons, Candance M., and Stuart P. Taylor. 1985. "The Control of Alcohol-Related Aggression: Redirecting the Inebriate's Attention to Socially Appropriate Conduct." *Aggressive Behavior* 11(2): 93–101.

Krull, Kevin R., Landgrave T. Smith, Rajita Sinha, and Oscar A. Parsons. 1993. "Simple Reaction Time Event-Related Potentials: Effects of Alcohol and Sleep Deprivation." *Alcoholism: Clinical and Experimental Research* 17: 771-777.

Lau, Mark A., Robert O. Pihl, and Jordan B. Peterson. 1995. "Provocation, Acute Intoxication, Cognitive Performance, and Aggression." *Journal of Abnormal Psychology* 104(1): 150–155.

Lau, Mark A., and Robert O. Pihl. 1996. "Cognitive Performance, Monetary Incentive, and Aggression." *Aggressive Behavior* 22: 417–430.

Lezak, Muriel D. 1985. "Neuropsychological Assessment." In *Handbook of Clinical Neurology: Vol. 1. Clinical Neuropsychology*, edited by Joseph Antonius M. Frederiks, 515–530. New York: Elsevier.

Lipsey, Mark W., David B. Wilson, Mark A. Cohen, and James H. Derzon. 1997. "Is There a Causal Relationship Between Alcohol Use and Violence? A Synthesis of Evidence." In *Recent Developments in Alcoholism, Volume13: Alcohol and Violence*, edited by Marc Galanter, 245–282. New York: Plenum Press.

Leonard, Kenneth E. 1989. "The Impact of Explicit Aggressive and Implicit Nonaggressive Cues on Aggression in Intoxicated and Sober Males." *Personality and Social Psychology Bulletin* 15: 390–400.

Levenson, Robert W., Kenneth J. Sher, Linda M. Grossman, Joseph P. Newman, and David B. Newlin. 1980. "Alcohol and Stress Response Dampening: Pharmacological Effects, Expectancy, and Tension Reduction." *Journal of Abnormal Psychology* 89: 528–523.

Loewenstein, George. 1996. "Out of Control: Visceral Influences on Behavior." *Organizational Behavior and Human Decision Processes* 65: 272–292.

Lukas, Scott E., Jack H. Mendelson, Elena Kouri, Michelle Bolduc, and Leslie Amass. 1990. "Ethanol-Induced Alterations in EEG Alpha Activity and Apparent Source of the Auditory P300 Evoked Response Potential." *Alcohol* 7: 471-477.

Luria, Alexander R. 1980. *Higher Cortical Functions in Man, Second Edition*. New York: Basic Books.

Maylor, Elizabeth A. and Patrick M. Rabbitt. 1993. "Alcohol, Reaction Time and Memory: A Meta-Analysis." *British Journal Of Psychology* 84: 301-317.

Miczek, Klaus A., Elise M. Weerts, and Joseph F. DeBold. 1993. "Alcohol, Aggression, and Violence: Biobehavioral Determinants." In *Alcohol and Interpersonal Violence: Fostering Multidisciplinary Perspectives. NIAAA Research Monograph 24*, edited by Susan E. Martin, 83–119. NIH 93–3496.

Moss, Howard B., Jeffrey K. Yao, and John M. Maddock. 1989. "Responses by Sons of Alcoholic Fathers to Alcoholic and Placebo Drinks: Perceived Mood, Intoxication, and Plasma Prolactin." *Alcoholism: Clinical and Experimental Research* 13: 252–257.

Murdoch, Douglas, R.O. Pihl, and Deborah Ross. 1990. "Alcohol and Crimes of Violence: Present Issues." *The International Journal of the Addictions* 25(9): 1065–1081.

Nagin, Daniel S., and Raymond Paternoster 1991. "The Preventive Effects of the Perceived Risk of Arrest: Testing an Expanded Conception of Deterrence." *Criminology* 29(4): 561–585.

Peterson, Jordan B. and Robert O. Pihl. 1990. "Information Processing, Neuro-psychological Function, and the Inherited Predisposition to Alcoholism." *Neuropsychological Review* 1:343–369.

Petrides, Michael, Bessie Alivisatos, Alan C. Evans, and Ernst Meyer. 1993. "Dissociation of Human Mid-dorsolateral from Posterior Dorsolateral Frontal Cortex in Memory Processing." *Proceedings of the National Academy of Sciences* 90: 873–877.

Pernanen, Kai. 1981. "Theoretical Aspects of the Relationship Between Alcohol Use and Crime." In *Drinking and Crime*, edited by James J. Collins, Jr., 1–69. New York: The Guilford Press.

Pihl, R.O., J. B. Peterson, and M. A. Lau. 1993. "A Biosocial Model of the Alcohol-Aggression Relationship." *Journal of Studies on Alcohol* 11:128–139.

Piliavin, Irving, Craig Thornton, Rosemary Gartner, and Ross L. Matsueda. 1986. "Crime, Deterrence, and Rational Choice." *American Sociological Review* 51: 101–119.

Quay, Herbert C. 1988. "The Behavioral Reward and Inhibition System in Childhood Behavior Disorder." In *Attention Deficit Disorder, Volume 3: New Research in Attention, Treatment, and Psychopharmacology*, edited by Lewis M. Bloomingdale, 176–186. Oxford, England UK: Pergamon Press

Raine, Adrian. 1993. *The Psychopathology of Crime: Criminal Behavior as a Clinical Disorder*. San Diego, California: Academic Press.

Roizen, Judith. 1997. "Epidemiological Issues in Alcohol-Related Violence." In *Recent Developments in Alcoholism, Volume13: Alcohol and Violence*, edited by Marc Galanter, 7–39. New York: Plenum Press.

Rule, Brendan G. and Andrew R. Nesdale. 1976. "Emotional Arousal and Aggressive Behavior." *Psychological Bulletin* 83: 851–863.

Sano, Mary, Peter E. Wendt, Ann Wirsen, Georg Stenberg, Jarl Risberg and David H. Ingvar. 1993. "Acute Effects of Alcohol on Regional Cerebral Blood Flow in Man." *Journal of Studies on Alcohol* 54: 369-376.

Sayette, Michael A. 1993. "An Appraisal-disruption Model of Alcohol's Effects on Stress Responses in Social Drinkers." *Psychological Bulletin* 114: 459-476.

Sayette, Michael A., Terence G. Wilson, and John A. Carpenter. 1989. "Cognitive Moderators of Alcohol's Effects on Anxiety." *Behaviour Research and Therapy* 27: 685-690.

Schmutte, Gregory T., and Stuart P. Taylor. 1980. "Physical Aggression as a Function of Alcohol and Pain Feedback." *Journal of Social Psychology* 110(2): 235-244.

Schwartz, Joseph A., Nancy M. Speed, Milton D. Gross, Michael R. Lucey, Andrew M Bazakis, Hariharan, M., and Thomas P. Beresford. 1993. "Acute Effects of Alcohol Administration on Regional Cerebral Blood Flow: The Role of Acetate." *Alcoholism: Clinical and Experimental Research* 17: 1119-1123.

Séguin, Jean R., Robert O. Pihl, Philip W. Harden, Richard E. Tremblay, and Bernard Boulerice. 1995. "Cognitive and Neuropsychological Characteristics of Physically Aggressive Boys." *Journal of Abnormal Psychology* 104(4): 614-624.

Shallice, Tim. 1988. *From Neuropsychology to Mental Structure*. New York: Cambridge University Press.

Shallice, Tim and Paul W. Burgess. 1991. "Deficits in Strategy Application Following Frontal Lobe Damage in Man." *Brain* 114: 727-741.

Stewart, Sherry H., Robert O. Pihl. 1994. "Effects of Alcohol Administration on Psychophysiological and Subjective-emotional Responses to Aversive Stimulation in Anxiety-sensitive Women." *Psychology of Addictive Behaviors* 8(1): 29-42.

Tannenbaum, Percy H. and Dolf Zillmann. 1975. "Emotional Arousal in the Facilitation of Aggression Through Communication." In *Advances in Experimental Social Psychology, Volume 8*, edited by Leonard Berkowitz, 149-191. New York: Academic Press.

Taylor, Stuart P. 1967. "Aggressive Behavior and Physiological Arousal as a Function of Provocation and the Tendency to Inhibit Aggression." *Journal of Personality* 35: 297-310.

Taylor, Stuart P., and Charles B. Gammon. 1975. "Effects of Type and Dose of Alcohol on Human Physical Aggression." *Journal of Personality and Social Psychology* 32(1): 169-175.

Taylor, Stuart P., and Charles B. Gammon. 1976. "Aggressive Behavior of Intoxicated Subjects: The Effect of Third-Party Intervention." *Journal of Studies on Alcohol* 37: 917-930.

Taylor, Stuart P., and Kenneth E. Leonard. 1983. "Alcohol and Human Physical Aggression." In *Aggression: Theoretical and Empirical Reviews*, edited by Russell G. Geen and Edward I. Donnerstein, 77-101. New York: Academic Press.

Taylor, Stuart P., Richard M. Vardaris, Allen B. Rawich, Charles B. Gammon, Jay W. Cranston, and Arvin I. Lubetkin. 1976. "The Effects of Alcohol and Delta-9–Tetrahydrocannabinol on Human Physical Aggression." *Aggressive Behavior* 2: 153–161.

Taylor, Stuart P., Gregory T. Schmutte, Kenneth E. Leonard, and Jay W. Cranston. 1979. "The Effects of Alcohol and Extreme Provocation on the Use of a Highly Noxious Electric Shock." *Motivation and Emotion* 3(1): 73–81.

Taylor, Stuart P., and James D. Sears. 1988. "The Effects of Alcohol and Persuasive Social Pressure on Human Physical Aggression". *Aggressive Behavior* 14(4): 237–243.

Tedeschi, James T. and Brian Quigley. 1996. "Limitations of Laboratory Paradigms for Studying Aggression." *Aggression and Violent Behavior* 1: 163–177.

Teuber, Hans-Lukas. 1972. "Unity and Diversity of Frontal Lobe Functions." *Acta Neurobiologia Experimentalis* 32: 615–656.

Turkkan, Jaylan S., Maxine L. Stitzer, and Mary E. McCaul. 1988. "Psychophysiological Effects of Oral Ethanol in Alcoholics and Social Drinkers." *Alcoholism: Clinical and Experimental Research* 12: 30–38.

Tyson, Paul D. 1998. "Physiological Arousal, Reactive Aggression, and the Induction of an Incompatible Relaxation Response." *Aggression & Violent Behavior* 3(2): 143–158.

Vogel, Gretchen. 1997. "Scientists Probe Feelings Behind Decision-making." *Science* 275(5304): 1269.

Warrington, Elizabeth K., Merle James, and Christina Maciejewski. 1986. "The WAIS as a Lateralizing and Localizing Diagnostic Instrument: A Study of 656 Patients with Unilateral Cerebral Lesions." *Neuropsychologia* 24: 223–239.

Weinstein, Sidney and Hans-Lukas Teuber. 1957. "Effects of Penetrating Brain Injury on Intelligence Test Scores." *Science* 125: 1036–1037.

Weisman, Adam M., and Stuart P. Taylor. 1994. "Effect of Alcohol and Risk of Physical Harm on Human Physical Aggression." *The Journal of General Psychology* 121(1): 67–76.

Welsh, Marlyn C., and Bruce F. Pennington 1988. "Assessing Frontal Lobe Functioning in Children: Views from Developmental Psychology." *Developmental Neuropsychology* 4: 199–230.

Wolfgang, Marvin E., and Rolf B. Strohm. 1956. "The Relationship Between Alcohol and Criminal Homicide." *Quarterly Journal of Studies on Alcohol* 17: 411–425.

Zacchia, Camillo, Robert O. Pihl, Simon N. Young and Frank R. Ervin. 1991. "Effect of Sucrose Consumption on Alcohol-induced Impairment in Male Social Drinkers." *Psychopharmacology* 105:49-56.

Zeichner, Amos, and Robert O. Pihl. 1979. "Effects of Alcohol and Behavior Contingencies on Human Aggression." *Journal of Abnormal Psychology* 88(2): 153–160.

Chapter 5

The Rational Choice Implications of Control Balance Theory

Alex R. Piquero and Matthew Hickman

INTRODUCTION

In the late 1980s, Charles Wellford observed that theoretical criminology was in a state of paralysis. Since the publication of this strong assessment, criminologists have witnessed the development of several general theories of crime and deviance, sparking a renewed interest in both theoretical and empirical research. These general theories have been developed within the dominant theoretical perspectives of criminology including strain (Agnew 1992), rational choice (Cornish and Clarke 1986; Nagin and Paternoster 1993), control (Gottfredson and Hirschi 1990; Sampson and Laub 1993; Tittle 1995), and developmental (Moffitt 1993; Patterson and Yoerger 1993; Vila 1994) theories. More important, and in line with Wellford's suggestions, several of these general theories are interdisciplinary in nature (Braithwaite 1989), recognizing the importance of not only sociological correlates of criminal behavior, but also psychological and biophysical perspectives as they relate to criminal and antisocial behavior (Raine et al. 1997).

One theoretical approach that has received a considerable amount of attention is the rational choice perspective. Unlike the rational choice theories arising from economics (Becker 1968), the rational choice perspective in criminology is rooted in the pioneering work of Cornish and Clarke (1986). In *The Reasoning Criminal*, these authors advance a perspective of crime that considers the situational context in which criminal events transpire. By focusing attention on the risks, rewards, opportunity structure, and causal influence of several variables for different types of crimes, Cornish and Clarke present a general framework for understanding all criminal acts.

85

A second but more recent general theory has been developed by Tittle (1995) in his award-winning book, *Control Balance*. The general theme of control balance is that the amount of control to which people are subject, relative to the amount of control they can exercise (the control balance ratio), will affect both the probability and type of deviant behavior they undertake. Individuals with a balanced control ratio are likely to conform. Unlike previous control theories, Tittle's control balance argues that *both* low control (control deficits) and high control (control surpluses) may be conducive to criminal and deviant acts. Thus, by focusing on control *im*balances, Tittle presents a theory designed to account for all criminal and deviant acts.

While elements of the rational choice perspective are discussed by Tittle, he leaves much room for elaboration with regard to the specific interrelationships between an individual's control ratio and their perceptions of the risks and rewards associated with criminal and deviant acts. Investigating these inter-relationships (what Tittle refers to as "contingencies") are important because the influence of individual control ratios on criminal and deviant behavior may be mediated by the risks, rewards, and opportunities of criminal and deviant acts. As Tittle (1995:50) observes:

> To understand deviance, even if it can be described with a cost-benefit formula, one must know what goes into the calculation. Why do some fear punishment more than others; why do some regard particular things as costly that others regard as rewarding; why do actual punishment probabilities vary from situation to situation; and how do group sanctions interact with individual sanctions? Moreover, what are the circumstances that allow deviance to occur, given a favorable cost-benefit calculation, and how do we account for the distribution of costs and benefits in various societies and across social situations?

From this discussion, we derive two rational choice implications from the control balance framework: (1) the control balance ratio affects assessments of the costs and benefits associated with particular actions; (2) given a cost/benefit ratio favorable to deviance, the control balance ratio affects the extent to which actual deviance may occur. In other words, the control balance ratio has an indirect effect on deviance through the costs and benefits associated with criminal and deviant acts.

In this chapter, we explore how the control ratio and the rational choice perspective are related. After reviewing both the rational choice perspective and Tittle's control balance theory, we present a series of predictions about the interrelationships between the control ratio and several rational choice variables. Then, we test these hypotheses using data collected for the specific purpose of assessing the control balance process.

RATIONAL CHOICE THEORY

Unlike other contemporary theories of crime that focus primarily on properties of the offender (Gottfredson and Hirschi 1990; Moffitt 1993; Agnew 1992), the rational choice perspective explains the conditions that are needed for specific crimes to occur, and thus emphasizes the role of crime opportunities in crime causation (Clarke and Cornish 2000). This is not to say that the rational choice perspective does not also pay attention to the "criminality" part of the "criminality-criminal event" distinction. When it focuses on involvement, the rational choice perspective is also a theory of criminality, "albeit one that gives a fuller role to current life circumstances, needs, and opportunities" (Clarke and Cornish 2000). When it focuses on the event and attempts to understand the situational characteristics that lead to the decision to commit a crime, it becomes a theory of crime. Several scholars have empirically demonstrated this particular point (Nagin and Paternoster 1993; Piquero and Tibbetts 1996).

The main premise underlying rational choice theory is that crime is a chosen activity because the anticipated benefit it brings to the offender outweighs the perceived cost associated with committing the crime. While all variants of rational choice theory assume that crime is the outcome of choice, most assume that an individual's behavior is characterized by "limited" or "bounded" rationality (Simon 1957). In other words, criminal decision-making is less than perfect because (1) it reflects imperfect conditions under which it naturally occurs, (2) human beings are imperfect processors of information, and (3) choices to engage in an act are often made very quickly without having all the necessary information regarding cost and benefit (see also Fattah 1993).

Under the rational choice perspective, would-be offenders are influenced by the costs and benefits of their actions, such as the anticipated financial reward of the crime and the certainty of formal and/or informal sanction threats. In addition, offenders are likely to be influenced by characteristics of the criminal event itself, such as the location of the offense and the possible response of the victim (Cornish and Clarke 1986). In sum, the rational choice perspective focuses on the situational characteristics associated with the criminal act. Since different criminal acts are a function of different situational characteristics, the rational choice perspective requires a crime-specific focus.

As a utility-based conception of criminal offending that focuses on a calculus of the risks and rewards of criminal offending, scholars have explored different dimensions associated with the benefits (thrill, excitement, money) and costs (formal and informal sanction threats, moral regret) of offending. The rational choice perspective has received a good deal of research attention in recent years, looking at a variety of different types of crimes such as sexual assault, theft, drinking and driving, and tax evasion (Bachman et al. 1992; Clarke and Felson 1993; Nagin and Paternoster 1993, 1994; Piquero and Tibbetts 1996). Much of the research in this area suggests that situational characteristics are important predictors of criminal behavior, and that the situational factors that are important for one type of criminal act may not necessarily equate with those that are important for another type of criminal act. Only recently have scholars argued that properties of individuals (e.g., self-control, etc.) influence the manner in which situational characteristics are interpreted (Nagin and Paternoster 1993; Piquero and Tibbetts 1996; Wright et al. 1999). For example, individuals with low self-control may be more likely to respond to the thrill associated with an act, as opposed to the probability of legal sanctions. Similarly, these individuals are more likely to see criminal and deviant acts as thrilling and exciting.

In sum, the rational choice perspective has helped criminologists to focus on the particulars of criminal acts and has renewed an interest in studying situational factors across different crimes.

CONTROL BALANCE THEORY

In *Control Balance*, Tittle (1995) presented a new method of theory construction termed "synthetic" theoretical integration. Control balance theory was offered as an exemplar of the new method. Although Tittle's primary intent was to introduce the synthetic method, many scholars have reviewed, critiqued, and commented on control balance theory (Braithwaite 1997; Curry 1998; Savelsberg 1996, 1999; Singer 1997; Jensen 1999), and some have undertaken initial empirical tests (Piquero and Hickman 1999). Collectively, these efforts have prompted Tittle to refine his initial thoughts and statement of the theory (see Tittle 1997, 1999, 2001), and a newly revised control balance formulation will be forthcoming. For the time being, however, our focus here is to provide a review of the original control balance framework and to investigate the implications of the rational choice perspective for control balance, on both theoretical and empirical levels.

The core of control balance theory is the control ratio, or the amount of control to which one is subject relative to the amount of control one can exercise. Exercising control is a continuous variable conveying the extent to which one can limit other people's realization of their goals or can escape limitations on one's own behavioral motivations that stem from the actions of others or from the physical and social arrangement of the world. Similarly, being controlled is a continuous variable conveying the extent to which the expression of one's desires and/or impulses is potentially limited by other people's abilities (whether actually exercised or not) to help, regulate, hinder, and/or punish, or by the physical and social arrangements of the world.

A balanced control ratio predisposes an individual toward conformity. A control imbalance in either direction predisposes an individual to one of two general forms of deviance, and within these general forms, a specific type of deviance depending on the magnitude of the control imbalance. A control deficit (when the amount of control to which one is subject is greater than the amount of control one can exercise) is likely to generate increasingly repressive forms of deviance, such as predation, defiance, or submission. A control surplus (when the amount of control one can exercise is greater than the amount of control to which one is subject) is likely to generate increasingly autonomous forms of deviance, such as exploitation, plunder, or decadence.

Deviance, defined as "any behavior that the majority of a given group regards as unacceptable or that typically evokes a collective response of a negative type" (Tittle 1995:124), is used to alter the control ratio in a favorable way (i.e., escape a control deficit or extend a control surplus), and will only result when several conditions are satisfied. First, the individual must be motivated toward deviance. Although Tittle contends that individuals are predisposed toward deviance by innate bodily and psychic needs, an "almost universal" (Tittle 1995:145) desire for autonomy, and the control ratio, actual deviant motivation results when an individual is reminded of his/her control imbalance through situational provocations of various forms and frequencies, such as verbal insults or similar debasing events. Second, there is an element of constraint, which is the probability (perceived or actual) that potential control will actually be exercised, and is a product of the control ratio, the seriousness of a given act, and the chance of discovery (i.e., situational risk) (see Tittle 1995:167–168). Motivation and constraint interact with each other in a balancing fashion, much like the control ratio (Tittle 1995:145, 168). Finally, there must be an opportunity for deviance to occur. Opportunity is a discrete and essential variable in control balance theory, and although Tittle (1995:177) asserts that the opportunity for some kind of deviance is almost always present, the theory recognizes that opportunities come in various frequencies and magnitudes. Thus, in order for deviance to occur, there must be a favorable configuration of motivation, constraint, and opportunity.

Interestingly, the constraint variable in control balance theory (influenced by situational risk, seriousness of the act, and the control ratio) subsumes the costs, risks, or pain highlighted by the rational choice perspective. Similarly, motivation in control balance theory subsumes the benefits, rewards, or pleasure highlighted by rational choice. In sum, control balance theory portrays deviant motivation as a product of situational cost-benefit assessments, and it is these assessments that are likely to mediate the relation between the control balance ratio and deviant acts.

Importantly, the control balance framework does not take for granted that individuals go through extensive mental calculation when arriving at motivating perceptions; rather, much like the rational choice framework, Tittle (1995:166) suggests that "most of the time" individuals are only afforded a momentary glimpse of the conditions under which they choose whether to engage in a deviant act.

RATIONAL CHOICE IMPLICATIONS OF CONTROL BALANCE THEORY

Tittle (1995:185) anticipates that the effect of the control balance ratio depends to a large extent on various contingencies, including the probability of activating countercontrolling responses and/or perceived sanction risk. At its core then, control balance theory is a contingent theory, and according to Tittle (1995:205) it must be tested with this feature in mind. What is a contingency? According to Tittle (1995:201), it includes: any aspect of an individual, social relationships, organizational structures, or the physical environment that influences how completely or strongly the control balancing process operates. That is, even though the control balance ratio is the most important variable in the framework, its effect on criminal and deviant acts is not independent of other influences. Although Tittle identifies several contingencies for control balancing and describes how they should influence the central causal effects, our focus is limited to the situational contingencies that emanate from the rational choice perspective. In particular, we focus on two of these contingencies: perceived risk and perceived pleasure.

Perceived Risk. The role of perceived risk has been studied in great detail within criminological circles (Paternoster 1987). Some scholars contend that the evidence in support of the deterrence doctrine, particularly the deterrability arising from formal sanction threats, is negligible (Decker et al. 1993; Williams and Hawkins 1986). However, recent research does suggest that individual perceptions of informal negative sanctions from significant others appears to inhibit criminal behavior (Nagin and Paternoster 1993; Piquero and Tibbetts 1996), and in some cases, formal sanction threats also serve in an inhibitory capacity (Grasmick and Bursik 1990; Nagin and Paternoster 1994).

In relation to control balance, Tittle (1995:222) defines risk as the probability that the act will be discovered and acted on, and risk is heavily dependent on situational characteristics. Since risk is individually and situationally variable, these variations will affect how well the control balance process will operate. According to Tittle (1995:223), when situational risk is large or small, predictions from the theory will be more or less effective, in a linearly interactive fashion. Thus, we would anticipate that for those individuals with control imbalances, deviance is most likely to occur in situations of low perceived risk; that is, when the probability of detection and sanction are lowest, the effect of the control balance ratio on deviance should be at its maximum; however, when the probability of detection and sanction are highest, the effect of the control balance ratio will be at its minimum. In other words, strong perceptual sanction threats will make the theoretical outcomes less likely while weak perceptual sanction threats will make the theoretical outcomes more likely.

Perceived Pleasure. The basic argument behind perceived benefits is simple: The benefits associated with an act (whether monetary, thrills, excitement, or otherwise) are likely to produce higher probabilities of offending, and may in fact be more salient than perceived sanction risk in the offenders' decision-making (Carroll 1978; Piliavin et al. 1986; Piquero and Rengert 1999). Although Tittle makes no explicit claim that perceived benefits derived from deviant acts can serve as a situational contingency, theoretical (Katz 1988; McCarthy 1995) and empirical research (Carroll 1978; Klepper and Nagin 1989; Nagin and Paternoster 1993; Piliavin et al. 1986; Piquero and Tibbetts 1996) within the rational choice perspective has shown this to be an important factor in the decision-making process.

With regard to control balance, we would anticipate that deviance among those with control imbalances is more likely when the perceived benefits are highest. Similar to the hypothesis for perceived risk, when perceived benefit is large or small, predictions from the theory will be overrespondingly more or less effective, in a linearly interactive fashion. Therefore, we would anticipate that for those individuals with control imbalances, deviance is most likely to occur in situations of high perceived benefit; that is, when the probability of benefit is high, the effect of the control balance ratio on deviance should be at its maximum; however, when the probability of benefit is low, the effect of the control balance ratio will be at its minimum. In other words, strong perceived pleasure will make the theoretical outcomes more likely, while weak perceived pleasure will make the theoretical outcomes less likely.

Although the above discussion allows that both perceived sanction risk and perceived pleasure are, by themselves, linearly interactive, it raises the possibility that their own interaction could influence the control balance process to a greater extent than either perceived sanction risk or perceived pleasure alone. Does the control balance framework accommodate this combination of linear, interactive effects?

Tittle (1995:223) argues that two or more contingencies may combine to affect the theoretical process—what he refers to as a second order contingency. Thus, in the context of the above discussion, the predicted deviant outcomes for an individual with high perceived risk and low perceived pleasure should be less than for individuals with either weak perceived risk or high perceived pleasure, or both. In other words, when weak perceived risk combines with high perceived pleasure, the effect of the control balance ratio should be at its maximum.

Consider the following example: An individual with a control deficit is standing beside an abandoned parking lot late at night when he sees a car with an unlocked passenger door. In the past, he has successfully hot-wired cars and taken them to chop shops to make some money on the side. He also derives a sense of thrill and challenge by hot-wiring cars that are thought to be foolproof. Since his rent is due next week, he decides to enter the car through the passenger door, hot-wire the car, and take it to the chop shop to earn some extra money.

In this scenario, the individual's control ratio exerted an effect on the decision to engage in the act in part because 1) the lot was abandoned (i.e., weak perceived risk), 2) he had successful experiences with hot-wiring cars in the past, 3) he derives a thrill from the act, and 4) he was motivated to earn money to pay the rent. The particular situation in which he found himself allowed the control balance ratio to exert maximum influence on stealing the car because of the favorable configuration of several contingencies. Consideration of the interaction of situational contingencies arising from the rational choice perspective should be of importance when evaluating the effect of the control balance ratio on deviant outcomes.

SUMMARY

At some level, control balance theory is designed to improve upon the failure of rational choice to explain or account for what happens before and after situational costs and benefits are taken into consideration (Tittle 1995:50). What makes control balance useful, from the perspective of rational choice and routine activities theories, is that it can help explain why some individuals fear punishment more than others, and how certain situational factors condition the effect of the control balance ratio on deviant outcomes.

In this line of thought, Tittle suggests that the control balance ratio, motivation, constraint, and opportunity effectively cover both rational choice and routine activities perspectives. The interesting theoretical point is that while the control balance ratio predisposes one toward deviance, actual deviance results only when a favorable configuration of motivation, constraint, and opportunity is present. The control balance ratio is postulated to have an indirect effect on actual deviance through the complex interaction of motivation, constraint, and opportunity. Therefore, the predictions of the theory may be more salient within certain contingency configurations. This is the process that we explore in the present effort.

DATA

Data used in this chapter come from a self-administered questionnaire given to students at a large, northeastern university in the Spring of 1998. The survey instrument contained a number of questions and offense scenarios designed to study the control balance process. Students in attendance on the day the survey was administered were asked to participate, and no student refused. One-hundred and sixty-five students responded to the survey, and through listwise deletion of missing cases, the sample was reduced to one hundred and forty-six subjects.

Although the use of student samples has come under some criticism (Hagan and McCarthy 1997; Jensen et al. 1978; Williams and Hawkins 1986), several researchers have argued in favor of their use (Mazerolle and Piquero 1997, 1998; Nagin and Paternoster 1993; Piquero and Hickman 1999; Piquero and Tibbetts 1996). Importantly, in the context of the current effort, no secondary sources of data exist for which to assess predictions from control balance theory. Since Tittle (1995:269) notes that limited assessments of the theory can make use of any sample of individuals and any realm of control, we believe that use of a student sample is acceptable so long as the data are collected with questions and behaviors geared toward such a sample.

SCENARIO METHOD

Following previous research (Rossi and Anderson 1982), we employed factorial survey methodology in which respondents read a series of scenarios and responded to a battery of questions regarding each scenario. The scenarios employed in the survey instrument included short third-person depictions of events that individuals may readily find themselves involved in at some point in their lives. Moreover, the scenarios were framed in settings and situations familiar to the respondents and with regard to detail and contextual specificity, such as presenting details of the circumstances of the offense, naming of locations, and so on. The strengths and weaknesses of the scenario approach have been discussed elsewhere (Bachman et al. 1992; Fishbein and Ajzen 1975; Nagin and Paternoster 1993; Piquero and Tibbetts 1996).

For present purposes we use a scenario portraying an aggravated assault, which we classify as a repressive act of predation. The aggravated assault scenario read as follows:

Brian is standing in Shampoo, a dance club, with his friends, drinking beer. Another patron, David, bumps into Brian from behind, causing him to spill beer all over his shirt and pants. Brian's friends can't help laughing at him. Brian turns around and David, smiling, says, "sorry" and spins around to continue dancing with his friends. Brian taps David on the shoulder and says, "Hey, you just made me spill beer all over the place!" David stops dancing, stares directly into Brian's eyes and asks him, "Do you have a problem?" Brian says, "Yeah, why don't you get me another beer?" David pushes his finger into Brian's chest and asks, "Why don't you get on your knees and beg?" Brian hits David in the face with his fist, and a fight breaks out between them.

After reading the scenario, respondents were asked to estimate the likelihood that they would do what Brian finally did. Responses were measured on a scale from zero (no chance at all) to ten (100 percent chance), but were later re-coded to 0/1 because control balance is designed to account for the probability of offending (Tittle 1995:171,177,194; Piquero and Hickman 1999:327). Thus, values registering a zero indicate a zero probability of engaging in the act portrayed in the scenario, while values of one or greater, re-coded to one, suggest some nonzero probability of engaging in the act portrayed in the scenario.[1]

Before proceeding, it is important to note that provocation plays a central part in the control balance framework. Although we have no measure of how each of the respondents differentially interpreted the provocation in the scenario, we attempted to construct a scenario in which provocation was present. For example, in the assault scenario above, David provoked Brian (i.e., made him aware of his relative control deficit) when he 1) spilled beer on him and 2) pushed his finger into Brian's chest.

INDEPENDENT VARIABLES

Although there are multiple methods by which the control balance ratio can be measured, we concentrated on the more global control balance ratio that Tittle (1995:267) argues is the "most important" overall measure. We measured the control balance ratio by asking respondents to rate the degree of control they exercise over specific others, objects and circumstances. (Tittle 1995:267). Response options ranged from 0 (no control) to 5 (medium control) to 10 (total control). Respondents were then asked to rate the degree of control the same items had over them. Items included: relationships with significant others, performance in school (grades), job/employment, recreational activities, society as a whole, and other people (such as neighbors, solicitors, repair people). Response options ranged from 0 (no control) to 5 (medium control) to 10 (total control). Following Piquero et al.'s (2001) revision of the control balance scale, we eliminated some of the original items and collapsed response categories into a four-point scoring system.

To construct the control balance ratio, we summed the items for the amount of control to which one is subject and obtained a total. Then, we summed the items for the amount of control one can exercise and obtained a total. Third, we took the ratio of the amount of control to which one is subject relative to the amount of control one can exercise. This produces the overall control balance ratio.

Before proceeding, it is important to bear in mind that since three of the key variables in control balance—opportunity, risk, and provocation—are largely contextual (Tittle 1995:221), analytic approaches must use an act-specific focus that is consistent with the aim of the rational choice perspective. Therefore, we also collected several other scenario-specific measures that are consistent with themes from the rational choice framework including perceived sanction risk and perceived pleasure.

Perceived sanction risk was obtained by an item measuring an individual's perception of the risk of being caught for each specific act: "On a scale of 1 to 10, rate the risk of getting caught by committing the act portrayed in the scenario." Response options ranged from 0 (not likely) to 10 (very likely). Perceived pleasure was measured by an item measuring an individual's perception of the excitement generated for each specific act: "On a scale of 1 to 10, how exciting would it be to engage in the act portrayed in the scenario?" Response options ranged from 0 (not exciting) to 10 (very exciting).

An important consideration in control balance theory is the role of opportunity. Since the scenario methodology affords each respondent the same opportunity to engage in the specific act, our analysis controls for opportunity by placing the respondents in the same situation. Thus, opportunity is held constant through the scenarios.

Finally, we control for age, sex, race, religiosity, low self-control, prior behavior, moral beliefs, and deviant peers. Age is measured continuously as reported. Sex is coded as male (0) and female (1), while race is coded as white (0) and non-white (1). Religiosity is coded 1 if the respondent practiced some sort of religion, 0 otherwise. Low self-control is measured by the Grasmick et al. (1993) scale. Prior behavior is measured as an individual's involvement (no/yes) in the past few months with assault (i.e., hitting another person). Moral belief is measured by a single-item indicator that followed each scenario: "On a scale of 1 to 10, how morally wrong is the act portrayed in each scenario?" Finally, deviant peers is measured by a single-item indicator that followed each scenario: "On a scale of 1 to 10, how many of your friends have engaged in the act portrayed in the scenario?" Response options ranged from 0 (none) to 10 (most).

HYPOTHESES

To study the contingencies hypothesized within the control balance framework, we examine the effects of the control balance ratio within sub-samples of individuals that differ with respect to the specific contingent variable. We proceed along three steps. First, we examine how the control balance ratio operates within two sub-samples partitioned by their level of perceived risk (high and low). The median score on the perceived risk measure was used as a cut-off to separate the groups. We will test the following hypothesis:

H1:   The effect of the control balance ratio will be strongest for the low perceived risk sub-sample, as compared to the high perceived risk sub-sample.

Second, we examine how the control balance ratio operates within two sub-samples partitioned by their level of perceived pleasure (high and low). Again, the median score on the perceived pleasure measure was used as a cut-off to separate the groups. We will test the following hypothesis:

H2:   The effect of the control balance ratio will be strongest for the high perceived pleasure sub-sample, as compared to the low perceived pleasure sub-sample.

Third, we examine a second-order contingency of favorable risk/rewards (high pleasure, low risk versus low pleasure, high risk). We will test the following hypothesis:

H3:   The effect of the control balance ratio will be strongest for the low risk, high pleasure sub-sample, as compared to the high risk, low pleasure sub-sample.

To the extent that the theory is correct, we would expect empirical confirmation of each of these hypotheses.

Since the control balance framework makes predictions that are non-linear in nature, our analytic approach takes the form of segmented, non-linear regression (Neter et al. 1985; see also Piquero and Hickman 1999). Specifically, we estimate the deficit and surplus segments of the control balance ratio separately. The model expression is as follows:

$$Y = (cbr<=1)^*\mu_1 + (cbr>1)^*\mu_2 + age^*\mu_3 + sex^*\mu_4 + race^*\mu_5 + religiosity^*\mu_6 + lsc^*\mu_7 + prior^*\mu_8 + morals^*\mu_9 + peers^*\mu_{10}$$

where Y refers to the dependent variable (probability of predation), cbr equals the control balance ratio (i.e., values less than or equal to one correspond to a surplus and values greater than one correspond to a deficit), age equals respondent age, sex equals respondent sex (0/1), race equals respondent race (0/1), religiosity equals respondent practices religion (0/1), lsc equals low self-control, prior equals prior involvement in the behavior, morals equals moral beliefs against the act, peers equals peer involvement in the behavior, and μ_{1-10} refer to parameters estimated by the model. Descriptive statistics for all variables may be found in Table 1.

Table 1: Descriptive Statistics

Variable	Mean	SD	Min.	Max.
Age	22.82	4.51	18	46
Sex	.52	.50	0	1
Race	.32	.47	0	1
Religiosity	.72	.45	0	1
Low Self-Control	36.74	10.56	16	67
Prior Behavior	.24	.43	0	1
Moral Beliefs	6.18	2.36	0	10
Peer Experience	5.04	3.06	0	10
CBR	.87	.30	.11	2.00
Risk	6.72	3.11	0	10
Pleasure	3.07	3.02	0	10
Predation (DV)	.72	.45	0	1

RESULTS

Table 2 presents the full sample estimation. As can be seen, five of the ten estimated coefficients are statistically significant at $p<.05$. Specifically, both segments of the control balance ratio exert significant and positive effects on predation (surplus estimate = .689, deficit estimate = .792). These results are only partially supportive of Tittle's (1995) prediction, since only control deficits should be related to repressive forms of deviance (see also Piquero and Hickman 1999). Among the other significant predictors in the model, males (estimate = .171) are more likely to report intentions to engage in predation, individuals having moral inhibitions against predation (estimate = -.070) are less likely to report intentions to engage in predation, and individuals having peers who have engaged in the behavior (estimate = .042) are more likely to report intentions to engage in predation. The amount of variation explained by this model is 36 percent.

Looking at the sub-samples defined by perceived risk (see Table 3), the exact same five coefficients retained their significance in the low perceived risk sub-sample. Note that the effects of the control balance segments are significant in the low perceived risk sub-sample (surplus estimate = 1.129, deficit segment = 1.306), but non-significant in the high perceived risk sub-sample. Low self-control (estimate = .015) is the only significant predictor among the high risk sub-sample. Taken together, this evidence provides support for H1; the effect of the control balance ratio is strongest for the low perceived risk sub-sample, as compared to the high perceived risk sub-sample.

Table 2: Non-Linear Regression Estimates, Full-Sample

Variable	EST	SE	EST/SE	95% CI
CBR (Surplus)	.689	.231	2.98 *	.232, 1.145
CBR (Deficit)	.792	.231	3.43 *	.336, 1.247
Age	-.005	.007	-.71	-.018, .009
Sex	.171	.065	2.63 *	.042, .300
Race	.071	.067	1.06	-.062, .203
Religiosity	.119	.071	1.68	-.020, .259
Low Self-Control	.004	.004	1.00	-.003, .010
Prior Behavior	.002	.003	.67	-.003, .007
Moral Beliefs	-.070	.014	-5.00 *	-.098, -.043
Peer Experience	.042	.011	3.82 *	.019, .064

R-square = .36
* p<.05

Table 4 presents the estimations for each sub-sample defined by level of perceived pleasure. Four of the coefficients retained their significance in the low perceived pleasure sub-sample, including both of the control balance segments. In the high perceived pleasure sub-sample, the effects of the control balance segments are not significant at $p<.05$, but are significant at $p<.10$. Males (estimate = .273) were more likely to report intentions to engage in predation, and those with moral inhibitions (estimate = -.042) were less likely to report intentions to engage in predation. Taken together, this evidence does not provide strong support for H2; the effect of the control balance ratio is not strongest for the high perceived pleasure sub-sample.

Table 5 presents the estimations for each sub-sample defined by both risk and pleasure. Among the low risk, high pleasure sub-sample (n=42), three of the coefficients retained their significance, including both segments of the control balance ratio. Among the high risk, low pleasure sub-sample (n=26), none of the coefficients were significant. Taken together, this evidence provides support for H3; the effect of the control balance ratio is strongest for the low risk, high pleasure sub-sample, as compared to the high risk, low pleasure sub-sample. Due to the relatively small sample sizes in this portion of the analysis, caution should be exercised in interpreting the coefficients.

Table 3. Non-Linear Regression Estimates, Low and High Risk Sub-Samples

Variable	Low Risk				High Risk			
	EST	SE	EST/SE	95% CI	EST	SE	EST/SE	95% CI
CBR (Surplus)	1.129	.304	3.71 *	.524, 1.734	.172	.386	.45	-.605, .949
CBR (Deficit)	1.306	.307	4.25 *	.695, 1.917	.237	.374	.63	-.517, .990
Age	-.010	.010	-1.00	-.029, .009	-.009	.012	-.75	-.033, .015
Sex	.152	.074	2.05 *	.005, .299	.227	.132	1.72	-.039, .493
Race	.030	.076	.39	-.121, .181	-.005	.145	-.03	-.297, .286
Religiosity	.099	.077	1.29	-.055, .253	.279	.158	1.77	-.040, .598
Low Self-Control	-.004	.004	-1.00	-.012, .005	.015	.006	2.50 *	.002, .028
Prior Behavior	-.013	.029	-.45	-.071, .045	.002	.003	.67	-.004, .009
Moral Beliefs	-.071	.016	-4.44 *	-.102, -.039	-.057	.029	-1.97	-.114, .001
Peer Experience	.049	.013	3.77 *	.023, .075	.024	.023	1.04	-.022, .071

R-square =   .38   .42

* p<.05

Table 4. Non-Linear Regression Estimates, Low and High Pleasure Sub-Samples

Variable	Low Pleasure				High Pleasure			
	EST	SE	EST/SE	95% CI	EST	SE	EST/SE	95% CI
CBR (Surplus)	.833	.348	2.39 *	.139, 1.528	.647	.337	1.92	-.027, 1.320
CBR (Deficit)	1.102	.352	3.13 *	.400, 1.805	.580	.334	1.74	-.087, 1.247
Age	-.003	.009	-.33	-.021, .016	-.000	.012	-.08	-.025, .024
Sex	.076	.104	.73	-.131, .283	.273	.088	3.10 *	.098, .449
Race	.072	.102	.71	-.131, .275	.107	.086	1.24	-.064, .278
Religiosity	.056	.113	.50	-.170, .282	.167	.089	1.88	-.010, .345
Low Self-Control	.004	.006	.67	-.008, .015	-.001	.004	-.25	-.009, .008
Prior Behavior	.063	.072	.88	-.081, .207	.003	.002	1.50	-.002, .007
Moral Beliefs	-.102	.022	-4.64 *	-.146, -.058	-.042	.018	-2.33 *	-.079, -.006
Peer Experience	.043	.016	2.69 *	.010, .076	.028	.016	1.75	-.004, .060
R-square =	.38				.26			

* p<.05

Table 5. Non-Linear Regression Estimates, Low Risk/High Pleasure and High Risk/Low Pleasure Sub-Samples

Variable		Low Risk, High Pleasure				High Risk, Low Pleasure		
	EST	SE	EST/SE	95% CI	EST	SE	EST/SE	95% CI
CBR (Surplus)	.940	.400	2.35 *	.125, 1.754	.750	.958	.78	-1.281, 2.780
CBR (Deficit)	.960	.412	2.33 *	.120, 1.800	1.010	1.084	.93	-1.288, 3.308
Age	.001	.015	.07	-.029, .031	-.002	.017	-.12	-.038, .035
Sex	.321	.085	3.78 *	.147, .494	.152	.257	.59	-.392, .696
Race	.049	.084	.58	-.122, .221	-.323	.342	-.94	-1.049, .402
Religiosity	.113	.081	1.40	-.051, .277	.203	.314	.65	-.463, .870
Low Self-Control	-.009	.005	-1.80	-.018, .001	.016	.015	1.07	-.016, .047
Prior Behavior	.014	.026	.54	-.039, .066	.164	.433	.38	-.754, 1.082
Moral Beliefs	-.030	.018	-1.67	-.066, .007	-.142	.076	-1.87	-.304, .020
Peer Experience	.024	.016	1.50	-.008, .057	-.012	.049	-.24	-.117, .092

R-square =   .42   .39

* p<.05

DISCUSSION

The purpose of this chapter was to examine three specific contingency hypotheses emanating from Tittle's control balance theory that share common-ground with many rational choice explanations of crime. Guided by Tittle (1995), we derived three rational choice implications from control balance theory. First, under conditions of low risk, the effect of the control balance ratio on predation should be at its maximum. Second, under conditions of high pleasure, the effect of the control balance ratio on predation should be at its maximum. Third, under conditions of high pleasure and low risk, the effect of the control balance ratio should be at its maximum. In general, the analyses supported the first and third hypotheses, but provided mixed evidence regarding the second hypothesis. Across all three estimation procedures, both sides of the control balance ratio (surplus and deficit) were predictive of predation intentions. Since Tittle argues that control deficits should be predictive of predatory acts, these analyses only partially support his theory. This notwithstanding, evidence was found regarding the single and second-order contingency hypotheses from control balance theory, and continued exploration appears worthwhile.

Several limitations with the current effort must be acknowledged. First, our sample was based on college students. Although this does not present a fatal flaw in our effort to assess the contingency hypotheses derived from the theory, other samples may provide unique and different estimates. Second, the measure of the control balance ratio in the present study made use of a global rather than situational measure. Although Tittle argues that this more global scale is the most important in obtaining estimates of control ratios, collection of more situationally-based measures of the control ratio appear important. Third, our exploration into the contingency hypotheses of control balance only made use of one deviant act. The extent to which these hypotheses hold for other criminal and deviant acts remains an open, empirical question. Finally, due to a relatively small sample, our analytic procedure was not able to examine the contingency hypotheses across race and/or gender sub-groups. Given Tittle's (1995) expectations in this regard, and extant research providing evidence of important gender differences in the control balance process (Hickman and Piquero 2001), future work in this area appears warranted.

With these limitations in hand, we see several promising areas for future empirical research as it relates to the contingency hypotheses derived from control balance. First, the exploration of the control balance process across other rational choice contingencies may be useful. Some of these other contingencies include moral beliefs, self-control, prior successes at criminal behavior, etc. We would expect that the effect of the control ratio should be at its maximum with samples of individuals who possess low moral beliefs, low self-control, and who have had successful criminal attempts. In the interest of space, we lay out expectations for one of these contingencies in particular, moral beliefs.

The importance of moral commitments for inhibiting criminal and deviant behavior have been described elsewhere (Bachman et al. 1992; Etzioni 1988; Grasmick and Bursik 1990; Tittle 1980); however, it may be instructive to re-state the main premise behind this particular decision-making factor: Persons may refrain from offending because they believe certain acts to be morally wrong. According to Etzioni (1988), rational choice theories of crime have failed to consider the role of persons' moral positions and beliefs, and as a result, have left the decision-making process of offenders and would-be offenders under-specified. But how do moral commitments relate in control balance theory?

According to Tittle (1995:282), ". . . the effects of a control imbalance are muted when moral feelings directed against a given type of behavior are strong." Thus, moral commitments signal to an individual's conscience that there will be an emotional penalty for committing (or even contemplating) a criminal and/or deviant act. Thus, strong moral inhibitions will decrease the chances of repressive deviance among those with minimal control deficits; however, among those with weak moral constraints, the effect of the control balance ratio should be at its maximum. Although this particular example relies on a single-order contingency, moral commitment may interact with several other contingencies to condition the effect of the control balance ratio on deviant acts.

In sum, theory progresses as better theoretical models are constructed and as theorists and researchers pay close attention to the relationship between empirical results, theoretical concepts, and the measurement strategies that are required by the theories developed (Wellford 1989:127). Tittle's control balance theory was designed with these premises in mind. Although conceived as an exemplar of integrated theory, control balance relates to the rational choice perspective in many ways. Hopefully, the preliminary research in which we have engaged with the present study will encourage other researchers to obtain the requisite data and extend our initial foray into the rational choice implications of control balance theory.

NOTE

1. Due to time constraints, males and females were given the same scenario. Initially, some readers may point out that the sex of the character in the scenario would likely influence survey response (i.e., intention). However, males and females reported similar estimates regarding the believability of the scenario ($p > .05$).

REFERENCES

Agnew, Robert. 1992. "Foundation for a General Strain Theory of Crime and Delinquency." *Criminology* 30:47–88.

Bachman, Ronet, Raymond Paternoster, and Sally Ward. 1992. "The Rationality of Sexual Offending: Testing a Deterrence/Rational Choice Conception of Sexual Assault." *Law and Society Review* 26:343–372.

Becker, Gary S. 1968. "Crime and Punishment: An Economic Approach." *Journal of Political Economy* 76:169–217.

Braithwaite, John. 1989. *Crime, Shame, and Reintegration.* Cambridge: Cambridge University Press.

Braithwaite, John. 1997. "Charles Tittle's Control Balance and Criminological Theory." *Theoretical Criminology* 1:77–97.

Carroll, John. 1978. "A Psychological Approach to Deterrence: the Evaluation of Crime Opportunities." *Journal of Personality and Social Psychology* 36:1512–1520.

Clarke, Ronald and Derek Cornish. 2001. "Rational Choice Theory." In *Explaining Criminals and Crime*, edited by Raymond Paternoster and Ronet Bachman. Los Angeles, CA: Roxbury.

Clarke, Ronald and Marcus Felson. 1992. "Introduction: Criminology, Routine Activity, and Rational Choice." In *Advances in Criminological Theory, Volume 5: Routine Activity and Rational Choice*, edited by Ronald Clarke and Marcus Felson. New Brunswick, NJ: Transaction.

Cornish, Derek and Ronald Clarke. 1986. *The Reasoning Criminal.* New York: Springer-Verlag.

Curry, G. David. 1998. "Book Review: Control Balance: Toward a General Theory of Deviance." *Social Forces* 76:1147–1149.

Decker, Scott, Richard Wright, and Robert Logie. 1993. "Perceptual Deterrence Among Active Residential Burglars: A Research Note." *Criminology* 31:135–147.

Etzioni, Amitai. 1988. *The Moral Dimension: Toward a New Economics.* New York: Free Press.

Fattah, Ezzat A. 1993. "The Rational Choice/Opportunity Perspectives as a Vehicle for Integrating Criminological and Victimological Theories." In *Advances in Criminological Theory, Volume 5: Routine Activity and Rational Choice*, edited by Ronald Clarke and Marcus Felson. New Brunswick, NJ: Transaction.

Fishbein, Martin M. and Icek L. Ajzen. 1975. *Belief, Attitudes, Intention, and Behavior.* Reading, MA: Addison-Wesley.

Gottfredson, Michael R. and Travis Hirschi. 1990. *A General Theory of Crime.* Stanford, CA: Stanford University Press.

Grasmick, Harold and Robert J. Bursik, Jr. 1990. "Conscience, Significant Others, and Rational Choice: Extending the Deterrence Model." *Law and Society Review* 24:837–862.

Hagan, John and Bill McCarthy. 1997. "Anomie, Social Capital, and Street Criminology." In *The Future of Anomie Theory*, edited by Nikos Passas and Robert Agnew. Boston, MA: Northeastern University Press.

Hickman, Matthew and Alex R. Piquero. 2001. "Exploring the Relationships between Gender, Control Balance, and Deviance." *Deviant Behavior*.

Jensen, Gary. 1999. "A Critique of Control Balance Theory: Digging into Details." *Theoretical Criminology* 3:339–343.

Jensen, Gary, Maynard Erickson, and Jack P. Gibbs. 1978. "Perceived Risk of Punishment and Self-Reported Delinquency." *Social Forces* 57:57–78.

Katz, Jack. 1988. *Seductions of Crime*. New York, NY: Basic Books.

Klepper, Stephen and Daniel S. Nagin. 1988. "The Deterrent Effect of Perceived Certainty and Severity of Punishment Revisited." *Criminology* 27:721–746.

Mazerolle, Paul and Alex R. Piquero. 1997. "Violent Responses to Strain: An Examination of Conditioning Influences." *Violence and Victims* 12:323–345.

Mazerolle, Paul and Alex R. Piquero. 1998. "Linking Exposure to Strain with Anger: An Investigation of Deviant Adaptations." *Journal of Criminal Justice* 26:195–211.

McCarthy, Bill. 1995. "Not Just "for the thrill of it": An Instrumentalist Elaboration of Katz's Explanation of Sneaky Thrill Property Crimes." *Criminology* 33:519–538.

Moffitt, Terrie E. 1993. "Adolescence-Limited and Life-Course Persistent Antisocial Behavior: A Developmental Taxonomy." *Psychological Review* 100:674–701.

Nagin, Daniel S. and Raymond Paternoster. 1993. "Enduring Individual Differences and Rational Choice Theories of Crime." *Law and Society Review* 27:201–230.

Nagin, Daniel S. and Raymond Paternoster. 1994. "Personal Capital and Social Control: The Deterrence Implications of a Theory of Individual Differences in Criminal Offending." *Criminology* 32:581–606.

Neter, John, William Wasserman, and Michael Kutner. 1985. *Applied Linear Statistical Models*. 2d ed. Homewood, IL: Irwin.

Paternoster, Raymond. 1987. "The Deterrent Effect of the Perceived Certainty and Severity of Punishment: A Review of the Evidence and Issues." *Justice Quarterly* 4:173–217.

Patterson, Gerald and Karen Yoerger. 1993. "Developmental Models for Delinquent Behavior." In *Crime and Mental Disorder*, edited by S. Hodgins. Newbury Park, CA: Sage Publications.

Piliavin, Irving, Graig Thornton, Rosemary Gartner, and Ross L. Matsueda. 1985. "Crime, Deterrence, and Rational Choice." *American Sociological Review* 51:101–119.

Piquero, Alex R. and Matthew Hickman. 1999. "An Empirical Test of Tittle's Control Balance Theory." *Criminology* 37:319–341.

Piquero, Alex R., Randall MacIntosh, and Matthew Hickman. 2001. "Applying Rasch Modeling to a Control Balance Scale." *Journal of Criminal Justice*, forthcoming.

Piquero, Alex R. and George F. Rengert. 1999. "Studying Deterrence with Active Residential Burglars: A Research Note." *Justice Quarterly* 16:451–472.

Piquero, Alex R. and Stephen G. Tibbetts. 1996. "Specifying the Direct and Indirect Effects of Low Self-Control and Situational Factors in Offender Decision-Making: Towards a More Complete Model of Rational Offending." *Justice Quarterly* 13:481–510.

Raine, Adrian, Patricia Brennan, David P. Farrington, and Sarnoff Mednick. 1997. *Biosocial Bases of Violence*. New York, NY: Plenum Press.

Rossi, Peter and Andy Anderson. 1982. "The Factorial Survey Approach: An Introduction." In *Measuring Social Judgements*, edited by Peter Rossi and Steven Nock. Newbury Park, CA: Sage Publications.

Sampson, Robert and John H. Laub. 1993. *Crime in the Making*. Cambridge, MA: Harvard University Press.

Savelsberg, Joachim J. 1996. "Review: Toward a General Theory of Deviance." *American Journal of Sociology* 102:620–622.

Savelsberg, Joachim, J. 1999. "Human Nature and Social Control in Complex Society: a Critique of Charles Tittle's Control Balance." *Theoretical Criminology* 3:331–338.

Simon, Herbert. 1957. *Models of Man*. New York, NY: Wiley.

Singer, Simon I. 1997. "Review: Control Balance: Toward a General Theory of Deviance." *Contemporary Sociology* 26:492–493.

Tittle, Charles R. 1980. *Sanctions and Social Deviance*. New York, NY: Praeger.

Tittle, Charles R. 1995. *Control Balance: Toward a General Theory of Deviance*. Boulder, CO: Westview.

Tittle, Charles R. 1997. "Thoughts Stimulated by Braithwaite's Analysis of Control Balance Theory." *Theoretical Criminology* 1:99–110.

Tittle, Charles R. 1999. "Continuing the Discussion of Control Balance." *Theoretical Criminology* 3:344–352.

Tittle, Charles R. 2001. "Control Balance." In *Explaining Criminals and Crime*, edited by Raymond Paternoster and Ronet Bachman. Los Angeles, CA: Roxbury.

Vila, Bryan. 1992. "A General Paradigm for Understanding Criminal Behavior: Extending Evolutionary Ecological Theory." *Criminology* 32:311–360.

Wellford, Charles. 1989. Towards an Integrated Theory of Criminal Behavior. In *Theoretical Integration in the Study of Deviance and Crime*, edited by Steven F. Messner, Marvin D. Krohn, and Allen E. Liska. Albany, NY: State University of New York Press.

Williams, Kirk R. and Richard Hawkins. 1986. "Perceptual Research on General Deterrence: A Critical Review." *Law and Society Review* 20:545–572.

Wright, Bradley R. Entner, Avshalom Caspi, Terrie E. Moffitt, and Phil A. Silva. 1999. "Low Self-Control, Social Bonds, and Crime: Social Causation, Social Selection, or Both?" *Criminology* 37:479–514.

Chapter 6

Sex Differences and Rational Choice: Traditional Tests and New Directions

Brenda Sims Blackwell and Sarah Eschholz

While the evolution of rational choice theory has made enormous advances in the past forty years, one key factor that structures the choice to commit crime has been virtually ignored. A number of articles have examined the influence of sex-roles on either perceived sanction threats (Blackwell 2000; Finley & Grasmick 1985; Grasmick, Blackwell, & Bursik 1993) or the decision to commit crime (Blackwell 2000; Grasmick, Finley, & Glaser 1984) within the rational choice perspective. We argue choice is structured by a number of factors and that the advancement of the rational choice perspective depends on including structural variables. In this paper, we begin by including sex-roles in a test of rational choice and conclude by advocating the inclusion of gender-roles and other structural variables in tests of rational choice. Before elaborating on the importance of sex and gender roles, we briefly chronicle milestones in deterrence/rational choice research.

DETERRENCE/RATIONAL CHOICE

Deterrence research revitalized many of the precepts first utilized by Betham and Beccaria in the Classical School of criminology. An emphasis was placed on the effects of punishment on future decisions to offend. While the decision whether or not to offend is made by individuals, most early tests of deterrence focused on the role of state sanctions in reducing crime rates using aggregate level data. With its focus on objective measures of punishment, deterrence theory was inevitably associated with research exploring the viability of capital punishment as a crime reducing policy. Macro-level tests provided little support for the hypothesis that punishment, particularly the death penalty, reduces crime rates (Sutherland and

Cressey 1978; Sellin 1959), until two separate tests of the deterrence model demonstrated a relationship between the certainty of legal punishment and crime rates (Gibbs 1968; Tittle 1969). Jenson (1969) and Waldo and Chiricos (1972) further advanced deterrence research by returning to the role of individual perceptions and choice in the decision to commit crime, reporting a relationship between perceived threats of legal sanctions and criminal decision making.

With this shift from exploring the impact of deterrence at the aggregate level to examining the salience of individual perceptions, deterrence research returned to its classical roots, emphasizing individual differences and opening the door for researchers to explore how choices are influenced by psychological *and* structural factors. As deterrence expanded into a rational choice model, scholars noted the importance of including the certainty and severity of perceived threats of not only formal (Grasmick and Bryjak 1980), but also informal sanctions (Tittle 1980; Grasmick and Green 1980; Grasmick and Bursik 1990). This line of research recognized that choices are not the same for everyone. Rather, choices are structured by individual characteristics, target characteristics and the structural characteristics of a given society (Clarke & Cornish 1985; Cornish & Clarke 1987).

Concurrent to the development of several variations of the rational choice model, the feminist movement of the 1960s and 1970s highlighted the role of women in society. Scholars began to focus on differences between men and women in structural opportunities along with sex-role socialization (Connell, 1990; Schur, 1984). Researchers such as Simon (1975) and Adler (1975) brought this line of inquiry to the subject of crime. The fact that females commit fewer criminal acts across time, societies, and age groups is widely acknowledged (Kruttschnitt 1996; Sutherland and Cressey 1978; Canter 1982; Gottfredson and Hirschi 1990; Chesney-Lind and Sheldon 1992). Yet, historically crime studies were conducted solely on male subjects, or merely included sex[1] as a control variable (Chesney-Lind 1989; Elliott 1988). In other words, researchers were less interested in the question of why women do not commit crime than the question of why men do. Simon and Adler challenged this myopic view as they separately reported that the crime rate for females was increasing at a faster pace than that of their male counterparts in the 1970s.

THE "OBJECTIVIST" AND "SUBJECTIVIST" POSITIONS

Simon (1975) and Adler (1975) both attributed this trend of convergence to the criminality of emerging "nontraditional" women. Their assumptions ran counter to the predominant view that sex differences in criminality were a result of the biological differences between men and women. Simon and Adler each assumed that while both traditional and nontraditional women commit less crime than do men, the difference between nontraditional women and men in criminality was less than the difference between traditional women and men. While each recognized the ability of women to take on different sex-roles, their explanations of the emergence of women's nontraditionalism were decidedly different. Simon (1975) posited a structural explanation focusing on the changing employment opportunities for women, while Adler (1975) explained sex convergence in criminality from a social-psychological viewpoint.

While both of these perspectives highlight factors that constrain the choices of individual actors (i.e., increased exposure to opportunities to commit crime and having psychological access to crime as a choice of possible behaviors), labor force participation and sex-role socialization rarely have been discussed or tested within the confines of a rational choice model. Even when sex-differences are acknowledged today, it generally is in the context of a control variable (Smith and Paternoster 1987) or only as a slight modification to an existing model (Richards and Tittle 1981; Grasmick et al. 1993).

In one exception, Grasmick and his colleagues (Grasmick et al. 1984; Finley and Grasmick 1985) explore the link between the perspectives offered by Simon (1975) and Adler (1975) and deterrence/rational choice. They identify the two positions as "objective" and "subjective," referring to Simon's structural labor-force participation position and Adler's sociopsychological sex-role explanation, respectively. While these tests describe the importance of sex differences for variables in the rational choice model, they do not explicitly outline the connection between these perspectives and the rational choice concepts of opportunity and guardianship.

We argue that the Objectivist perspective, offered by Simon, corresponds with the rational choice concept of opportunity. Individuals who work are more mobile and, more importantly, have greater access to situations where crime is possible than individuals who stay at home, particularly if they are staying home in the context of parenting. For parents, the Objectivist explanation also indirectly taps into the notion of guardianship. Specifically, women who stay at home spend more time with their children than their working counterparts (Hochschild 1989). While children do not act as guardians in the sense of watching over an adult, they arguably are moral guardians for parents concerned about modeling appropriate behaviors for their children. Increasing the time away from one's children may produce a decreased sense of moral guardianship, thereby freeing women to commit more crime. On the other hand, it is possible that employment outside the home decreases the economic need to commit crime.

The Subjectivist perspective, offered by Adler, relates to the rational choice concepts of criminal motivation and guardianship. Women with liberal sex-role attitudes concerning the division of the labor at work and in the household are psychologically more free to act like men in other arenas as well. It is necessary to recognize this symmetry between liberal feminist and rational choice concepts in order to understand the utility of the rational choice model for explaining not only criminality, but also as a framework for exploring sex differences in criminality.

While researchers previously examined the relationship between sex and perceived sanction threats (Grasmick et al. 1993; Richards and Tittle 1981) and sex and crime (Paternoster 1987; Smith and Paternoster 1987; Piquero and Paternoster 1998), a complete model connecting these concepts has not been explored, nor have the theoretical implications of both arguments been fully expounded. We examine the theoretical link between the Objectivist and Subjectivist perspectives and concepts found in rational choice theory. In so doing, we compare and contrast the efficacy of the operationalizations of traditionalism offered by these two perspectives for explaining sex differences in perceived sanction threats and crime. Specifically, we join sex, perceived sanction threats, and crime to examine the validity of the Objectivist and Subjectivist conceptualizations of the "changing female." Furthermore, we add a time element to our study to ascertain whether and where convergence is occurring.

SEX DIFFERENCES AND THE DETERRENCE/RATIONAL CHOICE MODEL

Through the early 1970s, the most frequently tested hypothesis of the rational choice model is that the perceived threat of legal sanctions deters criminal behavior (Paternoster 1987). By the mid-1970s, however, researchers began to explore the role of internal moral beliefs and attachments to significant others in providing sources of deterrence (Tittle 1980; Burkett and Jensen 1975; Jensen et al. 1978). While informal sanctions have been conceptualized in a variety of ways, Grasmick and Bursik (1990) formally introduced a rational choice model that includes measures of the perceived threats of shame and embarrassment, along with legal sanctions. The inclusion of informal sanction threats into the deterrence perspective has proven to be an important addition to the model. Indeed, research often yields stronger effects for the threat of informal than formal sanctions on crime (Burkett and Jensen 1975; Akers et al. 1979; Tittle 1980; Paternoster et al. 1983).

In their conceptualization of rational choice theory, Grasmick and Bursik (1990) assert that the perceived threats of shame and embarrassment should be combined with the perceived threat of legal sanctions to provide a more inclusive array of cost factors. In this model, shame is self-imposed and occurs when internalized norms are violated. When considering the commission of an illegal act, Grasmick and Bursik (1990) argue that individuals weigh the potential of feeling shame, or guilt, if they decide to engage in that behavior. On the other hand, embarrassment, a socially imposed sanction, occurs when actors violate norms endorsed by others whose opinions are valued by individuals. Embarrassment is experienced as a loss of respect from significant others.

Several steps have been taken to connect sex convergence in crime with rational choice theory. A number of researchers have posited that females perceive higher sanction threats than males. Because girls are more controlled by their parents (see discussions in Hagan et al. 1985 and Gottfredson and Hirschi 1990) than boys in early childhood, they perceive greater sanctions, both formal and informal (Braithwaite 1989; Finley and Grasmick 1985; Grasmick et al. 1993). Additionally, researchers have proposed that the sex difference in crime is the result of differences in perceived sanction threats (Silberman 1976; Smith 1979).

Focusing on the perceived threat of legal sanctions, Silberman (1976: 47–48, Richards and Tittle 1981; see also Tittle 1980; Finley and Grasmick 1985; Smith and Paternoster 1987) applied the deterrence model with the rationale that if females perceive greater sanction threats than males the relationship between sex and crime may be spurious. The majority of research, however, indicates that the effect of perceived certainty of legal sanctions on crime does not differ significantly for males and females (Jensen et al. 1978; Burkett and Jensen 1975; Anderson 1977; Smith 1979; Smith and Paternoster 1987).

In contrast, the revised deterrence/rational choice model, which includes informal sanction threats, has proven particularly useful in examining sex differences in individuals' decisions to engage in criminal activities. Drawing from the sex-role literature, numerous criminologists note that girls are taught to internalize shame, unlike boys, whose aggressive, independent, and self-assertive natures are nourished. These scholars contend that as a result of such early socialization females are likely to perceive greater threats of shame than males and consequently, have more conventional orientations toward the law (Shover et al. 1979; Simpson 1989; Braithwaite 1989; Jensen and Eve 1976; Tittle 1980; Blackwell 2000; Hagan et al. 1985).

Gilligan (1977) asserts that females are socialized to take responsibility for the maintenance of social relationships, therefore women have more to lose if caught committing a crime (Richards and Tittle 1981). Because the socialization experienced by female children focuses on relationships, females are expected to perceive greater costs of embarrassment than males when they consider status-threatening behavior. Additionally, women fear losing the relationships that are so important to their individual sense of identity. Men, whose socialization focuses on personal achievement, comparatively are less concerned with relationship maintenance (Gilligan 1977).

Tests of the relationship between sex and deterrence indicate that females report greater perceptions of shame than males (Jensen et al. 1978; Finley and Grasmick 1985; Grasmick et al. 1993; Tibbets and Herz 1996). Research also indicates females are more influenced by other's impressions of them than males (Macoby and Jacklin 1974; Gilligan 1977; Jensen et al. 1978; Grasmick et al. 1993). However, Grasmick et al. (1993) report that while in 1982 women scored higher on perceived threats of shame, embarrassment, and legal sanctions for theft and assault than men, this tendency is reduced by 1992. They assert that these findings support the claim that sex-role patterning of perceived threats of sanctions have changed over time.

In conclusion, research exploring the relationship between sex-roles and perceived sanction threats, both formal and informal, yields a mix of results, particularly concerning the claim that perceived sanction threats account for the sex difference in crime and delinquency. Nevertheless, generally consistent findings have been uncovered that females perceive greater risks of sanctions, both formal and informal, than do males. Tittle (1980: 296) argues that it is not enough to know that men and women are different in their perception of sanctions, criminologists should also explore the sources of these differences and the prospect that changes have occurred over time. Furthermore, "We must also be able to predict who will have greater or less perceptions of sanction threats and to do that we must understand how perceptions of sanctions are formed" (Tittle 1980: 296). Grasmick et al.(1984) made an initial step in this direction by borrowing from early work in feminist criminology.

LABOR FORCE PARTICIPATION, SEX-ROLES AND RATIONAL CHOICE

As previously mentioned, early work in feminist criminology produced two related explanations for the convergence in crime rates between the sexes. Grasmick and colleagues (Finley and Grasmick 1985; Grasmick et al. 1984) acknowledged that these arguments fit within the framework of a rational choice/deterrence model. The Objectivist position claims that changes in female participation in the labor force produced greater opportunities and an increased willingness for women to become involved in criminal behavior. Research indicates that women who are college-educated have made gains in the labor force in occupations that would tend to produce gender similarity in social control experiences (Grasmick et al. 1993). Sorensen (1991:13) notes that between 1978 and 1989, "the median weekly salary of full-time female workers increased from 61 percent to

79 percent that of full-time male workers," and concludes that there has been a decline in labor market discrimination against women, as well as an improvement in the quality of female labor relative to that of male labor. Therefore, as women become more like males in the workplace, given increased opportunities for crime, the Objectivist perspective predicts a decrease in perceived threats and an increase in criminal involvement.

Similarly, according to the Subjectivist perspective, as perceived sex-roles change for women, so to will their willingness to participate in traditionally male behavior such as crime (Hill and Harris 1981). In a recent meta-analysis of the sex-role literature, Twenge (1997) examined the results of sixty-three studies that assessed the sex-roles of college students. Twenge reported a positive relationship between year of administration and masculinity for females. As the psychological attributes of women become more like men, studies should yield evidence of convergence, assuming that men do not become more masculine/traditional at the same time.

These two explanations were first addressed by Grasmick et al. (1984). They conclude that convergence is most likely the result of a combination of the Objectivist (labor-force participation) and Subjectivist (non-traditional sex-role attitudes) explanations. In addition, they find support for Simon's claim that as women increasingly participate in the labor force, their opportunity to commit economic offenses increases; at the same time, their sense of powerlessness, and thus their motivation to commit violent crimes, decreases. Their results indicate the least similarity between non-traditional women and men on the offenses of assault. Further, they determine that convergence between men and women is "most characteristic of economic offenses" (p. 716).

Similarly, Finley and Grasmick (1985) tested the hypothesis that gender differences in the perceived threats of shame, embarrassment, and legal sanctions are accounted for by the changing climate of gender roles and the rise of "non-traditional" females. They reported that while nontraditional females do not significantly differ from males in perceived sanctions of shame and embarrassment, traditional females perceive higher certainty of shame and embarrassment than males. Both types of females perceive significantly higher threats of legal sanctions than males.

To further advance this line of research, we test the deterrence/rational choice model, including both objective and subjective measures of traditionalism for women. Additionally, we include two separate time periods to address the assumption that convergence is occurring. After presenting our final model, we critique the operationalizations derived from these perspectives and argue that future rational choice research should focus on crime as situated action that is structured by gender, race and class differences. Only when we recognize the ways in which choices are constrained can we predict how these choices will be made.

PRESENT STUDY

This research examines the effects of labor force participation and sex-role attitudes in the rational choice model. First, we measure the impact of sex on perceived sanction threats by testing: (1) the static hypothesis that there is a sex difference in the perceived sanction threats of shame, embarrassment, and legal sanctions, and (2) the dynamic hypothesis that the gap between men and women in these sanction threats converged between 1982 and 1992.

Second, we test these static and dynamic hypotheses using the Objectivist approach (focusing on employment status) to categorize women as traditional or not. Again, we propose (1) the static hypothesis that the gap between employed females and males in perceived sanction threats is smaller than the gap between unemployed females and males and (2) the dynamic hypothesis that there will be convergence between 1982 and 1992 between employed women and men; convergence between unemployed women and men is not expected.

Third, we examine these same static and dynamic hypotheses using the Subjectivist perspective (focusing on female sex-roles) to distinguish between women.

Fourth, we test the full rational choice model proposed by Grasmick and Bursik (1990) by including both perceived sanction threats and measures of female traditionalism to predict future offending decisions. We begin by using the traditional approach, including only a measure of sex to examine (1) the static hypothesis that there is sex difference in crime, (2) the dynamic hypothesis that women and men have converged in criminality, and (3) the hypothesis that the perceived threats of sanctions mediate the sex difference in offending. We next test these same hypotheses using the Objectivist and Subjectivist measures of female traditionalism.

METHODS
Data

The data come from the Oklahoma City Survey, an annual survey of adults. Several questionnaire items were included in both 1982 and 1992 surveys, providing the opportunity to examine the questions obtained from independent random samples in the same community separated by a decade, which arguably was a period of increased participation by women in the labor force and changing sex-roles. The total number of cases for the combined sample used for the analyses presented here is 746.[2]

Measures
Endogenous Variables—Future Theft and Future Assault

Both Adler and Simon posit that women are increasing in the level of offending for not only property, but also violent crimes. Later research, however, indicates that while women are committing more crime, it is primarily in the form of property, or economic-based offenses (Steffensmeier 1980). Thus, the two dependent variables explored in the final analyses were chosen as representative of economic/property offenses—theft, and personal/violent offenses—assault. Respondents were asked if they had committed each of the crimes in the past five years and if they would commit each of these offenses in the future.[3] The analysis here refers to future intentions, coded 1 for yes and 0 for no. Theft was presented on the questionnaire as "taking something from someplace worth less that $20 that did not belong to you," while assault was presented as "physically hurting another person on purpose." Separate analyses are reported for these variables.

Exogenous Variables
Perceived Threats of Sanctions

Measures of the perceived certainty and severity for the threats of shame, embarrassment, and legal sanctions for assault and theft were included on both surveys (Grasmick and Bryjak 1980; Miller and Simpson 1991; Grasmick et al. 1993). For the perceived certainty of legal sanctions, respondents were asked if they believed they "would get caught by the police" if they engaged in each of these behaviors. Responses were given on a 4-point Likert scale ranging from definitely would (4) to definitely would not (1). Measures of perceived certainty for shame were similar. A remark that some people might feel ashamed, guilty, or remorseful even if no one else found out, preceded the statement, "Generally, in most situations I would feel guilty if I . . . ," followed by the offense. Responses were given on a 4-point scale ranging from strongly agree (4) to strongly disagree (1). To tap the certainty of embarrassment, respondents were asked if people whose opinions they value most would lose respect for them if they committed the offense. Responses ranged from definitely would (4) to definitely would not (1).

The perceived severity of each of these punishments also was measured. For the perceived severity of legal sanctions respondents were asked to imagine they had been caught and to think about what punishment they would expect. They then responded to the question, "How much of a problem would this create for your life?" using a five-point Likert scale ranging from "a very big problem" (5) to "no problem at all" (1). Similarly, to tap the perceived severity of shame, respondents were asked to imagine they felt guilty or remorseful if they committed each of these offenses and to consider how big of a problem such a feeling would be for them. Finally, our measure of the perceived severity of embarrassment asked respondents to imagine that the people whose opinions they value would lose respect for them. A five-point scale ranging from a very big problem (5) to no problem at all (1) was utilized for responses to the measures of severity of shame and embarrassment.

Finally, following the expected utility model presented by Grasmick and Bursik (1990; see also Grasmick et al. 1993), we consider the product of perceived certainty and perceived severity for each of the sanction threats—legal sanctions, shame, and embarrassment—for the intent to commit theft and assault.

Sex

Sex of respondents is distinguished first on the basis of male (coded 1) versus female (coded 0). In the 1982 sample, 54.3 percent of the respondents were women while 53.8 percent of the respondents were women in the 1992 sample.

Objectivist Measures of Traditionalism

The Objectivist measure of nontraditionalism further delineates different kinds of women; women who were employed full-time, full-time and part-time, and retired were considered nontraditional, while women who were not employed or who were employed only part-time were classified as traditional. These variables were dummy coded to compare employed females (coded 1) to men (coded 0) and females who were not employed (coded 1) to men (coded 0). Using such coding, nontraditional women comprised 32 percent of the combined sample, whereas traditional women comprised 21 percent of the sample.

Subjectivist Measures of Traditionalism

The Subjectivist measure of nontraditionalism was based on the statement: "A wife should give up her job whenever it inconveniences her family." Responses were coded on a 4–point Likert scale ranging from strongly agree to strongly disagree. These categories were further collapsed to represent respondents who agreed with the statement (coded 1) representing traditional attitudes, and those who disagreed (coded 0) to represent nontraditional attitudes. For the final analysis, 23 percent of the sample is comprised of nontraditional women, using this measure, and traditional women comprise 31 percent.

Year

For these analyses, the two data sets were merged with year included as a dummy variable, coded 0 for 1982 and 1 for 1991. To test our dynamic hypotheses, that sex differences in perceived sanction threats have changed over time, we create a series of interaction terms by multiplying the variable year with the different representations of sex categories: Male X Year, Traditional Female (measured objectively) X Year with Nontraditional Female (measured objectively) X Year, and Traditional Female (measured subjectively) X Year with Nontraditional Female (measured subjectively) X Year. A positive interaction term will indicate convergence between the named category (e.g., traditional female) and males over the ten year period, while a negative coeffecient for the interaction term will indicate divergence.

Additional Controls

In the 1982 sample, the median age was thirty-eight, while the median age of the 1992 sample, as expected because of the aging of the population, was forty-four. Thus, age is included as a control variable. In addition, education is included in the analyses that follow; rational choice research indicates that education is linked to greater non-criminal opportunities (Tittle 1980) and education is positively correlated with more liberal sex-role attitudes for women (Faludi 1991). Finally, race is included as a control given findings in previous research that it is linked to both opportunity and perceived sanction threats (Blackwell et al. 1994). Because this sample is comprised primarily of whites, the variable included in these analyses was dichotomized into categories representing whites (86 percent of the combined sample) and non-whites (14 percent of the combined sample).

ANALYSES

The analyses are presented in two stages. First we present findings, in Tables 1 and 2, for our static and dynamic hypotheses for the perceived threats of sanctions for theft and assault. Second, we present our findings testing the static and dynamic hypotheses within the full rational choice model (Tables 3 and 4).

Sex and Perceived Sanction Threats for Theft and Assault

We test not only the traditional static hypothesis that males will score lower on perceived threats of sanctions than females, but also utilize Objectivist and Subjectivist categorizations of traditionalism for women. We expect the gap between traditional females and males to be greater than the gap between nontraditional females and males. Second, we introduce interaction terms in each of the models to test a dynamic hypothesis of convergence in the gap between nontraditional females and males in sanction threats between 1982 and 1992. This will be indicated by a significant positive coefficient for the interaction between year and nontraditional women. Significant convergence in the gap between traditional females and males during this time period is not expected. Analyses using the Objectivist perspective and the Subjectivist perspective are reported Panels 2 and 3 respectively.

Table 1 presents the OLS regression[4] results for sex differences in perceived sanctions for theft. In the first panel, females report significantly higher perceptions of shame (b = -1.469; p = .000), embarrassment (b = -.973; p = .009), and legal sanctions (b = -1.559; p = .000) than males. The interaction term, added in Equation II, suggests there was no convergence between males' and females' perceived threats over time.

The second panel presents our findings regarding the utility of the Objectivist perspective (e.g., comparing employed and unemployed females to males) in predicting perceived sanction threats. The coefficients for traditional and nontraditional females in Equation I are positive and significant across all types of threats (with the exception of the coefficient for nontraditional females for the perceived threat of embarrassment, which is nonsignificant). This indicates traditional females are significantly more likely to report the belief that they will be arrested, embarrassed, and shamed if they were to commit theft. While the coefficients for nontraditional females for shame and legal sanctions are positive and significant, because the magnitude of these coefficients is smaller than those for traditional females they still support our static hypothesis.

When we add the interaction terms, Equation II, we find support for the dynamic hypotheses only for perceived embarrassment (b = -2.192; p = .009). Nontraditional females report significantly higher perceptions of embarrassment than males in 1982 (b = 1.725; p = .005), but by 1992 this gap converged, with females reporting somewhat lower levels of perceived embarrassment than males (1.725 + -2.192 = -.467). There was no convergence between males and either type of females in the perceived threats of shame or legal sanctions.

The third panel of Table 1 presents the results of our analysis that categorizes females using the Subjectivist perspective. Contrary to our static hypothesis, both types of women report significantly higher threats of shame and legal sanctions than men when considering theft. Indeed, for all three perceived sanctions, the coefficients for nontraditional females are higher in magnitude than those for traditional females. Further, no convergence occurred between either category of females and males on any of the perceived sanction threats over the ten year period.

Table 1. OLS Regression of Perceived Sanction Threat Variables on Independent Variables for Theft: Traditional, Subjective and Objective Measures of Sex

	THEFT								
	Shame			Embarrassment			Legal Sanctions		
Traditional Measure of Sex									
Equation I	b	B	p	b	B	p	b	B	p
Male	-1.469	-.153	.000	-.973	-.088	.009	-1.559	-.163	.000
Year	-.078	-.008	.413	-.020	-.002	.481	-.081	-.008	.407
White	.573	.041	.133	.698	.043	.122	-1.106	-.079	.014
Education	-.144	-.082	.014	-.104	-.052	.084	-.292	-.167	.000
Age	.038	.135	.000	.040	.125	.000	.043	.154	.000
Intercept	16.201			12.988			16.849		
Equation II									
Male	-1.605	-.167	.001	-1.625	-.148	.003	-2.033	-.213	.000
Year	-.198	-.021	.341	-.597	-.054	.143	-.503	-.053	.143
Male*Year	.259	.023	.357	1.244	.097	.064	.908	.082	.093
White	.579	.041	.130	.725	.045	.113	-1.082	-.078	.016
Education	-.145	-.083	.013	-.112	-.056	.069	-.297	-.170	.000
Age	.038	.135	.000	.040	.124	.000	.043	.153	.143
Intercept	16.284			13.394			17.133		
Objective Measure of Traditionalism									
Equation I									
Non-Traditional female	1.123	.110	.003	.593	.051	.103	1.423	.140	.000
Traditional female	2.001	.170	.000	1.556	.116	.002	1.768	.151	.000
Year	-.111	-.012	.378	-.057	-.005	.445	-.094	-.010	.394
White	.523	.037	.155	.646	.040	.140	-1.124	-.081	.013
Education	-.134	-.077	.020	-.094	-.047	.108	-.288	-.165	.000
Age	.041	.146	.000	.043	.012	.000	.044	.158	.000
Intercept	14.533			11.790			15.213		
Equation II									
Non-traditional female	1.468	.143	.006	1.725	.147	.005	2.032	.199	.000
Traditional female	1.827	.156	.004	1.449	.790	.033	2.033	.174	.001
Year	.042	.004	.468	.625	.057	.148	.398	.042	.216
Non-Traditional Female*Year	-.668	-.052	.203	-2.192	-.148	.009	-1.181	-.092	.067
Traditional Female*Year	.307	.021	.370	.152	.009	.443	-.512	-.034	.286
White	.549	.039	.143	.716	.045	.115	-1.085	-.078	.016
Education	-.134	-.076	.020	-.097	-.048	.010	-.293	-.167	.000
Age	.040	.145	.000	.042	.133	.000	.044	.157	.000
Intercept	14.436			11.453			14.992		
Subjective Measure of Traditionalism									
Equation I									
Non-Traditional female	1.512	.145	.000	1.046	.088	.014	1.816	.175	.000
Traditional female	1.374	.120	.001	.802	.061	.065	1.137	.100	.005
Year	-.087	-.009	.403	-.030	-.003	.471	-.108	-.011	.377
White	.570	.041	.134	.692	.043	.124	-1.125	-.081	.017
Education	-.146	-.083	.013	-.108	-.053	.079	-.297	-.170	.000
Age	.038	.137	.000	.041	.127	.000	.045	.160	.000
Intercept	14.756			12.052			15.340		
Equation II									
Non-traditional female	1.345	.129	.013	1.517	.127	.015	2.192	.212	.000
Traditional female	1.856	.162	.002	1.627	.124	.015	1.708	.150	.003
Year	.036	.004	.472	.608	.055	.156	.364	.038	.235
Non-Traditional Female*Year	.303	.024	.357	-.888	-.060	.176	-.709	-.055	.189
Traditional Female*Year	-.943	-.063	.147	-1.611	-.093	.062	-1.123	-.075	.100
White	.615	.044	.117	.740	.046	.110	-1.089	-.078	.015
Education	-.141	-.081	.015	-.111	-.056	.072	-.301	-.172	.000
Age	.038	.135	.000	.040	.126	.000	.044	.159	.000
Intercept	14.609			11.759			15.123		

Table 2. OLS Regression of Perceived Sanction Threat Variables on Independent Variables for Assault: Traditional, Subjective, and Objective Measures of Sex

	ASSAULT								
Traditional Measure of Sex	*Shame*			*Embarrassment*			*Legal Sanctions*		
Equation I	b	B	p	b	B	p	b	B	p
Male	-1.543	-.151	.000	-1.723	-.157	.000	-1.132	-.117	.001
Year	.497	.049	.093	.572	.052	.078	.369	.038	.152
White	.914	.061	.047	1.753	.110	.001	.746	.053	.078
Education	.007	.036	.167	.043	.022	.278	-.089	-.051	.088
Age	.006	.195	.000	.052	.162	.000	.041	.147	.000
Intercept	12.104			10.390			12.978		
Equation II									
Male	-1.569	-.153	.002	-2.275	-.207	.000	-1.066	-.110	.020
Year	.474	.046	.177	.083	.008	.439	.427	.044	.191
Male*Year	.050	.004	.473	1.056	.083	.094	-.126	-.011	.430
White	.916	.061	.047	1.776	.111	.001	.743	.053	.078
Education	.067	.035	.168	.037	.019	.308	-.088	-.050	.091
Age	.058	.195	.000	.051	.161	.000	.041	.147	.000
Intercept	12.120			10.730			12.937		
Objective Measure of Traditionalism									
Equation I									
Non-Traditional female	1.127	.103	.005	1.166	.100	.005	1.088	.106	.004
Traditional female	2.192	.174	.000	2.581	.192	.000	1.200	.102	.005
Year	.460	.045	.110	.521	.048	.098	.364	.038	.156
White	.848	.057	.061	1.679	.105	.002	.740	.052	.079
Education	.078	.042	.130	.058	.029	.216	-.088	-.050	
Age	.062	.207	.000	.056	.177	.000	.042	.148	
Intercept	10.326			8.346			11.819		
Equation II									
Non-traditional female	1.276	.117	.019	1.804	.154	.003	.909	.088	.061
Traditional female	2.051	.163	.002	3.045	.227	.000	1.330	.113	.028
Year	.501	.049	.181	1.109	.101	.029	.299	.031	.283
Non-Traditional Female*Year	-.290	-.021	.367	-1.235	-.084	.088	.348	.027	.335
Traditional Female*Year	.257	.016	.397	-.880	-.051	.201	-.230	-.015	.403
White	.859	.058	.058	1.709	.107	.002	.726	.051	.084
Education	.078	.042	.129	.052	.026	.242	-.088	-.050	.092
Age	.062	.207	.000	.056	.176	.000	.042	.149	.000
Intercept	10.293			8.111			11.864		
Subjective Measure of Traditionalism									
Equation I									
Non-Traditional female	1.777	.160	.000	1.819	.153	.000	1.216	.116	.002
Traditional female	1.179	.097	.007	1.593	.122	.001	1.021	.089	.013
Year	.474	.046	.104	.559	.051	.083	.358	.037	.159
White	.898	.060	.050	1.751	.109	.001	.742	.053	.078
Education	.062	.033	.186	.041	.553	.290	-.091	-.052	.083
Age	.060	.200	.000	.052	.164	.000	.042	.149	.000
Intercept	10.604			8.679			11.859		
Equation II									
Non-traditional female	1.907	.172	.001	2.408	.203	.000	.866	.083	.079
Traditional female	1.071	.088	.058	2.119	.162	.002	1.319	.115	.021
Year	.499	.049	.182	1.134	.103	.027	.296	.031	.287
Non-Traditional Female*Year	-.241	-.018	.391	-1.105	-.075	.118	.645	.050	.220
Traditional Female*Year	.212	.013	.412	-1.034	-.060	.156	-.580	-.038	.261
White	.886	.059	.053	1.773	.111	.001	.777	.055	.070
Education	.059	.031	.199	.034	.017	.326	-.084	-.048	.103
Age	.060	.201	.000	.052	.164	.000	.041	.148	.000
Intercept	10.634			8.473					

Table 3. Logistic Regression of Crime Variables on Independent Variables for Theft and Assault

| | TRADITIONAL MODEL OF SEX | | | | | |
| | Theft | | | Assault | | |
Equation I	b	B	p	b	B	p
Male	.952	2.59	.010	.457	1.580	.055
Year	-.194	.824	.318	.196	1.216	.246
White	.193	1.212	.366	.037	1.038	.464
Education	.080	1.083	.156	-.029	.971	.301
Age	-.055	.946	.000	-.034	.967	.000
Intercept	-2.780			-1.045		
Equation II						
Male	2.185	8.887	.002	.110	1.116	.395
Year	1.395	4.034	.043	-.172	.842	.343
Male*Year	-2.306	.098	.003	.664	1.942	.124
White	.157	1.167	.391	.054	1.055	.447
Education	.088	1.092	.129	-.034	.967	.276
Age	-.055	.946	.000	-.034	.966	.000
Intercept	-3.838			-.807		
Equation III						
Male	1.833	6.255	.010	.146	1.158	.328
Year	1.458	4.299	.046	.282	1.326	.196
Male*Year	-2.167	.115	.016	---	---	---
White	.794	2.212	.124	.580	1.787	.119
Education	.076	1.079	.187	.049	1.050	.229
Age	-.048	.953	.003	-.025	.975	.011
Threat of Shame	-.131	.877	.001	-.173	.842	.000
Threat of Embarrassment	-.100	.905	.024	-.077	.926	.026
Threat of Legal Sanctions	-.096	.909	.042	-.014	.986	.362
Intercept	-.554			.438		

Table 4. Logistic Regression of Crime Variables on Independent Variables: Objective and Subjective Measures of Traditionalism.

| | OBJECTIVE MEASURES | | | | | | SUBJECTIVE MEASURES | | | | | |
| | Theft | | | Assault | | | Theft | | | Assault | | |
	b	(exp)B	p	b	(exp)B	p	b	(exp)B	p	b	(exp)B	p
Equation I												
Non-Traditional female	-.437	.646	.157	-.257	.773	.214	-.733	.480	.052	-.049	.952	.458
Traditional female	-2.400	.091	.010	-.774	.461	.031	-1.480	.228	.025	-.190	.827	.366
Year	-.173	.841	.327	.211	1.234	.231	-.194	.824	.308	.494	1.638	.101
White	.264	1.303	.329	.063	1.066	.438	.195	1.215	.364	.052	1.053	.449
Education	.073	1.076	.182	-.035	.966	.271	.074	1.076	.175	-.035	.966	.269
Age	.073	.943	.001	-.035	.965	.000	-.054	.947	.001	-.034	.967	.000
Intercept	-1.699			-.495			-1.766			-.685		
Equation II												
Non-traditional female	-1.581	.206	.020	.098	1.102	.416	-1.722	.179	.013	-.049	.952	.458
Traditional female	-8.026	.000	.339	-.462	.630	.219	-7.604	.000	.332	-.190	.827	.366
Year	-.899	.407	.038	.500	1.649	.096	.911	.402	.036	.494	1.638	.101
Non-Traditional Female*Year	2.208	9.101	.012	-.689	.502	.146	1.979	7.235	.023	-.695	.499	.148
Traditional Female*Year	6.909	1001.7	.361	-.580	.560	.242	7.438	1698.8	.385	-.636	.529	.212
White	.1939	1.214	.366	.085	1.088	.418	.160	.389	1.174	.052	1.053	.449
Education	.079	1.082	.159	-.038	.962	.251	.083	.145	1.086	-.035	.966	.269
Age	-.058	.943	.000	-.035	.965	.000	-.054	.947	.000	-.034	.967	.000
Intercept	-1.459			-.611			-1.596			-.685		
Equation III												
Non-traditional female	-1.104	.332	.086	.019	1.020	.479	-1.309	.270	.053	-.054	.947	.442
Traditional female	-2.053	.128	.026	-.497	.608	.165	-1.054	.349	.089	-.294	.745	.263
Year	-.503	.605	.164	.282	1.325	.197	-.394	.674	.212	.277	1.319	.402
Non-Traditional Female*Year	1.685	5.393	.051	---	---	---	1.561	4.652	.067	---	---	---
Traditional Female*Year	---	---	---	---	---	---	---	---	---	---	---	---
White	.755	2.127	.137	.586	1.797	.116	.839	2.314	.110	.590	1.803	.116
Education	.063	1.065	.233	.041	1.042	.268	.073	1.075	.198	.046	1.047	.241
Age	-.048	.953	.002	-.026	.974	.008	-.047	.954	.003	-.025	.976	.013
Threat of Shame	-.129	.879	.002	-.170	.844	.000	-.128	.880	.002	-.172	.842	.000
Threat of Embarrassment	-.103	.902	.019	-.074	.929	.032	-.105	.900	.017	-.077	.926	.025
Threat of Legal Sanctions	-.098	.907	.040	-.019	.981	.323	-.092	.912	.046	-.014	.986	.364
Intercept	1.441			.726			1.099			.597		

Table 2 reports the corresponding analyses for assault. Consistent with the findings for theft, males score significantly lower on the perceived threats of shame (b = -1.543; p = .000), embarrassment (b = 1.723; p = .000), and legal sanctions (b = -1.132; p = .001). Furthermore, these gaps between males and females have not significantly converged.

The comparison of traditional and non-traditional females to males using the Objectivist perspective to categorize women is presented in the second panel. Similar to theft, we find support for our static hypotheses. Both employed and unemployed women score lower on perceived sanction threats than men, and the gap between unemployed women and men is consistently larger. Our results yield no support, however, for the dynamic hypotheses. Employed women have not converged with men in perceived sanctions when considering assault.

Using subjective measures (panel 3), there is no support for the static hypothesis. The magnitude of the coefficients for nontraditional females are slightly larger than the coefficients for traditional females across all threat categories. Similarly, there is no evidence of convergence found in Equation II.

In sum, only when we distinguish between women using employment status (Objectivist measure), do we find that the gap between traditional females and males in their perceived threats of sanctions is greater than the gap between nontraditional females and males for both theft and assault. The dynamic hypothesis is supported only for the perceived threat of embarrassment for theft; employed women became more like men between 1982 and 1992. These data provide no support for the Subjectivist perspective in predicting sanction threats for either theft or assault.

Sex and Future Offending: Theft and Assault

We next present the full rational choice model. To begin, we present the traditional rational choice model, with a specific focus on sex differences in crime. Next, we suggest that not only do men commit more crime than women, explained in large part by females' higher perceptions of shame, embarrassment, and legal sanctions, but also that the degree to which women adhere to traditional statuses influences whether or not such differences exist. Thus, for the final set of analyses, we present first a comparison of the sexes on the likelihood of committing the offenses of assault and theft in the future, and second, comparisons of traditional and non-traditional women (using objective and subjective measures) to men. Because the dependent variables are binary, logistic regressions are used to test these hypotheses.

The Traditional Model

In Table 3, the analyses comparing men to all women in the intent to offend are presented. Equation I yields support for the static hypothesis that men are significantly more likely to report the inclination to commit theft (b =.952; p = .010). Men also are more likely to commit assault than are women (b = .457) and this relationship approaches significance (p = .055). In Equation II, the interaction term is significant and positive for theft, supporting the dynamic hypothesis (b = -2.306; p = .003). Specifically, men were significantly more likely than women to report an inclination toward theft in 1982 (b = 2.185; p = .002), but by 1992 the gap between men and women converged (2.185 + -2.306 = -.121). There is no significant convergence in the effect of sex on assault (b = .664; p = .124).

Perceived threats of sanctions are added in the final equation.[5] The addition of these variables does not alter the findings in the second equation. Males were significantly more likely to report an intent to commit theft in 1982, but significant convergence occurred. By 1992, females were more likely than males to report this intent. As expected from previous research on this rational choice model, each of the perceived sanction threats is negatively and significantly related to future theft. In other words, those who experience higher threats of shame, embarrassment, and legal sanctions—male or female—score lower on the intent to steal.

The coefficients for the perceived threats of shame and embarrassment are negative and significant, as expected, however, the perceived threat of legal sanctions does not reduce the intent to commit assault. Furthermore, the inclusion of these variables attenuates the effect of sex on future assault.

In Tables 4 and 5, both Objectivist and Subjectivist measures of female traditionalism are introduced in the full model. Drawing on our static hypothesis, the unstandardized coefficients for both types of women should be negative, indicating women are less likely than men to commit crime, and the coefficient should be smaller for nontraditional than traditional women. Second, according to our dynamic hypothesis, we expect a significant positive coefficient for the product term of year X nontraditional women, but we do not expect a significant positive coefficient for the product term for traditional women.

Objective Measures

In Table 4, employed and non-employed women are compared to men on the intent to offend (both theft and assault). In Equation I, we find support for our static hypotheses for both offenses—nontraditional women do not significantly differ from men in their intent to offend, while traditional women are significantly less likely than men to indicate future offending.

The interaction terms, added in Equation II to test the dynamic hypotheses, do not yield support for assault. However, the coefficient for the interaction term of nontraditional female X year is significant and positive for theft (b = 2.039; p = .017), indicating convergence in the likelihood of committing theft between these females and males. Specifically, both types of females were significantly less likely than males to indicate they would commit theft in 1982. By 1992, nontraditional females were more likely to report the intent to steal than males (-1.581 + 2.208 = .627). Consistent with our expectations, convergence did not occur between traditional females and males (b = 6.909; p = .361).[6]

The mediating variables are added in the fourth equation. The perceived threats of shame and embarrassment diminish the likelihood that individuals will offend. The direct effect of legal sanctions, however, is significant only when individuals are considering stealing (b = .098; p = .040); it does not impact the intent to commit assault (b = -.019; p = .323). The coefficients for traditional and nontraditional females are not altered with this addition.

Subjective Measures

The data using a subjective measure to distinguish women yield the same substantive conclusions as found with the Objectivist perspective. In Equation I, the static hypotheses are upheld, with traditional women significantly less likely to report an intent to steal than men (b = -1.480; p = .025), while the difference between nontraditional women and men approaches significance (b = -.733; p = .052). The interaction terms added in Equation II to explore the dynamic hypotheses indicate there was not significant convergence between traditional females and males in theft (b = 7.438; p = .385). However, there was a significant amount of convergence between nontraditional females and males during this period (b = 1.979; p = .023). In 1982, nontraditional females were significantly less likely to report that they would likely commit theft than were males (b = -1.722; p = .013), but were somewhat more likely than males to report the intent to commit theft by 1992 (-1.722 + 1.979 = .257).

As before, the insignificant interaction term for traditional females X year is eliminated in the final equation and the perceived sanction variables are added. The coefficients for the three sanction threat variables significantly reduce individuals' intent to commit theft at a future date. More importantly, including these variables both reduces the magnitude and renders insignificant the coefficients for the direct effects of nontraditional and traditional females as well as the coefficient for the interaction term between nontraditional females X year.

The models presented for assault yield support for neither our static nor our dynamic hypotheses. Both traditional and nontraditional females do not significantly differ from males in their intent to offend. In addition, there is no convergence or divergence between either of these groups and males over the ten year period examined here. Finally, in the full model, it is notable that only the perceived threats of shame and embarrassment significantly reduce the likelihood that individuals believe they will commit assault in the future; the coefficient for threat of legal sanctions is not significant ($b = -.014$; $p = .364$).

In sum, it appears that for assault there is no difference between men and women in the likelihood of committing this offense in the future. Furthermore, there is no difference between males and either traditional or nontraditional females in the likelihood of assault. This is maintained regardless of the approach taken to define traditionalism. No convergence or divergence in the gap between men and women is apparent from 1982 to 1992.

For theft, however, there is a significant gap between males and females in the likelihood that they will offend. More importantly, this gap not only exists, but persists, between men and nontraditional women. However, the gap between men and nontraditional women, either in terms of employment status or female sex-role attitudes, reveals that such women were significantly less likely to commit theft in 1982, but significant convergence occurred by 1992. This convergence is explained, in large part, by the perceived threats of shame, embarrassment, and legal sanctions. Grasmick and Bursik's (1990) rational choice model is supported by the these data.

CONCLUSION

In conclusion, this research establishes the importance of Simon's operationalization of traditionalism among women. The gap between non-employed women and men in both perceived sanction threats and the intent to steal is greater than the gap between males and employed females. Furthermore, the gap between non-employed women and men persists between 1982 and 1992, but the gap between non-employed females and males significantly converges. This convergence is explained in large part by changes in the gap in the perceived threat of embarrassment across this same time period.

No support for differentiating women based on female sex-role attitudes was found for either perceived sanction threats or offending decisions. Nor do we find support for either Simon's or Adler's claim that women are becoming more like men in the types of offenses they commit. Specifically, using both objective and subjective definitions of traditionalism, all women score higher on perceived threats of sanctions and lower on the intent to commit assault than men, and there has been no convergence over time.

We also conclude that the full rational choice model explains the intent to commit theft better than assault. This is not particularly surprising given the economic considerations involved in the decision to steal compared to the emotional nature of violent offenses, such as assault. Likewise, employment differences among women had a greater impact on theft than violence, lending support to the argument that labor force participation provides women with more opportunities to commit crime. This contradicts Steffensmeier's (1980) position that increases in female crime rates are basically a result of increased economic need. In our study, women who do *not* work, and consequently do not have their own economic resources, were *less* likely to steal than women who do work. We believe that future research must address the viability of the rational choice model for explaining violent crime.

More importantly, support for Simon's hypothesis within the rational choice model lends credence to the proposition that choice is structured (Cornish and Clarke 1987; Friedman and Diem 1993). Future research should develop, include, and refine structural variables in tests of rational choice theories to address the frequent criticism that rational choice frequently ignores the effects of social stratification in terms of race, gender, class, and age (England and Kilborn 1990; Folbre 1993; Frank 1990). While these criticisms are in many instances valid, critics rarely explore the possibility of combining structure and choice in one model (Friedman and Diem 1993). A constrained choice model may help explain differences in rationality, without labeling individuals who deviate from predicted patterns irrational.

Assuming that rationality is the same for all individuals is a gross misrepresentation of reality and denies the fact that groups differ in their conceptions of opportunities, costs, and rewards. Friedman and Diem (1993, p.95) draw attention to the misuse of rational choice theory when considering the impact of sex as they note that "utility is purely subjective." This highlights the usefulness of including the perceived threats of shame and embarrassment in a deterrence/rational choice model. However, as demonstrated in our research, perceived choices are not only structured by sex, but also by class (employment status). In other words, while women differ from men in the choices that they both have and perceive to have available to them, the degree to which women differ also is impacted by their class status (Wright 1997).

Moreover, while criminologists point out that women do not have the same opportunities as men, both legal and criminal (Steffensmeier 1980; Danner 1996), we note that women actually may have access to more non-crime alternatives than men, making crime less attractive for them. Hence, we propose that women choose non-crime alternatives not solely because they *fear potential sanctions*, but also because of the *benefits* that alternatives may provide. This is particularly relevant today because as women face costs that are increasingly similar to those experienced by men—in terms of legal sanctions (Daly 1987; Crew 1991); the benefits, or reward structures, of alternatives to crime likely have not changed.

Several researchers demostrate that female sex-roles are changing (Beutel and Marini 1995; Marini 1990). Since the 1970s women increasingly have entered the paid labor market. For many women, working is a choice and not solely a necessity, and they are now more likely to believe that they belong in the workforce than they did in the past (Danner 1996). While our study addresses changes in female sex-roles in our measures, we fail to incorporate changes in male sex-roles in our model. Men are increasingly participating in childrearing (Coltrane 1996), and this ultimately impacts their treatment in the criminal justice system. Indeed, Daly (1987) notes that all primary childcare providers, whether male or female, receive preferential treatment in sentencing. Thus, it is clear that male sex-roles should be explored in future research.

In addition to the sex-role literature, there is a growing body of research on gender. Because gender is a dynamic social structure, work in this area offers important insights into future rational choice research (Wright 1997). Arguably, many sex-roles have significantly changed over the past fifty years, and our measure of sex-roles is, as a result, inadequate for explaining gender dynamics. Gender measures explore how individuals construct both femininty *and* masculinity through social interaction (Connell 1990; 1995). Messerschmidt (1998) argues that crime is a way to "do" masculinity. Crime provides the added benefit of reinforcing masculinity for individuals who are trying to construct a masculine identity. In directing future models toward including structural variables that likely influence the perceived "utility," and therefore "rationality," of behavior options, we suggest that researchers must look beyond sex and sex-roles to consider the effect of "gender" on criminality.

Furthermore, because gender is a social construction, and not a biological trait, criminologists consistently reduce the utility of the rational choice model in accounting for variation within one sex. In other words, while we, like others, focused on the viability (Hagan et al. 1985) of the rational choice model in predicting sex differences, or solely on the differences between individuals—controlling for variables such as sex, class, and race, by not considering "gender" and the importance of "doing" gender to individuals, we likely misspecified the model at a structural level. Twenge (1997) demonstrates that both males and females have become more masculine since the 1970s. In contrast, men are not becoming more feminine, nor are women becoming less feminine. This may help to explain the sex gap in male and female criminality.

Finally, while the present study focuses on the importance of sex-roles in structuring choice, we argue that gender, race, age, and class operate in a similar manner. We contend that only when the ways in which choices are structured and constrained are recognized, can these choices, both to engage in crime and to abstain from crime, be predicted.

NOTES

1. Although sex and gender are frequently used interchangeably in criminological literature, we recognize they are separate concepts. Throughout this paper we distinguish between "sex"—a biologically based dichotomy—and "gender"—a situationally constructed attribute that is developed through the process of socialization. Likewise "sex-roles" are social roles based on the traditional division of labor in patriarchal societies while women occupy the homefront and men occupy the paid labor market, and gender-roles are based on psychological attributes associated with masculinity and femininity (which are not mutually exclusive).

2. Because these two samples are independent, we are not proposing that individuals' attitudes have changed over time. This would require a longitudinal sampling design. Rather, we note that the trend of female participation in the labor force has changed generally across time. This change should be reflected in the independent samples of these two time periods.

3. The analyses run on measures of whether these same offenses had been committed in the past five years produced comparable results. However, due to the issue of time order in rational choice theory, and the measurement of the key theoretical variables of perceived threats of shame, embarrassment, and legal sanctions, the use of these measures of future offending is more causally appropriate (Tittle 1980; Paternoster et al. 1983; Grasmick and Bursik 1990).

4. Because the variables measuring the perceived sanction threats for these two offenses are truncated, the analyses were replicated using tobit regressions. The results of these analyses led to the same substantive conclusions.

5. Since the interaction term was not significant in Equation II for assault, it is dropped in Equation III.

6. Because this interaction term is not significant, it is omitted in Equation IV.

REFERENCES

Adler, Freda. 1975. *Sisters in Crime*. New York: McGraw-Hill.

Akers, Ronald L., Marvin D. Krohn, Lonn Lanza-Kaduce, and Marcia Radosevich. 1979. "Social Learning and Deviant Behavior: A Specific Test of a General Theory." *American Sociological Review* 44: 635–655.

Anderson, E. 1977. "A Comparison of Male and Female Adolescents' Attachment to Parents and Differential Involvement with Marijuana." *International Review of Modern Sociology* 7: 213–223.

Beutel, Ann M. and Margaret Mooney Marini. 1995. "Gender and Values." *American Sociological Review* 60: 436–448.

Blackwell, Brenda Sims. 2000. "Perceived Sanction Threats, Sex, and Crime: A Test and Elaboration of Power-Control Theory." *Criminology* 38(2):439–488.

Blackwell, Brenda Sims, Harold G. Grasmick, and John K. Cochran. 1994. "Racial Differences in Perceived Sanction Threat: Static and Dynamic Hypotheses." *Journal of Research in Crime and Delinquency* 31: 210–224.

Braithwaite, John. 1989. *Crime, Shame and Reintegration*. Cambridge: Cambridge University Press.

Burkett, S., and E. Jensen. 1975. "Conventional Ties, Peer Influence, and the Fear of Apprehension: A Study of Adolescent Marijuana Use." *Sociological Quarterly* 16: 522–523.

Canter, Rachelle J. 1982. "Family Correlates of Male and Female Delinquency." *Criminology* 20: 149–167.

Chesney-Lind, Meda. 1989. "Girls' Crime and Women's Place: Toward a Feminist Model of Female Delinquency." *Crime and Delinquency* 35: 5–29.

Chesney-Lind, Meda and Randall G. Shelden. 1992. *Girls, Delinquency and Juvenile Justice*. Pacific Grove, CA: Brooks/Cole.

Chiricos, Theodore G. and Gordon P. Waldo. 1970. "Punishment and Crime: An Examination of Some Empirical Evidence." *Social Problems* 18: 200–217.

Clarke, Ronald and Derek Cornish. 1985. "Modeling Offenders' Decisions: A Framework for Research and Policy." In *Crime and Justice: An Annual Review of Research*, edited by M. Tonry and N. Morris, 147–185. Chicago: University of Chicago Press.

Coltrane, Scott. 1996. *Family Man: Fatherhood, Housework, and Gender Equity*. New York: Oxford.

Connell, R. 1995. *Masculinities*. Berkely: University of California Press.

———.1990. "The State, Gender , and Sexual Politics: Theory and Appraisal." *Theory and Society* 19: 507-44.

Cornish, Derek, and Ronald Clarke. 1987. "Understanding Crime Displacement: An Application of Rational Choice Theory." *Criminology* 25: 933–947.

Crew, Keith. 1991. "Sex Differences in Criminal Sentencing: Chivalry or Patriarchy?" *Justice Quarterly* 8: 59–81.

Daly, Kathleen. 1987. "Discrimination in the Criminal Courts: Family, Gender, and the Problem of Equal Treatment." *Social Forces* 66: 152–175.

Danner, Mona. 1996. "Gender Inequality and Criminalization: A Socialist Feminist Perspective on the Legal Social Control of Women." In *Race, Gender, and Class in Criminology: The Intersection,* edited by Martin D. Schwartz and Dragon Milovanovic, 29–48. New York: Garland.

Elliott, Doreen. 1988. *Gender, Delinquency, and Society.* Chapters 1 and 2. Brookfield, Vermont: Gower.

Eron, L.D. 1980. "Prescription for Reduction of Aggression." *American Psychologist* 3: 244–252.

Faludi, Susan. 1991. *The Undeclared War Against American Women.* New York: Doubleday.

Finley, Nancy J., and Harold G. Grasmick. 1985. "Gender Roles and Social Control." *Sociological Spectrum* 5: 317–330.

Folbre, Nancy. 1993. "Micro, Macro, Choice, and Structure." In *Theory on Gender: Feminism on Theory,* edited by Paula England, 323–331. Hawthorne, NY: Aldine de Gruyter.

Frank, Robert. 1990. "Rethinking Rational Choice." In *Beyond the Marketplace: Rethinking Economy and Society,* edited by Roger Friedland and A.F. Robertson, 53–87. Hawthorne, NY: Aldine de Gruyter.

Friedman and Diem. 1993. "Feminism and the Pro- (Rational-) Choice Movement: Rational-Choice Theory, Feminist Critiques, and Gender Inequality." In *Theory on Gender: Feminism on Theory,* edited by Paula England, 91–114. Hawthorne, NY: Aldine de Gruyter.

Gibbs, Jack. 1968. "Crime, Punishment, and Deterrence." *Southwestern Social Science Quarterly* 48: 515–530.

Gilligan, Carol. 1977. *In a Different Voice.* Cambridge, Massachusetts: Harvard University Press.

Gottfredson, Michael R., and Travis Hirschi. 1990. *A General Theory of Crime.* Stanford: Stanford University Press.

Grasmick, Harold G., Brenda Sims Blackwell, and Robert J. Bursik, Jr. 1993. "Changes in the Sex Patterning of Perceived Threats of Sanctions." *Law and Society Review* 27: 679–705.

Grasmick, Harold and George Bryjak. 1980. "The Deterrent Effect of Perceived Severity of Punishment." *Social Forces* 59: 471–491

Grasmick, Harold G. and Robert J. Bursik, Jr. 1990. "Conscience, Significant Others, and Rational Choice: Extending the Deterrence Model." *Law and Society Review* 24: 837–862.

Grasmick, Harold G., John Hagan, Brenda Sims Blackwell, and Bruce J. Arneklev. 1996. "Risk Preferences and Patriarchy: Extending Power-Control Theory." *Social Forces* 75: 177–199.

Grasmick, Harold G., Nancy Finley and Deborah Glaser, 1984. "Female Crime, Labor Force Participation, and Sex Role Attitudes: Evidence from a Survey of Adults." *Social Science Quarterly* 65: 703–718.

Grasmick, Harold G., and D. E. Green. 1980. "Legal Punishment, Social Disapproval and Internalization as Inhibitors of Illegal Behavior." *Journal of Criminal Law and Criminology* 71: 325–335.

Hagan, John, A.R. Gillis, and John Simpson. 1985. "The Class Structure of Gender and Delinquency: Toward a Power-Control Theory." *American Journal of Sociology* 90: 1151–78.

Hill, Gary D., and Anthony R. Harris. 1981. "Changes in the Gender Patterning of Crime, 1953–77." *Social Science Quarterly* 62: 658–671.

Hoschild, Arlie. 1989. *The Second Shift*. New York: Avon.

Jensen, Gary F. 1969. "'Crime Doesn't Pay': Correlates of a Shared Misunderstanding." *Social Problems* 17: 189–201.

Jensen, Gary F., Maynard L. Erickson, and Jack P. Gibbs. 1978. "Perceived Risk of Punishment and Self-Reported Delinquency." *Social Forces* 57: 57–78.

Jensen, Gary F., and Raymond Eve. 1976. "Sex Differences in Delinquency: An Examination of Popular Sociological Explanations." *Criminology* 13: 427–428.

Kruttschnitt, Candace. 1996. "Contributions of Quantitative Methods to the Study of Gender and Crime, or Bootstrapping Our Way into the Theoretical Thicket." *Journal of Quantitative Criminology* 12: 135–159.

Macoby, Eleanor, and Carol Nagy Jacklin. 1974. *The Psychology of Sex Differences*. Stanford, CA: Stanford University Press.

Marini, Margaret Mooney. 1990. "Sex and gender: What do we know?" *Sociological Forum* 5: 95–120.

Messerschmidt, J. 1998. *Masculinities, Crime and Criminology*. London: Sage.

Paternoster, Raymond. 1987. "The Deterrent Effect of the Perceived Certainty and Severity of Punishment: A Review of the Evidence and Issues." *Justice Quarterly* 4: 173–217.

Paternoster, Raymond, Linda E. Saltzman, Gordon P. Waldo, and Theodore G. Chiricos. 1983. "Perceived Risk and Social Control: Do Sanctions Really Deter?" *Law and Society Review* 17: 457–480.

Piquero, Alex and Paternoster, Raymond. 1998. "An Application of Stafford and Warr's Reconceptualization of Deterrence to Drinking and Driving." *Journal of Research in Crime and Delinquency* 35: 3–40.

Richards, Pamela, and Charles Tittle. 1981. "Gender and Perceived Chances of Arrest," *Social Forces* 59: 1182– 1199.

Schur, E. 1984. *Labeling Women Deviant: Gender, Stigma and Social Control.* New York: McGraw Hill.

Sellin, Thorsten. 1959. *The Death Penalty.* Philadelphia: American Law Institute.

Shover, Neil, S. Norland, J. James, and W. Thornton. 1979. "Gender Roles and Delinquency." *Social Forces* 58: 162–175.

Silberman, Matthew. 1976. "Toward a Theory of Criminal Deterrence." *American Sociological Review* 41: 442–461.

Simon, Rita. 1975. *Women and Crime.* Lexington, MA: Lexington Books.

Simpson, Sally. 1989. "Feminist Theory, Crime, and Justice." *Criminology* 27: 605–627.

Smith, Douglas and Raymond Paternoster. 1987. "The Gender Gap in Theories of Deviance: Issues and Evidence." *Journal of Research in Crime and Delinquency* 24: 140–172.

Sorenson, 1991. *Exploring the Reasons Behind the Narrowing Gender Gap in Earnings.* Washington, DC: Urban Institute Press.

Steffensmeier, Darrell. 1980. "Sex Differences in Patterns of Adult Crime, 1965–77: A Review and Assessment." *Social Forces* 58: 1080–1108.

Sutherland, Edwin H. and Donald R. Cressey. 1978. *Criminology.* (10th ed.) Philadelphia: Lippincott.

Tibbetts, Stephen G., and Herz, Denise C. 1996. "Gender Differences in Factors of Social Control and Rational Choice." *Deviant Behavior* 17: 183–208.

Tittle, Charles. 1980. *Sanctions and Social Deviance: The Question of Deterrence.* New York: Praeger.

———.1969. "Crime Rates and Legal Sanctions." *Social Problems* 18: 409–423.

Twenge. 1997. "Changes in Masculine and Feminine Traits Over Time: A Meta-Analysis." *Sex Roles* 36: 305–325.

Waldo, Gorden P. and Theodore G. Chiricos. 1972. "Perceived Penal Sanction and Self-Reported Criminality: A Neglected Approach to Deterrence Research." *Social Problems* 19: 522–540.

Wright, Eric Olin. 1997. *Class Counts: Comparative Studies in Class Analysis.* Cambridge, NY: Cambridge University Press.

Chapter 7

Premature Affluence, Rational Choice, and Delinquency: Examining the Darker Side of Affluence*

John Paul Wright

For over the last fifty years, American adolescents have ascended from relative economic obscurity to one of the largest and most lucrative markets of consumers in modern society (McNeal 1999). Contemporary youths command substantial economic clout and exercise unprecedented levels of financial power. Although reliable estimates are in short supply, available data indicate that adolescents represent a prosperous 122 billion dollar market (Teenage Research Unlimited 1998).

The significant acquisition of wealth gained and controlled by adolescents represents one of the most substantial, but least studied, social transformations that affected youth in the twentieth century. This newly found affluence came primarily from three sources. First, over the last forty years adolescent labor-market participation reached unprecedented levels (Steinberg 1996). It is now a common feature of adolescent life to balance educational requirements against the demands of employers. Indeed, Schneider and Schmidt (1996, 17) state that "working is perhaps the most common out-of-school activity among American teenagers." At any given time, more than half of all students sixteen to nineteen year olds are paid workers; nine out of ten students will become employees before leaving high school (Schneider and Schmidt 1996; see also, Steinberg 1996). From 1947 to 1980, adolescent male participation in the labor market had increased some 65 percent, while females increased their rates of participation over 240 percent. The United States, moreover, is the only industrial-

---

*Ideas embedded within this paper were influenced by several thought provoking conversations with Francis T. Cullen, Neal Shover and Mickey Braswell. Anything unique is largely due to their insight, any errors or omissions are mine alone.

ized nation that allows youth to mix working with going to school (Reubens Harrison and Rupp 1981; Steinberg 1996).

Second, income transfers from parents, commonly known as "allowances," have reached surprisingly high levels for certain youths. Analyzing data on 9,000 children from the National Longitudinal Survey of Youth, Zagorsky and Hering (2000) found that youths between the ages of twelve and eighteen reported an average of more than $100 in weekly allowances and other income transfers from their parents. Extrapolated out, Zagorsky's data indicate that the ten million U.S. teenagers receive approximately $1.05 billion per week in transfers.

Finally, the advent and wide dissemination of credit cards, and the ability they provide to purchase goods without necessary funds, have also influenced adolescent society. Although data are sparse, St. John (1996) reports that by age nineteen, thirty-nine percent of youths possess their own credit card. For youth under the age of eighteen, parents commonly grant their adolescents access to their line of credit.

The large sums of money commanded by young people have not gone unnoticed. Intense marketing campaigns are now directed at adolescents; all with the intent of making attractive the latest articles of clothing, the most popular musical groups, and the most impressive stereo systems, to name just a few. Interestingly, these campaigns also attempt to trigger impulsive, hedonistic decision-making; factors clearly related to crime and offending (Gottfredson and Hirschi 1990). The evidence of this fact is overwhelming; one need only to watch television or to read an adolescent magazine to understand that adolescents have been targeted by pervasive and systematic advertisement campaigns that stimulate their economic desires and corresponding concerns. According to McNeal (1999), marketing and advertisement expenditures by American companies now pinpoint $2 billion per year on youth, twenty times the amount spent just ten years ago (Cohen 2000).

Unfortunately, the subtle conversion of adolescents into powerful economic actors has received little empirical or theoretical attention. Although the reasons for this oversight are likely varied and numerous, part of the explanation points to the fact that most Americans believe that economic empowerment and the acquisition of wealth brings with it certain benefits, including a higher standard of living, and, for our purposes, less crime (Greenberger and Steinberg 1985; Steinberg 1996). Simply put, there is, as Robert Reich (1988) would call it, an underlying "public idea" that affluence can cure social ills.

There can be little doubt that most Americans view the accrual of wealth as a positive feature of adulthood, a time when home ownership and family responsibilities demand the ability to earn a sufficient income to meet living expenses. However, there is also some evidence, derived from large national samples of families, that adults, particularly parents, also believe that the accrual of wealth by adolescents engenders greater social responsibility. Parents of employed teens, for example, strongly support and believe that their youth's employment makes them more socially conforming and will ease their child's transition into adulthood (Manning 1990; Phillips and Sandstrom 1990).

Another key indicator showing widespread belief in the power of affluence to cure the social problems of adolescents can be found in policy decisions to create and maintain job programs for youth. Many accept uncritically that unemployment creates crime and, conversely, employment reduces crime. As such, without any evidence of effectiveness, hundreds of millions of tax dollars have been poured into job programs with the intent of bettering the lives of adolescents by teaching them skills useful in the adult world of work (National Commission on Youth 1980). Moreover, criminologists have typically endorsed such efforts and provided the necessary theoretical justifications. Greenberg (1993, 1977), for example, has argued that juvenile crime became pervasive throughout the 1960s and 1970s primarily because adolescents couldn't adequately participate in a culture that valued spending and consumption. For Greenberg, the key to alleviating the criminogenic stresses and strains originating from a youth's desire to participate fully in adolescent culture could be found in better integrating young people into the economic system of production—that is, by opening the once restricted labor-market to adolescents. Once armed with enough money to satisfy their consumption desires, the argument goes, delinquency would be reduced (see also, Stephens 1979).

Even so, it is not entirely clear that the economic empowerment of adolescents has had the expected positive effects—that is, has reduced rates of crime or individual levels of misbehavior. As I'll show, adolescent employment rates reached their peak in the late 1970s, precisely the time when rates of juvenile delinquency were also increasing. Moreover, a growing body of research has recently called into question the assumption that economic affluence engenders prosocial, healthy adolescent development (Agnew 1986, 1990, 1994; Bachman 1983; Cullen Mathers and Larson 1985; Wright Cullen Agnew and Brezina in press). Although still in its infancy, this body of research suggests that premature affluence may also come with a cost: particularly *higher* levels of misbehavior.

RATIONAL-CHOICE AND AFFLUENCE

Individual level studies into the decision-making processes associated with offending rely heavily on understanding the situational inducements that make crime more or less likely (Tunnell 1992). While valuable, this approach overlooks the normalizing influence of mass culture, those values and viewpoints that lead substantial proportions of people to make common, similar decisions. From a rational choice viewpoint, affluence likely has reshaped adolescent society in ways that have fundamentally altered youths' rudimentary calculations of the benefits and costs associated with certain choices. Given the substantial number of youth who now pursue their own economic betterment by fully participating in our economic system of earning and spending, it should be safe to argue that a clear cultural shift has occurred that has normalized adolescent economic pursuits. Where, for instance, school and employment were once segregated, most youth now face a choice between investing their time in school, with its tenuous link to an ill-defined future payoff, or in spending numerous hours on a job where they earn an immediate reward for their participation.

Working and possessing money generally opens an enticing array of lucrative and alluring opportunities for crime. With money in hand, youths are better able to meet their consumption desires, including purchasing automobiles, alcohol, and illicit drugs (Bachman 1983; Steinberg 1996). Moreover, possessing money for the sake of pursuing immediate, hedonistic desires may establish an exaggerated sense of entitlement; an orientation that may make difficult the transition from adolescence to adulthood (Bachman 1983). For these reasons and more, crime and delinquency may appear to be a rational extension of the darker side of affluence. This possibility is not entirely new. Bonger (1916:26), writing at the turn of the twentieth century, questioned the impact working had on youths. In his words:

> The paid labor of young people has a bad influence. . . . while still very young it forces them to think only of their own interests; then, brought into contact with persons who are rough and indifferent to their well being, they follow these only too quickly, because of their imitative tendencies, in their bad habits, grossness of speech, etc. Finally, the paid labor of the young makes them more or less independent at an age where they have the greatest need for guidance. . . . Certainly, this increase of juvenile crime is chiefly due to influences of bad domestic conditions, but the labor of the young people themselves also plays a part.

The following paragraphs examine the social transformation that has created the wealthiest group of youths in history. Longitudinal data on aggregate levels of labor-market participation are used to examine the large-scale movement of adolescents into the shared world of school and work. These data demonstrate the general association between labor-market participation rates and rates of criminal behavior. While these data are not without limitations, they graphically illustrate the substantial increases in working by adolescents and provide tentative evidence that youth employment is correlated with *more* crime, not less.

Aggregate data show trends over time, but they cannot tell us about the effects of affluence on individuals. For this I turn to an expanding body of literature that paints a mixed picture of the effects of work and money on the behavior of youth. Contrary to those who view the economic enhancement of adolescents as a panacea to delinquency, numerous studies now call into question whether working and possessing substantial amounts of disposable income are in the long-term best interest of most adolescents.

My goal in this chapter is to paint a portrait of youth, hopefully accurate, that escapes most contemporary criminological discussions. For too long, criminology has been captivated with the misbehavior of the poor and economically disenfranchised, avoiding the pathologies that are masked by wealth and economic security. The linkage to rational choice theory comes from recognizing that wealth and affluence are potentially criminogenic precisely because they may affect youths lives in ways that make the choice for crime more appealing, and conversely, the cost of crime less threatening.

The Social Transformation of Youth Into Workers

Youth labor-market participation became a substantial political issue in the 1960s. Framed within the context of class inequality, youth unemployment was publically and academically viewed as a major social problem rooted in the exclusion of adolescents from the marketplace (Greenberg 1977; Steinberg 1996). It is, therefore, likely not a coincidence that the 1960s were also a time when strain and anomie theories of crime gained widespread attention and political acceptance (Cloward and Ohlin 1961; Cohen 1955). Strain theories share a common assumption about the causes of crime; the causes are rooted in the frustration associated with the inability to pursue and obtain conventionally valued goals, in this case a good job and disposable income. While the details of these theories vary, they generally point to common policy conclusions, namely eliminating the roadblocks to employment faced by youths. As Steinberg and Cauffman (1995) note, numerous governmental programs were put into place to provide jobs to youth (see, Steinberg 1982 for a review).

What could not have been predicted at the time, however, was the onset and rapid macroeconomic changes that would occur beginning in the 1970s. These changes, particularly the advent of the service-based economy and the decline in traditional manufacturing jobs, did more to create employment opportunities for youth than any national program could have achieved. Unlike the production jobs found in mills and factories that excluded youths from the labor-market because of their age and inability to commit to long hours of manual work, adolescents were welcomed into the emerging sector of low wage, no benefits, part-time employment (Steinberg 1996).

To provide a cautious assessment of the movement of youth into the marketplace, I collected data from the Bureau of Labor Statistics on youth employment rates. Although these data are far from perfect, they tend to underestimate actual levels of youth employment for instance, they do provide a basis from which to analyze the effects of adolescent employment rates (see Steinberg and Cauffman 1995 for a review). Moreover, to assess the covariation between moving large numbers of youth into the labor-market and crime, I also utilized data from the well-known Uniform Crime Reports. The Uniform Crime Reports represent crimes known to the police and are collected by the Federal Bureau of Investigation. It is worthwhile to note that appropriate caution should be utilized in interpreting the following findings. Better data and more sophisticated analyses may yield different results.

Figure 1 shows the overall employment rates for adolescents age sixteen to nineteen for the years 1948 through 1996. For sake of comparison, the data are broken down into categories to reflect differences in levels between younger, sixteen to seventeen years old, and relatively older, eighteen to nineteen year old, workers.

Starting in 1948, perhaps partially due to the enforcement of child-labor laws, overall adolescent employment rates declined through the mid 1960s, at which time they began a steady increase through the late 1970s and into the early 1980s. Throughout this time period, on average 52 percent of all youths aged sixteen to nineteen were gainfully employed. This reached a peak of 58 percent in 1978, after which the recession of the early 1980s brought the levels back down.

Substantial differences, however, can be seen when the employment rates of older, compared to younger, workers are examined. Older youth are far more likely to be employed throughout this time period, perhaps owing to the end of their compulsory public education requirements. On average, 62 percent of older youths, compared to just 42 percent of younger adolescents, were officially employed during this time period. For both groups, however, the peak employment rates occurred in the late 1970s, where 49 percent of sixteen to seventeen year-olds were officially employed and 67 percent of eighteen to nineteen year-olds were employed.

Figure 2 shows the employment rates for males only, again broken down by age. Overall employment rates for all males appear to have declined since 1948, when 63 percent of all male adolescents were officially employed. This trend holds for younger, as well as older, youths. The downturn in male employment rates was especially pronounced after the mid-to-late 1970s, where in 1996, 65 percent of eighteen to nineteen year-

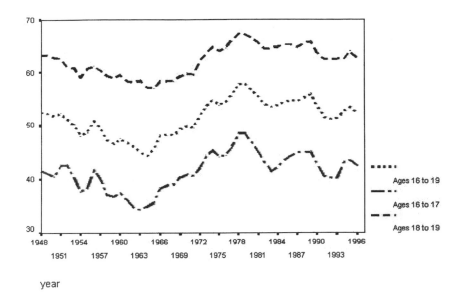

Figure 1: Adolescent Labor Market—Participation Rates

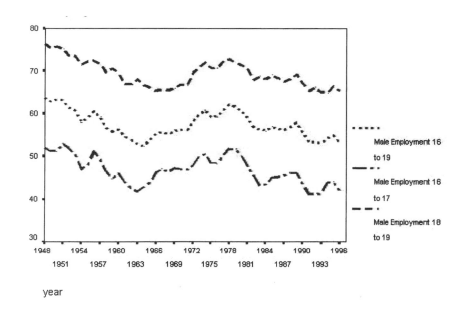

Fig. 2: Male Labor Market— Employment Rates

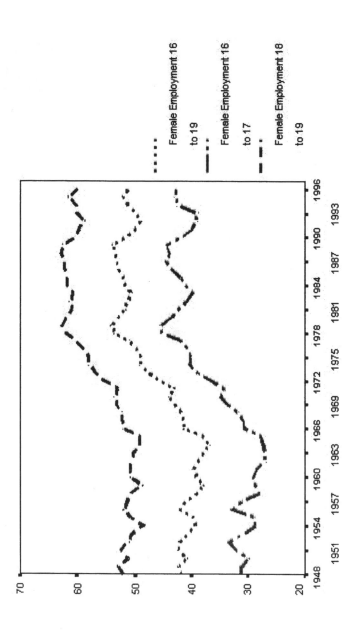

Fig. 3: Female Labor Market—Participation Rates

olds and 42 percent of sixteen to seventeen year-olds were counted as employed.

In stark contrast, however, the labor-market participation rates of females have increased substantially. Figure 3 graphically depicts the substantial changes that have occurred in adolescent female employment. From 1948 through the mid 1960s, the employment rates overall and by each age group were relatively stable. Beginning in the late 1960s however, employment rates escalated overall, and for older and younger females. Unlike their male counterparts, female rates have not noticeably declined since the late 1970s. While differences still exist between levels of female and male adolescent employment, those differences have narrowed substantially or, in the case of 16–17 year-olds, have been nearly equalized.

Adolescent Labor-Market Participation Rates and Crime

What has this change brought? From a rational choice perspective, modern youths are now faced with a dizzying array of economic options and financial opportunities. While some of these options may be beneficial, it is not clear that moving large numbers of youth into the economy has had the desired effect of lowering crime rates. The issue is no doubt complicated and difficult to assess. To gain some appreciation of the possible effects youth employment rates have had on crime rates, correlation coefficients were calculated to determine the amount of covariation between aggregate levels of adolescent employment and age-specific youth crime. That is, employment rates for sixteen to seventeen year olds, for example, were correlated with Uniform Crime Reports of crimes known to the police for sixteen to seventeen year olds.

Table 1 presents the results. For the entire sample, youth employment is *positively* related to rates of homicide for younger and older teenagers, positively related to robbery for the younger group, and positively associated with aggravated assault, burglary, larceny and alcohol offenses for the older sample of youth. Rates of employment for the younger sample were also positively associated with alcohol and drug offenses. In only one case was adolescent employment related to *reduced* crime, that being the case of auto-theft for sixteen to seventeen year-olds.

Just as the data presented earlier on trends in employment masked the differences between males and females in their rates of change over time, these data also provide at least tentative evidence that rates of youth employment generate different effects on males and females. In the case of males, the significant correlations are generally negative. Specifically, increased male labor-market participation was associated with reduced levels of homicide and aggravated assault for both age groups of males. In only one case was employment of older males related to increased offend-

Table 1: Correlations between Adolescent Employment Rates and Crime.

	Homicide	Robbery	Aggravated Assault	Burglary	Larceny	Auto Theft	Alcohol Offense	Drug Offenses
Youths 16–17	.307*	.377*	.267	.234	-.133	-.463*	.686*	.425*
Youths 18–19	.381*	.141	.373*	.569*	.493*	.356	.777*	.216
Males 16–17	-.581*	-.221	-.394*	.231	-.078	-.057	-.138	.129
Males 18–19	-.645*	-.064	-.464*	.213	.234	.363*	-.223	-.157
Females 16–17	.645*	.530*	.501*	.132	-.106	-.480*	.827*	.396*
Females 17–18	.725*	.153	.606*	.452*	.358*	.159	.908*	.278

ing, that being auto-theft. It is also important to note that in the majority of instances, labor-market participation rates have no significant correlation with rates of male crime.

Even so, the findings relating female employment rates to female crime rates show a startling contrast. For the majority of crimes, higher levels of adolescent female employment correlate *positively* with higher levels of female crime, especially for relatively younger females. The results are particularly noticeable for alcohol offenses and homicide. Apparently, the substantial increases in female labor-market participation have altered female adolescence in ways that increase crime and offending among young women. The clear implication is that the onset and rapid escalation of adolescent female labor-market participation altered choices and opportunities for females that once were relegated solely to males.

Understanding Aggregate Level Change and Crime

At first glance, it may seem incongruent that employment could be related positively to crime. However, it is important to recall that the focus here is on adolescent employment, and not with adult employment. The difference is not merely a matter of chronological age but of varying social contexts, opportunities, and available choices. On one hand, adults, particularly those with the added responsibility of raising children, spend considerable amounts of time at work in order to meet necessary expenses, such as a mortgage or rent payment, and to provide a standard of living for their children. Most of their income is spent paying for basic services. Moreover, adult work often is a source of self-identification. For many adults, their work is the result of years spent in college or apprenticeship programs where they received their training and credentials.

Adolescents, on the other hand, have available to them a wider range of economic options and opportunities than do adults. First, most youth jobs require few skills and only limited education or training (Greenberger and Steinberg 1980). The amount of personal investment in their work is minimal, thus they are free to move from job to job with little apparent loss to their income base or to their self-identity. Second, for most youths any money they earn is generally disposable income. Several studies, to be examined later, consistently find that youths immediately spend most of the money they earn on wanted luxury items, particularly clothes and electronic goods. Very few save any of their income and even fewer report helping out with family expenses (Bachman 1983; Wright et al. in press). Finally, adolescents typically spend much of their time at school, at work, and at play in the presence of peers, often in pursuit of thrill-seeking and partying (Hagan 1991; Warr 1993). The consequences of risky behavior, which for adolescents includes alcohol consumption and drug-use, do not entail the same costs that adults may face. Adults may lose their job if convicted of a crime, for example, but juveniles are often shielded from the deleterious effects associated with adjudication. If anything, a steady employment record may be viewed as sufficiently conventional to warrant less severe treatment for youths apprehended by the police (Sullivan 1989). It is no small irony, therefore, that available evidence indicates that adolescent employment is another domain where youths collectively associate and even commit crime (Ruggerio Greenberger and Steinberg 1982; Wright and Cullen 2000).

The social meaning of work thus takes on a different understanding when applied to adolescents. For most youths, working is unnecessary as their parents are able to meet their needs and most of their wants. However, those so motivated often make the choice to work against a backdrop of competing alternatives, which includes not working; participating in clubs, organizations, or athletics; working only a limited amount of time; or working extensively.

Thus to understand how moving large numbers of youths into the labor-market may create crime, we have to understand the enticement working offers to adolescents. Money is an obvious attraction. However, the opportunities that possessing money offers to youths may be more important. The purchase of an automobile, for example, is an important status symbol in adolescent culture, as is wearing "good" clothes and maintaining an active party life (Freedman and Thornton 1990; Steinberg 1996). Money and cars also allow for an extra degree of social independence—that is, youths are able to spend more time away from parents, who may place limits on their activities, and spend more time with their friends (Hirschi 1969; Steinberg and Cauffman 1995; Wright et al. in press). The point is, working allows youths to pursue hedonistic, short-term utilitarian interests, potentially to the detriment of long-term goals. Rational choice theorists have traditionally argued that individuals will pursue their immediate interests when other competing long-term alternatives are not as attractive (Cornish and Clarke, 1986). In essence, the movement of youths into the labor-market may have created such a condition by encouraging a culture of crass economic consumption that, in turn, altered the routine activities of young people by expanding the choices available to them. This transition has likely had its greatest impact on females, whose rates of employment and crime have increased precipitously since the 1960's.

INDIVIDUAL LEVEL STUDIES ON YOUTH EMPLOYMENT

While the movement of youths into the labor-market started in the 1960s, it was not until the early 1980s that empirical research began to investigate the effects of employment on the lives of adolescents. Although still limited in number and scope, the studies that have emerged over the last twenty years paint a complex and disturbing picture that implicates youth employment in a range of problem behaviors, including increased drug-use and delinquency. While the findings are generally small to modest in magnitude and must still be considered tentative, there is sufficient evidence to call into question whether "Our Children Should be Working" (Stephens 1979).

Collectively, a range of studies converge to show that adolescent employment is a rather innocuous event if limited to a few hours per week (typically between ten and fifteen hours). A sizeable portion of youth are, however, heavily invested in part-time jobs during the school year. In most samples, between twenty to thirty percent of surveyed youths report working over twenty hours per week. Unfortunately, the deleterious effects of youth employment appear to hinge on the number of hours per week adolescents spend at work, or what is frequently termed "work intensity." For instance, youths who spend a sizeable portion of their time at work generally report poor educational attainment, including earning lower grades, lower levels of school commitment, fewer hours studying outside of class, missing class more frequently, and cheating more often (Bachman, Bare and Frankie 1986; Bachman and Schulenberg 1993; Crowley 1984; Gottfredson 1985; Greenberger and Steinberg 1986; Steinberg, Greenberger, Garduque, and McAuliffe 1982; Marsh 1991; McNeil 1984; Mortimer and Finch 1986; Ploeger 1997).

Even so, "If there is reason to be concerned about the possible deleterious consequences of extensive employment" writes Steinberg and Cauffman (1995, 158), "it is to be found in studies of working and problem behavior." Contrary to conventional wisdom, as well as most criminological theories of delinquency, working long hours per week is generally associated with higher levels of delinquency (Cullen, Williams and Wright 1997; Elliott and Wofford 1991; Ruggiero 1984; Ruhm 1995; Shannon 1982; Steinberg and Dornbusch 1991; Steinberg et al. 1993; Wright Cullen and Williams 1997), with higher levels of risk-taking preferences (Yamoor and Mortimer 1993), with higher levels of occupational delinquency (Ruggerio et al. 1982; Wright and Cullen 2000), and with higher levels of drug-use and abuse (Bachman and Schulenberg, 1993; Mortimer, Finch, Shanhan, and Rue 1992; Steinberg et al. 1993).

These findings have been derived from multiple samples, including national and community samples, and across different methodological designs. While consistent in suggesting that high levels of work intensity are associated with greater misbehavior, out of these findings has emerged a serious debate. In essence, the debate questions whether the association between work intensity and misbehavior is the product of socialization or, conversely, self-selection—that is, whether traits that exist prior to entrance into work explain both higher levels of work intensity and delinquency. Some scholars point to the fact that early levels of misbehavior predict future levels of work intensity (Bachman and Schulenberg 1993). These studies show that delinquent and drug-using youths find employment an attractive alternative to other conventional pursuits, such as school. Bachman and Schulenberg (1993) and Newcomb and Bentler (1988) suggest, for example, that youths who work at high levels while of school age are already predisposed toward deviance. This predisposition, which Bachman and Schulenberg label as "pseudomaturity," is part of a larger collection of problem behaviors. Newcomb and Bentler make a similar argument, suggesting that "precocious" development, or the hastened onset of adult social roles, accounts for delinquency as well as labor force participation.

There are, however, two problems with the self-selection position; the first is empirical, the second theoretical. First, contrary to those who interpret the correlation between work intensity and illegal behavior as the product of pre-existing individual differences, much research suggests that high levels of working leads to *increases* in imprudent and delinquent conduct, even while controlling for pre-existing traits and behaviors. In one study, Steinberg and his associates (1993) found that preexisting differences in drug-use did not predict changes in levels of work intensity but did predict increased use of drugs and alcohol. Their findings are particularly important because they also show that youth who reduced their level of work intensity also reduced their levels of illegal behavior. Similarly, analyzing data from the National Youth Survey, Cullen et al. (1997) found that the deleterious effect of employment on delinquency remained even after prior levels of misbehavior were statistically controlled. Finally, youth who begin to work long hours per week appear to accelerate their misbehavior, especially when compared to youths who do not work or youths who work relatively few hours. For example, Steinberg et al's. (1993) longitudinal analyses of a sample of adolescents from Orange County, California, found that one year after entering the labor market, youths who worked more than twenty hours per week used drugs and alcohol 33 percent more often than unemployed adolescents (see also, Steinberg and Cauffman 1995). Thus, there is empirical evidence that suggests "increases in delinquency follow, rather than precede, employment in part-time jobs" (Steinberg and Cauffman 1995, 160).

Second, the notion that levels of work intensity and delinquency can be accounted for by preexisting individual differences fails to provide a motivating and compelling reason why youth who are delinquent would find working so enticing. If this perspective is true, and there is evidence to suggest that at least *part* of the correlation can be accounted for by pre-existing individual differences, then why would delinquent youths, who largely do not do well in school and who typically have problems relating to authority, desire to spend much of their time in the ordered and disciplined environment of the labor-market? Moreover, if delinquent youths welcome the workplace as an alternative to participation in other conventional activities, then, at a minimum, this suggests that the adolescent workplace may not be the social prophylactic typically thought.

For delinquents, employment may be particularly risky to their long-term adjustment. In one study, Wright and his colleagues (1996) found that the effects of employment were especially adverse for "high-risk" males. Their analysis of data from the National Survey of Families and Households showed that employment had particularly deleterious direct effects on the delinquency of males, and important indirect effects on misbehavior by reducing parental supports and school commitment. Although their findings were based on cross-sectional data, taken in conjunction with the findings from other studies, it seems reasonable to believe that employment may hasten, or at least continue, the social failures of delinquent adolescents.

We are left to speculate why delinquent youths may choose to work at higher levels than their more conforming counterparts, largely because research has not taken the next step to examine adolescents' motivations to work. Nonetheless, it appears likely that youth do not make the choice to either work or to commit crime; they can do both. Working may offer an attractive way for youths to spend much of their time away from home where adult oversight is less likely. Several studies have found that adolescent employment typically involves monotonous, repetitive work and is accompanied by little adult supervision. Employment may, therefore, be viewed as an escape from the rigid and demanding structure found in schools. Moreover, employment has the obvious accompanying benefit of earned income. Thus, the immediate acquisition of wealth may be very tempting for youths already involved in delinquent behavior, especially when we consider that much adolescent delinquency involves drug and alcohol use.

Yet to focus our concern only on already delinquent youth overlooks the possible negative consequences employment may have on relatively prosocial adolescents. Indeed, even for conventional youth there is cause for concern. In general, the adolescent workplace is likely filled with youth of varying propensities to commit crime. If there is a nonrandom selection effect that systematically places delinquent youths into premature work roles, then conventional adolescents are likely to find the workplace replete with delinquent peers. In other words, the adolescent workplace may establish the context where delinquent and nondelinquent youths coexist. In one test of the possibility, Wright and Cullen (in press) found that the acquisition of delinquent coworkers had effects on youths, regardless of their individual differences, by increasing their delinquency on the job as well as their misbehavior away from the workplace. Their analysis also showed that for youths low in self-control, the acquisition of delinquent coworkers had especially damaging consequences.

In sum, available evidence calls into question whether adolescent employment is beneficial to the long-term development of youths. At the individual level, working long hours per week is negatively associated with educational success, positively associated with illegal and imprudent behavior, and positively associated with increased drug-use. From a rational choice perspective, employment may offer an enticing array of possibilities for adolescents, some of which include escaping the rigors of public school life, avoiding adult oversight, earning money, and, therefore, creating opportunities to participate with coworkers in activities that breach or break conventional and legal norms. Thus, it may not be the case that youthful employment teaches responsibility and self-control as much as it extends and intensifies the adolescents' social life. Indeed, scholars such as Greenberger (1977) and Coleman (1961) have drawn attention to the fact that participation in the adolescent lifestyle is an economically costly and time-consuming process. Money is a necessary ingredient for many adolescent activities, including dating, going to the movies, and purchasing drugs and alcohol. In the next section, I briefly review the limited research on the effects of possessing money and adolescent behavior. Adolescents, it appears, are far wealthier than criminologists have acknowledged.

MONEY AND YOUTH CRIME

Borrowing heavily from Merton's (1938) conceptualization of the American Dream, Messner and Rosenfeld (1994) have recently drawn attention to America's "fetishism for money." "Money," they argue, "is awarded special priority in American culture." So much so, they contend, that it is now inextricably tied to the socialization of young children and adolescents, or, in their language, modern youth have been "penetrated" by economic motives and concerns. Interestingly, other disciplines have also drawn attention to the potential costs associated with affluence. O'Neil (1997), for example, in a aptly titled book, *The Golden Ghetto: The Psychology of Affluence*, provides a powerful commentary against the superficial personal existence derived out of what she labels as "affluenza," or America's dysfunctional relationship with money.

As I've discussed already, all available evidence shows that contemporary adolescents are sophisticated economic actors in control of substantial resources (McNeil, 2000). To rely completely on statistics relating youth socialization to labor-market participation, however, fails to capture the extent of the consumer culture that now envelopes adolescents. Other indicators also point to the importance of adolescents as consumers and draw attention to the current tug-of-war now underway between inculcating impulsive, hedonistic decision-making in youths on one hand, and greater appreciation for delayed gratification and self-control on the other. The available data suggest the battle may be highly one-sided. For example, in a recent book titled *The Kids' Market: Myths and Realities,* James McNeal (1999) reports that over the last thirty years, youths between the ages of twelve to fourteen doubled their spending; in the 1990s their spending was tripled. According to McNeal, in 1962, youth twelve to fourteen spent $2.2 billion. This number climbed to $4.2 billion by 1982 and to $17.1 billion by 1994. As of 1997, their spending topped $23.4 billion. When older youth are included in these estimates, adolescents twelve to nineteen years old spent $63 billion of their own money in 1994; by 1998 this number had climbed to $94 billion.

The increased economic power of young people has gained the attention of powerful economic forces. Sophisticated advertisement campaigns commonly target the consumption desires of youths, elevating "wants" into "needs" and creating dissatisfaction with their current economic plight (Swimme 1998). Advertisements, it appears, are omnipotent: Modern youths, who spend more time watching television than in school (Annenberg Public Policy Center 1999), view 20,000 to 40,000 commercials every year (Leonhardt and Kerwin 1997). Even schools, once sanctuaries from crass economic forces, now invite sponsors and advertisers. Channel One, an educational program transmitted directly to school rooms across the nation, fills 42 percent of its broadcast with commercials (Channel One Network 1999). Comparably, Channel One has a daily adolescent audience as large as that of the Superbowl; over the course of the year, fifty times more youths watch Channel One than MTV.

As advertisers know well, youth spend their own money, spend their parents' money, and hold considerable sway in the economic decisions of their parents. Again turning to McNeal (1999), survey data reveal that youths influenced about $5 billion of their parents purchases in the 1960s. Since then, their influence has increased ten-fold, by 1984 to $50 billion and tripling to $188 billion in 1997. McNeal estimates that it will reach $290 billion by year 2000 (Swimme 2000).

ECONOMIC SOCIALIZATION AND CHOICE

The primary contexts for youth socialization traditionally resided in neighborhoods, peer groups, families, and churches. Today, we must add one more context to this, our economic system. To understand modern American adolescence is to recognize the ubiquitous role of economic socialization and its corresponding incentives, motives, and consequences.

Unfortunately, unlike most families our economic system likely does not hold the best interest of youth as a priority. The differences are striking. While average parents do not appear to reject pursuing economic self-interest (Manning 1990), they do tend to reject the reckless pursuit of crass utilitarian self-interest, especially when it creates harm. Other differences exist: Where parents value self-control, adolescent economic culture values, if not relies on, impulsivity; where many parents value delayed gratification, adolescent culture emphasizes a "here and now" orientation; and where most parents value responsible altruism, contemporary adolescent economic culture values selfishness and greed.

Modern youths thus face choices that prior cohorts didn't face. Understanding these alternative choices may give some insight into why such a high proportion of American adolescents engage in crime and delinquency. Against the backdrop of choices available to youths, two come immediately to mind—that is, participating in the economic youth culture or in "adult" culture. The incentives are obvious for participating in the first; more money, more spending, more time spent with friends, more partying, and more status. The immediate incentives are not as clear for the second, where some youths are admonished for being too "geeky" if they take too seriously their role as student and their social responsibilities. In one survey youths were asked to describe their peers and the type of crowd to which they would like to belong. Summarizing the results, Steinberg writes (1996, 146), "five times as many students say [they would rather be in] the populars or jocks, as say the brains. Three times as many say they would rather be partyers or druggies. It should not, therefore, be surprising to find a greater proportion of youths mired in adolescent economic culture than integrated into the adult economic world of working and spending.

If extensive employment is associated with a range of problem behaviors, is possessing and spending money as well associated with maladjustment? Although the number of studies are limited, it does not appear that possessing money is universally beneficial to adolescents. Youths generally secure money in two ways: through an income transfer from their parents, termed an "allowance," or through paid employment outside of the family (Miller and Yung 1990). Common assumptions concerning parental allowances are (1) that parents provide only a small level of enumeration, and (2) that parents provide their youth with an allowance contingent on their youth's conduct. On closer inspection, these assumptions appear completely wrong. First, it appears that for youths who receive allowance from their parents, that, at least for some youths, the numbers are far from small. Examining data from the National Longitudinal Survey of Youths, Zagorsky and Hering (2000) found the median allowance for youths twelve to eighteen equaled $50 per week. Youths at the lower end of this continuum, typically younger adolescents from economically poor families, averaged only $7 per week. However, youths at the top end of the distribution, usually older youths from economically well-off families, secured $222 per week in allowance. Adolescents whose parents earned $100,000 or more per year report an average weekly allowance of $175; 59 percent of youths in this group reported receiving an allowance.

Second, other research shows that parents believe making an allowance contingent on conduct or the completion of chores around the home teaches responsibility. However, the same research shows that few parents actually follow through in withholding their child's allowance if their conduct is questionable or their chores not complete (Miller and Yung 1990). Moreover, youths apparently view their allowance as an "entitlement" rather than as the result of fulfilling a contractual arrangement with their parents (Miller and Yung 1990).

Data also show that having money and desiring money may foster delinquency and unreasonable expectations (Wright, Cullen, Agnew, and Brezina in press). First, research conducted by Cullen, Mathers, and Larson (1985) found that youths with more financial resources scored higher on a measure of delinquency than youths who had limited economic resources. Second, using the Youth in Transition data, Agnew (1994) found that a strong desire for money was positively correlated with higher levels of theft and vandalism, and higher levels of aggression. Third, similar to Agnew's study, Ruggiero, Greenberger, and Steinberg (1992) report that "materialism, defined in terms of placing a high value on money and material goods and spending money compulsively," was predictive of work-related delinquency. Fourth, from a sample of high achieving students in New York, Miller and Yung (1990) found that a youth's allowance was positively associated with risk-taking, a factor typically associated with crime and delinquency (Hagan 1991). Fifth, Bachman (1983) found that adolescents spend most of the money they earn from a job on their own entertainment. His analysis of data from the longitudinal Monitoring the Future survey also revealed the possibility that "premature affluence" led to a "decline in the standard of living during the years immediately following high school" (67). Or, more broadly stated,

> the pattern of spending a large proportion of income on relatively immediate sources of pleasure may reduce the ability to "delay gratification." More specifically, the sometimes expensive tastes developed in the teen years may be very hard to give up a few years later (67).

Finally, analyzing data from a sample of high school seniors, Wright et al. (in press) found that money earned from work and money received from parents in the form of allowance was predictive of greater, not less, delinquent involvement and greater, not less, drug-use. Their study was particularly important because it controlled for individual traits typically associated with crime, such as low self-control. Thus, it is less probable that their findings can be accounted for by pre-existing individual differences in criminal behavior.

The available data suggest that possessing money has fundamentally altered adolescent culture. For many youths, their routine activities, including much of the time they spend with their friends, center around earning money, spending money, and consuming resources. While there may be some benefits to allowing youths to exercise control over their finances, there also appear to be some drawbacks. Along with the acquisition of wealth comes an array of delinquent and criminal opportunities made available to youths. Youths with money appear more likely to smoke cigarettes, to use and abuse alcohol, and to use drugs. Even so, the real danger of adolescent "affluenza" may not have much to do with criminal behavior; the real threat looms in socializing youths into such a high standard of living that they divorce themselves from the institutions designed to prepare them for their future occupational and intellectual endeavors, namely their family and school. Tasting the "good life" prematurely, with its nice cars, nice clothes, parties, and large disposable incomes, may make the transition from youth to adulthood more difficult and less pleasurable.

CONCLUSIONS

Adolescence has been deeply penetrated by powerful and alluring economic forces. Possessing money, desiring brand name clothes, new cars, and electronics goods, and working long hours at boring jobs is now a common feature of adolescent development. Indeed, economic motives and extensive financial means are now so pervasive in adolescence that economic socialization can and should be viewed as a fundamental part of the life-course development of modern youth. This is not currently the case.

Criminology has largely neglected this core area of adolescent development; instead retaining its focus on traditional institutions on individual development, such as neighborhoods, families and peers. This oversight is important to notice for four reasons: First, criminologists have typically rallied around efforts to elevate the economic standing of adolescents. Employment is widely thought to alleviate the stresses and strains associated with economic marginality and to facilitate greater individual responsibility by allowing youths to more fully participate in *adult culture* (Greenberg 1977; Wright and Cullen 2000). While the potential for sustained economic disenfranchisement to negatively affect youthful misbehavior must be realized, an abundance of data now call into question the conventional wisdom that views youths as marginalized economic actors of limited means.

Second, these same data point to the deleterious impact economic influences have on adolescent development. Possessing money and an inflated desire for money may be a byproduct of an adolescent culture that values money for the sake of associating with peers in activities that include delinquency and drug-use. Money alters the lifestyle and behaviors of youths by expanding opportunities for deviance, by bringing criminally motivated youths together in time and space, and by allowing for the expression of immediate desires through the purchasing of goods and services to meet wants, cravings, and passions (Felson 1994). Money, in short, may be the key to participating in the more disreputable side of adolescent culture.

Third, corporations target adolescents with sophisticated and pervasive advertisements. Designed to stimulate their consumption desires, advertising serves as a major source of information for youths concerned with purchasing the latest and most popular products. As Williams, Cullen, and Wright (1997) note, a byproduct of economic socialization may be that impulsive behavior, a characteristic of adolescents' "low self-control" may be the product of systematic, organized campaigns designed to increase the profit margins of corporations (Wright and Cullen 2000). Advertisement serves to make certain choices more likely by increasing the likelihood that youths will act on impulse, without regard to their long-term goals.

Finally, premature affluence may carry with it deleterious consequences that extend into adulthood. Youths who chose to systematically mortgage their education for the immediate gratification of participating in the earn and spend culture of adolescence will likely find it more difficult to gain entrance into top universities, and consequentially, into well paying jobs. Future research may benefit by examining how the economic choices made by youths influence their long-term adjustment, including their levels of education and occupational status.

Youth are subject to various sources of influence. In turn, these influences shape and sometimes alter their decisions, even if their decisions may short-change their long-term development (Granovetter 1985, 1992). At least part of these influences can be located in the powerful pushes and pulls emanating from economic desires. The process of earning money, spending it on wanted items, and purchasing the most popular products may be so enticing and alluring that many youth simply choose to participate in the adolescent culture because of the immediate and gratifying rewards that it provides over adult culture.

Understanding the economic socialization of adolescents thus draws attention to how their choices are shaped, formed and determined amid a range of other economic possibilities. A rational choice perspective that includes a recognition of the opportunities, enticements and associated rewards that accompany participating in our economic system offers potential insight into adolescent misbehavior specifically, and youth socialization generally. Clearly, modern American adolescents are having their choices heard by businesses, employers and parents alike. Perhaps it is time for criminologists to reconcile their imagery of youths as unsophisticated and marginalized economic actors with the reality constructed by wealth and retained by choice.

REFERENCES

Agnew, Robert. 1986. "Work and Delinquency Among Juveniles Attending School." *Journal of Crime and Justice* 9:19–41.

———. 1990. "Adolescent Resources and Delinquency." *Criminology* 28:535–66.

———. 1994. "Delinquency and the Desire for Money." *Justice Quarterly* 11:411–27.

Anneberg Public Policy Center. 1999. *Media in the Home 1999: The Fourth Annual Survey of Parents and Children.* Http://appcpenn.org/kidstv99/survey5.htm.

Bachman, Jerald. 1983. "Premature Affluence: Do High School Seniors Earn Too Much?" *Economic Outlook* Summer:64–67.

Bachman, Jerald G., Dawn E. Bare, and Eric I. Frankie. 1986. *Correlates of Employment Among High School Seniors.* Ann Arbor, MI: Institute for Social Research.

Bachman, Jerald G. and John Schulenberg. 1993. "How Part-Time Work Intensity Relates to Drug Use, Problem Behavior, Time Use, and Satisfaction Among High School Seniors: Are These Consequences or Merely Correlates?" *Developmental Psychology* 29:220–35.

Bonger, William A. 1916. *Criminality and Economic Conditions.* Boston: Little, Brown.

Channel One Network. *The Fact Book 1997–1998.* New York: Channel One Network.

Crowley, Joan E. 1984. "Delinquency and Employment: Substitutions or Spurious Associations." Pp. 239–95 in *Youth and the Labor Market: An Analysis of the National Longitudinal Survey*, edited by M. E. Borus. Kalamazoo, MI: W. E. Upjohn Institute for Employment Research.

Coleman, James. 1961. *The Adolescent Society.* New York: Free Press.

Cornish, Derek B. and Ronald V. Clark, eds. 1986. *The Reasoning Criminal: Rational Choice Perspectives on Offending.* New York: Springer.

Cullen, Francis T., Nicolas Williams, and John Paul Wright. 1997. "Work Conditions and Juvenile Delinquency: Is Youth Employment Criminogenic?" *Criminal Justice Policy Review* 8:119–44.

Elliott, Delbert and S. Wofford. 1991. *Adolescent Employment*. Brief prepared for press release available from the authors. Boulder, CO: Institute for Behavioral Science, University of Colorado.

Freedman, Deborah S. and Arland Thornton. 1990. "The Consumption Aspirations of Adolescents: Determinants and Implications." *Youth and Society* 21:259–81.

Gottfredson, Denise C. 1985. "Youth Employment, Crime, and Schooling: A Longitudinal Study of a National Sample." *Developmental Psychology* 21:419–32.

Gottfredson, Michael R. and Travis Hirschi. 1990. *A General Theory of Crime*. Stanford, CA: Stanford University Press.

Granovetter, Mark. 1985. "Economic Action and Social Structure: The Problem of Embeddedness." *American Journal of Sociology* 91:481–510.

———. 1992. "The Sociological and Economic Approaches to Labour Market Analysis: A Social Structural View." Pp. 233–263, in *The Sociology of Economic Life*, edited by Mark Granovetter and R. Swedberg. Boulder, CO: Westview Press.

Greenberg, David F. 1993 [originally published in 1977]. "Delinquency and the Age Structure of Society." Pp. 334–56 in *Crime and Capitalism: Readings in Marxist Criminology*, edited by D. F. Greenberg. Philadelphia: Temple University Press.

Greenberger, Ellen and Laurence Steinberg. 1981. "The Workplace as a Context for the Socialization of Youth." *Journal of Youth and Adolescence* 10:185–210.

———. 1986. *When Teenagers Work: The Psychological and Social Costs of Adolescent Employment*. New York: Basic Books.

Greenberger, Ellen, Laurence Steinberg, and Mary Ruggiero. 1982. "A Job is a Job is a Job . . . or is It?" *Work and Occupations* 9:79–96.

Hagan, John. 1991. "Destiny and Drift: Subcultural Preferences, Status Attainments, and the Risks and Rewards of Youth." *American Sociological Review* 56:567–82.

Leonhardt, David and Kathleen Kerwin. 1999. "Hey Kid, Buy This: Is Madison Avenue Taking 'Get 'em While They're Young' Too Far?" *Business Week* June 30.

McNeal, James. 1999. *The Kids Market: Myths and Realities*. Ithaca: Paramount Marketing Publishing, Inc.

Messner, Steven F. and Richard Rosenfeld. 1994. *Crime and The American Dream*. Belmont, CA: Wadsworth.

Mortimer, Jeylan T. and Michael D. Finch. 1986. "The Development of Self-Esteem in the Early Work Career." *Work and Occupations* 13:217–39.

Mortimer, Jeylan T., Michael Finch, Michael Shanahan, and Seongryeol Ryu. 1992. "Adolescent Work History and Behavioral Adjustment." *Journal of Research on Adolescence* 21:59–80.

National Commission on Youth. (1980). *The Transition of Youth to Adulthood: A Bridge Too Long.* Boulder: Westview Press.

Newcomb, Michael D. and Peter M. Bentler. 1985. "The Impact of High School Substance Use on Choice of Young Adult Living Environment and Career Direction." *Journal of Drug Education* 15:253–261.

O'Neill, Jessie. 1997. *The Golden Ghetto: The Psychology of Affluence.* Http//www.affluenza.com/gghetto.html.

Phillips, Sarah and Kent L. Sandstrom. 1990. "Parental Attitudes Toward Youth Work." *Youth and Society* 22:160–83.

Ploeger, Matthew. 1997. "Youth Employment and Delinquency: Reconsidering a Problematic Relationship." *Criminology* 35:659–76.

Reich, Robert B. 1988. *The Power of Public Ideas.* Cambridge, MA: Harvard University Press.

Reubens, Beatrice G., John A. C. Harrison, and Kalman Rupp. 1981. *The Youth Labor Force 1945–1995: A Cross National Analysis.* Totowa, NJ: Allenheld, Osmun.

Ruggiero, Mary, Ellen Greenberger, and Laurence D. Steinberg. 1982. *Occupational Deviance Among Adolescent Workers. Youth and Society* 13:423–48.

Ruhm, Christopher J. 1995. "The Extent and Consequences of High School Employment." *Journal of Labor Research* 16:293–302.

Schneider, Barbara and Jennifer A. Schmidt. 1996. "Young Women at Work." Pp. 17–21 in *Women and Work: A Handbook*, edited by P. J. Dubeck and K. Borman. New York: Garland.

Shanahan, Michael J., Michael Finch, Jeylan T. Mortimer, and Seongryeol Ryu. 1991. "Adolescent Work Experience and Depressive Affect." *Social Psychology Quarterly* 54:299–317.

Steinberg, Laurence. 1996. *Beyond the Classroom: Why School Reform Has Failed and What Parents Can Do About It.* New York: Simon and Schuster.

Steinberg, Laurence and Elizabeth Cauffman. 1995. "The Impact of Employment on Adolescent Development." *Annals of Child Development* 11:131–66.

Steinberg, Laurence and Sanford M. Dornbusch. 1991. "Negative Correlates of Part-time Employment during Adolescence: Replication and Elaboration." *Developmental Psychology* 27:304–13.

Steinberg, Laurence and Ellen Greenberger. 1980. "The Part-time Employment of High-School Students: A Research Agenda." *Children and Youth Services Review* 2:161–85.

Steinberg, Laurence, Ellen Greenberger, Laurie Garduque, Mary Ruggiero, and Alan Vaux. 1982. "Effects of Working on Adolescent Development." *Developmental Psychology* 18:385–95.

Stephens, W. (1979). *Our Children Should be Working*. Springfield, IL: Charles C. Thomas.

St. John, Warren. 1996. "They Blow Money". *George* (June-July): 101, 129.

Sullivan, Mercer L. 1989. *"Getting Paid": Youth Crime and Work in the Inner City*. Ithaca: Cornell University Press.

Swimme, Brian. 2000. *How Do Our Kids Get So Caught Up in Consumerism? Center For the American Dream*. Http//www.new-dream.org/newsletter/swimme.html.

Tunnell, Kenneth D. 1992. *Choosing Crime: The Criminal Calculus of Property Offenders*. Chicago: Nelson-Hall Publishers.

Warr, Mark. 1993. "Age, Peers, and Delinquency." *Criminology* 31:17–40.

Wright, John Paul and Francis T. Cullen. 2000 "Juvenile Involvement in Occupational Delinquency." *Criminology*. In press.

Wright, John Paul, Francis T. Cullen, Robert Agnew, and Tim Brezina. In Press. "The Root of All Evil"? Money and Delinquent Involvement: An Exploratory Study". *Justice Quarterly*

Wright, John Paul, Francis T. Cullen, and Nicolas Williams. 1997. "Working While in School and Delinquent Involvement: Implications for Social Policy." *Crime and Delinquency* 43:203–221.

Yamoor, C., and Jeylan T. Mortimer. 1990. "An Investigation of Age and Gender Differences in the Effects of Employment on Adolescent Achievement and Well Being." *Youth and Society* 22:225–40.

Zagorsky, Jay and Jennifer Hering. 2000. *How Much Allowance Do U.S. Teenagers Get?* Columbus, Ohio: Center for Human Resource Research.

Chapter 8

Decision Making in Violent Events among Adolescent Males: An Examination of Sparks and Other Motivational Factors*

Deanna L. Wilkinson

I n recent years, there has been a growing interest in studying violent phenomena as interactional events (Fagan and Wilkinson 1998b; Felson
1993; Griffin 1993; Katz 1988; Meier and Kennedy 2000; Oliver 1994;
Polk 1994; Sullivan 1997; Tedeschi and Felson 1994; Wright and Decker
1997). Several studies have employed a situational approach to the study
of violence using a variety of research methods and samples. Most of what
we know about violent events comes from studies of adult males (Felson
and Steadman 1983; Luckenbill 1977; Oliver 1994; Wright and Decker
1997). These studies have three main foci: illustrating the violence process,
examining proximal motivations for violence, and isolating the influences
of third parties on violent outcomes (Decker 1995; Felson 1982; Felson,
Ribner, and Siegel 1986). Several studies are reviewed briefly below.

The interactions between victims and offenders, and the importance of
situational factors in homicide and other interpersonal violence, suggest
that a focus on *events* may be appropriate (Felson 1993). Violence
researchers have come to understand dispute-related violent events as a
process of social interactions with identifiable rules and contingencies.
Using this framework with respect to violence, numerous studies have

---

*Support for this research was provided by grants from the Harry Frank
Guggenheim Foundation, the Centers for Disease Control and Prevention, the
National Science Foundation, and the National Institute of Justice. An earlier version of this paper was presented at the American Society of Criminology in 1997. I
thank Bob Meier for his helpful comments and feedback on that early paper. The
points of view in this paper are solely those of the author. I would like to acknowledge the many contributions of my interview crew and research staff. Special thanks
to Jeffrey Fagan, principal investigator, for his support, suggestions, and comments.

focused on the interactional dynamics of situated transactions (Campbell and Gibbs 1986; Felson 1982; Felson and Steadman 1983; Luckenbill 1977; Luckenbill and Doyle 1989; Oliver 1994). Violent behavior can be viewed as a non-verbal method of communicating social meanings within contexts where such action is expected, or at least tolerated. Violence theory and research have paid little attention to the meaningful differences in the forms of violent acts, especially among teenagers. Violence research often has failed to acknowledge the heterogeneity of violent interactions. Empirical research shows that teens are involved in a wide range of violent acts. Miethe and Meier (1994), make the observation that a general theory of criminal events, and violent events more specifically, would be less useful than a more systematic inquiry of the variety of events across contexts and populations. The current research is consistent with that viewpoint.

This paper includes empirical data on decision-making and situational factors in violent events reported by a sample of 125 urban youth aged sixteen to twenty-four. The author and her colleague, Jeffrey Fagan, collected the study data beginning in September of 1995 and continued through the end of 1997. The analyses of the interview narratives focused on elaborating social processes of violent events by focusing on the heterogeneity of such events. It focuses specifically on disentangling the sparks or motivations in 306 violent or near violent events described by respondents. The paper highlights the complexity of decision-making in violent situations by examining the social and situational contexts in which these events are situated. This paper also focuses on the role that guns play in shaping decision-making among adolescent males.

BACKGROUND

Most explanations of violence include some type of dichotomy with "instrumental" and "expressive" forms of violence. Instrumental violence has been considered to be extrinsically motivated (i.e., a means to an end), while expressive (angry, hostile, or impulsive) violence is defined as intrinsically motivated (i.e., an end in itself) (Tedeschi and Felson 1994). Meaningful distinctions must go beyond this simple dichotomy and seek to locate violence within a framework where motivation interacts with social context to produce a violent act. Typically, these distinctions separate the "rational" and "irrational" forms to enable a better understanding of each type. Tedeschi and Felson argue that if one carefully examines the sequence of activities in events that have been previously classified as "irrational," "impulsive," or non-goal directed from the actor's point of view, one will usually find that the behavior is instrumental. This type of imperfect decision-making that appears irrational is simply what Clarke and Cornish

(1987) refer to as "bounded rationality." One researcher suggests that even the most seemingly irrational violent acts have a logical and predictable sequence (Katz 1988). Tedeschi and Felson's (1994) introduction of the social interactionist perspective departs greatly from previous work in the area of violence research, primarily because of their claim that all violent behaviors (coercive actions) are instrumental, or goal-oriented behavior. Tedeschi and Felson (1994) suggest that several factors affect the decision-making process, including cognitive processes (scripted behavior), emotion, alcohol/drug consumption, and impulsivity.

The social interactionist perspective also emphasizes the role of social interaction over other "personality" explanations in aggressive behavior. This perspective interprets all aggressive behavior as goal-oriented or instrumental, that is, as an attempt to achieve what is valued. Social interaction is examined in terms of a rational choice or decision-making model. Both Katz and Felson identified three main goals of aggressive actions: to compel and deter others, to achieve a favorable social identity, and to obtain justice (Felson 1993; Katz 1988). An interactionist perspective, concerned with the actor's point of view, focuses on describing the factors that produce conflict and those that inhibit it. This approach focuses on three central issues for understanding violence: the escalation of disputes, the role of social identities, and the role of third parties. Felson describes the dynamics of violent incidents similarly to Luckenbill and Doyle (1989), calling the sequence of events a social control process. Violence is a function of events that occur during the incident and therefore is not predetermined by the initial goals of the actors (Felson and Steadman 1983). Instrumental behavior is considered learned behavior because individuals learn about expectations, incentives, and inhibitions. The actor has expectations about what actions should follow his use of threats and/or punishment, as well as the probable costs of that action. These expectations, based on whatever information is processed at the time of the event, may be incomplete or distorted.

The "predatory" versus "dispute-related" dichotomy offers another heuristic for disentangling the heterogeneity of violent situations. Felson distinguishes "predatory" violence from dispute-related violence and suggests that dispute-related violence includes processual factors that are not evident in "predatory" assaults (Felson 1993). Predatory violence is defined as physical aggression committed without provocation, while dispute-related violence involves a reaction to some alleged wrong. The distinction is fuzzy; for example, a dispute may exist between the aggressor and the victim, although there appears to be no interaction between the two parties prior to the violent act. In these cases, the victim may be a proxy, surrogate, or symbolic target for the other disputant. Additional research is needed to more clearly identify the different types of violent situations and the interactional processes across event types.

A Brief Review of Studies of Violent Events

Studies of violent events as situated transactions examine the intersection of individual personality and situational factors in which violent outcomes result, what Toch has called "contingent consistency" (Toch 1986: 28). As Campbell explains:

> The notion of aggression as a form of interpersonal transaction is a relatively new one. Not only have we largely failed to see it as a process rather than an outcome, but we have also fallen into the belief, common in criminology, that 'bad' outcomes must have 'bad' causes so we continue to search for the predictors of aggression in static intrapersonal attributes such as under-controlled hostility or defective ego strength. . . . The factors that researchers studying interpersonal processes have found to be important are the setting, the relationship between the participants, their mutual goals for the interaction, and the extent to which they share a similar cultural understanding of the propriety and meaning of social actions. . . . People and situations are not logically independent of one another in the real world. (Campbell 1986: 115–116)

Luckenbill's Analysis of Homicide Records

Luckenbill employed a situational approach to the study of criminal homicide using data for the years 1963 through 1972 from one county in California. The homicide files contained a variety of information sources, including "police, probation, psychiatric, and witness reports, offender interviews, victim statements, and grand jury and court testimony" (Luckenbill 1977:177). Seventy cases met the study criterion and were analyzed for content. Luckenbill analyzed the step-by-step development of each transaction to prepare case reports for the event. Based on continued analysis of Luckenbill's homicide event data, Luckenbill and Doyle offered one such conceptual framework of interpersonal disputes (Luckenbill and Doyle 1989). They argue that such disputes were the product of three successive events: "naming," "claiming," and "aggressing." At the naming stage, the first actor identifies a negative outcome as an injury that the second actor has caused (i.e., assigning blame). At the claiming stage, the injured party expresses his grievance and demands reparation from the adversary. The final stage determines whether or not the interaction is transformed into a dispute. The third event is the rejection of a claim (in whole or in part) by the adversary. The researchers use these data to develop the *disputatiousness* theme in homicide events. According to their categorization, "disputatiousness" is defined as the likelihood of naming and claiming, and aggressiveness is defined as the willingness to preserve and use force to settle the dispute (Luckenbill and Doyle 1989). They claim that violence is triggered by norms within the code of personal honor and that differential disputatiousness and aggressiveness depend on the situation. Homicide research, including gun homicides, has begun to examine situational factors in violent behavior to some extent. However, homicide research is limited in several ways. It includes incarcerated offenders and offenders only in completed events. Homicides also represent a single event in a sequence of events that may have included other instances of non-lethal firearm use or other weapons.

Felson and Steadman's Study

Felson and Steadman used a similar event-centered approach to examine the interactive process leading to criminal violence (Felson and Steadman 1983). Using official data from 159 incidents of homicide and assault (after which suspects were incarcerated), the authors developed a detailed action-unit coding scheme for the data to identify different actions that were classified into eight general categories: physical attack, influence attempts, noncompliance, explicit identity attacks, threats, including verbal threats and brandishing a weapon without using it, evasive actions, mediation, and instigation (Felson and Steadman 1983: 63). Next, each situation was coded in what they termed a "sequence of unit-actions in which the actor(s) engaged in a particular behavior toward a target according to this format: actor-action-target" (Felson and Steadman 1983: 65). A trichotomous variable (offender, victim, and third party) representing actors and another representing targets was created for each action. Four rules guided their coding process. The ostensible nature of the action was coded; each stage of the interaction was coded, beginning with the first interaction of the parties and ending with the final attack on the victim; actions (not emotions or feelings) were coded; and exceptional events were excluded from the analysis. The study has provided an important analytic framework for examining situational and processual factors in violent events by developing an actor-action-target coding schemata.

They found that the incidents tended to follow systematic patterns. They usually began with identity attacks, were followed by attempts and failures to influence the opponent, then included verbal threats and finally, ended in physical attack. Retaliation, escalation, and aggressiveness of the victim were found to be important factors.

In this study, the researchers relied on offender statements to investigators, victim statements in non-homicide cases, and third-party statements. Biases evident in those statements were carried over into the researchers' coding decisions. Biases may be expected, since statements to investigators can influence the outcomes of cases, including important sentencing decisions. It is understandable if offenders or victims put a unique "spin" on their statements to investigators. This study, albeit limited methodologically, illustrates the usefulness of a processual analysis of violent events. Detailed narratives on incidents that were volunteered without any prejudicial motive may provide insights that previous research using official data could not.

Oliver's Study of Black Men in Bars and Bar Settings

Oliver (1994) used detailed narratives of violent confrontations between black males in bars and bar settings. Oliver employed both participant observation and interview methods over a five-year period (1983–1987) to "systematically examine the social functions of the black bar and how black males interacted with each other and with females in this setting" (Oliver 1994: 44). Oliver's sample consisted of forty-one black men twenty-eight to forty-five years old who frequented the research locations.

Oliver examined violent behaviors to identify the "rules" of engagement and situational causes of violence in the bar setting. The work also focused on articulating the social processes of violence. He observed a five-stage sequence of events similar to Felson and Steadman's previous classification. The first stage was characterized by "a respondent (who) perceived his antagonist as having committed an act that was defined as representing a potential threat to his manhood, physical safety and/or reputation" (Oliver 1994: 153). The second stage involved an attempt to clarify the antagonist's intentions and also included an attempt to confirm one's definition of the situation. Stage three was the development of a plan of action and the actual physical confrontation. The fourth stage was the conclusion of the confrontation that included three types of endings: symbolic, overt, and internal. The final stage of the sequence of events was described as the post-incident aftermath, including psychological and behavioral adjustments. This analysis again illustrates the importance of situational factors.

Although Oliver did not specifically focus on gun-use events, many of the events described involved the use of weapons. In his interviews with older respondents (men in their 30s and 40s), Oliver's respondents explained that weapons had changed the dynamics of interpersonal violence. Fighting on the street was characterized as being unfair because of the power of guns. He also found that carrying a weapon often resulted from a lack of closure in an ongoing interpersonal conflict. Oliver concluded that respondents carried a weapon because they anticipated violence or retaliation in the future and/or they knew from previous transactions that the antagonist had a weapon. According to the narrative, respondents often stashed weapons in handy locations nearby so that they could quickly arm themselves if the need arose. This tactic was recounted, at least in part, as a strategy to reduce the severity of possible criminal justice sanctions. Unfortunately, the incidents described were limited in scope and number; therefore, Oliver's study provides only a tiny glimpse of gun-use events. A more detailed analysis of the many important micro-decisions that influence gun-use events is needed.

The Role of Third Parties or Bystanders

The role of bystanders and third parties in the evolution of interpersonal disputes contributes significantly to the outcome (Black 1993; Decker 1995; Felson 1982; Felson, Ribner, and Siegel 1986; Oliver 1994; Riedel 1993). In their comprehensive review, Tedeschi and Felson (1994) describe a variety of roles that third parties play, including instigator, peacekeeper, cheerleader, and bouncer. In a public dispute, third parties constitute the audience, and their reaction has a strong effect on youthful actors. In dispute situations, the identities and associations of observers of potential conflict can deeply influence the thoughts, feelings, and behavior of the actors. For example, Felson (1982) found that when a dispute occurred between parties of the same sex, the presence of third parties increased the likelihood that a verbal disagreement would turn into a physical fight.

Oliver's (1994) subjects described three primary roles for third parties: "mediators, instigators, and instigating audiences." According to Oliver, "mediators" were third parties who actively attempted to intervene in an encounter between a respondent and an antagonist to de-escalate conflict toward a nonviolent termination (Oliver 1994: 98). Instigators were third parties who assumed a proactive stance in violent incidents by provoking one participant to argue or fight with another participant (1994: 100). An "instigating audience" consists of bystanders who encourage one or both participants in a dispute to resort to violence (Oliver 1994: 103).

Black (1993) identified two roles (supportive and settlement) and two dimensions (degree of partisan intervention and degree of authoritative intervention) that are useful to consider when analyzing third-party involvement in violence (Black 1993). Supportive roles include the *informer, adviser, advocate, ally,* and *surrogate,* and the settlement roles include the *friendly peacemaker, mediator, arbitrator, judge,* and *repressive peacemaker* (Black 1993: 97–124). The role of third parties often depends on their personal allegiance (or lack of it) to the main actors. Audience members allied with either the protagonist or the antagonist may each contribute to the escalation or de-escalation of a dispute through verbal statements, body language, cheering, nonverbal social pressure, or physical acts of violence.

Given the nature of peer relations during adolescence and their social activity patterns (frequent interaction with peers), third parties or bystanders may play an even greater role in "co-producing" violent events. Narratives presented in this chapter and elsewhere, allow for detailed examinations of these influences on the focal respondents' involvement in violent actions.

METHODOLOGY

Interviews were conducted with a targeted sample of 125 active violent offenders from two New York City neighborhoods. The primary field methods were in-depth interviews and biographical methods focusing on the social and symbolic construction of violent events (Cornish 1993; Cornish 1994). "Peer" interviewers were used to increase interviewer-respondent rapport and enhance data collection efforts (for a detailed discussion of the methodology for this study see Wilkinson 1998). The study design included sampling from two primary targeted pools: a recently released sample of young violent offenders and a matched sample drawn from the study neighborhoods. Eligible respondents were males, from sixteen to twenty-four years of age, who either are convicted of illegal possession of handguns or other violent offenses (criminal justice sample), or who, upon screening, were identified as actively involved in these behaviors in the past six months (neighborhood sample). The recently released sample consists of young men who were released from Rikers Island Academy between April, 1995 and December, 1996[1] and who, upon release, entered a membership program called *Friends of Island Academy*, Guys Insight on Imprisonment For Teenagers (G. I. I. F. T.).[2] The neighborhood samples were generated using chain referral or snowball sampling techniques (Biernacki and Waldorf, 1981; Watters and Biernacki, 1989). We purposefully sampled on the dependent variable in this study. The primary justification for including only active violent offenders in our sample was that we were interested in the social processes of violent events among individuals who had multiple events to report (to overcome the base rate problem). While the results will not be generalizable to the larger adolescent male population or even the neighborhoods, information concerning the cognitive landscapes of active violent offenders can be gained. Two neighborhoods were selected for this study primarily to control for the effects that neighborhood differences may have on violent behavior. The two neighborhoods are among the worst in terms of poverty and violent crime in the City of New York (NYC Department of Planning, 1993).

The sample for this analysis was exclusively minority and male, 44.8 percent African American, 41.6 percent Puerto Rican American, and 13.6 percent Caribbean or mixed ethnicity. Fifty-eight percent resided in East

New York or Brownsville, Brooklyn and 41.6 percent resided in the South Bronx. Forty five percent were recently released from Rikers Island or other correctional institutions, while 55 percent were recruited from the study neighborhoods. The average age was 19.29 with 24.8 percent at the modal age 18 years old. Respondents provided detailed descriptions of a total of 306 violent events that occurred in the two-year period prior to the interview. Respondents described an average of 2.44 events per interview, the range went from one event (16 percent) to ten events (.8 percent). See Table 1 for additional information on the characteristics of the sample.

Table 1: Sample Characteristics

Variable	%	N
Neighborhood		
East New York	58.4	125
South Bronx	41.6	125
Sample Source		
Recently Released (Jail)	45.0	125
Neighborhood Chain Referral	55.0	125
Age		
Mean	19.3	125
Median	19	125
Mode	18	125
Race/Ethnicity		
African American	44.8	125
Puerto Rican American	41.6	125
Other Islands or Mixed Ethnicity	13.6	125
Structural Position		
Completed High School or GED	19.4	120
Enrolled in School	26.4	120
Currently Employed (legal work)	11.4	114
Raised in 2 Parent Family	16.8	119
Mean Family Size	5.4 members	104
Respondent is a Father	46.9	104
Risk Factors/Violent Behaviors		
Ever Owned a Gun	96.8	125
Median Age of First Gun	14.0 years old	73
Involved in Violence	99.0	125
Involved in Drug Economy	84.3	121
Ever been Incarcerated	89.7	117
Ever Witnessed a Serious Violent Incident	91.4	125
Reported about a Gun Event	79.2	125
Experienced feeling like a Punk/Herb	72.9	96

Narrative interviews took one to two hours to complete. They were tape-recorded, fully transcribed, and analyzed using QSR NVIVO, NUD*IST 4.0, and SPSS software. The interview protocol focused on identifying the interpersonal dynamics of neighborhood violence, identity and status issues, representations of self-identity, attacks on identity, negotiating survival, and the role of contexts and circumstances in shaping violent outcomes. Respondents were asked to describe the process of social interaction with other young males on the street around issues such as image, reputation, respect, and identity attacks. In addition, they were asked to reconstruct three violent events: one where guns were present and they were used, one where guns were present and they were not used, and one where guns were not present. Events included both "completed" and non-completed violent situations. The latter group included events where violence was avoided in a variety of situational and social contexts.

DESCRIPTIVE FINDINGS

Research using a transactional framework has consistently found the following characteristics of violent events to be relevant: the context, the relationship between combatants, actors' definitions of the situation, motivations, antecedent factors, arousal state, the role of third parties, weapons, and alcohol or drug use. The interactional process (actor by action sequences) by which an interaction escalates toward a violent outcome is important. To date, there is little available information on violent events in which adolescent and young adult males are main participants. The developmental literature (Steinberg and Caufmann 1996) would suggest that the violence process may be different during this period reflecting immature decision-making by younger actors and other contingencies.

Prior research on violent events has shown that violence reflects a variety of motivational and situational concerns. The event data included in this analysis were coded on thirteen major dimensions including:

- type of weapon;
- type of weapon use;
- who was armed (respondent, opponent, respondent's companions, or opponent's associates);
- role of the respondent;
- role of the opponent;
- relationship between combatants;
- role of the other parties present, including: the respondent's associates, the opponent's companions, and neutral bystanders;
- a classification of collective decision making in violent events (co-offending);

- reason or spark of the event;
- location or context;
- role of alcohol and/or drug use in the event;
- role of the police; and
- an analysis of outcomes of the violent event including injuries and conflict resolution.

The data were presented by each of these domains in an effort to illustrate the heterogeneity of violent situations among adolescents (Wilkinson 1998). The detailed examples provided in the current paper often illustrate more than one theme requiring multiple references to specific event descriptions across domains. Excerpts of selected narratives will be presented to demonstrate the richness of the qualitative interview data. Weapon type was centrally important to the research questions of this study thus, all categories were examined across type of weapon.

Type of Weapon and Weapon Use in Violent Events

Respondents were asked to describe violent events with guns, knives, and other weapons that were either "completed" or "defused." They also were asked to describe fights without weapons. In total, respondents described 151 gun events, 37 knife events, 14 including other weapons, and 111 events with no weapon (just hands). Events were classified by type of weapon according to whether or not a weapon is part of the interaction between actors. For example, if any person in the situation had a gun, the event would be classified as a gun event. Weapons could have been brought into the situation by either the respondent, the respondent's companions, the opponent, or the opponent's companions. Each of these situations was coded for level of lethality.

Gun Events

Research on gun violence tends to confound gun carrying with gun use. To overcome this problem, each gun event was classified by different types of gun "use." Respondents reported having guns in 102 violent events, opponents having a gun in 88 situations, respondents' companions having guns in 69 events, and opponents' companions having guns in 35 situations. Of the 151 gun events, guns were used to threaten 23 percent (n=34), to beat 7 percent (n=10), and to shoot or shoot at someone 71 percent (n=107) of the time.

Respondents described both offensive and defensive moves in gun events. For example, seventy gun events were initiated by respondents (both alone and as a group) while sixty-three events were started by an opponent. According to our analysis of the data, the "options" available when armed with a gun included pulling out (to threaten), shooting in the air (to threaten), pistol whipping, shooting to injure, shooting to kill, attempting to shoot (failure), and drive-by shootings. The "options" available when confronted with an armed opponent included stalling or talking one's way out of the situation (with no retaliation), stalling or talking one's way out of the situation (with planned retaliation), negotiating another type of violence (disarming), pulling out a gun and facing off (no shooting), having a shootout, friends pulling out guns and forcing the opponent to back down (overpowering arms), and fleeing the situation to escape harm. Respondents decided which action to take based upon their prior knowledge of an opponent's willingness or ability to use violence (or their on-the-spot impression of the opponent), the respondent's assessment of his own ability to outperform the opponent, the likelihood that other parties would get involved to aid either party if needed, the level of anger/emotion during the event by both parties, and the respondent's assessment of risks and benefits to his social identity by using or avoiding violence. Guns clearly tip the scales of power in favor of the person who is armed.

Reasons or Sparks: Respondents' Definitions of the Situation

This section examines the causes or sparks of violent events. These situational definitions reflect a variety of issues and concerns for the actor(s) that are both situational and normative. The reasons or justifications respondents offered include both motivational and interactional domains; the two are often difficult to disentangle. Respondents described a number of reasons or sparks for conflict including: challenges to identity/status, jealousy/competition over females, self-defense, robbery, drug business transactions, revenge/retaliation, defense of others, rumors, territory/neighborhood honor, money/debts, unfair play (e.g., sports and gambling situations), misunderstandings, and fun or recreation. Descriptive statistics for the sample of events are presented, followed by an examination of the detailed narratives of the most common contingencies within each type of event. The excerpts provide a glimpse into the content and context of these violent events. Some of the events are used to illustrate multiple domains; in these cases, the event descriptions are presented in sections throughout the chapter. As shown in Table 2, many violent events involved more than one reason or spark.

Existing data on offender motivations often make broad claims about the overlapping existence of several motivational factors. A correlation matrix of the different types of motivations is presented below to illustrate the degree to which respondents' motives did or did not overlap. The data show that violent events among adolescent males in these two neighborhoods reflect a wide variety of issues and contextual dynamics. As shown

Table 2. Intersection of Type of Weapon by Spark or Reason for Event (n=306)*

Spark or Reason for Event:	Total		Gun		Other Weapon		No Weapon	
	n	%	n	%	n	%	n	%
Identity/Status	129	42.2	61	41.2	21	41.2	48	43.2
Girl	94	30.7	38	25.7	20	39.2	39	35.1
Self-Defense	67	21.9	30	20.3	17	33.3	20	18.0
Robbery	61	19.9	42	28.4	8	15.7	10	9.0
Drug Business	53	17.3	40	27.0	3	5.9	9	8.1
Revenge	53	17.3	32	21.6	9	17.6	13	11.7
Defense of Others	34	11.1	16	10.8	8	15.7	10	9.0
Rumors	18	5.9	7	4.7	3	5.9	8	7.2
Territory (non-drug)	16	5.2	10	6.8	3	5.9	3	2.7
Money or Debt	16	5.2	12	8.1	1	2.0	3	2.7
Unfair Play	15	4.9	9	6.1	3	5.9	13	11.7
Misunderstanding	5	1.6	0	0.0	1	2.0	4	3.6
No Reason	5	1.6	3	2.0	0	0.0	2	1.8
Fun or Recreation	4	1.3	3	2.0	0	0.0	1	0.9

*Data were missing on different domains. Percentages are for valid cases only. Reflects multiple sparks per event.

Table 3. Correlation Matrix Spark or Reason for Event & Weapon Type

	1	2	3	4	5	6	7	8	9	10	11	12	13	14	15
1 Identity/Status	1.00	.02	.09	-.19**	-.13**	.06	-.09	.07	-.05	-.08	.00	-.02	.04	-.06	.02
2 Girl		1.00	-.01	-.20**	-.21**	-.08	.08	.04	-.09	-.13*	-.10	-.10	.09	-.01	.08
3 Self-Defense			1.00	.02	-.05	-.05	.04	.04	.02	-.09	-.11	-.03	.05	.11	-.07
4 Robbery				1.00	.07	-.04	-.13*	-.13*	-.08	.03	-.10	.20**	-.04	-.03	-.18**
5 Drug Business					1.00	-.07	-.08	-.00	.16**	.16**	-.02	.24**	-.14*	-.02	-.16**
6 Revenge						1.00	.09	-.04	-.03	.01	.11	.10	.07	-.10	-.11
7 Defense of Others							1.00	.04	-.08	-.04	-.11	-.01	.00	.07	-.03
8 Rumors								1.00	-.06	-.06	-.03	-.05	-.01	.01	.04
9 Territory (non-drug)									1.00	.01	-.02	.06	.01	.02	-.08
10 Money or Debt										1.00	-.02	.09	-.09	.02	-.05
11 Unfair Play											1.00	-.06	-.08	.05	.09
12 Gun												1.00	-.36**	-.18**	-.72**
13 Knife													1.00	-.08	-.23**
14 Other Weapon														1.00	-.16**
15 No Weapon															1.00

* Significance level of .05
** Significance level of .01

in Table 3, some economically motivated violent events were significantly correlated with each other; specifically, drug business transactions correlate with events coded as igniting over neighborhood or turf concerns and the repayment of debts. Both drug business violence and robberies were negatively correlated with events erupting out of identity or status concerns or over females. The results suggest at minimum two separate motivational trajectories—identity or status and economic. Consistent with prior research, both robberies and violence associated with the drug business are significantly correlated with guns as the weapon of choice.

Challenges to Social Identity or Status

This section comprises narrative reconstructions of violent events classified as erupting out of some type of challenge or test to one's social identity or status. These events could be called "character contests," strategies of "impression management" and/or "face saving" situations. An event was coded as sparking out of identity or respect concerns if either the opponent or respondent felt "dissed," challenged, or "played." These situations typically involve the denial of personal status or identity manifested through insults, ridicule, bump, slight, ice grill (hard looks), lack of proper acknowledgment, cheating, deception, domination, cunning, unwarranted threats, or unprovoked physical attack. One hundred twenty-nine situations (67 percent of the total) reflected identity or respect concerns, according to respondents.

Personal Attacks

Respondents described a variety of situations in which nonverbal communication between two or more parties in a setting resulted in violent conflict. These situations most often involved a direct challenge to the rights of each individual over defining and controlling both the situation and space. In some cases, the initial exchange was simply an attempt at defining a situation, what Luckenbill (1977) called the "naming" stage. As illustrated by the examples below, many factors affect situational definitions in potential conflict situations. Several examples below show how violent events can erupt out of what respondents call "ice grills," "icing," "grilling," "hard profiling," or "staredowns." This form of communication between strangers within certain age-demographic groups is common on the street. In some situations, a look may be targeted at an individual with the goal of discovering more about his intentions in the setting. In other cases, ice grills are aggressive attempts to defend against any potential threat anticipated by the presence of a stranger in the neighborhood. These gestures speak loudly in a variety of settings to ward off attacks and identify situations in which attacks may be successful.

In the first example, the opponent is ice grilling the respondent and he becomes angry to the point of thinking about getting his gun. He interprets the opponent's ice grill as an extremely hostile threat and anticipates the opponent's return to the scene with a gun. This conflict may have escalated further if a mutual friend had not intervened:

> Interviewer (DB): Tell me what happen.
> Respondent (ENYN09): We went to the spot to buy weed.
> Interviewer (DB): Mmm-hmm.
> Respondent (ENYN09): So this dude came up start ice grilling me.
> Interviewer (DB): What caused the beef?
> Respondent (ENYN09): He was grilling (me). Then he ran up straight to the block. He went for his gun and I was gonna go for mine but my man came over. My man right there, (we) use to go to school with each other. So we just dead that, squashed it.
> Interviewer (DB): What made you decide not to hurt your opponent?
> Respondent (ENYN09): 'Cause he my man's peoples.

Looking back on the situation, the respondent feels that "if I had a gun and was by myself I probably woulda shot him." The ice grill was perceived as a serious personal insult. The respondent was only willing to drop his grievance with the opponent because of his relationship with the third party.

Many violent events result from taunting and ice grills between the combatants. One such event occurred during a baseball game in jail. The respondent "iced" his opponent for making a "slick comment" and paid for his transgression against this powerful individual with a physical injury.

> Interviewer (DB): All right. I want you to describe the scene so I could picture it. . . .
> Respondent (ENYN20): The fight, the main fact I can remember is when I got jumped and I had to get 140 stitches across my eye. Right at the bottom. And the situation was . . . it started on a baseball field where someone said a slick comment towards me and I turned around and I iced him and that person was well known . . . basically he ran (in) the building and he got all his peoples that was on my unit, my wing (in jail), to take care of his business, so when he was there, I was fighting at least eight people, guys who was doing 18 to life, lifers and there was not no skinny, you know, they wasn't no skinny puny people. They've been there, they've been working out . . . . it was a rough battle.
> Interviewer (DB): How the fight had started?
> Respondent (ENYN20): I already told you how it started, it started because. . . .
> Interviewer (DB): I mean like in your unit, how did they approach you?

Respondent (ENYN20): They approach me, they approached the way, you know, handled their business, they just said, 'pardon me may I speak to you,' and once I came inside that room then, we got it on.

Outsider Status and Identity Uncertainty

One central theme in identity- or status-related violent events is that identity challenges resulting in violent events are more often between strangers. The examples presented below illustrate how these conflicts unfold in a variety of situations.

In the setting in which these occurred, bumping into someone represents a personal attack. One respondent reacted to a bump by swinging at the opponent. While this seemingly spontaneous conflict could have resulted in a physical fight without weapons, the opponent chose instead to get his gun. He explained the situation:

Interviewer (DB): Can you tell me about a gun event that you was involved in? I want you to tell me what happened, what it was over, everything.
Respondent (SBN71): I was walking through the projects one day. I was going to a party. It's not around my 'hood, (I) ain't know nobody around there. And this kid bumped me. And I swung at him. Then he ran to go get his people. And he came back and he shot at me twice.
Interviewer (DB): So you . . . said he bumped you?
Respondent (SBN71): Yeah.
Interviewer (DB): And then what you did?
Respondent (SBN71): I swung at him.
Interviewer (DB): And then he ran and and got his gun?
Respondent (SBN71): Yeah.
Interviewer (DB): Um, was there some type of argument before the gun got involved?
Respondent (SBN71): Nah just when he bumped me and I swung at him.
Interviewer (DB): Why you swung at him for?
Respondent (SBN71): 'Cause he bump me and then he look back like he was going to do something. So I swung.
Interviewer (DB): What he say?
Respondent (SBN71): 'What's the fuck wrong with you, man?'
Interviewer (DB): What was it about this situation that made it necessary to handle it the way you did?
Respondent (SBN71): They way he talk to me. And he never knew me before.
Interviewer (DB): Who made the first move toward violence?
Respondent (SBN71): Actually, I did.
Interviewer (DB): You swung at him?
Respondent (SBN71): Yeah.
Interviewer (DB): What did he do after that?
Respondent (SBN71): He ran to get his gun.
Interviewer (DB): Was anybody else around?
Respondent (SBN71): His peoples.

Interviewer (DB): What kind of stuff was they sayin'?
Respondent (SBN71): 'Kill that nigga.'
Interviewer (DB): How did you feel about what his friends was sayin? Were you afraid?
Respondent (SBN71): I was. Man with a gun, shooting.

The other individuals in the situation clearly were against the respondent and verbally encouraged the opponent's gun use. The event escalated to a gun incident quickly and the respondent fled the scene without injury. Two factors made the respondent's presence in that neighborhood problematic: he was vulnerable to attack because of his outsider status and he did not have a gun.

Another respondent became involved in a gun conflict when his opponent bumped him in a party. The respondent was high and refused to accept the apology of the opponent. The event unfolded in the following way:

Interviewer (DT): All right, let's talk about the gun event. What happened? Can you describe the situation? And how did it happen, what started it?
Respondent (ENYN56): It's like I said before, you know, just me and my man was just jiving and bugging out, dancing and shit, you know, drinking, smoking. Shit, some niggas just wanted to try to play you and shit, make us look stupid. So, you know, (they) pulled out the gun and started shooting in the fucking house and shit, everybody screaming and shit. Me and the niggas shot back at them. They shot my man twice. So then after that, like, everybody just started screaming and running, so we, like, just started shooting.
Interviewer (DT): Was there some kind of argument before the guns was used?
Respondent (ENYN56): Nah. Yeah, of course, you know, of course, you know.
Interviewer (DT): So tell me, like, everything that was said.
Respondent (ENYN56): All right, like me and my man, right, we was dancing and shit, smoking, all that, drunk like a motherfucker, you know? So like one punk, you know, like, bumped my man and shit, you know. So, you know, they came out arguing and shit, you know, pussy and this and that, you know. So we was like, all right, so then I went up to my man, I was like 'what's the deal and shit,' he was like 'I don't know, somebody just trying to play you.' So I just started shooting at them, you know? Fuck it.
Respondent (ENYN56): We was high and shit, so I was like, 'I'ma shoot these motherfuckers', so that's that . . .

In the next example, the respondent immediately sensed the opponent's hostile stance toward him as soon as he entered a party. Again, the respondent was an outsider to the neighborhood and put himself in a risky situation by attending the party. In this case, however, he brought his gun. He explained:

> Interviewer (JM): You wasn't scared or nothing?
> Respondent (G-80): Nah I wasn't scared I was thinking about murdering the nigga. Nigga came up to my face talking shit.
> Interviewer (JM): So that night, so, how did Y'all get into that beef?
> Respondent (G-80): We went in the party . . . we walked up in the party.
> Interviewer (JM): Who started it?
> Respondent (G-80): Ain't nobody really start it. As soon as I walked in the party niggas was looking at me hard.
> Interviewer (JM): True.
> Respondent (G-80): So I tried to ignore that . . . So I started with this chick in there, kid. Niggas was looking at me wrong from when I first stepped in the party. Niggas was playing themselves. Talking about 'look at the new faces up in here,' 'Cause I ain't from around there.
> Interviewer (JM): So what, true true. Who made first moves out there?
> Respondent (G-80): When we was in the party, I made the first move. I told money 'let's go outside.' He came up to me, so I told him 'let's go outside.' It was in a small-ass little apartment. A little room. With the lights off. All his peoples were there. But I wasn't sweating it 'cause I had my gun on me.
> Interviewer (JM): True. You know if money was strapped?
> Respondent (G-80): Nah, he wasn't strapped. 'Cause when he went outside, he went back . . . he ran back inside when I pulled out. He ran back inside.
> Interviewer (JM): You don't know if he had a joint in there?
> Respondent (G-80): Yeah. He musta have a joint inside there. Yeah. I'm saying. It was his party.

Accusations: Attacks of Honor

Many violent events result from situations in which one or more individuals make accusations or claims to the other for some wrong that supposedly has been committed. The accused typically responds with a hostile reaction that almost always pushes the dispute toward violence. These exchanges could be classified as attempts at obtaining justice, or as what Donald Black (1983, 1993) has called "self-help." In the following example, the accusations anger the respondent and the respondent's denial of the claim fuels a physical fight between the two parties.

> Interviewer (RM): What was y'all fighting for, y'all money? Drugs?
> Respondent (G-41): The nigga came home talking some bullshit, talking about this drug king and his girlfriend or whatever. He can't find his girlfriend or whatever. (That) we killed her or whatever, some bullshit. It was over bullshit.
> Interviewer (RM): It was. . . . it was bullshit.
> Respondent (G-41): Yeah. It ain't nothing to die for.
> Interviewer (RM): I mean, when you think about it now.

Respondent (G-41): Yeah. I think about it now and psss . . . It's like you saying, 'it was bullshit,' that ain't nothing to die for, man. Not for bullshit, man. Word up! I'd die for my moms, my kids, that's it. I ain't dying for no words, man.

The description above recounts only the middle event in a series of related exchanges that resulted in several deaths, illustrating the serious consequences of accusations.

Hostility is a common response to accusations of stealing or dishonesty. False accusations in front of others are often taken extremely personally and are usually denied by actors in the situations described. Being accused is typically perceived as a personal threat or attack on one's name or personal honor. Among our sample, accusations often instigated confrontations that eventually became violent.

Interviewer (DB): Tell me what happened, describe the situation so I could picture it, how it happened, what it was over.
Respondent (ENYN64): I remember I got in a fight at school. 'Cause me and my man, we was cutting and shit. And somebody coat got stolen out they locker. The kid approached me and he was like 'I heard you got my coat.' I told him I didn't have it. So he started getting loud and shit. So I snuffed that nigga. So he went and told his peoples and then they came back and they tried to jump us. My man was there so we just was fighting. We got beat up and all, but we got him back.
Interviewer (DB): Was there a specific point you realized you was going to have to get violent?
Respondent (ENYN64): Yeah.
Interviewer (DB): How did you know?
Respondent (ENYN64): 'Cause I was like 'I ain't got your coat' and he stood up in my face trying to yell and shit. So I was 'yo man back the fuck up,' you know, and the nigga was still talking shit, so I was like, all right, we going to have to brawl. We going to have to do this shit.

Respondents explained that the way in which an individual makes a claim or accusation influences the response. Depending on the situation, there is a "right" way and a "wrong" way to express a grievance. Fighting or other violence is an important part of defining these contests.

Material Attacks

Identity attacks often include the taking of another's possession as a statement of dominance or control. Respondents described a variety of situations in which they had taken the possessions of others, or vice versa, and many described the battles that were waged to keep possessions. These material attacks reflect attempts to identify, maintain, and degrade social identity. Three examples are provided below. In the first example, the respondent defended himself and his cousins against a personal and material attack that occurred as they sat on the stoop of a tattoo parlor in another neighborhood.

> Interviewer (RM): So tell me about the time you had to pistol-whip somebody?
> Respondent (G-42): Oh. We went downstairs. We was chilling in front of the place. It was kind of hot upstairs, we was getting bored. So we wanted to go outside. So we just stepped outside and sat right outside on the stoop. And, I don't know, for one reason or another there was, like, four black kids walking on the block. We over talking amongst ourselves, we not paying attention to them, you know what I'm saying. They a little older than us too, so we like, yo, they ain't acknowledging us, we ain't acknowledging them. We carrying on our conversation. And so me and my cousin in front of one stoop and about, like, two feet over there's another stoop and my man was sitting there, and he had on a little New York Knickerbocker hat, a little phat hat that just came out. The first two set of kids walk by and they was just kind of looking, but I kind of ignored them 'cause I was talking to my cousin. But my man, he's a little guy too so he wasn't looking for no trouble or nothing like that, but he ain't going to let nobody disrespect him neither. So the first two walked by. They ain't even look at nobody. The second two that's walking behind them, they just looking and, you know, carrying they little conversation too. They walked by me and my cousin and as they passing my friend they just, one of them snatched his hat off his head, and put it on his head. He was like 'what, money, what you want to do for this?' So my man kind of stepped up and he was like 'yo, what's up, man, I ain't trying to have that,' and kind of snatched it back, he got a chance to grab it back and my cousin had stepped up too. It was four of them and it was like three of us, so we was like 'damn, whatever, whatever. They going to have to leave us here on the floor, leave all of us here. So they was like 'what?' and then the other two that was in the front turned around they was like, 'oh, what's up, man, y'all niggas want to do these niggas or what?' They tried to treat us like we was herbs. So that's kind of like, I kind of felt funny.

The respondent who reported "they tried to treat us like we was herbs" felt disrespected and became angry. As the respondent explained, he took a gun from his aunt's purse and pulled it out to protect his friend from the opponents' threats. The gun gave him the ability to counter-challenge his opponents' personal and material attack.

> Respondent (G-42): For one reason or another, my aunt just happen to be coming down the steps and at that point, soon as she open the door I just grabbed straight for the purse and I pulled the joint out and I was like 'yo, what, man, what y'all niggas want to do now?'
> Interviewer (RM): Umm.

Respondent (G-42): And the first two, they was like 'yo,' and they started taking off, and the other two, they was like yo they didn't know whether to run or if I was going to bust or not. So I got kind of close to him where I could swing on him and I swung on him with the joint boom. And I hit him in his head and that was it. He had to step after that. Then after that I turned around and it was kind of like a cop car coming down the block, and I'm glad my aunt grab the joint again and she put it back in her purse and she went upstairs.

Competition over Girls, Social Identity, and Violent Events

Social interaction among adolescent males reflects a growing interest and preoccupation with sexuality and heterosexual companionship (Brown 1994; Eder, with Evans, and Parker 1995; Gulligan 1982). Violence is one of many strategies used by young males to create and sustain relationships with females in a context where competition is perceived as intense. "Girls" were cited as the subject of violent disputes in 94 of the 306 incidents described by our respondents. These situations typically resulted from sexual competition (both maintenance and acquisition), the protection of a girl's honor or reputation, the defense of a female after physical victimization, the spread rumors and the escalation of disputes through gossip, and the amplification of impression management in the presence of a relevant female. Like toughness, relations with females may provide males with opportunities for developing valued social identities.

Competition over females involves a number of interesting social processes reflecting both a normative system and violations of those rules. The competition for females often reflects multiple definitions of a situation, including: those of a young man who perceives himself as having a particular girl, those of another young man who wants a particular girl, those of female (who may or may not consider herself to be in a relationship with a particular male), and those observers who may make public judgments and pronouncements. Conflicting definitions of a female's relationship status often result in violent encounters among competitors.

The social world and attendant status-conferring of dating and sexual behavior among young males is highly competitive, and potentially dangerous. Respondents characterized the implicit rules of the dating game as such: don't look at, talk to, talk about, befriend, touch, have sex with, or attempt to have sex with another man's girl. Although these norms were understood by the young males in the sample, they were frequently violated when the opportunity presented itself.

Respondents generally avoided selecting potential "mates" from among those females who were in relationships with members of the respondent's own social networks. Girls who were not part of this social network were considered "fair game" for competition. It is evident that respect (in this case, applied to the rules of dating competition) is granted almost exclusively to members of one's social network. Violations of dating competition among members of the same social network frequently were characterized as a reason for serious violence among associates and the dissolution of long-lasting male friendships. Some such disputes resulted from the ambiguity associated with determining exactly *when and how* a female became one man's girl. Meanings attached to "dating" situations and female "commitment" to these males typically were defined by males, who often internalize definitions of monogamous relations with females (regardless of females' definitions of the relationship and often despite outward evidence to the contrary).

Violence stems from sexual competition in two ways: defending existing relationships and challenging others for the right to new relationships with females. Once an individual has an established relationship or has made clear his intentions to pursue such a relationship, respondents described the need to defend that status at any cost. It seems that the rules of competition for females depend on whether one is defending a relationship or seeking a new one.

Sexual Competition

Respondents described many scenarios in which rule violations regarding relationships with females resulted in violence. The escalation of these situations seems to follow certain patterns, including the identification of an advance on one's girl by another man, the lack of a respectful account to the "boyfriend," and physical rebuttal without a verbal account by the opponent. The example below illustrates the "don't talk to my girl" rule.

> Interviewer (JM): Tell me one that you remember the most?
> Respondent (G-83): One time I was chillin', we was chillin', me and my companions on the fucking corner, . . . chillin,' talking to fucking girls. Next thing you know, nigga fucking roll up in a fucking Lexus, and niggas said 'yo, you niggas talking to the fucking wrong bitches. These bitches are trouble, kid.' So we ain't pay no attention, we just keep on talking to bitches, them bitches looked good. We wanted to hit the bitches up.
> Interviewer (JM): True.
> Respondent (G-83): So we keep on talking to them . . . and their fucking men came . . . and them niggas just started fucking talking shit, kid. So we just pulled out, and they pulled out. Niggas started running and shit, so we just did some crazy shit. Shot and shit...and the cops came and we all broke out, man.

The next example illustrates the "don't touch" rule and what happens when one party does not properly account for his actions. The respondent interpreted the touching of his girl as disrespect and asked the opponent for acknowledgment of his transgression. Instead he was challenged to step outside to fight for the girl. The event unfolded into a shooting, as described by the respondent:

Respondent (G-76): Yeah, man, we was at a party, man. This cat started throwing his arm around . . . this girl I was with and everything. He was trying to rub up against her. . . .
Interviewer (DT): What, he was trying to dance with her?
Respondent (G-76): Yeah, man, but she didn't wanna dance with him, and he was rubbing up. He was drunk and shit. Boom, I tell him, you know how you be trying to avoid shit? I tell him 'you know I'm with her, don't disrespect me like than, man,' and he was like 'what son, what what? Let's take this outside, son, what you want!' I'm like 'say no more, say no more.' Everybody go outside, and once I walk out. Bong, he snuffed me. He caught me. I wasn't really dazed. I was upset though. Boom, my man passes me the .380 and shit, the chrome. Bong, I hit him with the butt of it. I pistol-whipped him, right in his head. Then he snuffs me. So then, um, his man is going to get him something. I don't know what it was look like it was a revolver. His man hit him off, right when he hitting him off, bong. I blazed him, I hit him two times. I caught him right there, on his back, his stomach and his back, his stomach first. Then he turned around and I caught him in the back. Then I bounced. I got caught half an hour later.

The next example illustrates what happens when a guy befriends another man's girlfriend with the intention of winning her away from the other man. Friendship is used to cloak ulterior motives. The respondent who explained this event was pulled into the beef to assist his brother, who had become friendly with another man's girl. He explained:

Interviewer (RM): What? Tell me about that what happen?
Respondent (G-44): All right um. One time my brother, he was messing with this girl in the projects. . . . She had a man and um, every time her man used to go there, it's like my brother used to give him this dirty look. . . . And one time the dude just got sick and tired of it and um, pssst, screamed on my brother. My brother shut up and he didn't say nothing.
Interviewer (RM): All right. Where they was when he screamed on him?
Respondent (G-44): They was in the projects. At the girl house.
Interviewer (RM): And he was there? Your brother was with the girl?
Respondent (G-44): Yeah.
Interviewer (RM): And her man came?
Respondent (G-44): Her man came, yeah. 'Cause they act . . . let me tell you. Her girl, I mean Duke girl, always told him that 'nah, we just friends, we been friends for a while,' after that it was dead. My brother used to give him this dirty looks. He not supposed to, he supposed to be some DL nigga, but my brother wanted more from her, you know, cause she used to tell him that she

wanted more from him, too. So my brother was trying to get her to leave him and come to him. So the dude, um, I guess he was (not) trying to hear it. . . . Like a week later or two, a week later or two he flipped on him. He flipped on him and, um, then.

Interviewer (RM): You all beat him up?

Respondent (G-44): Yeah.

Interviewer (RM): Why?

Respondent (G-44): I guess 'cause of what he said. My brother never went out, kid.

Interviewer (RM): 'Cause of what he said, 'cause he just screamed on him? So y'all jumped him?

Respondent (G-44): Yeah. We jumped him. And then. . . .

Interviewer (RM): I mean, what made you do that? What was going through your mind, you know when you did something like that?

Respondent (G-44): What was going through my mind?

Interviewer (RM): Yeah.

Respondent (G-44): I mean, I was upset..

Interviewer (RM): You was upset?

Respondent (G-44): I was upset. I was just upset at the fact that, um, that he played, that Duke played my brother and shit. I wasn't thinking about that he had probable cause or nothing.

Interviewer (RM): Yeah. You was just rolling with your brother?

Respondent (G-44): Yeah. I was just down with my brother. I was just down for my brother.

Interviewer (RM): All right.

Parties, clubs, and other social settings where members of different social cliques intermingle often are hotbeds of violence. Competition over the attention of females frequently was cited as a source of this conflict. Respondents' described how public gatherings are integral to gaining and maintaining male-female relationships. Males who already have girlfriends perceive these situations as opportunities to show off their girls and have a good time; those without girlfriends perceive parties or clubs as locations for picking up or hitting on women. As respondents explained, females at clubs and parties are fair game:

Interviewer (JM): . . . What was they saying when the beef went down?

Respondent (SBN33): My man . . . one man was talking to . . . dancing with this girl, and he was like, 'nigga it's a party, niggas is dancing with everybody, I didn't know that was your girl. Don't bring your girl to a party if you don't want a nigga dancing with her.'

Interviewer (JM): So what you was telling that kid?

Respondent (SBN33): Nah, I'm saying I just explained . . . the girl was in the party, . . . so we was just dancing. He wanna act (hard), come out his face, talking 'bout that's his girl. I'm saying straight up and down I don't care if that's your girl. She's was in the party, . . . she looking good, . . . that's about it.

According to respondents, many neighborhood or territorial disputes also were connected closely with females. Many respondents described frequenting other projects or parts of the neighborhood, where they were generally not welcome by the young men who live there, in the pursuit of females. Of course, this was considered an outward display of disrespect toward the young men who live there. Many conflicts erupted between different groups whose "interests" were at stake:

> Interviewer (RM): So what you was saying about, you know, using the projects?
> Respondent (G-18): Yeah. We was walking through there and shit. Actually, one of my peoples went up to see a girl, that's mostly what beefs come from too. Girls and shit. Niggas do the weirdest things for girls. But we went up there. He told us 'wait outside' and shit. We had some weed and shit. We was smokin', mindin' our own business and shit. Then the niggas from the other side come up and ask mad questions, 'who this?' you know, like 'who the fuck are you?' And I'm like, you know, 'who the fuck are YOU!?' and shit. What the hell are you, what's the problem, man, we just chillin'. So, you know, we started with the lip and shit. And one thing led to another and we was fightin' and everybody started pullin' out and we started bustin' each other, and I think nobody got hit. One person got hit from the Brownsville side, 'cause my man hit him up against the chest. I didn't get hit. So it was a lot of gunplay and shit. And we started blastin', not really paying. . . . When people blast I don't think they really aimin' at anyone, you know, a blast is just a blast. A lot of stray bullets be going everywhere, you know. I'm glad we got out of that situation.

Projecting the Right Image in Front of your Girl

Identity attacks in front of one's girl also were sources of conflict, according to sample members. The presence of females increases the stakes of impression management and shows of disrespect by other men. As illustrated in the example below, the display of disrespect may have been an intentional effort to make the respondent look bad in front of his girl. He explains:

> Interviewer (DT): . . . tell me about you pulling out on somebody, son.
> Respondent (G-62): Pulling out on people who try to act hard, try to put my style down and who I represent.
> Interviewer (DT): But why they wanna try to diss you though, son?
> Respondent (G-62): 'Cause they see I got a fly chick, they call me a faggot or pretty boy, pretty boy loose. Nigga tried to put me down one day when I was with this chick, so I pulled out on him.

Interviewer (DT): So, you was with the chick, you pulled out on him?
Respondent (G-62): Yeah. He tried to play me in front of a shorty.
Interviewer (DT): Why he tried to play you though, son? . . .
Respondent (G-62): This nigga was jealous, man.
Interviewer (DT): Oh, jealousy?
Respondent (G-62): Jealousy. Jealous ones envy all the time, that why a lot of shit be happening, 'cause jealousy. They see you got this, they ain't got it, they want and they wanna do something about it.
Interviewer (DT): So, was it good for the girl when you pulled out?
Respondent (G-62): Nah, she was kind of scared, but I had to calm her down. After all that I ain't never seen Duke again.

Protecting Her Reputation

A young man is supposed to fight for the honor of his girl whenever possible, because her image reflects directly on his own status among peers. When one individual ridicules or insults another man's girl, it is taken as a disrespect of him and becomes a source of conflict. The next example illustrates this process.

Interviewer (RM): What happen? A shootout?
Respondent (ENYN02): Not a shootout, but I shot at somebody.
Interviewer (RM): What happen?
Respondent (ENYN02): We was chasing after this kid that I beef with. He live on the other side in the back of this building.
Interviewer (RM): Why you got beef with him?
Respondent (ENYN02): 'Cause I told some stupid shit. I told this girl to take off the wig.
Interviewer (RM): You told a girl to take her wig off?
Respondent (ENYN02): (Laughing) Yeah. Then he came in my face riffing, and I was like ah-ight, I'ma see you again. So I saw him walking, started just shooting at him. Hit a little kid in his leg.
Interviewer (RM): You hit a little kid in the leg?
Respondent (ENYN02): Yeah, the kid, like, thirteen.

The confrontation described below started over a comment about a girl and escalated into a knife event between multiple participants. The respondent's seventeen-year-old friend did not like the way a stranger on the train was talking about his female companions. After this first confrontation, the friend relayed the story to his clique and they went back to find the man, who frequently sold incense on the subway. He explained:

Respondent (ENYN04): This Muslim man was selling incense on a train, and my man was on the train with his girl and another girl. So the Muslim man was going through the car and he's like, 'oh , you a pimp.' My man was like—the nigga big, that's why I don't think my man didn't nothin' by himself. So my man is like, 'fuck you talking about, that's my fucking girl, you trying to call my girl a whore? What the fuck wrong with you, man?'

Self-Defense

An event was coded "self-defense" if the respondent reported that the main reason for using violence in the situation was to protect his own safety and health. Self-defense was cited as the main reason for respondents' involvement in sixty-seven incidents (approximately 22 percent). Young men in the sample were willing to fight back when attacked by another for his possessions. In the following example, a respondent ignored the risk of injury and fought an opponent who is armed with a knife at the time. The respondent describes his efforts to keep his bike:

> Interviewer (JM): So, um what happened? Can you tell me from the beginning?
> Respondent (SBN30): We was riding the bike and he wanted to fight me so I was like for what and he was like 'cause I wanted your bike and you didn't want to give it to me. So I was like, 'nah, I couldn't give it to you. It's not yours.' So he started fighting me.
> Interviewer (JM): So how did the knife get involved?
> Respondent (SBN30): He pulled it out and I was like, 'you really want to kill me?' He was like, 'yeah, give me your bike.' So I was like, 'well then, let's throw the hands if, you know, you got the knife.' He was like 'nah, nah,' and so he started swinging with the knife and I picked up a bottle and we started fighting, and I hit with the bottle and he cut me and dropped the knife, and we started fighting with the hands.
> Interviewer (JM): So how did this situation end?
> Respondent (SBN30): We started fighting and he didn't get to take my bike and he left. It ended—he left. He was like, 'I'll catch you next time.'
> Interviewer (JM): He told you?
> Respondent (SBN30): Yeah. I was like yeah whatever. You know?

Similarly, events in which the respondent believed he was drawn into a conflict to assist or defend others are classified as "defense of others" events. In these situations, respondents were uninvolved until stepping in to fight for a friend or fight on behalf of a friend; in thirty-four situations, respondents came to the defense of others.

Drug Business Transaction

An event was classified as a drug business transaction if it took place in a drug spot or area, occurred as direct result of the buying or selling of drugs, or occurred between workers in the drug business. Fifty-three violent events in the sample were attributed to some aspect of the drug business. A variety of drug business-related gun events were described by our sample, including disputes over turf and customers, product price, quantity and quality, shortages of drugs or money, retaliation for dishonest business practices, or protection from robberies during the course of drug selling. The situations included shootouts involving two or more parties, either or both armed, as well as drive-bys, sniper attacks from rooftops or other distant locations, and setups. In the next example, conflict stemmed from an attempt by a competing drug dealer to take over the respondent's drug spot while he was out of town. He described his feelings and his need to retaliate for the transgression:

Respondent (ENYN05): I got a little story. I got into some shit. I will run it to you real quick. When I had went away—my aunt was sick, I went down South with my cousin. God bless him, he dead right now. Me and him went down South to see my aunt. I came back—I had a spot, you know what I'm saying. My spots was making two, three G's a day. Each spot. I came home, niggas was telling me all they sold was 100 dollars. I had been gone 10 days, I'm like, 'yo, what is going on?' Niggas was telling me these niggas was in the store, tell my worker that they can't be out there hustling. So I stepped to the niggas, and the nigga was like 'yeah.' The nigga gabbed me, and that is the worstest thing he could do. And I went and got my joint and I came back. I put the shit in his mouth but it wouldn't go off, right. So I was like all right, cool. Then he went and told the cops on me. He was hustling, too. The cops was looking for me. Boom, he tell my little sister 'tell your brother I'm going to kill him.' So I was like all right, it was snowing and I told my father I'm going to sit out there. I hope it snow, 'cause I'm going to lay in that snow and when they open that store I'm going to murder them. Whatever, whatever happen. The next day came, I went down there and I took care of what I had to. I did what I had to do and you know the rest.
Interviewer (DT): Tell me about the guy that you did your thing with. Did you know him?
Respondent (ENYN05): I'm saying—yeah I knew him. I didn't know him personally but I knew him from the store. I knew the guy that owned the store. Me and him was raised together, he was my man. And I told him 'yo, that nigga can't disrespect me, son. Before you all, even you all, even moved around, I been around here hustling.
Interviewer (DT): So he had a store and he was selling drugs in the store?
Respondent (ENYN05): Yeah, they was selling in the store and we was selling on the corner.
Interviewer (DT): So he told your workers not to?
Respondent (ENYN05): Yeah, and yo, was touching me, touching me. I don't like when nobody touching me, yo.
Interviewer (DT): So what did you know about him besides?
Respondent (ENYN05): Yo, I'm saying the nigga was working in the store, but he was smoking crack and shit. Stupid motherfucker, talking shit. Always talking shit. And then what was so fucked up, the nigga wouldn't even buy

they crack. He would come to me and buy my crack but tell my workers that they buy—he telling other people that is coming in the store they can't buy from me, but he buying from me.

Interviewer (DT): When you pulled the gun on him and put the gun in his mouth, what were you thinking at the time?

Respondent (ENYN05): 'Word, son, I'm going to smoke this nigga.' I just turned on him and he was like 'oh, oh, oh, you going to shoot me' and I just clicked the gun and said 'shut up' but shit just didn't work. Shit had a double safety on it, but the shit didn't go off that time so whatever but I got him I took care of my business.

Interviewer (DT): Were you concerned about whether you would kill him or something and get locked up?

Respondent (ENYN05): Nah, I wasn't thinking about that, I wasn't thinking about that because whatever happened cops didn't find out what I did. I wasn't never concerned, I wasn't afraid to kill, yo, because, you know why I wasn't afraid to kill? Because I'm saying I sat and analyzed killing. I know everybody done killed, from the smartest person in the world to the illiterate. Why? Because you done killed a roach or a bug. So everybody can kill.

Interviewer (DT): Were you concerned whether he had a gun that day, when you pulled out a gun and it didn't go off?

Respondent (ENYN05): Yeah, I was concerned, actually, because I knew he did have guns, so I knew. That is why I want to take care of what I had to, because I knew he was going to try to smoke me.

Revenge or Retaliation

Events coded as being motivated by revenge or retaliation were precipitated by the outcome of a previous interaction with the opponent or his associates. These prior incidents typically were unsuccessful, incomplete, or unsatisfactory to the respondent, resulting in the "need" for additional violence. Respondents often were drawn into these situations as "torch-takers" or "avengers" seeking justice for wrongs committed against the individual and/or his group. Unlike the self-defense code, this domain includes both parties' involvement in revenge. Fifty-three events were sparked out of issues of revenge or retaliation.

The example below shows how an individual may rally the support of a peer to increase the chances of successful retaliation. In this case, initial transgression was the theft of a pair of sneakers:

Interviewer (DB): Tell me about a gun event, the last gun event that you did. Tell me what happened. Describe the situation—how it happened and what it was over.

Respondent (ENYN81): The last gun event—that was probably when I got robbed for my sneakers. I called my cousin and shit. And then he seen the kid again—he had the sneakers on. Me and my cousin just asked him 'what's the deal?' He went to reach (for a gun), and we shot him.

Interviewer (DB): He went to get his gun?

Respondent (ENYN81): Yeah, and we shot him.

Interviewer (DB): You don't know nothing about the guy you was fighting, right?

Respondent (ENYN81): Yeah. He lived in my cousin's projects.

Interviewer (DB): Oh, you knew the dude, and he knew you when he robbed you?

Respondent (ENYN81): Yeah. He just played hisself, that's what he did right there. Yeah. That's what the whole point was. He disrespected me.

CONCLUSIONS

This paper focused on the systemic patterns of violent events by examining the sparks or motivational factors that initiated the majority of events. The narratives presented in this paper shed new light on understanding the social processes of "bounded rationality" among adolescent males in two inner-city neighborhoods in New York City. While the data presentation was limited to two main dimensions, additional insights about other situational factors were also explored. The heterogeneity of violent events was examined focusing specifically on context, motivations, relationship to the opponent(s), the role of co-offenders in violent situations, the role of third parties, the linkages of violent events to subsequent events, and arousal states. After reading the event descriptions carefully, the question of what is *rational* in rational choice decision-making among adolescent males becomes increasingly complex. The data suggests that several situational factors have a powerful influence on adolescent decision-making, including the availability of guns, perception of likelihood others would have a gun, the participation of peers in violent encounters, the use of drugs and/or alcohol, the lack of social controls in locations frequented by young people, and the cost and benefits associated with violence for one's social identity in the neighborhood.

In an earlier paper, I presented a summary of the role of the thirteen different situational dimensions collected in this study (Wilkinson 1997). Specifically, I found that violent events were described as public performances, often with serious implications beyond the immediate interaction. Violent events where guns were involved included the active participation of "co-offenders" in nearly 67 percent of the cases compared with only 33 percent of the non-weapon events. The violent performances described by our respondents reflected concerns about gains or losses in individual and group status among other possible outcomes. Respondents were more likely to engage in gun violence with a stranger or rival rather than a friend, co-worker, or neighborhood acquaintance. Gun events were more likely to occur on street corners, in unregulated clubs or parties, or other public spaces with limited social controls. Gun-use events were less common in schools or jails. Respondents frequently got involved with gun events while under the influence of alcohol or some type of drug. The ratio of being high or drunk to not being high/drunk was 3.8 for gun events vs. 1.2 for events where no weapon was involved. Naturally, serious injuries were more likely in situations with firearms compared to no weapons. Situations where knives and other weapons were used also resulted in a high rate of injury. As discussed above, gun events were less likely to reach resolution while fights without weapons were much more likely to achieve closure.

NOTES

1. The interviews were conducted from June, 1995 and March, 1997.

2. *Friends of Island Academy* (Friends) is a non-profit organization founded in 1992. Friends provides educational, vocational, and mentoring services to young men and women who have left the educational Academy (alternative high school) at Rikers Island. Guys Insight on Imprisonment for Teenagers (G. I. I. F. T.) Pack is a program for youth run by the youth membership of Friends. The main approach is peer counseling and outreach where ex-offenders assist soon-to-be released offenders to make positive changes by learning from their mistakes. G. I. I. F. T. Pack members regularly engage in public speaking at Rikers Island Academy, New York City schools, community based organizations, and in local media outlets.

REFERENCES

Black, Donald. 1993. *Crime as social control.* New York: Cambridge University Press.

Brown, B., M.S. Mory, and D.A. Kinney. 1994. "Casting Adolescent Crowds in a Relational Rerspective: Caricature, Channel, and Context." In *Personal Relationships during Adolescence*, edited by R. Montemayor, Adams, G.R., and Gullotta, T.P. Thousand Oaks, CA: Sage Publications.

Campbell, Anne. 1986. "The Streets and Violence." In *Violent Transactions: The Limits of Personality*, edited by Anne Campbell and Jack Gibbs. New York: Blackwell.

Campbell, Anne, and Jack Gibbs, eds. 1986. *Violent Transactions: The Limits of Personality.* New York: Basil Blackwell.

Cornish, Derick. 1993. "Crimes as Scripts." Paper read at Second Annual Seminar on Environmental Criminology and Crime Analysis, at University of Miami, Coral Gables, FL.

Cornish, Derick. 1994. "The Procedural Analysis of Offending." In *Crime Prevention Studies*, edited by R. V. Clarke. NY: Criminal Justice Press.

Decker, Scott H. 1995. "Reconstructing Homicide Events: the Role of Witnesses in Fatal Encounters." *Journal of Criminal Justice* 23 (5):439–450.

Eder, Donna with C. C. Evans, and S. Parker. 1995. *School Talk: Gender and Adolescent Culture*. New Brunswick, NJ: Rutgers University Press.

Fagan, Jeffrey, and Deanna L. Wilkinson. 1998b. "Guns, Youth Violence, and Social Identity in Inner Cities." In *Crime and Justice: A Review of Research*, edited by Michael Tonry and Mark Moore. Chicago: University of Chicago Press.

Felson, Richard B. 1982. "Impression Management and the Escalation of Aggression and Violence." *Social Psychology Quarterly* 45:245–254.

Felson, Richard B. 1993. "Predatory and Dispute-Related Violence: A Social Interactionist Approach." In *Routine Activity and Rational Choice, Advances in Criminological Theory*, edited by Ronald V. Clarke and Marcus Felson. New Brunswick, NJ: Transaction Press.

Felson, Richard B., Stephen A. Ribner, and Merryl S. Siegel. 1986. "Age and the Effect of Third Parties during Criminal Violence." *Sociology and Social Research* 68 (4):452–462.

Felson, Richard B., and H.J. Steadman. 1983. "Situational Factors in Disputes Leading to Criminal Vviolence." *Criminology* 21:59–74.

Griffin, Larry J. 1993. "Narrative, Event-Structure Analysis, and Causal Interpretation in Historical Sociology." *American Journal of Sociology* 98 (5):1094–1133.

Gulligan, Carol. 1982. *In a Different Voice: Psychological Theory and Women's Development*. Cambridge, MA: Harvard University Press.

Katz, Jack. 1988. *Seductions of Crime: Moral and Sensual Attractions of Doing Evil*. New York: Basic.

Luckenbill, David F. 1977. "Homicide as a Situated Transaction." *Social Problems* 25:176–186.

Luckenbill, David F. and D.P. Doyle. 1989. "Structural Position and Violence: Developing a Cultural Explanation." *Criminology* 27 (3):419–436.

Meier, Robert and Leslie Kennedy, eds. 2000. *Advances in Criminological Theory: The Criminal Event*. Vol. 9. New Brunswick, NJ: Transaction.

Oliver, William. 1994. *The Violent Social World of Black Men*. New York: Lexington Books.

Polk, Kenneth. 1994. *When Men Kill: Scenarios of Masculine Violence*: Cambridge University Press.

Riedel, Marc. 1993. *Stranger Violence: A Theoretical Inquiry*. New York: Garland.

Steinberg, Laurence and Elizabeth Caufmann. 1996. "Maturity of Judgment in Adolescence: Psychosocial Factors in Adolescent Decision Making." *Law and Human Behaviors* 20 (249–272).

Sullivan, Mercer L. 1997. "Social and Symbolic Interactionist Approaches to the Study of Adolescent Violence." Paper read at American Society of Criminology, at San Diego, CA.

Tedeschi, James T., and Richard Felson. 1994. *Violence, Aggression, and Coercive Actions*. Washington, D.C.: American Psychological Association.

Wilkinson, Deanna L. 1997. "Decision Making in Violent Events among Adolescent Males: A Comparison of Ggun and Non-Gun Events." Paper read at The American Society of Criminology meeting, at San Diego, CA.

Wilkinson, Deanna L. 1998. "The Social and Symbolic Construction of Violent Events Among Inner City Adolescent Males." Unpublished doctoral dissertation Rutgers University. Ann Arbor, MI: UMI Dissertation Services.

Wright, Richard, and Scott Decker. 1997. *Armed Robbers in Action: Stick Ups and Street Culture*. Boston: Northeastern University Press.

Chapter 9

"I'm Down for My Organization": The Rationality of Responses to Delinquency, Youth Crime, and Gangs

Scott H. Decker and G. David Curry

INTRODUCTION

The rationality of the behavior of individual offenders has repeatedly been the object of research on crime (Cornish and Clarke 1987; Clarke and Felson 1993; as well as the rest of this volume). Far less attention has been devoted to the study of the rationality of agencies and communities in responding to the law breaking of offenders. The rationality of institutions, particularly those that are part of the justice "system," is often taken as a given, despite evidence that the institutional response to crime and delinquency is highly variant over time (Bernard 1992; Howell 1997), location (Feld 1991; Kempf, Decker, and Bing 1990; Burrus and Kempf 2000), and coordination (Spergel 1997). Here, we assess the degree to which comprehensive community responses to crime and delinquency involving a diversity of partner agencies can be characterized as rational. Specifically, we examine the community response to gangs and youth violence in St. Louis.

PROBLEM AND RESPONSE
Gangs and Youth Violence

From 1985 until the mid-1990s, the U.S. experienced substantial increases in the levels of youth and gang violence. Gangs represent a substantial challenge to criminal justice and social service agencies. Justice Department estimates (National Youth Gang Center, forthcoming) suggest that there are more than 26 thousand gangs and over 800 thousand gang members in the United States. In the 1990s, gangs have greater access to automobiles and high-powered firearms than did their predecessors. And the conditions of urban areas, particularly the growth of the urban underclass (Jackson 1991; Hagedorn 1988; Klein 1995), portend greater difficulties in ending the conditions that spawn gangs. There is also evidence that gangs are spreading beyond the boundaries of cities and gaining a foothold in suburban and rural communities (Klein 1995). These circumstances make responding to gangs a difficult task for criminal justice and social service agencies.

A crucial factor that shapes our ability to respond to gangs is the way the problem is defined. Unfortunately, perceptions of gangs on the part of the public and agencies charged with responding to gangs are shaped more by images from popular culture including the evening news or movies, than by objective facts. Decker and Leonard (1991) found that members of an Anti-Gang Task Force based their knowledge of gangs on the source they considered least reliable, the media. Gangs and gang members have been "over-rationalized" by a number of commentators who see them as more organized, more purposive and more rational than the research record would document (Skolnick 1990; Sanchez-Jankowski 1991; Taylor 1990). The popular perception sees gangs as well-organized groups of men (and sometimes women) who are committed to a common set of goals. From this perspective, gangs are rational enterprises that behave in a manner consistent with long term goals. However, there is not much support for these views (Klein 1995; Curry and Decker 1998).

Gangs in St. Louis

This paper examines the rationality of responses to gangs in St. Louis. In 1991 St. Louis first participated in a Justice Department gang survey. St. Louis reported thirty-three gangs and eight gang homicides. For 1993 and 1994, the University of Missouri-St. Louis Violence Project tabulated thirty-three and fifty-four gang-related homicides for St. Louis, or respectively, 13.7 percent and 25.5 percent of all homicides. The 1994 proportion is comparable to the Chicago statistic of 26.2 percent. The disproportionate cost of the gang crime problem for St. Louis' African-American community is reflected in the over-representation of blacks among the victims of gang-related homicides. In 1993, all but one (97.0 percent) of the victims were African-Americans. In 1994, fifty-two (96.3 percent) of the fifty-four victims were African Americans.

In St. Louis, the gangs that have emerged in the last decade share names and symbols with gangs in California and Chicago, yet the existence of structural connections between gangs in St. Louis and the gangs in these cities is highly improbable. The gangs in St. Louis are very loosely organized. Decker and Van Winkle (1996) found gang cohesion and organization to be governed by recurring cycles of collective violence and individual reactions to the threat of violence. Decker and Curry (2000) observed that youth marginally involved in gangs perceive the St. Louis gangs to be more organized than do youth who are members of the same gangs.

Developing Research-Based National Policy Responses to Gangs and Delinquency

In 1987, the Office of Juvenile Justice and Delinquency Prevention (OJJDP) funded the National Youth Gang Suppression and Intervention Program at the University of Chicago. The following year, the research team led by Irving Spergel surveyed 254 agency representatives from 45 cities and six institutional sites as part of this study. Respondents answered open-ended questions on program activities, priority of strategies employed, and estimates of effectiveness of agency efforts. The goal of the program survey was to identify promising programs that existed in 1988. Those promising projects studied by Spergel and his colleagues from 1988 to 1991 were used to develop prototypes and models for new programs (Spergel et al. 1994).

From their analysis of respondent answers, Spergel and Curry (1993) identified five categories of response strategies: (1) suppression, (2) social intervention, (3) opportunities provision, (4) community mobilization, and (5) organizational change. Some coordinated combination of all five strategies were essential to successful gang response programs. Agencies for which prototype manuals were developed included (1) the police, (2) prosecution, (3) judiciary, (4) corrections, (5) probation/parole, (6) schools, (7) community-based youth agencies, and (8) employment programs (Spergel, et al. 1996). While the participation of all these agencies could contribute to the success of a comprehensive community program, the participation of the police was essential so that support programs could be coordinated with suppression efforts. Some provision of employment opportunities were needed to provide alternatives to gang involvement for gang members and youths at risk, and the involvement of grass roots organizations was necessary to ensure connections between program and community residents. OJJDP's Comprehensive Community-Wide Approach to Gangs that is described in the manuals and prototypes produced by the National Youth Gang Suppression and Intervention Program is generally referred to as the "Spergel" model.

At the same time that OJJDP was supporting the development of the Spergel model, separate initiatives were underway to identify the causes and correlates of delinquency and develop systematic program responses to reduce serious, chronic, and violent offending by juveniles. A social development model that incorporated the key influences of family, school, and community and emphasized protective and risk factors emerged (Hawkins 1996). If serious, chronic, and violent offending were to be reduced, OJJDP

(Howell et al. 1995) concluded that the juvenile justice system would have to become part of comprehensive continuum of services and sanctions. Protective factors would have to be enhanced (not just in the family, but in the womb), and risk factors would have to be diminished or at least mediated. Like the Spergel model, the Comprehensive Strategy for Serious, Chronic, and Violent Juvenile Offenders (or "Comp" Strategy as it is generally known) became part of official OJJDP policy.

Rationality and Comprehensive Community Strategies

Together the Spergel model and the Comp Strategy came to be the basis for major contemporary federal and local responses to gangs and delinquency. Both models require responses that are comprehensive in two ways. First, both models include elements that respond to gang members and young offenders as part of a single youth population that ranges from at-risk youth who may only marginally be involved in gangs and delinquency to serious, violent, and chronic offenders who may be deeply involved in gangs and crime. Second, both models establish inter-agency partnerships that require coordination and cooperation.

There are a number of assumptions about organization that underlie both the Spergel model and the Comp Strategy. One assumption is that institutions that make up the juvenile and criminal justice systems have some commonality of rational structure across jurisdictions. Another assumption is that given a general set of goals shared across organizations, partner agencies can fulfill their separate operational objectives while contributing to the success of the overarching plan. Likewise it is assumed that the organizational structures of each agency constitute systems of rational behavior that can be linked into a system of rational behavior operating at a higher level of complexity.

The characterization of organizations as rational has a long history in the social sciences. Max Weber (1946) is noted for his analyses of the structure of social organizations existing across historical and geographic settings. Among the types of social orders, Weber (p. 245) described bureaucracy as traditional or patriarchic organizations "made rational." All bureaucracies share particular features. Among these are stability and the conduct of business by particular rules and regulations. As Weber (p. 197) noted, "modern organizations" consist of a set of hierarchical authority positions for each of which is prescribed a set of specific duties, responsibilities, and restrictions. Bureaucratic forms characterize private, public, and communal organizations. The existence of organizational rationality is fundamental to the success of comprehensive programs that would attempt to effect system change.

As the 1990s brought record increases in levels of juvenile violence, national policy makers became more convinced that the problems of serious, violent, and chronic offending and gang-related crime were becoming increasingly intertwined. National policy makers decided that a major effort needed to be undertaken to test both the utility of the Spergel Model and the Comprehensive Strategy in specifically targeted geographic settings. OJJDP became the lead agency in implementation efforts. OJJDP incorporated the Spergel model and the Comp Strategy into its Community Mobilization, Caring Communities, and SafeFutures Programs. The systematic nature and elements of these strategies have also served as the basis for the Bureau of Justice Assistance's Comprehensive Communities programs and Response to Gangs in American Indian and Alaska Native Communities and the Office of Community Oriented Policing Services Anti-Gang Initiative. With funding from OJJDP, SafeFutures Programs have been established in four urban sites (Boston, Seattle, Contra Costa County [California], and St. Louis), one rural site (Imperial Valley, California), and one Indian Reservation (Fort Belknap, Montana). Funding for SafeFutures projects is larger and extended over a longer period of time than funding for previous comparable efforts. In 1995, the St. Louis program was funded for five years at $1.4 million per year.

SafeFutures Model as a Rational Response

One key to understanding the response to youth crime and delinquency is to assess the extent to which those responses target problematic behaviors in ways that have a chance of succeeding. To the extent that responses are capable of doing so, they may be termed rational. In our review of responses to gangs (Decker and Curry 1999), we documented that "fit" between the problem of gangs and the dose, or response to that problem. In general, our review found that responses generally failed to include one (or more) essential ingredients for the successful response to gangs. In most cases a social service response did not have a suppression or law enforcement component. In other cases a suppression-only intervention was mounted. Some gang responses are short-term and as a consequence have little chance of delivering reductions in gang membership or gang crime. Other responses fail to integrate the services of multiple agencies, thus failing to meet the needs of children for multiple services.

By these criteria, SafeFutures appears to be a rational response to the problems of gang involved and delinquent youth. As a multiple year intervention, SafeFutures has the potential to maintain services over a sustained period of time and not leave children in the lurch when funding dries up. Equally important, the program integrates suppression, social opportunities provision, and social interventions. This comprehensive range of services is buttressed by a fifteen agency umbrella of services that have an MIS system designed for case management and client data base sharing. In addition, SafeFutures is funded at a substantial level and is geographically targeted at about forty percent of the city population, ensuring that the intervention dose is not spread too thinly over too large a population group.

The St. Louis SafeFutures Program

Prior to the renewed national attention to gangs, a core of St. Louis partner agencies had viewed with distress what they perceived as an increasingly serious delinquency problem. Representatives from the St. Louis Metropolitan Police Department, the Family Court, the public schools, and a range of community-based youth service agencies and grass roots organizations had convened public meetings around child safety and the emerging gang problem. An Anti-Gang Task Force had been established in which the police played a central role (Decker and Leonard 1991). That a coalition of these concerned agencies would apply for federal assistance was almost inevitable.

In 1995, St. Louis was selected by OJJDP as a SafeFutures site. By mandate, the grant recipient was the St. Louis city government. Extra points were awarded to applicants for whom the target area was a federally designated enterprise zone, so the grant application defined the service area as the portion of the city that constituted such a zone. There were a number of ways in which the development of the St. Louis SafeFutures program substantiated the hopes for a rational inter-agency model to improve community response to gangs and serious juvenile offending. However, there were also a number of unanticipated instances in which the rational operation of individual agencies failed in bringing about collective success.

The Application of a Systematic Response Model (SafeFutures) in St. Louis

As the SafeFutures model developed in St. Louis, the conceptual goals of the Spergel model and Comp Strategy were integrated. These goals included: identification and dissemination of program goals, an assessment of the gang problem in the community, development of a set of common definitions, identifying and serving gang members, a systematic procedure for record-keeping, and integrating preliminary evaluation results into program development.

Agreement on Shared Goals

From its initial proposal to OJJDP through the development of its Strategic Plan, St. Louis SafeFutures has made implementation of OJJDP's

Comprehensive Community Approach to Gangs (the Spergel model) and the Comprehensive Strategy for Serious, Violent, and Chronic Youth Offenders (Comp Strategy) central to its goals and objectives. One of the first in-service training sessions for SafeFutures partner agency directors and staff focused on the requirements of the Spergel model. The training was provided by a member of the local evaluation team who was very familiar with the model including its implementation in Chicago's Little Village and the five pilot projects. Initially SafeFutures' agency partners were comfortable with the Spergel model. For them, it represented a flexible model that provides communities the opportunity to respond to gangs within each community's specific gang problem context and with each community's existing and potential resources. The Comp Strategy likewise reflected a common belief among partner agency representatives. To them, it seemed that most agencies were accomplishing their objectives with individual youths, but there was a lack of coordination between agencies that resulted in gaps in service for youth who needed a continuum of services most.

At the beginning of Year II of the SafeFutures program, the Illinois Criminal Justice Information Authority provided a workshop on applying the Spergel Model in the local context. The workshop stressed that the five Spergel model strategies are community mobilization, social intervention, opportunities provision, suppression, and organizational development and change. The intent of this workshop was to create an understanding among St. Louis SafeFutures agency partners that the Spergel model requires the identification and coordination of strategies as well as community agency partners. Following this training, the SafeFutures administrators began to enjoin each partner agency to view its part in SafeFutures in terms of its specific strategic responsibilities. Also important to SafeFutures staff becoming aware of the Spergel model was a field visit of selected staff (particularly street outreach workers) to Spergel's Little Village project in Chicago (Spergel and Grossman 1997). For SafeFutures administrators and agency partner directors by the end of Year II, the Spergel model provided a terminology and conceptual framework that could be used to describe program activities.

In the second year of SafeFutures, Shay Bilchek, the Director of OJJDP, visited St. Louis and stressed the importance of the Comp Strategy in reducing youth violence and delinquency. The Director met with the Mayor of St. Louis, the Chief of Police, and a range of other key leaders in the city. During the third year, the same kind of emphasis that had been given to the Spergel model in the second year was placed on generating an understanding of the Comp Strategy among SafeFutures partners. Among program administrators, the stated quest for a continuum of services and sanctions for youthful offenders became as important as the Spergel model strategies.

Effective Assessment of the Problem

Assessment of the nature of the local gang problem within its unique community context is the first step in developing a response to gangs that is in conformity with the Spergel model. During Year I, Decker and Van Winkle's (1996) ethnographic study of gangs in St. Louis was published. The book was read (or at least bought) by many agency directors. For many SafeFutures directors and staff, *Life in the Gang* served as a qualitative and comparative source of information on the nature of the St. Louis gang problem. In collaboration with the UM-St. Louis Homicide Project, a GIS (Geographical Information System) analysis of gang homicides from 1992 through 1994 was conducted by the local evaluation team. The result of integrating these two perspectives was an assessment of the St. Louis gang problem that incorporated both official law enforcement information and perspectives of active gang members and their families.

Common Definitions

A major requirement of the Spergel model is the development of a set of definitions that is shared across the agencies involved. For St. Louis, the conclusions of the study conducted by Decker and Leonard (1991) (described above) confirmed the level of disorganization in defining the problem that prevailed in that early stage of the St. Louis community's effort to respond to the city's gang problem. From its outset, the St. Louis SafeFutures Program struggled with the issue of systematically defining what it means by gang problems. In Missouri, there is a definition of a gang and a gang member that are mandated by state law. More important definitions had to be arrived at through collective multiple-agency decision-making, mediation, and compromise.

A COPS funded initiative facilitated the development of a systematic definition of a gang-related offense. The greatest division has been between member-based definitions and motivation-based definitions (Maxson and Klein 1990). In a member-based definition, law enforcement agencies identify gang members, and when a "known" gang member commits any crime, that crime is identified as gang-related. In a motivation-based definition, specific crimes are identified as "gang-motivated," that is, serving the interests of the gang in some way such as expanding territory or reputation or protecting a criminal enterprise. In St. Louis, the gang unit has developed a prototype multi-level classification that counts both crimes involving gang members as offenders and victims and the subcategory of "gang-motivated" crimes.

Under the Spergel Model and the Comprehensive Strategy, OJJDP requires courts and social service providers to expend extra resources in bringing drug treatment, job preparation, support in school, and family services to gang-involved youths and serious, violent, and chronic juvenile offenders. Identifying offenders in gang-related crimes and serious, violent, and chronic offenders is a matter of law. More troublesome, particularly for social service providers and school officials was the issue of systematically identifying gang-involved youths. For program purposes, it was resolved through much negotiation to base the delivery of social services on a three-tiered classification of youths. Gang offenders were youths identified by the juvenile justice system as offenders in gang-related crime or delinquency. Gang-involved youths were identified using a set of research-based measures of gang-involvement (Curry and Spergel 1992) that include wearing gang colors or symbols, flashing hand signs, and having gang member friends or siblings. Since these gang-involved youths (who with the offenders are targeted for the majority of SafeFutures resources) are not themselves identified as offenders in their involvement in SafeFutures, the gang-involvement classification is used only for the provision of social services and is not shared with the law enforcement partners in the overall program. The third group is non-gang involved offenders.

Identifying and Serving Gang-Involved Youth

Another primary tenet of the Spergel model is identifying and serving gang members and gang-involved youths who are marginal to gangs. Agency partners such as the Family Court and youth corrections (Division of Youth Services in Missouri) already had processes in place for recording gang involvement of their clients. Gang membership was already considered an important risk factor for youths under juvenile justice jurisdiction. Many staff from other SafeFutures partner agencies outside the juvenile justice system were initially intensely resistant to identifying their clients as gang members.

During Year II, however, the increased sensitivity to gang issues through exposure to the Spergel model made program staff much more aware of the gang activity in which their clients were involved. Through this process of problem recognition came the development of skills needed to serve gang-involved youths. Another factor that contributed to outreach skills for serving gang and delinquent youth was a series of training programs provided by Dr. Booker Yelder, a veteran administrator of street outreach in Washington, D.C., and Dietrich Smith, a veteran observer of gang life in St. Louis.

By the middle of Year IV, SafeFutures staff had identified 527 clients receiving wrap-around services as gang-involved. That represents 53.7 percent of all clients provided wrap-around services over the four years of the program to date. The Spergel Model makes a distinction between two types of gang members who are to be served. The two groups are younger marginally gang-involved children and older more heavily involved gang members. Clients served by St. Louis SafeFutures represented both of the kinds of gang members. Analyses (excluding clients who entered SafeFutures through a justice system agency) reveal that clients identified as gang-involved by SafeFutures staff are significantly more likely than clients not designated as gang-involved to have official records of delinquency and of serious, violent, and chronic offending. Identifying gang-involved youth was one mandate in which St. Louis SafeFutures excelled.

The Computerized Management Information System (MIS)

During the first two years of operation, SafeFutures administrators and staff assisted the local evaluation team in developing a system of paper forms for keeping track of clients and their contacts with the program. Initially, it was understood that a city agency would computerize this record-keeping system, but that arrangement did not work. Finally, a special contract for technical assistance was made with the evaluation team to computerize the record-keeping system and keep it running at a local university. Subsequently, all records since the first services provided in 1996 have been input into the computerized MIS. St. Louis SafeFutures may be one of the best-documented comprehensive community response programs ever.

The Role of Evaluation in SafeFutures Planning and Operation

Each SafeFutures program was required to incorporate a local evaluation and cooperate with a national evaluation. Especially in the first two years, the local evaluation team provided more technical assistance than evaluation. The gang member identification procedures and the computerized MIS were both products that depended on local evaluators as technical assistance providers.

Thanks to the evaluation team's preliminary analysis of the data that eventually became part of the MIS, major changes in the program were made. At the end of Year III, agencies that had not been effective in serving gang involved youths in earlier years or had not provided required services were replaced with new agency partners willing to service the appropriate population of youth and their special needs. During Year III, the St. Louis SafeFutures Program was enhanced and expanded by the creation of a broader coalition of agencies bearing the name of St. Louis Cease Fire. The St. Louis Cease Fire Program was directly modeled on the Boston program (Kennedy, Piehl, and Braga 1996) and supported by the U.S. Attorney's office working in cooperation with the Office of the Mayor. During Year IV, SafeFutures and St. Louis Cease Fire continued to mobilize the community against crime and delinquency. This alliance of community agencies continues to represent the best principles of the Spergel model and the Comp Strategy. Under this umbrella of city-wide cooperation, SafeFutures programs are now being linked with newly implemented programs such as the St. Louis Mental Health Board and Family Court's Juvenile Justice Mental Health Initiative (sponsored by funding from the state of Missouri Department of Mental Health), the St. Louis Juvenile Accountability Incentive Block Grant (JAIBG) program, and the St. Louis Safe Schools/Healthy Schools Program.

Failures in Rationality in the St. Louis SafeFutures Program

Despite a number of ways in which St. Louis SafeFutures constituted a rational manifestation of a rational organizational model, there were also a number of ways in which rational agencies following a rational model fell short. These include implementation problems, the match between clients and services, agencies' not fully playing their role in a continuum of services and sanctions, program drift, organizational disorganization, and budgetary management.

Implementation Problems

From the start, several of the participating agencies had difficulty integrating their goals with SafeFutures goals. This probably should not have been unexpected in an umbrella of fifteen agencies, but it did pose several problems during the implementation phase of the project. It took nearly a full year for full program implementation to occur, not surprising in a project of this magnitude with such broad reaching goals. Some agencies were not capable of reaching or serving the at-risk population. For example, one agency had as its main goal the provision of parental training to gang members and delinquent youths who were teen parents. Despite this prescribed role in the overall range of services, its internal practices prohibited it from reaching gang members or teen parents. Instead, the primary service group was nongang members who were not prospective or actual teen parents.

Another of the agencies (a local Boys and Girls Club) did not believe that youth needed multiple services other than those already provided by the club. Another problem was the club's unwillingness to share their service records and client identities. The club was willing to share their records with the evaluation team, but not the other partner agencies. As a consequence, referrals to this agency and from this agency to other agencies were not possible.

Perhaps the most substantial implementation problem was encountered during the first year. Workers at the participating juvenile court often cited court rules as a reason for non-participation in the activities they were funded to complete. As a consequence referrals from the court to other services were slow in coming. This led to roadblocks in placing court supervised youth with other participating agencies.

Match between Clients and Services

One of the service providers, contracted to provide the job opportunities provision fundamental to the Spergel model, had high referral numbers from the network of social service agencies and schools. This reflected the conventional wisdom that most of the at-risk juveniles and seriously involved criminals really wanted a job, and that the key to finding a job was good training and placement. These facts conspired to make the job agency a very popular placement target. However, during one meeting a member of the job training group claimed that no one could find job placements for the population of youths who were the target of SafeFutures Program intervention. In addition, one administrator offered that, "Our program wasn't designed to reach that kind of kid."

Another of the groups hired to provide mentoring services (with a national reputation for providing such services) indicated that it did not have appropriate mentors for the kind of youth targeted by the program. In particular, the agency suffered from the availability of minority mentors to match with minority youths. Instead the agency proposed providing a form of "group mentoring."

In most cases this inability to provide required services to the appropriate youth population resulted in the partner agency not being invited to apply for funding in a subsequent year of the program. Other of these agencies worked with SafeFutures administrators to reconfigure their methods of providing services.

"Court Supervision for Compliance"

A number of agencies complained at monthly management meetings about the habits of the juveniles referred to their agencies. It appears that many of the youth failed to show up for their placements, were often late for appointments, and when they arrived were disruptive. A member of one social service agency offered a unique approach, and asked why all of the youth couldn't just be placed under court supervision so that they could be compelled to appear for services, be on time and behave appropriately. We title this "sanction envy," the desire on the part of social service agencies and programs to punish kids for noncompliance.

Inability of Police to Join the Model

A key to the Spergel model, and therefore to SafeFutures, is the participation of the police. However, early on the police declined to become full participants. The police didn't want to work with community-based agencies that employed former criminals and gang members as outreach workers. Some of those employees also didn't want to work with the police because of past stress in relationships with them. During the first year of the project a "road trip" to Chicago was held for police and outreach workers to observe the Gang Outreach workers at work in the Little Village neighborhood. However, in the days before the trip the police were prohibited to travel, despite the fact that no police funds were committed to the travel costs. To this date, the start of Year V, the police have not drawn down the money provided for them in the annual budget. There is concern about the possibility of a state or federal audit, and some in the police department don't want the extra paperwork and feared a federal audit. Still, law enforcement has been represented primarily in an advisory capacity or through the bridge between police and SafeFutures provided by St. Louis Cease Fire.

Program Drift

One of the common observations of social programs is that they "drift" over time. That is, many social programs—and institutions—move from their stated or original goals to new goals as they meet the realities of program implementation and operation. One of the unfortunate instances of program drift in the life of SafeFutures was the loss of an afterschool gang outreach program. This program was located in an "outbuilding" of an urban church within the service area. For three years it had provided direct services to the most at-risk youth. Indeed, this agency was one of the first in the SafeFutures partnership to provide services to gang-involved youth. There was evidence that many of the most delinquent and younger gang members attended programs and received services at this facility. Through this afterschool program, many of its clients saw marked improvements in their behavior. Three years into the project, however, the church elders declared that they didn't want a program for that "sort" of children in their buildings and the program was unceremoniously closed. This cost the intervention effort a valuable resource, but it also sent a message to the participating youths that trusting institutions was not such a good idea. These two clients had been viewed as SafeFutures success stories and are now serving lengthy sentences in state prison for dealing drugs. In the months immediately following the closing of the afterschool program, two clients (brothers) were involved in gang-related shootings, the older dead as a victim and the younger as the shooter in the retaliation.

Perhaps the greatest drift in the program occurred early in Year III. At this time there was a change in Project Director from an administrator to a practitioner. As a consequence of this few of the requirements of a rationally organized bureaucracy or complex organization were met. The Administrator had, by all acclaim, done quite a good job holding the fabric of the organization together, preparing the annual requests for funding, and negotiating the political minefield that was the project's home territory. However, owing to many of the "irrationalities" noted here, this person decided to terminate their employment. Their replacement was elevated from the program closed by the church elders; by all accounts this individual was the best in the network at working with seriously delinquent and criminally-involved gang members. This is not a set of qualifications that directly translates into an administrative job, and the communication, processing of paperwork, and preparation of annual applications suffered considerably.

One of the conclusions of service providers in Year I was that girls needed more programming and emphasis than they were receiving. This conclusion led to the development of gender-specific training and identifying gender-specific services. The emphasis on girls led to a weekend "sleepover" conference at a local hotel. Two of the girls were accused of shoplifting in the hotel store, and a member of the research team who was present reports that much of the informal activities glorified the actions and belief systems of the girls most heavily involved in gangs.

Organizational drift does not always come from programs. The federal funding agency had decided to fund a substantial national evaluation. The first year of this evaluation the decision was made to support a process evaluation. The daunting task of running process evaluations in six sites across the country from Washington, D.C. was not considered in full. At the end of Year I an outcome evaluation was mandated, and local evaluators were charged with collecting data to support that evaluation. All participating agencies were to sign on as participants, and their funding was tied to providing data for this evaluation. Despite this, the participating school partner has yet to turn over their data and in some cases can not identify the location of such mundane data elements as attendance records or grades.

Service Model for Referral to Multiple Agencies

Central to the models upon which SafeFutures was based is the coordination of client services from multiple agencies. Early on the SafeFutures administrators, with the assistance of the evaluation team, constructed a complex graphic showing a child at the center, a "caring adult" (a SafeFutures agency staff member) wrapped around the child. Through the supervision and intervention of the caring adult, a myriad of different services delivered by SafeFutures partner agencies were channeled to the child based on the caring adult's assessments of the child's needs. The administrators and evaluators assumed that the referral of clients to and from partner agencies would be as easy to implement as it is to understand.

By February 1997, only 12.1 percent of all SafeFutures clients were being served by multiple agencies. At a meeting of SafeFutures partner agency directors, this statistic was presented by a member of the evaluation team to the agency partners. The directors promised to try harder to get the referral process working. In May 1997, the percentage of clients being served by multiple agencies reached 20.7 percent. Unfortunately that percentage was the peak. Of youths served by the SafeFutures partner agencies from January to June 1999, only 10.3 percent had been served by multiple partner agencies. When this statistic was presented to the directors, the "we'll do better" response had become "my agency is providing every service that these youths need." This unwillingness to "share" clients across agencies may the greatest failure of the St. Louis SafeFutures Program.

St. Louis Public Schools: An Agency Impoverished of Organization

Unfortunately, the public schools lacked the infrastructure to participate in SafeFutures in a rational fashion. The school system could not locate children in their data system and could not identify the correct school in which children were located. In addition, when service providers and members of the research team appeared at one school, the gang members controlled a class more than the principal and teacher, preventing access to other students. When computers were provided as part of the MIS system for case management, schools could not put computers in space where SafeFutures workers were located and document their services. When the local research team turned to the key service provider at the public schools for assistance in accessing data they received a sobering lesson. This individual had requested aggregate data on student suspensions from his central administration for a grant renewal that meant several hundred thousand dollars to the district. He was rebuffed in this request, only to find the very data he had been denied published on the front page of the daily newspaper the next day, provided by the Central Administration of the school district.

Budget Issues

From the start of the project, reimbursing the participating agencies has been a matter of great concern. Some of the agencies went more than nine months before their vouchers were acted on. In the case of small not-for-profit agencies, this effectively put them out of business. Even for the larger participants in the project, such as the juvenile court, the slow action on reimbursement vouchers caused considerable problems. Indeed, the Year II application could not request specific amounts because it was not known how much had been spent on any given activity during Year I.

ANALYSIS

Considerable effort has been expended in the study of the rationality of the behavior of individual offenders (Cornish and Clarke 1987; Clarke and Felson 1993; as well as the rest of this volume) but little of the agencies that respond to law breaking of offenders. In criminology, studies of burglary (Bennett and Wright 1984; Wright and Decker 1994; Cromwell, Avery and Olsen 1991; Shover 1985); robbery (Wright and Decker 1997; Jacobs and Wright 199) and other offenses (Cornish and Clarke 1987; Clarke and Felson 1993) have examined the extent to which offenders are rational decision makers. From this perspective, offenders make decisions and choose options in the face of external conditions that mediate or determine their actions. Offenders are seen as recipients of external stimuli who respond to those stimuli and make decisions about offending based on a calculus. This calculus is the basis for assessing the rationality of offenders. Where offenders sense the opportunity for gain in the face of diminished risks, they will offend. Alternatively in those circumstances where offenders sense that their opportunity for gain is limited, they will desist from offending. This decision will be based largely on the balance between the chances of being apprehended and the level of gain from the offense. Here we have attempted to apply the same kinds of analysis to institutions involved in a multiple-year, multi-million dollar comprehensive community response to youth crime.

A recurring theme in the rational choice literature focuses on conceptualizing the transition from individual-level rational relationships to macro-level behavior. This kind of "micro-to-macro problem . . . is pervasive throughout the social sciences" (Coleman 1990, p. 6). As Coleman points out, "one of the central deficiencies in economic theory is the weakness of the linkage between microeconomic theory and macroeconomic theory. Not only is the theoretical transition from micro-level to macro-level one that is often "papered over," there are a number of known paradoxes that plague the interpretation of transitions between rational behavior at the individual level and collective, or organizational, behavior.

One of the best known and simplest paradoxes in theories of rational choice involves the process of collective decision-making for three actors with different rankings of utilities for each of three possible outcomes A, B, and C (Sen 1970). Actor 1 prefers A > B > C. Actor 2 prefers B > C > A. Actor 3 prefers C > A > B. A simple vote on any two particular outcomes by the three actors is totally determined by which two pairs of outcomes are chosen for comparison. In a vote between outcome A and outcome B, Actor 1 and Actor 3 vote for A, and Actor 2 votes for B, resulting in outcome A. In a vote between outcome B and outcome C, Actor 1 and Actor 2 vote for B, and Actor 3 votes for A, resulting in outcome B. In a vote between outcome B and outcome C, Actor 2 and Actor 3 vote for C, and Actor 1 votes for B, resulting in outcome C. The same kinds of paradoxes can develop even when there are only two actors involved.

An outcome from a collective action for which all actors achieve the maximum utility possible without some other actor achieving less than optimal utility is identified as "Pareto optimal." Paradoxes that emerge from combinations of utilities at one level and social action on another level frustrate the achievement of Pareto optimality. Coleman (1990 p. 337) suggests that the way to avoid such paradoxes is to allow actors more flexibility in negotiating collective outcomes. With appropriate decision-making strategies, Pareto optimality can be reached. The rational choice problem as it emerges in comprehensive community response programs requires reconciling potentially contrary agency goals (or utilities) in a process of collective action that occurs at the trans-agency or community level. In practical terms, this may mean that organizations must forge cooperation in times of tight budgets, or be able to work together in those (rare) circumstances when resources and support increase. From an organizational perspective, achieving more flexibility in agency-level behavior to affect community-level optimality is constrained by the organizational structure of contemporary community agencies.

Comprehensive community approaches requiring inter-agency cooperation and collaboration call for specific kinds of collective behavior among agency representatives. Perhaps the key element in this collective behavior is the definition of common goals, followed closely by agreement about the techniques by which goals are to be achieved. The common goal of such agency partnerships is the protection and nurturance of at-risk children and adolescents. This may mean taking advocacy roles, working in conjunction with other groups, fighting existing structural arrangements, or giving up certain domains of power and influence. There is a danger that community agencies become "too rational" in pursuing agency goals to be successful in arriving at optimal solutions through collective action. Under such a scenario agencies may be "hemmed in" by the rationality of their internal logic and fail to adequately respond to an external environment.

In his description of the emergence of capitalism, Weber (1958, pp. 181–183) quoted a contemporary who suggested that the emerging forms of order should lie upon "the shoulders" of participants "like a light cloak, which can be thrown aside at any moment." Weber concluded, "But fate decreed that the cloak should become an iron cage." Thus the structural rules of organizations come to determine the function of such organizations and often prevent them from achieving external rationality.

We are not the first to document this kind of problem. In one of his overviews of how comprehensive programs should be structured so as to be successful, Irving Spergel (et al. 1994, p. 5) noted:

Failures or delays in community mobilization occur primarily because agencies and local community organizations seek to protect or enhance their particular agency or group interests, which may or may not be related to the gang problem. Issues of organizational turf and interpersonal or interagency rivalry and conflict may prevent discussion of common goals and objectives and the means for collaborative endeavors.

Resolving turf issues may be more difficult for rational organizations than it is for loosely structured gangs.

CONCLUSIONS

This paper has reviewed the behavior of a comprehensive delinquency and gang intervention program. We noted the many occasions in which the behavior of one constituent agency failed to meet the expectations of the program model, or areas in which the arrangements between agencies failed to meet the requirements. A primary actor in the response model, the police, has not been integrated into the referral and follow-up process. The public schools, a key player in the identification and referral of problem youth, was unable to track students and utilize technology and other resources made available to them. The most successful gang outreach agency was unceremoniously closed, despite considerable objective evidence that the agency was the most successful in the service delivery in meeting the goals of the intervention. In a number of cases serious program drift was observed. The service network was designed to ensure that youths were referred to multiple agencies and that the number of youth served by multiple agencies would increase over time. It failed to achieve either of these goals.

In this context, it may be important to distinguish between a *program* and a group of *services*. The logic model that underlies SafeFutures describes a program, a well-integrated web of interventions in which information, decision-making and youth are shared in a seamless manner across programs. However, SafeFutures in operation more closely resembles a series of services, that are related only because they are funded through the same mechanism and because their members attend the same meetings. The absence of a strong client focus distinguishes programs from services in this regard.

Despite these apparent irrationalities, the program continues to exist. Indeed, in many senses the program appears to be thriving, and is often held up by federal monitors as a successful intervention. Representatives from other sites have been sent to St. Louis to observe the local operation, and in at least two of these sites the program appears to be floundering. There also appears to be estimable support for sustaining the program beyond the flow of federal funding. In the context of this review at least one important question comes to mind, What accounts for the irrational elements of organizational behavior? That is, how can it be that a program with the necessary ingredients for success fails to even put all of the pieces together.

A prominent current of organizational analysis (Perrow 1979) suggests that the Weberian view of organizations as rational may be overstated. That is, like individuals organizations adapt to their environments, and such adaptation is normal in the life cycle of organizations and agencies. Coleman (1990) suggested that the links between micro- and macro-level economic theory are often not well specified, and that as a consequence both individuals and organizations are characterized as overly rational. Indeed, much of the criminological research that has examined offender behavior has concluded that criminals are not particularly calculating or rational in their choices of targets, motives for offending, or patterns of offending (Cromwell, et al. 1991; Shover 1985; Wright and Decker 1994; 1996). Indeed the robbers and burglars studied by Wright and Decker were characterized as "encapsulated," that is enclosed in a self-limiting and self-perpetuating lifestyle that created circumstances from which offenders were often incapable of extricating themselves. In this context it hardly seems appropriate to characterize their behavior as rational, at least in the sense that micro-economic theory would postulate.

Our analysis has demonstrated that the quotient of "rational" organizational behavior seems comparable to that of individual offenders, though motivated by several different concerns. In their review of Youth Violence Prevention in St. Louis, Rosenfeld and Miles (1997:1) note that comprehensive interventions are limited by the reluctance of organizations to share "information, expertise, resources, clients, and other organizational capital." They observe that collaborative ventures achieve success when the number of participants is small, when there are few concerns about the underlying values of the intervention, and few resources are present. They conclude that narrowly focused interventions based on a single service provider or limited partnerships are most likely to achieve rational operating status. In this way, the observation from Spergel (1994: 5) noted above might be countered that the issues of turf, goals and interests may be more effectively addressed by attending to single issues in a single-minded fashion.

REFERENCES

Bennett, Trevor and Richard Wright. 1984. *Burglars on Burglary*. Hampshire, England: Gower.

Bernard, Thomas. 1992. *The Cycle of Juvenile Justice*. New York: Oxford University Press.

Burrus, George and Kimberly Kempf-Leonard. 2000. Attorney Representation and Impact in Serious Delinquency Cases: An Evaluation of Three Missouri Circuits. Final Report Submitted to the Missouri Governor's Juvenile Justice Advisory Group and the Missouri Department of Public Safety.

Clarke, Ronald V. and Marcus Felson. 1993. *Routine Activity and Rational Choice*. Volume 5, Advances in Criminological Theory. New Brunswick, New Jersey: Transaction Books.

Coleman, James S. 1990. *Foundations of Social Theory*. Cambridge, MA: Harvard University Press.

Cornish, Derek B. and Ronald V. Clarke. 1986. *The Reasoning Criminal: Rational Choice Perspectives and Offending*. New York: Springer-Verlag.

Cromwell, Paul, D'Aun Avary, and Phil Olsen. 1991. *Breaking and Entering: An Ethnographic Analysis of Burglary*. Newbury Park, CA: Sage.

Curry, G. David and Scott H. Decker. 1998. *Confronting Gangs: Crime and Community*. Los Angeles: Roxbury.

Decker, Scott H. and Barrik Van Winkle. 1996. *Life in the Gang: Family, Friends and Violence*. New York: Cambridge.

Decker, Scott H. and Kimberly Leonard. 1991. "Constructing Gangs: The Social Construction of Youth Activities". *Criminal Justice Policy Review*, 4: 271–291.

Decker, Scott H. and G. David Curry. 1999. "Responding to Gangs: Does the Dose Match the Problem?" in J. Sheley Ed. *Criminology*. Belmont, CA: Wadsworth.

Decker, Scott H., and G. David Curry. 2000. "Addressing Key Features of Gang Membership: Measuring the Involvement of Young Members." *Journal of Criminal Justice*, 28: 473–482

Feld, Barry. 1991. "Justice by Geography: Urban, Suburban, and Rural Variation in Juvenile Justice Administration." *Journal of Criminal Law and Criminology*, 79: 1185–1246.

Hagedorn, John. 1988. *People and Folks: Gangs, Crime and the Underclass in a Rustbelt City*. Chicago: Lakeview Press.

Hawkins, J. David, ed.. 1996 *Delinquency and Crime: Current Theories*. New York: Cambridge University Press.

Howell, James C. 1997. *Juvenile Justice and Youth Violence*. Thousand Oaks, CA.: Sage.

Howell, James C., Barry Krisberg, J. David Hawkins, and John L. Wilson. 1995. *Serious, Violent, and Chronic Juvenile Offenders: A Sourcebook*. Thousand Oaks, CA.: Sage.

Jackson, Pamela Irving. 1991. "Crime, Youth Gangs and Urban Transition: The Social Dislocations of Postindustrial Economic Development." *Justice Quarterly*, 8:379–397.

Jacobs. Bruce and Richard Wright. 1999. "Stick-up, Street Culture, and Offender Motivation." *Criminology*, 37:149–173.

Kempf, Kimberly, Scott H. Decker and Robert L. Bing. 1990. An Analysis of Apparent Disparities in the Handling of Black Youth within Missouri's Juvenile Justice Systems. St. Louis: University of Missouri-St. Louis, Department of Administration of Justice.

Kennedy, David, Anne Piehl, and Anthony Braga. 1996. "Youth Violence in Boston: Gun Markets, Serious Youth Offenders, and a Use-Reduction Strategy." *Law and Contemporary Problems*, Volume 59: 147–196.

Klein, Malcolm W. 1995. *The American Street Gang*. New York: Oxford University Press.

Maxson, Cheryl and Malcolm Klein. 1990. "Street Gang Violence: Twice as Great, or Half as Great." IN C. Ronald Huff ed., *Gangs in America*. Newbury Park, CA: Sage Publications, 71–100.

National Youth Gang Center. Forthcoming. *1998 National Youth Gang Survey: Summary.* Washington, D.C.: U.S. Department of Justice, Office of Juvenile Justice and Delinquency Prevention.

Perrow, Charles. 1979. *Complex Organizations: A Critical Essay.* Glenview, IL: Scott, Foresman.

Rosenfeld, Richard and Troy Miles. 1997. "Youth Violence Prevention in St. Louis: The Challenge of Community Partnerships." Paper Presented at the National Weed and Seed Conference. St. Louis, MO.

Sanchez-Jankowski, Martin. 1991. *Islands in the Street: Gangs and American Urban Society.* Berkeley, CA.: University of California Press.

Sen, Amartya Kumar. 1970. *Collective Choice and Social Welfare.* Amsterdam: Elsevier Science.

Shover, Neal. 1985. *Aging Criminals.* Beverly Hills, CA: Sage.

Skolnick, Jerome. 1990. "The Social Structure of Street Drug Dealing." *American Journal of Police*, 9: 1–41.

Spergel, Irving. 1995. *The Youth Gang Problem: A Community Approach.* New York: Oxford University Press.

Spergel, Irving A., Ron Chance, Kenneth Ehrensaft, Thomas Regulus, Candice Kane, Robert Laseter, Alba Alexander, and Sandra Oh. 1994. *Gang Suppression and Intervention: Community Models.* Washington, DC: Office of Juvenile Justice and Delinquency Prevention, U.S. Department of Justice.

Spergel, Irving A. and G. David Curry. 1993. "The National Youth Gang Survey: A Research and Development Process." In Arnold Goldstein and C. Ronald Huff Eds.. *Gang Intervention Handbook.* Champaign-Urbana: Research Press.

Taylor, Carl. 1990. *Dangerous Society*. East Lansing, MI: Michigan State University Press.

Weber, Max. 1946. *From Max Weber: Essays in Sociology*. Translated and edited by Hans H. Gerth and C. Wright Mills. New York: Oxford University Press.

Weber, Max. 1958. *The Protestant Ethic and the Spirit of Capitalism: The Relationship between Religion and the Economic and Social Life in Modern Culture*. Translated by Talcott Parsons. New York: Charles Scribner's and Sons.

Wright, Richard and Scott H. Decker. 1994. *Burglars on the Job*. Northeastern University Press. Boston: MA.

Wright, Richard and Scott H. Decker. 1996. *Armed Robbers in Action*. Northeastern University Press. Boston: MA.

Chapter 10

Reconciling Feminism and Rational Choice Theory: Women's Agency in Street Crime

Jody Miller

Feminist theories of women's lawbreaking are very much concerned with how traditional criminological theory constitutes "the female offender." Every theoretical perspective has within it both explicit and hidden assumptions about human nature and the individuals or groups in question. In criminology, assumptions about gender—and about the "nature" of females and males—have shaped the evolution of theories about women and crime. Often these assumptions are grounded in long-standing cultural beliefs about differences between women and men. For instance: men are more rational, women more emotional; men are more aggressive, women more passive; men are stronger, women weaker. As taken-for-granted suppositions, these stereotypes about what distinguishes women from men often are reflected in criminological theory.

Feminist critiques of traditional criminological approaches are grounded in a recognition of the limitations of this work to adequately address women's involvement in crime. Several limitations in particular have been highlighted. First, much criminological theory has either ignored *women*—focusing exclusively or implicitly on explaining male participation in crime and defining females as unimportant or peripheral—or has ignored *gender*. Ignoring gender results both when theories of male crime don't seek to account for how gender helps to structure and shape male involvement in crime, and when theories assume to be generalizable—that is, theories derived from the study of men are assumed to be able to account for female crime or female offenders. As theories derived from studies of women are not seen as generalizable to men, implicit in the assumption that male theories are generalizable to women is the notion that women are a subcategory of men.

A second critique is aimed at theories that do the opposite: theories that are based on beliefs about fundamental differences between women and men. It is precisely women's greater emotionality, passivity, and weakness, according to these theories, which account for both their involvement in crime and the nature of that involvement. Early theories about female crime, for example, focused on individual pathologies such as personality disorders and sexual or emotional maladjustment. This approach contrasts with theories of male crime, which have historically been much more likely to define males in relation to the broader social world around them. Because many of the gender-based assumptions that have guided criminological theories are hidden or taken-for-granted, it has taken a feminist lens to bring many of these biases to light (for feminist critiques of criminological theory, see Belknap 1997; Daly and Chesney-Lind 1988; Simpson, 1989).

Though feminist approaches to the study of women and crime themselves draw from diverse theoretical traditions regarding the nature and root causes of women's oppression (see Tong 1998), there are a number of central beliefs that guide feminist inquiry. Daly and Chesney-Lind (1988: 504) list five aspects of feminist thought that distinguish it from traditional criminological inquiry:

> • Gender is not a natural fact but a complex social, historical, and cultural product; it is related to, but not simply derived from, biological sex difference and reproductive capacities.
> • Gender and gender relations order social life and social institutions in fundamental ways.
> • Gender relations and constructs of masculinity and femininity are not symmetrical but are based on an organizing principle of men's superiority and social and political-economic dominance over women.
> • Systems of knowledge reflect men's views of the natural and social world; the production of knowledge is gendered.
> • Women should be at the center of intellectual inquiry, not peripheral, invisible, or appendages to men.

Thus, feminist criminology highlights the significance of gender inequality as a structural feature of American society that both shapes women's and men's participation in crime and shapes criminological theory and knowledge systems. Rational choice theory, with its primary focus on individual decision-making, may at first glance appear antithetical to feminist goals. However, my aim in this chapter is to highlight facets of this approach relevant for advancing feminist theories of women's offending. I focus on two interrelated issues. First, I discuss the utility of a rational choice approach for providing a framework that recognizes women's agency. Second, I do so by emphasizing the crime-specific and situational aspects of rational choice theory. Drawing on several studies based on qualitative interviews with active female offenders, I frame my discussion in the context of three forms of street offending: robbery, drug sales, and gang violence. While I address the benefits of adopting some facets of a rational choice approach, I do so while also highlighting the dangers of adopting a wholly rational choice model.

FEMINIST ACCOUNTS OF FEMALE STREET CRIME

Feminists have thoroughly critiqued the ways that some criminological theories have constituted "the female offender" as pathological or maladjusted. Though feminist scholars have challenged the longstanding view of women's crime as resulting from maladjustment to appropriate femininity, the theme of women's victimization continues to permeate some feminist accounts, such that women continue to be framed as passive victims—in this case, not of their own pathology, but of patriarchal systems and relationships. Recognition of women's victimization within male-dominated society is a necessary feature of any theory that attempts to take gender seriously and place relations of sex and gender at the foreground of inquiry. Nonetheless, focusing narrowly on women's victimization is problematic because it "tend[s] to create the false impression that women have *only* been victims, that they have never successfully fought back, that women cannot be effective social agents on behalf of themselves or others" (Harding 1987: 5). Moreover, even when feminist inquiries focus on *resistance* to victimization, a strategy adopted to overcome the implied passivity resulting from an exclusive focus on victimization, the "constitution" of female offenders remains problematic. Often women's lives—or their criminal activities—are still framed as governed exclusively by gendered victimization, or fear and response to such victimization. This is an approach often found in feminist accounts of women's use of violence (but see Simpson 1991; Simpson and Elis 1995).

Several examples should help to illustrate this problem. Campbell (1993), in her study of gender and aggression, suggests that while men routinely adopt instrumental aggression, women's aggression is primarily expressive, unless they find themselves in contexts in which instrumental aggression is necessary for self-protection. Turning her attention specifically to gangs, Campbell differentiates between gang girls' use of violence and the violence of their male counterparts. Among young men, Campbell (1993: 131–2) suggests, "[v]iolence is power, and it is directed at other gangs and local youth because gang members want recognition and respect on their own turf. Violence is a measure of being someone in a world where all hope of success in conventional terms is lost." In contrast, she describes young women's aggression in a very different manner:

> Fear and loneliness—in their families, their communities, and their schools—are the forces that drive young women toward an instrumental view of their aggression. They know what it is to be victims, and they know that, to survive, force must be met with more than unspoken anger or frustrated tears. Less physically strong and more sexually vulnerable than boys, they find that the best line of defense is not attack but the threat of attack. . . . There is nothing so effective as being in a street gang to keep the message blaring out: "Don't mess with me—I'm a crazy woman" (Campbell, 1993: 133).

Similarly, in her ethnography of a Brooklyn drug market, Maher (1997) notes that women adopt violent presentations of self on the street as a strategy of protection. She explains: "'Acting bad' and 'being bad' are not the same. Although many of the women presented themselves as 'bad' or 'crazy,' this projection was a street persona and a necessary survival strategy" (Maher 1997: 95). She notes that the women in her study were infrequently involved in violent crime, and most often resorted to violence in response to threats or harms against them. Maher (1997: 95–6) concludes: "unlike their male counterparts, for women, reputation was about 'preventing victimization.'"

These explanations of women's behavior shift the frame of reference from individual maladjustment to structural gender inequalities and move beyond the early image of individual pathology. But they nonetheless keep women thoroughly and almost exclusively bound by gendered victimization. Here women are not victims of biology and maladjustment, but are victims of male oppression—victims whose actions always reflect resistance or response to that oppression. Women's agency is thus narrowly defined. While I do not wish to discount the significance of the "blurred boundaries" of women's victimization and offending (see Chesney-Lind 1997; Gilfus 1992; Richie 1996), and these accounts may be accurate in some situations, I nonetheless suggest that feminist theories must leave sufficient space to account for other facets of women's offending and women's lives. For example, in certain contexts situational norms favorable to women's use of violence may exist that are not simply about avoiding victimization but also result in economic gain, status, recognition, or emotional rewards such as alleviation of boredom, excitement or revenge (see also Simpson 1991; Simpson and Elis 1995). Taking such situational norms and motivations into account can be done, I suggest, without sacrificing a gendered inquiry. I further outline these ideas below.

RECONCILING FEMINISM AND RATIONAL CHOICE THEORY

Feminist theories are explicitly political approaches in that they are critical of gendered structures of inequality both in society and in the body of ideas that comprises and shapes mainstream criminological thought. Rational choice theories, as well, have implicit within them political implications that are in many ways disparate from feminist goals. Core concepts guiding rational choice theory include the belief in free will, hedonism and individual choice. Politically, this emphasis can result in a narrow individualistic approach that calls for individual responsibility for lawbreaking. Moreover, rational choice theory is often joined with "constitutional" theories which further shift the frame of reference to individuals and away from structural inequalities in society that shape the "choices" members of various segments of the population have available to them (see, e.g., Wilson and Herrnstein 1985). Such an approach reifies precisely those conservative political views that feminist scholars seek to challenge.

However, it may not be necessary to wholly accept a rational choice approach in order to draw from relevant features of rational choice theory. Some mainstream (e.g., nonfeminist) theorists, for example, rather than rejecting rational choice approaches, suggest that insights from this theory can be incorporated into other theoretical approaches (see, for example, Akers 1990). Though feminist theorists have been critical of traditional criminological approaches, there is nonetheless recognition that "many seminal ideas that have emerged in criminological thought can be integrated and/or elaborated in ways that can inform gendered criminological theory" (Simpson 2000). I would argue that rational choice theory may provide a means of strengthening feminist accounts of women's agency. That is, there are elements in the rational choice approach that may provide useful tools in integrating feminist concerns with gender inequality with the desire to recognize women as more than simply passive victims of male oppression.

The rational choice perspective is widely recognized as having advanced criminological theory specifically through its emphasis on the need for a crime-specific approach that "concentrat[es] chiefly on the decision-making process of offenders confronted with specific contexts" (Einstadter and Henry 1995: 70). As Cullen and Agnew (1999: 254) summarize: "The leading crime theories have paid little attention to those factors that influence the decision to commit a particular criminal offense, and one of the leading contributions of rational choice theory has been to focus attention on this area." In several recent essays on feminist criminology, Daly (1998, 2000) suggests that there are four significant areas of inquiry for the development of feminist theories: the gender ratio of crime, gendered pathways to lawbreaking, gendered crime, and gendered lives.

Inquiries into "gendered crime," she notes, should address the following questions: "What are the contexts and qualities of boys'/men's and girls'/women's illegal acts? What is the social organization of particular offenses?" (Daly 2000). Thus to the extent that "gendered crime" is an important arena for feminist inquiry, there is overlap in the emphases of rational choice and feminist approaches.

A primary means through which feminists have dealt with "gendered crime" has been the utilization of sociological theory on gender as situated accomplishment (West and Zimmerman 1987; West and Fenstermaker 1995). According to this perspective, gender is "much more than a role or an individual characteristic: it is a mechanism whereby situated social action contributes to the reproduction of social structure" (West and Fenstermaker 1995: 21). Women and men 'do gender' in response to normative beliefs about femininity and masculinity. These actions are "the interactional scaffolding of social structure" (West and Zimmerman 1987: 147), such that the performance of gender is both an indication of and a reproduction of gendered social hierarchies.

This approach has been incorporated into feminist accounts of crime as a means of explaining differences in women's and men's offending (Newburn and Stanko 1994; Messerschmidt 1993, 1995; Simpson and Elis 1995). Here, violence is described as "a 'resource' for accomplishing gender—for demonstrating masculinity within a given context or situation" (Simpson and Elis 1995: 50). Though the concept of gender as situated accomplishment has primarily been brought to bear on male offending and constructions of masculinity, feminist theorists recently have attempted to account for female crime based on the same framework. Messerschmidt (1995: 172), for example, suggests that "'doing gender' renders social action accountable in terms of normative conceptions, attitudes and activities appropriate to one's sex category in the specific social situation in which one acts." Theorizing about young women in gangs, Messerschmidt argues that girls engage in gang activities, including violence, with the goal of enacting normatively appropriate femininity:

> For girls in the gang, doing femininity means occasionally, and in appropriate circumstances, doing violence. However, because participation in violence varies depending upon the setting, girls are assessed and held accountable as 'bad girls' differently. Given that gang girls realize that their behavior is accountable to other girls and boys in the gang, they construct their actions in relation to how those actions will be interpreted by others in the same social context (Messershmidt 1995:183).

Already, this approach draws from elements of rational choice theory: males and females make decisions to engage in particular acts of law-breaking as a means of enacting masculinity or femininity. Their decision-making is guided, according to these theorists, by how their actions will be read by others around them, who have the ability to sanction or approve their success in "doing gender."

While this particular application of the concept of gender as situated accomplishment has proven to be of some utility, it nonetheless continues to give primacy exclusively to gender as the most salient factor guiding or motivating behavior. It may be instead that, even when crime is recognizably gendered, this is the case not because of gendered situational motives. As I noted earlier, in many instances, more universal goals than enacting femininity (or resisting victimization) may guide women's criminal decision-making at the situational level. Nonetheless, because women's and men's decision-making processes occur within the context of gender stratification, their actions are likely to remain "gendered" even when the motives guiding behavior and decision-making are not.

Though Messerschmidt (1995) notes the reciprocal relation of gender and other social practices, this conceptual theme has not been fully explored. For example, rather than crime simply being a resource for accomplishing gender, the converse may also be true: gender may be used as a resource for female lawbreakers to accomplish their participation in and avoidance of crime. Again, this is precisely an arena in which a rational choice perspective on criminal events is of utility. One of the situational factors guiding women's decisions about whether and how to engage in crime is gender stratification within criminal and street networks. There is compelling evidence that gender inequality remains a salient feature of the urban street scene (Maher 1997; Steffensmeier 1983; Steffensmeier and Terry 1986). As Maher (1997) documents, gendered status structures both women's and men's participation in street crime. Taking a rational choice approach provides a means to examine how women negotiate within gender-stratified environments, and how they accommodate and adapt to gender inequality in their commission of crime.

THE STUDIES

To illustrate the approach I have just outlined, I draw from several qualitative studies in which I have been involved over the past five years. In each case, women and girls were interviewed at length about their involvement in street crime.[1] The first study (Miller 2001) is based on interviews with forty-eight young women who are members of street gangs. In these interviews, we discussed both young women's participation in gang conflict and violence, and their participation in drug sales. The second study (Jacobs and Miller 1998) is drawn from interviews with twenty-five female crack dealers, and focuses on women's drug selling strategies. Finally, the third study (Miller 1998; see also Wright and Decker 1997) is drawn from interviews with fourteen women actively involved in street robbery (along with a comparative sample of male robbers). These interviews focused on situational motivations, target selection, and the accomplishment of robbery.

At the outset, I should highlight the unique populations of which these samples are illustrative. Studying women and girls involved in the types of street-level offending I discuss in this chapter means studying exceptional groups of women and of female lawbreakers. For example, despite the growth in gangs throughout the United States since the 1980s (see Klein 1995), studies that attempt to gauge the prevalence of gang participation among youths have found that only a small percentage of young people are active gang members. For example, longitudinal results from the Gang Resistance Education and Training Program, based on a sample of youth from six cities across the United States, report prevalence rates of only three percent of youths in a school-based sample (Esbensen 2000). Based on a stratified sample of youths from high-risk, high crime neighborhoods, the Rochester Youth Development Study found 22 percent of girls in the earliest waves of the project reported gang membership—a figure that declined precipitously in subsequent waves of the study (Bjerregaard and Smith 1992; Thornberry 1999). Estimates suggest that females account for approximately 20 to 46 percent of gang members (see Esbensen and Winfree 1998; Moore 1991; Winfree et al. 1992). Moreover, studies of female gang members' participation in delinquency find a bimodal distribution, with equal numbers of multiple-index offenders and petty delinquents (see Fagan 1990; Miller 2001). Overall, female gang involvement is not widespread; gang girls who participate in serious gang crime are even less common.

This is also the case with regard to female drug sellers and women who participate in street robberies. Urban crack markets, for example, remain highly stratified by gender, with women's activities heavily restricted by male-dominated street drug networks (Bourgois 1995; Maher 1997). Research has documented the relative rarity of successful independent female dealers (Dunlap, Johnson, and Manwar 1994; Fagan 1994; Maher 1997). Maher and Daly (1996: 472), for example, report that of the 200–plus women they came into contact with during three years of fieldwork in a Brooklyn drug market, they "did not discover any woman who was a [drug] business owner, and just one who worked as a manager." When women are involved in drug sales, they typically are relegated to peripheral roles such as irregular selling, selling or renting drug paraphernalia, or copping drugs for others (see Maher 1997; Maher and Daly 1996). Likewise with street robbery, which is one of the most gender-differentiated serious crimes in the United States. According to the FBI's Uniform Crime Report for 1995, women accounted for only 9.3 percent of robbery arrestees (Federal Bureau of Investigation 1996).

It is important to emphasize the unique nature of the types of female lawbreaking I examine in the discussion that follows in order to put these women's offending in a broader context. They do not represent *typical* female offenders, nor are they representative of a so-called "new violent female offender" whose participation in serious and violent crime has escalated in recent years (see Chesney-Lind 1993; Chesney-Lind, Shelden, and Joe 1996). Despite their relative rarity, women and girls who engage in street crime have something significant to teach us about women's place in the urban street world, as does the examination of how situational decision-making within criminal events is shaped by gender. The in-depth interview techniques utilized in these studies are particularly fruitful ways to examine these issues. Qualitative interviews provide one of the best methods for gaining information from the points of view of study participants, as well as detailed descriptive information about the nature and contexts of lawbreaking (Glassner and Loughlin 1987; Miller and Glassner 1997).

CRIME AS GENDERED ACCOMPLISHMENT

As noted above, my goal in this chapter is to draw from the rational choice focus on the situational aspects of crime-specific decision-making processes to examine women's agency within the context of gender-stratified street and criminal networks. I do so with a specific emphasis on how women and girls accommodate and adapt to these gender inequities in their decisions about whether and how to engage in gang violence, drug selling, and robbery. Kandiyoti (1988) coined the phrase "bargaining with patriarchy" to highlight women's strategies of action as they arise within particular sets of gendered constraints. She notes: "Different forms of patriarchy present women with distinct 'rules of the game' and call for different strategies to maximize security and optimize life options with varying potential for active or passive resistance in the face of oppression" (Kandiyoti 1988: 274). My interest here is in women's and girls' "gender strategies" for crime-commission in male dominated street settings.

YOUNG WOMEN AND GANG VIOLENCE

Because of the group processes in operation within gangs, they are often recognized as social contexts that facilitate violence. Scholars who discuss the facilitation or enhancement effects of gangs on delinquency and violence emphasize the strength of gang members' associations with violent peers, but also gang norms and group processes that encourage youths to engage in these activities (Battin et al. 1998; Thornberry 1997). In fact, Klein (1995) suggests that violence, particularly in the form of intergang conflict, is more than just an outcome of gang membership; instead, it serves as a source of group cohesion for its members. An important element of gang life involves challenging and fighting with rival gangs. It is often at the level of these antagonisms that youths stake out the identity of their gang: having common enemies facilitates members' perceptions of themselves as a unified group (see Decker 1996). Thus, gang involvement "may directly facilitate violence by virtue of the public and participatory nature of gang conflicts" (Rosenfeld, Bray, and Egley 1999: 514).

What is notable about gangs, however, is that the most serious forms of gang violence, including gun use and homicide, are almost the exclusive purview of *male* gang members. For example, in a recent analysis of gang homicides in St. Louis from 1990 to 1996 (Miller and Decker 2001), *none* of the 229 gang homicides committed during that period were attributed to a female gang member. One reason for young women's lack of participation in serious gang violence is the structural exclusion of female gang members by their male gang peers (Bowker, Gross, and Klein 1980; Miller and Brunson 2000). This results from the fact that most street gangs are male-dominated. However, my research suggests that male exclusion of female participation in serious gang violence doesn't fully account for young women's limited involvement in serious violent confrontations. Instead, young women engage in active decision-making to participate in particular kinds of gang conflicts and avoid others.

Young women's accounts of gang-related conflict shed some light on these issues. While girls are involved in altercations with rival gangs, they rarely escalate to violence, and even more rarely escalate to serious violence involving weapons. Opposition to rival gangs is a central theme in the cultural imagery and symbolism that gang youths adopt. Often confrontations with rivals are a consequence of these displays, particularly in conjunction with the defense of neighborhood boundaries. For instance, Crystal explained, "if a Blood come on our set and we Crips, as long as they come on our set saying, 'what's up Blood,' they . . . just gonna start a fight. 'Cause they diss [disrespect] us by coming on our set and saying 'what's up Blood.' There ain't nobody no Blood over there." Vashelle concurred: "A dude come over [to our neighborhood from a rival gang], he know what kind of 'hood it is to begin with. Any dude that come over there from a gang and know that's a Blood hood, you try to come over there Cripped out [wearing Crips colors, symbolism], you know you gonna eventually have it some way."

The vast majority of confrontations in which girls were engaged involved fists, occasionally knives, but not guns. However, most young women said when they encountered rivals, as long as they weren't met with a direct challenge, they were willing to tolerate their presence rather than escalate into a fight. Pam explained:

We going to the show or skating, to the mall. We be seeing some of our enemies too when we do those things, clubs and stuff, we be seeing a lot of our
enemies. [If] they don't say nothing to us, we don't say nothing to them. They
say something to us, we say something to them. So that way everybody just
go they own little way if they don't want nothing to happen.

Many young women echoed Pam's account. While violence and confrontations with rivals were normative features of their gangs, and things
on which gang girls placed value, they were not activities young women
typically chose to engage in themselves. Instead, they were often content to
leave such activities to young men. That these activities were normative features of girls' gangs is reflected in their discussions of status hierarchies in
their groups, as well as their descriptions of individuals they looked up to
in their gangs. These included individuals who "did dirt" for the gang by
committing gang-motivated assaults and participating in the confrontation
of rivals. Status emerged in part from having proven oneself on these
grounds.

That young women described looking up to individuals in the gang
who had such qualities is an indication of their acceptance of these gang
norms. For example, Heather described the most influential girl in her set
as "the hardest girl, the one that don't take no crap, will stand up to anybody." Likewise, Diane described a highly respected female member in her
set as follows:

People look up to Janeen just 'cause she's so crazy. People just look up to her
'cause she don't care about nothin'. She don't even care about makin' money.
Her, her thing is, "Oh, you're a Slob [Blood]? You're a Slob? You talkin' to
me? You talkin' shit to me?" Pow, pow! And that's it. That's it.

Nonetheless, most girls saw males as the group members most likely to
carry through these activities at their most extreme. As Tonya exclaimed,
"we ain't no supercommando girls!" Young women held males and females
to different standards based on their perceptions of what "femaleness" or
"maleness" brought to their interactions and behaviors, and some girls
used this as a basis for limiting their participation in serious gang violence,
particularly gun violence. Crystal noted, "girls don't be up there shooting
unless they really have to." Keisha explained, "Guys is more rougher. We
have our G's back but, it ain't gonna be like the guys, they just don't give
a fuck. They gonna shoot you in a minute." And Pam suggested that girls
don't use guns because "we ladies, we not dudes for real . . . *we don't got
to be rowdy*, all we do is fight" [my emphasis].

As Pam's comments suggest, it's not just that gang girls participated in
or avoided certain crimes as a means of *enacting* femininity. Rather, they
also used norms about gender to temper their involvement in serious and

dangerous gang violence—because they were girls, they "don't got to" engage in serious violence. Girls could gain status in the gang by engaging in those violent activities that mark members as "hard" and "true" to the set. But many young women drew on the gender inequalities that permeated status hierarchies and expectations about member behavior within gangs in order to avoid such activities. Moreover, they played on beliefs about gender in other circumstances, using their presence to shield suspicion from the actions of their gang. For instance, Tonya described:

> Like when we in a car, if a girl and a dude in a car, the police tend not to trip off of it. When they look to see if a car been stolen, police just don't trip off of it. But if they see three or four niggers in that car, the police stop you automatically, boom. . . . [Girls have] little ways that we got to get them out of stuff sometimes, we can get them out of stuff that dudes couldn't do, you know what I'm saying.

Thus gender—and gender stereotypes—were often resources that young women drew from both to negotiate and limit their involvement in gang violence, and to facilitate the success of gang members' crimes.

WOMEN'S INVOLVEMENT IN STREET-LEVEL DRUG DEALING

As I noted above, the street-level drug economy is highly stratified by gender. Its institutional structure, including homosocial reproduction, gender segregation, and gender-typing, limits women's participation in street-level drug dealing (Maher 1997; Steffensmeier 1983; Steffensmeier and Terry 1996). Within this gender-stratified context, a small number of women have managed to carve out a selling niche of their own, but in doing so, they face unique circumstances that shape and mediate their dealing experiences. Similar to the evidence I presented with regard to gang violence, women often draw on gender as a resource to successfully negotiate their participation in drug sales.

Returning first to female gang members' involvement in drug sales, only about a quarter of the young women in my sample sold drugs on a regular basis. Though young women viewed drug sales as a viable means of making money, most described their involvement as sporadic rather than an everyday activity, indicating some difference between their activities and those of young men. Shandra said, "the times when I sold I only did it for a short while. I only did it to make a little money to do something big. I ain't never really made it a career or nothing like that." Likewise, Pam explained:

> Some girls just sell some drugs and then they'll quit. They just sell it just to get them some money 'cause they need some. Whatever they need they'll

make they money and then probably won't sell drugs no more until they need something else. And then they'll go buy them some drugs and sell it and that's it. The dudes, they keep on, keep on, keep on. They like to sell it and stash they money, cards and all that.

Young women typically described their suppliers as older members of the gang. A likely consequence of both these factors was that young women were not viewed as serious competition for male drug sellers, thus lessening the risks associated with violence in the drug marketplace. Nonetheless, young women did report the problem of potential predators, which they suggested made it more difficult for females to sell drugs on the streets than males. Pam explained that this was because women were viewed as particularly easy targets for drug robberies:

A dude, they [robbers] ain't too quick to run up on you and rob you, take your stuff. See, you a girl, they be like, "well she ain't gonna do nothing, she ain't got no clout [reputation], she ain't nothing but a girl. All I got to do is tell her to up it and she gonna give it here." They just can't come up to a dude like that, especially if he know them and he got some clout. They be scared to run up on you if he a dude. By you being a girl, they'll rob you quicker, take everything, your drugs, your money, anything else they want.

Consequently, young women had to accommodate to these circumstances in order to be successful in their endeavors. They described two methods to deal with such problems. One was to avoid selling drugs alone. Some young women would sell with young men, and rely on these male peers to protect them. Mia said the young men in her gang assisted in her drug sales by watching her back to "make sure don't nobody do nothing to take nothing from me when I'm on the streets." Likewise, Pam said sometimes girls would "have somebody standing by, one of your boys or something." Jennifer was a member of an all-female gang, and also described selling in a group context rather than individually:

Everybody would think that if some boys were goin' to buy some bud from us, the first one that comes to mind, "I ain't paying her for it, I'm gonna jack her for it." But then they see how many girls, like when we go out we always have like three or four girls with us 'cause, especially with the tiny people. Like I'm one of the tinier people. So I have to have a couple big people with me.

Young women involved routinely in drug sales also described adopting discreet methods of selling, which not only decreased their risk of danger from others on the streets, but also drew less police attention. Vashelle explained, "the police, they don't be on the girls for real, females, but if they see a whole crowd of niggers sitting out, they gonna get down on them. But I'm saying if there are niggers out there and I'm with them too they gonna shake me too. If I'm walking up the street by myself they ain't gonna trip off me 'cause I'm a gal." She said she avoided such scrutiny by not "sit[ting] out with a crowd. I sit out by myself . . . on the back porch." Vashelle sold drugs in a way that avoided calling attention to herself, and also used beliefs about gender to conceal her activities and avoid being caught.

Our interviews (Jacobs and Miller 1998) with female crack dealers who were not selling in the context of gangs revealed similar discretionary techniques, though these women did not describe selling in groups as a protective strategy. In order to succeed in the drug trade, all street level crack sellers must adopt a variety of strategies to minimize their risks of both police detection and other dangers (see Jacobs 1999). The female crack dealers we studied employed a variety of techniques that paralleled those of male crack dealers, and they also adopted a number of gendered techniques to successfully accomplish their activities. They did so by creating images of themselves and their behavior consistent with popular beliefs about women's place in (or absence from) the street-level drug economy.

One technique women employed was to project a self-image that contradicted that of the more indiscreet behavior of many male dealers— "standin' on the streets, seein' a car go by, runnin' behind them, flaggin' 'em down." Women rejected these techniques, and instead described affecting a physical appearance that was mundane, and thus unlikely to attract attention. One woman described dressing "like a lady, you know, sandals, hair down, a dress." In addition, because the primary image of women in the crack economy is that of an "addict" and not of a dealer, women used this gender stereotype to their advantage. Latisha, one of the young women from the gang study, noted that if "you be a girl, the police think that if you selling dope or something, a girl, you smoking it, stuff like that." Likewise, another woman from the drug study explained that when the police "see a woman on the streets, walkin' or somethin', they think she lookin' for somethin' or is prostitutin' [and are not likely to stop her]." Though the particular details varied, all of the women in Jacobs and my (1998) study presented a self-image at odds with that of the prototypical dealer as a means of successfully selling drugs.

These women described using other gendered techniques as well. Their choices for stashing drugs so as to avoid their detection are one example. Though public strip searches were a practice often utilized by the police for males suspected of drug dealing, the same was not the case for women. Police could not conduct strip searches of female suspects unless or until they took them to the station, where a female officer had to do the search. Consequently, a number of women utilized on-person stashing techniques as a means of concealing their drugs. In addition, some women described selling crack during hours of the day in which their presence on the streets could be legitimately explained, for example during the time that stores were open so that the police would "just think you be goin' to the store."

In fact, many women described assimilating into the routine activities of the environment as a means to minimize risks by either integrating their drug sales into other social activities or staging performances to camouflage their drug sales and allow them to proceed unnoticed. Female drug sellers (in Lauderback, Hansen and Waldorf 1992) for example, brought their infants to drug transactions in order to avoid detection: "[It's] kind of like a decoy, we have our strollers and stuff and babies, they [police] don't usually bother us." Likewise, a woman in our sample said she brought boxes of food, household cleaner, or grocery bags to customers' homes, making it appear as if she were running an errand. Or she acted as if she were coming over to pick up something either owed her, or left there by her sometime before. "You got those canned goods and boxes I left in the basement?" she would reportedly say loudly enough to be heard. After going inside and making the sale, she would exit with the aforementioned items, affirming the apparent mundane purpose of her visit. Though any of these techniques *could* be employed by males, Jacobs' (1996, 1999) studies of male crack dealers did not uncover male adoption of these approaches.

WOMEN'S ACCOMPLISHMENT OF STREET ROBBERY

As with my discussion of the situational and group dynamics facilitating gang violence, the study of women's involvement in street robbery solicited information about proximate and immediate motivations guiding women's decisions to commit robberies. This study was also benefited by a comparison group of male robbers,[2] which provides a better tool for feminist theory-building than is permitted by single sex research (Simpson 2000). In fact, most notable in the robbery study was that women's and men's discussions of the reasons they committed robbery was more a case of gender similarities than differences. At least for this set of offenders, this calls into question the utility of an approach that describes robbery as a means of enacting or accomplishing gender (see Katz 1988; Messerschmidt 1993), or as gendered resistance to victimization (see Maher 1997). The majority of women and men in this sample said their immediate reasons for committing robberies was to get status-conferring goods such as gold jewelry, spending money, and/or for excitement.

Despite these similarities, there were clear differences in how women and men accomplished robberies. These differences appeared to be the result of women's strategic choices in the context of gender-stratified environments. The men in the sample described committing robberies in a strikingly uniform manner—using physical violence or its threat and most often a gun placed on or at close proximity to the victim in a confrontational manner. In male robberies, in fact, physical violence could sometimes be avoided because of the compliance achieved from the presence of a firearm. This method was employed regardless of whether men robbed male or female victims, though the former were more common targets than the latter. In contrast, women's techniques for committing robberies varied considerably depending upon whether they were targeting male or female victims, and whether they were working with male accomplices.

When women robbed other women, they did so either alone or with female accomplices, but not with male accomplices. Women's robberies of other females occurred in a physically confrontational manner that typically involved no weapon or (less frequently) a knife. They described targeting female victims because they were seen as less likely to resist than males. CMW explained, "see women, they won't really do nothing. They say, 'oh, oh, ok, here take this.' A dude, he might try to put up a fight." The use of weapons in these robberies was often deemed unnecessary, though other forms of physical violence were quite common. According to Janet Outlaw, "we push 'em and tell them to up their shit, pushing 'em in the head. Couple of times we had to knock the girls down and took the stuff off of them." She explained the reason this type of physical force was necessary: "It's just a woman-to-woman thing and we just . . . letting them know like it is, we let them know we ain't playing."

In contrast, women's robberies of men nearly always involved guns, and did not involve physical contact. Janet Outlaw, who described a great deal of physical contact in her robberies of other women, described her robberies of men in much different terms: "If we waste time touching men there is a possibility that they can get the gun off of us, while we wasting time touching them they could do anything. So we just keep the gun straight on them. No touching, no moving, just straight gun at you." The circumstances surrounding female-on-male robberies differed as well. Women's strategy for robbing men involved pretending to be sexually interested in their male victims, with the dropping of the man's guard providing the opportunity for the crime to occur. In particular, women played upon men's beliefs about women in order to accomplish these robberies. Such beliefs included the assumption that women wouldn't be armed, wouldn't attempt to rob men, and could be taken advantage of sexually. Quick explained:

> They don't suspect that a girl gonna try to get 'em. You know what I'm saying? So it's kind of easier 'cause they like, she looks innocent, she ain't gonna do this, but that's how I get 'em. They put they guard down to a woman. . . .

Most of the time when girls get high they think they can take advantage of us so they always, let's go to a hotel or my crib or something."

Men's actions, and their attitudes about women, thus made them vulnerable targets.

The final method women employed to commit robberies occurred when they worked in tandem with male partners. When they committed street robberies with men, women described using the same techniques that men routinely employ—physical contact that typically involved the display and placement of a gun on the victim. Moreover, women suggested that it was because of the presence of their male accomplices that they were able to avoid the challenge or resistance likely to occur when using the same technique on a male victim alone. In fact, only one woman described employing this technique without the presence of a male accomplice. Ne-Ne explicitly indicated that she was able to complete the robbery because the victim did not know it was a woman who was robbing him. Describing herself as physically large, Ne-Ne said she dressed and adopted mannerisms that masked her gender. She wore a baseball cap "pulled down over my face and I just went to the back and upped him. Put the gun up to his head. . . . He don't know right now to this day if it was a girl or a dude."

DISCUSSION

The studies I have just discussed—of young women's participation in and avoidance of gang violence, women's drug dealing, and commission of street robberies—illustrate the range of gender strategies upon which women draw in order to negotiate within the gender stratified world of the streets and successfully participate in street-level lawbreaking. For women, gender stratification—and its requisite stereotypes of women as weak and vulnerable—is one of the specific situational contexts that must be confronted in the decision-making processes of lawbreaking. As I have described, in each case, women's gendered techniques and actions represent practical choices they make while taking into account the gendered nature of their environments.

Feminist theories of women's lawbreaking have been particularly critical of those approaches that fail to take gender into account; in the context of studying crime at the situational level, this has often meant an overemphasis on women's volition, in conjunction with inattention to how gendered status structures and circumscribes the opportunities available to women on the streets (see Maher 1997). At first blush, a rational choice approach would appear to be in line with the approaches feminist scholars have vigorously critiqued. However, I have suggested that many of the concepts feminist scholars currently utilize—resistance to victimization, 'doing gender,' and gender strategies—share assumptions about agency and decision-making with rational choice models. Regardless of the particular explanatory concept employed, women are seen as actively involved in decision-making processes in order to "maximize security and optimize life options" (Kandiyoti 1988: 274) in the context of male oppression.

Criminological theory remains a thoroughly gendered field of knowledge-building, whereby androcentric approaches are brought to bear primarily on male or presumably "universal" offenders. Because of the challenges inherent in bringing these biases into the frame of inquiry, feminist scholars have often tended to focus on gender as *the* explanatory factor shaping women's involvement in lawbreaking. At the situational level this is the case, as I have suggested, whether the focus is on gendered victimization, or on crime as a resource for accomplishing gender. While these approaches hold some utility, my studies provide one of a series of alternate conceptual frameworks, drawing from the larger criminological literature on lawbreaking. Taking situational norms and motives shared between women and men into account does not preclude the use of a gendered inquiry. As a starting point of gendered inquiry, however, feminist scholars must recognize that gender "may be more or less relevant, and relevant in different ways, from one social context to the next" (Thorne 1993: 29). This does not mean that gender is unimportant, or that gender doesn't shape criminal behavior, but that its significance can't be assumed at the outset, and needs to be empirically discovered (Thorne 1998).

Drawing from the insights of traditional criminological theories, such as in my case rational choice theory, does not require a whole-hearted acceptance of these approaches, particularly given their evolution as gender-neutral theories and the androcentric bias that results. My goal here has been to show that there are elements of the rational choice approach that may provide useful tools for integrating feminist concerns with gender inequality with the desire to recognize women as more than simply passive victims of male oppression. Nonetheless, to the extent that rational choice theory focuses primarily on the individual decision-making side of the equation, rather than on the range of structural constraints (e.g., gender inequalities, racial inequalities, class inequalities) that shape and limit opportunities and guide the choice to engage in lawbreaking, this approach remains useful but insufficient. In drawing on the larger body of criminological literature, the key for feminist scholars is to recognize that "those theories were not developed with a sophisticated theory of sex/gender in mind," (Daly 2000) and a number of challenges result. Nonetheless, when examined rigorously, particularly in comparative analyses between women and men, traditional theories remain an important source of concepts and ideas for developing gendered analyses that do not reify gender as the only feature governing women's lives.

NOTES

1. Due to space constraints, I do not discuss the study methodologies in this chapter. For detailed descriptions, see Jacobs and Miller 1998; Miller 1998, 2001; Wright and Decker 1997.

2. In both of the other studies comparative data is available for males (see Jacobs 1996; Miller and Brunson 2000), but in neither case was this comparative component built into the original research design as was the case with the robbery study.

REFERENCES

Akers, Ronald. 1990. "Rational Choice, Deterrence and Social Learning in Criminology: The Path Not Taken." *Journal of Criminal Law and Criminology.* 81: 653–676.

Battin, Sara R., Karl G. Hill, Robert D. Abbott, Richard F. Catalano, and J. David Hawkins. 1998. "The Contribution of Gang Membership to Delinquency Beyond Delinquent Friends." *Criminology.* 36: 93–115.

Belknap, Joanne. 1997. *The Invisible Woman: Gender, Crime and Justice.* Belmont, CA: Wadsworth.

Bjerregaard, Beth and Carolyn Smith. 1993. "Gender Differences in Gang Participation, Delinquency, and Substance Use." *Journal of Quantitative Criminology.* 4: 329–355.

Bourgois, Philippe. 1995. *In Search of Respect: Selling Crack in El Barrio.* Cambridge: Cambridge University Press.

Bowker, Lee H., Helen Shimota Gross, and Malcolm W. Klein. 1980. "Female Participation in Delinquent Gang Activities." *Adolescence.* 15: 509–519.

Campbell, Anne. 1993. *Men, Women and Aggression.* New York: Basic Books.

Chesney-Lind, Meda. 1997. *The Female Offender: Girls, Women, and Crime.* Thousand Oaks, CA: Sage Publications.

Chesney-Lind, Meda. 1993. "Girls, Gangs and Violence: Anatomy of a Backlash." *Humanity & Society.* 17: 321–344

Chesney-Lind, Meda, Randall G. Shelden and Karen A. Joe. 1996. "Girls, Delinquency, and Gang Membership." Pp. 185–204 in *Gangs in America, 2nd Edition,* edited by C. Ronald Huff. Thousand Oaks, CA: Sage Publications.

Cullen, Francis T. and Robert Agnew. 1999. *Criminological Theory: Past to Present.* Los Angeles: Roxbury Publishing Company.

Daly, Kathleen. 2000. "Feminist Theoretical Work in Criminology." *DivisioNews.* Newsletter of the Division of Women and Crime, American Society of Criminology, August. (http://www.ou.edu/soc/dwc/newsletter.htm).

Daly, Kathleen. 1998. "From Gender Ratios to Gendered Lives: Women and Gender in Crime and Criminological Theory." Pp. 85–108 in *The Handbook of Crime and Justice,* edited by Michael Tonry. Oxford: Oxford University Press.

Daly, Kathleen and Meda Chesney-Lind. 1988. "Feminism and Criminology." *Justice Quarterly.* 5: 497–538.

Decker, Scott H. 1996. "Collective and Normative Features of Gang Violence." *Justice Quarterly.* 13(2): 243–264.

Dunlap, Eloise, Bruce D. Johnson, and Ali Manwar. 1994. "A Successful Female Crack Dealer: Case Study of a Deviant Career." *Deviant Behavior.* 15: 1–25.

Einstadter, Werner and Stuart Henry. 1995. *Criminological Theory: An Analysis of Its Underlying Assumptions.* Fort Worth, TX: Harcourt Brace College Publishers.

Esbensen, Finn-Aage. 2000. "The National Evaluation of the Gang Resistance Education and Training (G.R.E.A.T.) Program." in *The Modern Gang Reader,* 2nd Edition, edited by Jody Miller, Cheryl L. Maxson, and Malcolm W. Klein. Los Angeles: Roxbury Publishing Company.

Esbensen, Finn-Aage and L. Thomas Winfree, Jr. 1998. "Race and Gender Differences Between Gang and Non-Gang Youths: Results from a Multi-Site Survey." *Justice Quarterly* 15: 505–526.

Fagan, Jeffrey. 1994. "Women and Drugs Revisited: Female Participation in the Cocaine Economy." *Journal of Drug Issues.* 24: 179–225.

Fagan, Jeffrey. 1990. "Social Processes of Delinquency and Drug Use Among Urban Gangs." Pp. 183–219 in *Gangs in America,* edited by C. Ronald Huff. Newbury Park: Sage Publications.

Federal Bureau of Investigation. 1996. *Crime in the United States, 1995.* Washington DC: U.S. Government Printing Office.

Gilfus, Mary E. 1992. "From Victims to Survivors to Offenders: Women's Routes of Entry and Immersion in to Street Crime." *Women and Criminal Justice.* 4: 63–89.

Glassner, Barry and Julia Loughlin. 1987. *Drugs in Adolescent Worlds: Burnouts to Straights.* New York: St. Martin's Press.

Harding, Sandra, ed. 1987. *Feminism and Methodology.* Bloomington: Indiana University Press.

Jacobs, Bruce A. 1999. *Dealing Crack: The Social World of Streetcorner Selling.* Boston: Northeastern University Press.

Jacobs, Bruce A. 1996. "Crack Dealers' Apprehension Avoidance Techniques: A Case of Restrictive Deterrence." *Justice Quarterly.* 13: 359–381.

Jacobs, Bruce A. and Jody Miller. 1998. "Crack Dealing, Gender, and Arrest Avoidance." *Social Problems.* 45: 550–569.

Kandiyoti, Deniz. 1988. "Bargaining with Patriarchy." *Gender & Society.* 2: 274–290.

Katz, Jack. 1988. *Seductions of Crime.* New York: Basic Books.

Klein, Malcolm W. 1995. *The American Street Gang: Its Nature, Prevalence and Control.* New York: Oxford University Press.

Lauderback, David, Joy Hansen, and Dan Waldorf. 1992. "'Sisters Are Doin' It For Themselves': A Black Female Gang in San Francisco." *The Gang Journal.* 1: 57–70.

Maher, Lisa. 1997. *Sexed Work: Gender, Race and Resistance in a Brooklyn Drug Market.* Oxford: Clarendon Press.

Maher, Lisa and Kathleen Daly. 1996. "Women in the Street-Level Drug Economy: Continuity or Change?" *Criminology.* 34: 465–492.

Messerschmidt, James W. 1995. "From patriarchy to gender: feminist theory, criminology and the challenge of diversity." Pp. 167–188 in *International Feminist Perspectives in Criminology: Engendering a Discipline,* edited by N.H. Rafter and F. Heidensohn. Philadelphia: Open University Press.

Messerschmidt, James W. 1993. *Masculinities and Crime.* Lanham, MD: Rowman & Littlefield.

Miller, Jody. 2001. *One of the Guys: Girls, Gangs and Gender.* New York: Oxford University Press.

Miller, Jody. 1998. "Up It Up: Gender and the Accomplishment of Street Robbery." *Criminology.* 36: 37–66.

Miller, Jody, and Rod K. Brunson. 2000. "Gender Dynamics in Youth Gangs: A Comparison of Male and Female Accounts." *Justice Quarterly* 17(3): 801–830.

Miller, Jody and Scott H. Decker. 2001. "Young Women and Gang Violence: An Examination of Gender, Street Offending and Violent Victimization in Gangs." *Justice Quarterly.* 18(1): 115–140.

Miller, Jody and Barry Glassner. 1997. "The 'Inside' and the 'Outside': Finding Realities in Interviews." Pp. 99–112 in David Silverman, ed. *Qualitative Research.* London: Sage Publications.

Moore, Joan. 1991. *Going Down to the Barrio: Homeboys and Homegirls in Change.* Philadelphia: Temple University Press.

Newburn, Tim and Elizabeth Stanko, eds. 1994. *Just Boys Doing Business?* New York: Routledge.

Richie, Beth E. 1996. *Compelled to Crime: The Gender Entrapment of Battered Black Women.* New York: Routledge.

Rosenfeld, Richard, Tim Bray, and Arlen Egley. 1999. "Facilitating Violence: A Comparison of Gang-Motivated, Gang-Affiliated, and Non-Gang Youth Homicides." *Journal of Quantitative Criminology.* 15: 495–516.

Simpson, Sally. 2000. "Gendered Theory and Single Sex Research." *DivisioNews*. Newsletter of the Division of Women and Crime, American Society of Criminology, August. (http://www.ou.edu/soc/dwc/newsletter.htm).

Simpson, Sally. 1991. "Caste, Class and Violent Crime: Explaining Differences in Female Offending." *Criminology*. 29: 115–135.

Simpson, Sally. 1989. "Feminist Theory, Crime and Justice." *Criminology*. 27: 605–631.

Simpson, Sally and Lori Elis. 1995. "Doing Gender: Sorting out the Caste and Crime Conundrum." *Criminology*. 33: 47–81.

Steffensmeier, Darrell J. 1983. "Organizational Properties and Sex-Segregation in the Underworld: Building a Sociological Theory of Sex Differences in Crime." *Social Forces*. 61: 1010–1032.

Steffensmeier, Darrell J. and Robert Terry. 1986. "Institutional Sexism in the Underworld: A View from the Inside." *Sociological Inquiry*. 56: 304–323.

Thornberry, Terence P. 1999. Personal Correspondence, April 2.

Thornberry, Terence P. 1997. "Membership in Youth Gangs and Involvement in Serious and Violent Offending." Pp. 147–166 in *Serious and Violent Juvenile Offenders: Risk Factors and Successful Interventions,* edited by Rolf Loeber and David P. Farrington. Thousand Oaks: Sage Publications.

Thorne, Barrie. 1998. Personal correspondence. September 17.

Thorne, Barrie. 1993. *Gender Play: Girls and Boys in School*. New Brunswick, NJ: Rutgers University Press.

Tong, Rosemarie. 1998. *Feminist Thought*. 2nd Edition. Boulder, CO: Westview Press.

West, Candace and Sarah Fenstermaker. 1995. "Doing Difference." *Gender & Society*. 9: 8–37.

West, Candace and Don H. Zimmerman. 1987. "Doing Gender." *Gender & Society*. 1: 125–151.

Wilson, James Q. and Richard J. Herrnstein. 1985. *Crime and Human Nature*. New York: Simon and Schuster.

Winfree, L. Thomas Jr., Kathy Fuller, Teresa Vigil, and G. Larry Mays. 1992. "The Definition and Measurement of 'Gang Status': Policy Implications for Juvenile Justice." *Juvenile and Family Court Journal*. 43: 29–37.

Wright, Richard T. and Scott H. Decker. 1997. *Armed Robbers in Action: Stickups and Street Culture*. Boston: Northeastern University Press.

Chapter 11

Assessing the Rationality of Criminal and Delinquent Behavior: A Focus on Actual Utility*

Timothy Brezina

At the heart of the rational choice perspective lies the assumption that criminal and delinquent offenders are goal-oriented and seek to benefit themselves by their behavior. Offenders, then, are said to exhibit a measure of rationality—on some level they consider the potential costs and benefits of crime and act accordingly (Cornish and Clarke 1986).

This assumption is important for several reasons. First, it challenges popular assumptions about the nature of offending behavior and is of particular interest in context of the "medicalization of deviance." As documented by a number of scholars, pathological accounts play an increasingly influential role in the interpretation of criminal and delinquent conduct (Conrad and Schneider 1992; Peele 1995; Sykes 1992). A noteworthy example is the most recent edition of the Diagnostic and Statistical Manual of Mental Disorders (American Psychiatric Association 1994), which lists a broad range of criminal and delinquent behaviors as indicators of possible disorder, including frequent lying, stealing, truancy, and running away (Richters and Cicchetti 1993).

While rational choice theorists do not deny the existence of pathological elements in the etiology of offending behavior, they imply that such behavior is more often guided by rational considerations (Cornish and Clarke 1986; see also Moffitt 1993). Indeed, as stated by one of its leading proponents, the rational choice approach "employs an explicit presumption of rationality as a safeguard against premature pathologization" (Cornish 1993, 365). The assumption of rationality, then, is of potential

* I would like to thank Edgar Kiser and the editors of this volume for their helpful comments on earlier versions of this chapter.

value to the extent that it restrains a tendency to "overpathologize" offend-ing (Cornish and Clarke 1986). To the extent that this assumption is cor-rect, the rational choice perspective is likely to provide a more constructive approach to the analysis of criminal and delinquent behavior.

The assumption of rationality is also important for a second reason. Assumptions about the essential nature of offending behavior have impli-cations for the effective control of crime and delinquency. If, on the one hand, offending behavior is best interpreted as a symptom of underlying disorder, then interventions designed to address the clinical needs of indi-vidual offenders are indicated. If, on the other hand, offending behavior is best interpreted as a rational and, therefore, predictable response to the offender's life situation, then interventions should address criminogenic features of the social environment.

In short, the assumption of rationality has important implications for the etiology and control of crime and delinquency. Consequently, research designed to evaluate this assumption should be of general interest to theo-rists and policy makers. The purpose of this chapter is to supplement and extend previous research on the rationality of offending behavior. This goal is achieved by examining the personal consequences of criminal and delin-quent involvement. Whereas previous studies have focused mainly on the decision-making processes of offenders and the concept of expected utility, an examination of personal consequences allows us to gauge the *actual utility* of crime and delinquency. I argue that this approach is superior in certain respects and helps to shed greater light on the rational (or irra-tional) components and possible adaptive (or maladaptive) properties of offending behavior.

The remainder of this chapter is divided into four sections: (1) the meanings of rationality, (2) the rationality debate, (3) empirical evidence, and (4) tentative conclusions. First, I begin with a brief review of "ration-ality" and the meaning of this term as found in the crime and rational choice literature. I also discuss the results and limitations of previous stud-ies that have attempted to assess the rationality of offenders. Second, I pres-ent the two sides of the rationality debate in greater detail (i.e., pathologi-cal and rational choice accounts). To help adjudicate between pathological and rational choice interpretations of crime and delinquency, the third sec-tion examines relevant evidence on the actual utility of offending behavior. Finally, in the fourth section, I draw some preliminary conclusions and pro-pose a tentative resolution of the rationality debate.

THE MEANINGS OF RATIONALITY
The Narrow Model of Rational Choice

Studies on the rationality of offenders are informed by one of two models of rational choice: the "narrow model" or the "wide model" (Opp 1997). The narrow model is associated with neoclassical economic theory and is based on the assumption that rational actors behave in ways that would be expected, from an objective point of view, to maximize personal gain or utility. According to this model, rational actors consider possible courses of action based on an appreciation of objective constraints. Each course of action is ranked in terms of its expected utility, based on the extent and probability that it will satisfy preferences for tangible gains such as money or promotion. To act rationally is to choose the highest-ranked option within the feasible set of alternatives (Elster 1986, 4).

One advantage of the narrow model is that it erects a clear and relatively unambiguous standard for judging the rationality of behavior. This advantage, however, is also one of its major drawbacks. According to the narrow model, rational action requires full awareness of possible options. Rational action also requires accurate and complete information, which is needed to calculate such things as the probability of punishment. In short, the narrow model of rational choice assumes the existence of optimal conditions for decision-making and erects an ideal standard of rationality. Proponents of the narrow model recognize that this approach is not necessarily realistic—at times individuals may face situations of uncertainty, be forced to act on incomplete or distorted information, and draw faulty conclusions. Nevertheless, it is argued that the straightforward assumptions of the narrow model capture the essential features of competition and market-oriented action, these assumptions are relatively easy to model and, therefore, this approach can be useful in the explanation of human behavior (Opp 1997).

The Wide Model of Rational Choice

Leading proponents of the rational choice perspective of crime do not suggest that offenders operate under optimal conditions of decision-making, nor do they claim that offenders are particularly competent decision-makers. Rather, their intent is simply to highlight the "rational and adaptive *aspects* of offending," which are said to involve the processing of information, strategic decision-making, and the choice of actions based on their expected utility or adaptive value to the offender (Cornish and Clarke1986, vi, emphasis added). This view is associated with the wide model of rational choice, which embraces the assumption of "bounded" or limited rationality.

The wide model of rational choice departs from the narrow model in a number of ways. First, unlike the narrow model, the wide model of rational choice does not assume that actors are fully informed, that they necessarily possess accurate information, or that they engage in extensive cost-benefit calculations. Instead, the wide model emphasizes the importance of perceived or subjective constraints in the decision-making process and merely presumes some set of logical beliefs about the causal structure of the situation which, in the actor's mind, links feasible courses of action to some anticipated outcome. Second, the wide model recognizes a diversity of possible motives including intangible incentives, such as a desire for excitement, thrills, or a sense of power and control (Katz 1988; Piquero and Hickman 1999; Tittle 1995). Third, at least certain versions of the wide model appear to soften the assumption of utility maximization. Instead of maximizing utility, it is recognized that actors may settle for anticipated outcomes that simply promise enough gain to satisfy immediate requirements (Walsh 1986). Rational action, in this view, can take the form of utility "satisficing."

From the standpoint of the wide model, rationality is thus a matter of degree. The degree and extent of information processing, strategic decision-making, and, hence, rationality may vary "from offender to offender and from crime to crime" (Cornish and Clarke 1986, vii). Moreover, rationality in this model is relative and subjective and must be assessed from the offender's point of view—taking into account his or her individual preferences, circumstances, perceptions of these circumstances, and what might seem reasonable. According to the wide model, then, behavior is rational to the extent it involves a process of reasoning and offers, or is expected to offer, some benefit to the offender.

Not surprisingly, the wide model of rational choice has been criticized for its lack of elegance and precision. In contrast to the narrow model, it suggests a relatively non-restrictive and hence ambiguous standard of rationality and one might question its usefulness—even if the assumptions underlying this approach are more realistic. Yet, if we shift our point of reference, and contrast the wide model of rational choice with models of criminal and delinquent *irrationality*, the significance of the wide model can be appreciated. As stated above, the assumption of rationality is intended to discourage premature "pathologization" and this purpose is not compromised by adopting a less restrictive model of rational choice. Like the narrow model of rational choice, the wide model depicts offenders as fundamentally goal-oriented actors for whom criminal and delinquent involvement is intended to serve some meaningful or constructive purpose (Opp

1997). As described below, this image of the offender contrasts sharply with pathological accounts.

PREVIOUS RESEARCH ON THE RATIONALITY OF OFFENDING BEHAVIOR
Crime and Decision-Making

To assess the rationality of offending behavior, numerous studies have examined the decision-making processes of shoplifters, robbers, drug users, and other offenders (e.g., Bennett 1986; Carroll and Weaver 1986; Feeney 1986; Jacobs 1999; Jacobs and Wright 1999; Piquero and Rengert 1999; Wright and Decker 1997). Although the results of these studies are somewhat mixed, at least one general conclusion can be drawn with reasonable confidence: there is little evidence that offenders meet the standard of rationality erected by the narrow model of rational choice. While certain accounts suggest that experienced offenders possess detailed crime-relevant information and act on this information in order to minimize risk, evade apprehension, and/or manipulate the legal system, this does not necessarily mean that offenders are optimal decision-makers (Carroll and Weaver 1986).

Consistent with the expectations of behavioral decision theory and the wide model of rational choice, the bulk of the evidence suggests that, while offenders may be sensitive to such elements as risks and payoffs, they "do not combine this information optimally" (Carroll and Weaver 1986, 21). Rather, people in general tend to employ a number of cognitive "shortcuts" designed to simplify available information, reduce the number of behavioral possibilities to be taken seriously, and otherwise bring the complex demands of information-processing in line with their limited cognitive capacity (Johnson and Payne 1986; Trasler 1993). When estimating the odds of apprehension, for example, individuals might focus on information that comes most readily to mind, such as the number of people they know who were caught (Stafford and Warr 1993). While this strategy increases cognitive efficiency, it also increases the likelihood that estimates will be influenced unduly by a particularly vivid memory, or by the facts of a single case. Given limited mental capacity, cognitive shortcuts of this nature are reasonable, but they nevertheless increase the odds of making a mistake (Carroll and Weaver 1986; Johnson and Payne 1986).

Offenders are no exception in this regard and relevant research points in the direction of limited rationality. Interviews with experienced shoplifters, for example, suggest that they typically gather and assess a wide range of information before considering a shoplifting attempt, including information about the size and accessibility of the target item, the presence of observers and other obstacles, and the likelihood of outwitting various security measures (Carroll and Weaver 1986; see also Nagin and Paternoster 1993). These offenders, however, pay little attention to seemingly relevant considerations beyond the immediate situation, such as the possible consequences of apprehension, arrest, or jail (Carroll and Weaver 1986).

Research in this vein also points to the importance of intangible incentives, which are recognized exclusively by the wide model of rational choice. Feeney's (1986) interviews with robbers in northern California uncovered a host of motives besides money, including a desire for excitement, a desire to intimidate others, and a felt need to retaliate against an opponent during a fight or argument. Feeney (1986) also observes that "most of the robbers appear to have taken a highly casual approach to their crimes," with little or no advance planning (p. 59). Nevertheless, he concludes that the robbers under study can be viewed as rational in a limited sense; their offenses were deliberate and were intended to satisfy various goals.

Expected versus Actual Utility

Studies that focus on the decision-making processes of offenders are revealing and can help to identify effective crime-control strategies. But studies of this nature appear to be limited in at least one respect. These studies tend to examine the nature and extent of planning and deliberation leading up to the criminal event and, thus, focus predominantly on the expected rather than actual utility of offending behavior. This focus on expected utility, in turn, tends to be joined with the assumption that offending behavior is rational only to the extent that it involves planning and deliberation.

These observations are particularly significant in light of Feeney's (1986) study of robbers, described above. This study not only finds limited evidence of planning and deliberation on the part of robbers but, interestingly, this was especially true of the more experienced offenders. Based on a forward-looking approach, one might be tempted to conclude that the most experienced robbers are the least rational. Yet Feeney recognizes an alternative interpretation: the more extensive experience of these robbers may serve as a substitute for detailed planning and deliberation. It is possible that they "simply followed an existing pattern for their offenses" and "did little new planning for their current offenses because they already had an approach they liked" (Feeney 1986, 59). Indeed, the wide model of rational choice recognizes that decision-making can be forward looking (based on expected utility) or backward-looking—that is, based on actual utility, as judged on the basis of past experience (Opp 1997; Mueller 1986).

A further illustration is provided by Bennett's (1986) study of opioid addicts. Bennett observes that decisions to try an opioid drug (e.g., opium, heroin) represent meaningful and purposeful lifestyle choices for users and, in some cases, even the process of becoming addicted is intentional and planned. In the words of one addict, "Drugs fascinated me from an early age, especially the junkie culture. . . . Let's put it this way: I wasn't worried about becoming an addict, I wanted to become one" (Bennett 1986, 95). Bennett also identifies the self-medicating properties of opioid drugs as a conscious reason for persistent drug use. It was the experience of many users that these drugs served to alleviate anxiety, depression, and provided a sense of well-being. Decisions to continue the use of opioid drugs, then, appear to be have been based largely on past experience with their mood-altering effects or, in other words, their actual utility.

The above observations are also significant in light of the criteria of psychopathology outlined in the mental health literature. As described below, one of the more powerful criterions of psychological disorder is the extent to which a particular behavior or behavior pattern causes distress to self (Raine 1993; Richters and Cicchetti 1993). Thus, according to this criterion, the actual rather than expected utility of behavior provides a basis for assessing the self-defeating (or irrational) nature of a particular course of action and, hence, the presence of disorder. For this reason, evidence pertaining to the actual utility of offending behavior should prove to be more decisive in the context of the larger rationality debate.

Below, I take a closer look at the actual utility of offending behavior. In particular, I examine evidence on the personal consequences of crime and delinquency, consider the extent to which such behavior is beneficial or self-defeating, and, on this basis, draw tentative conclusions about the rationality of offenders. But first, it is necessary to examine both sides of the rationality debate in greater detail.

TWO SIDES OF THE RATIONALITY DEBATE
Crime as Fundamentally Irrational Behavior

In light of rational choice arguments, it is intriguing to observe that criminal and delinquent behaviors are currently listed as symptoms of psychopathology in the Diagnostic and Statistical Manual of Mental Disorders, Fourth Edition (DSM-IV) (American Psychiatric Association 1994). Young people meet the criteria for "Adolescent-Onset Conduct Disorder" if their behavior causes significant impairment in social, academic, or occupational functioning and if three or more of the following criteria have been present during the past year, with at least one of these criterion present in the past six months: frequent lying; truancy from school (beginning before age thirteen); running away from home on repeated occasions; frequent violation of curfew (beginning before age thirteen); theft of property; property destruction; breaking into a house, building, or car; involvement in purse snatching, mugging, extortion, or armed robbery; arson; initiation of physical fights; use of a weapon during a fight; forcing someone into sexual activity; physical cruelty to animals; physical cruelty to people.

Older offenders meet the criteria "Antisocial Personality Disorder" if they exhibit some evidence of conduct disorder before the age of fifteen and if at least three of the following traits have been present since age fifteen: deceitfulness; repeated performance of acts that are grounds for arrest; repeated physical fights or assaults; impulsivity or failure to plan ahead; failure to sustain consistent work behavior or honor financial obligations; recklessness and disregard for the safety of self and others; lack of remorse. Offenders involved in particular types of criminal involvement (e.g., indecent exposure, compulsive shoplifting, arson, periodic aggression/loss of control) may meet the criteria for more specific disorders such as "Exhibitionism," "Kleptomania," "Pyromania," and "Intermittent Explosive Disorder."

In short, most criminal and delinquent acts have been incorporated in the DSM-IV, either as indicators of larger "behavioral syndromes" such as conduct disorder or as individual disorders in their own right (Raine 1993). Although specific justifications for each disorder are not provided, the DSM-IV states that the following definition of mental disorder helped to guide decisions regarding classification: "each of the mental disorders is conceptualized as a clinically significant behavioral or psychological syndrome or pattern that occurs in an individual and that is associated with present distress (e.g., a painful symptom) or disability (i.e., impairment in one or more important areas of functioning) or with a significantly increased risk of suffering death, pain, disability, or an important loss of freedom" (American Psychiatric Association 1994, xxi). Additional qualifications stipulate that the syndrome or pattern must not represent a culturally sanctioned response to a particular event (e.g., death of a loved one) and must be considered a manifestation of dysfunction in the individual.

This conceptualization of disorder emphasizes the personal consequences of behavior, with special attention given to behavior patterns that jeopardize the social, psychological, or physical well-being of the individual. In short, the presence of mental disorder is indicated by behavior patterns that are judged to be self-defeating and, hence, irrational. Criminal and delinquent behaviors appear to be self-defeating in a number of ways and therefore represent likely indicators of psychopathology according to this conceptualization. Such behaviors threaten to disrupt interpersonal relationships, academic performance, employment, and increase the risk of arrest and incarceration—especially when serious and persistent. As Raine (1993) observes, "a very high proportion of criminals" is likely to meet the criteria for one of the disorders described above (p. 16). According to

Raine, this fact provides partial justification for the view of serious and persistent criminality as an overarching clinical disorder.

Crime as Fundamentally Rational Behavior

Critics of the above view contend that the listing of criminal and delinquent acts in the DSM-IV "decontextualizes" crime, focuses attention away from the life circumstances that may promote deviant behavior, and strips away any meaning that such involvement may have for the offender. In certain social contexts, for instance, criminal and delinquent behavior may be rewarded or encouraged (Richters and Cicchetti 1993). In other contexts, such behavior may represent a coping technique or problem-solving response (Brezina 1996, 2000a).

To be sure, the DSM-IV is not insensitive to these concerns. The authors of the DSM-IV stress that its diagnostic criteria are meant to serve as guidelines for clinicians and are not to be applied mechanically. Assessing the clinical significance of behavioral patterns, especially in terms of functional impairment, is described as an "inherently difficult clinical judgement" (American Psychiatric Association 1994, 7). In certain instances, the social context in which a particular behavior occurs is mentioned as an important consideration. For example, it is said that runaway behavior does not typically qualify as a criterion for conduct disorder if it is a consequence of family abuse. Otherwise it is left to the clinician to distinguish between individual and environmental pathology, with the suggestion that it "may be helpful for the clinician to consider the social and economic context in which the undesirable behaviors have occurred" (American Psychiatric Association 1994, 88).

As implied by the treatment of runaway behavior in the DSM-IV, the rationality of a particular course of action may not be apparent without an adequate appreciation of contextual factors. For this reason, theorists who emphasize the normal and rational aspects of offending tend to highlight the specific challenges and interactional problems that are believed to evoke criminal and delinquent responses from otherwise normal persons.

Rational interpretations of violence and aggression provide a useful illustration. In the context of socially disorganized neighborhoods—where individuals may face a relatively high risk of personal victimization—the presentation of an aggressive demeanor can serve an important protective function. By demonstrating a willingness and capacity for violent counter-attack, an important message is sent to harmdoers: "I'm not to be messed with" (Anderson 1994). In fact, individuals may find functional value in a strategy of "rational irrationality." By campaigning for a reputation as crazy, unpredictable, and out of control, one can intimidate potential victimizers and deter challenges to self (Fagan and Wilkinson 1998; Katz 1988).

Aggression may serve similar functions in the context of a dysfunctional family environment. According to Patterson (1982), children exposed to hostile treatment by parents or siblings (e.g., teasing, slapping, and hitting) may learn to adopt aggressive behavior patterns because violent responses can facilitate the termination of undesired treatment, help to deter future attacks, and thus provide a means to control the behavior of family members. Moreover, to the extent that aggressive counterattacks are successful and force others to retreat, such behavior is likely to be rewarded and reinforced.

While aggressive behavior in the above contexts cannot be described as utilitarian in the classical sense of the term, it is implied that such behavior can nonetheless be purposeful, beneficial, and directed toward the realization of non-economic goals, such as control over the social environment. This observation highlights the importance of intangible incentives associated with the wide model of rational choice.

The emphasis on intangible incentives is particularly apparent in criminological works that stress the symbolic functions of crime and delinquency. For example, a common interpretation of juvenile delinquency is that it represents a means used by adolescents to assert control in an adult world that undermines their autonomy. As Moffitt (1993) describes, contemporary adolescents find themselves trapped in a maturity gap, "chronological hostages of a time warp between biological and social age" (p. 687). As the importance of personal power becomes increasingly evident and is impressed on them as never before, the denial of real autonomy, the inability to influence decisions of major import, and the remoteness of social ascribed maturity become "painfully apparent" (Moffitt 1993, 687). Delinquency is one possible response and is interpreted by Moffitt as a statement of personal independence.

Delinquency may allow youths to realize a sense of control and independence in a number of ways. First, delinquent involvement may symbolically affirm the offender's autonomy in the face of adult constraints, restrictions on behavior, and authority that is perceived to be coercive, demeaning, or unjust. By flouting adult rules, the offender shows disdain for those in control as well as the capacity to defy their commands (Brezina 2000b; Marwell 1966; Matza 1964; Tittle 1995). Second, delinquent behavior may enable youths to increase the amount of objective control they exercise over the social environment (Agnew 1984). Delinquency, for example, may allow adolescents to avoid or escape environments where their control is undermined (e.g., truancy and running away) or to obtain the resources necessary for autonomy and control (e.g., money and other goods).

Whereas some theorists emphasize the possible control-enhancement or control-maintenance functions of criminal and delinquent behavior, others have emphasized self-enhancement as an underlying motive. According to Kaplan (1980), much delinquency is motivated by a desire to protect or enhance self-esteem. Delinquent involvement is appealing to self-derogating youths because it may enable them "to attack (symbolically or otherwise) the perceived basis" of self-rejecting attitudes, avoid self-devaluing experiences and relationships, or it may offer "substitute patterns with self-enhancing potential" (Kaplan 1978, 256). Likewise, Katz (1988) suggests that, in the offender's eyes, criminal involvement may signify a particular brand of competence or daring and thus contribute to a sense of personal accomplishment.

Similarly, social-psychological strain theorists interpret much crime and delinquency as a form of "corrective action" in response to aversive environments, or "strain" (Agnew 1992). Criminal and delinquent responses to strain may be appealing because they can facilitate the regulation of negative emotions such as anger and despair. In an earlier work (Brezina 1996), I suggested that delinquency may allow youths to cope with strain and negative affect for a number of reasons. First, delinquent escape attempts such as truancy and running away allow youths to minimize time spent in environments that give rise to high levels of negative affect. Second, drug and alcohol use may allow youths to ward off depression and despair and compensate for a lack of positive affect (see also Newcomb and Harlow 1986). Third, delinquency may allow youths to satisfy desires for retaliation and revenge, and certain data indicate that retaliatory behavior is associated with a subsequent reduction in angry arousal (see Patterson 1982, 146–147).

Rational interpretations of crime and delinquency, then, suggest that such behavior may fulfill a number of protective functions in response to various psychosocial problems. Moreover, the above interpretations assume that crime and delinquency can be *effective*, allowing individuals to maintain real or perceived control, protect or enhance self-esteem, and manage negative affect (Brezina 2000a). In other words, criminal and delinquent behaviors have adaptive value or utility in certain contexts. Furthermore, these functional interpretations have been pitched as general accounts of criminal and delinquent behavior (e.g., Agnew 1992; Kaplan 1980; Tittle 1995) and therefore imply that, once sufficient attention is given to contextual factors, much if not most criminal and delinquent behavior can be explained in rational terms.

CRIME, DELINQUENCY, AND ACTUAL UTILITY: A REVIEW OF THE EVIDENCE

In essence, the larger rationality debate appears to hinge on the personal consequences of criminal and delinquent offending. Some theorists emphasize the dysfunctional or self-defeating properties of criminal and delinquent involvement and imply that it is best viewed as irrational behavior (Raine 1993). Other theorists emphasize the adaptive properties and functional utility of criminal and delinquent behavior—at least in certain contexts—and therefore endorse a rational interpretation.

To help adjudicate between these competing interpretations, it is useful to consider the actual extent to which criminal and delinquent behavior is associated with beneficial or detrimental outcomes for the offender. In the course of testing various criminological theories, a sizable body of research has accumulated on the personal consequences of criminal and delinquent involvement. This research provides a basis for assessing the actual utility of offending behavior and, although a definitive resolution of the rationality debate remains elusive, such research can point in the direction of one view or the other. Relevant studies have tended to focus either on the short-term or the long-term (life-course) consequences of criminal and delinquent involvement.

Short-Term Consequences

A number of studies suggest that, for some offenders, criminal and delinquent behaviors represent successful adaptations—at least in the short run. Data presented by Wood et al. (1997) indicate that the offending experience is typically associated with a range of positive emotional sensations. Offenders in their study indicated that the commission of various crimes often contributes to feelings of power, personal accomplishment, of feeling "alive," and "on top of the world." The authors conclude that the pursuit of deviant and risky behavior (also referred to as "edgework") may represent one way that persons on the margins of society achieve a sense of self-determination and self-actualization. In other words, criminal involvement may represent an alternative means of goal attainment for individuals who associate conventional relations with adversity, have a disdain for conventional pursuits, and turn elsewhere "for symbolistic situations that provide meaning to their lives" (Wood et al. 1997, 343; see also Agnew 1990; Katz 1988).

Likewise, in a recent study (Brezina 2000b), I found qualified empirical support for the control-maintenance interpretation of delinquency. Data indicate that male adolescents tend to respond to adult constraints and impositions (e.g., parental authoritarianism) with a diminished sense of personal control, or fatalism. However, the control-deflating consequences of adult constraints are minimized when delinquent involvement is extensive. Delinquency, then, appears to "neutralize" or negate the mood of fatalism that ordinarily stems from the impositions of adult society. Presumably, delinquency affirms the autonomy of youths in the face of adult constraints, symbolically or otherwise.

Although the control-related benefits of crime and delinquency may be largely symbolic in nature, as the above studies suggest, some evidence indicates that offending behavior may allow individuals to realize objective control. Patterson (1982) presents data showing that, in the context of dysfunctional family dynamics, aggressive counterattacks by children are often successful in terminating noxious treatment by family members. My own study of teenage violence toward parents indicates that parent assault may serve a similar function—enabling youths to intimidate parents and forcing them to "back off" (Brezina 1999).

Studies inspired by Kaplan's (1980) self-derogation theory of delinquency also point to certain positive outcomes of delinquent involvement. Drawing on longitudinal data, Rosenberg Schooler, and Schoenbach (1989) observe a reciprocal relationship between self-esteem and delinquency among lower-class male youths, characterized by countervailing effects. Low levels of self-esteem are associated with elevated levels of delinquency. But delinquency, in turn, appears to lead to the enhancement of self-esteem. This pattern of results is consistent with the view that, in certain contexts, delinquency represents a successful adaptation to problems involving self-derogation (see also Kaplan 1978; Wells 1980).

In a study inspired by social-psychological strain theory (Brezina 1996), I examined the coping properties of delinquent behavior, especially in terms of emotion regulation. The results of this study suggest that delinquent involvement allows adolescents to minimize the deleterious consequences of strain, as indexed by family and school problems. In comparison to their non-delinquent counterparts, delinquent adolescents were found to be less vulnerable to the negative emotional consequences of strain as evidenced by lower levels of strain-induced anger, resentment, anxiety, and depression. Presumably, delinquent involvement minimizes the psychic toll of strain because it enables youths to escape or avoid strain (e.g., truancy and running away from home), compensate for the adverse effects of strain (e.g., drug use to ward off depression and despair), and/or satisfy desires for retaliation and revenge (see also Agnew 1990; Novacek, Raskin, and Hogan 1991).

Long-Term Consequences

While the above findings highlight the short-term benefits of offending behavior and therefore lend support to a rational choice interpretation, concerns about the long-term consequences of criminal and delinquent involvement discourage a premature resolution of the rationality debate. With the exception of the above studies, criminologists have typically emphasized the long-term maladaptive properties of criminal and delinquent behavior. For various reasons, persistent criminality is likely to exact a high price in relationships with parents, teachers, employers, and others. Agnew (1997) raises the possibility that persistent delinquency by strained individuals may antagonize others and lead to more strain in their relationships over time (see also Caspi, Bem, and Elder 1989). Sampson and Laub (1993) observe that "delinquency tends to mortgage one's future by generating negative consequences for life chances" (p. 142) (see also Hagan 1991, 1997; Moffitt 1993).

Studies on the life-course consequences of criminal and delinquent involvement tend to confirm the existence of a relatively bleak future for individuals with a long history of antisocial conduct. While participation in a delinquent subculture may satisfy the immediate social-psychological needs of adolescents, several studies show that this type of involvement tends to be associated with diminished life chances, as indicated by negative effects on education and occupational status attainment (Hagan 1991; Sampson and Laub 1990; Tanner, Davies, and O'Grady 1999). Former delinquents also tend to experience relatively high levels of hopelessness and despair by early to mid-adulthood, perhaps because they have come to grips with their entrapment in menial, unstable, and unrewarding jobs (Hagan 1997). Among individuals with an especially long and persistent history of antisocial behavior, later outcomes also include high rates of drug and alcohol dependence, unstable relationships, victimization, accidents, poor health, homelessness, and other troubles (Bardone et al. 1996; Moffitt 1993; Robins 1966).

It is not yet clear why criminal and delinquent histories tend to be associated with these negative outcomes (Tanner, Davies, and O'Grady 1999). One possibility involves a "labeling" effect. The stigma attached to a criminal record, for example, may lead to difficulties in securing stable and meaningful employment. Consistent with this explanation, Hagan (1991) finds that police contacts mediate the effect of male subcultural preferences (e.g., favorable orientations toward fighting, theft, and vandalism) on future occupational prestige. Another possibility involves the persistence of subcultural attitudes or orientations that make adjustment in the conventional world problematic, even if individuals are no longer active in crime. As Jencks (1992) observes, "Few employers want unskilled workers who are assertive. . . . Even fewer want assertive workers from an alien culture they don't understand" (p. 129). A related explanation involves the possibility that serious and persistent criminal involvement may be symptomatic of underlying traits or deficits—such as impulsivity, hyperactivity, and learning problems—which interfere with long-term adjustment (Moffitt 1993).

While life-course research paints a fairly consistent picture, it is important to note the existence of substantial variation in the long-term effects of offending behavior. For example, some studies draw attention to the existence of "successful" criminal careers, involving high-rate offenders who manage to avoid arrest and incarceration (Johnson, Natarajan, and Sanabria 1993). Likewise, research by Hagan (1991) suggests that the negative occupational consequences of delinquency accrue mainly to lower-class males. Presumably, middle-class males enjoy greater access to "second chances." Most of the research in this area suggests that negative consequences accrue disproportionately to the most serious and persistent offenders (Hagan 1991; Moffitt 1993).

It is also important to note that offenders are not necessarily oblivious to the long-term negative consequences of criminal and delinquent involvement. It appears that many offenders become increasingly sensitive to the negative consequences of crime as they age, and their behavior is responsive to this fact. This sensitivity may stem from a humiliating experience involving alcohol or other drugs, an experience with arrest or jail, rejection by a significant other, getting "burned" by delinquent associates, the experience that delinquencies and substance use are interfering with life goals, or a general culmination of a series of negative life events (Cusson and Pinsonneault 1986; Labouvie 1996; Mulvey and LaRosa 1986; Waldorf 1983). With experience, offenders develop greater sensitivity to the "law of averages." They come to realize that the more crimes they commit, the greater the cumulative probability of their being caught and of experiencing other troubles (Cusson and Pinsonneault 1986). As Shover (1983) observes, the aging process of ordinary offenders typically includes a redefinition of their youthful behavior as "foolish," "dangerous," "self-defeating," and of "limited value for constructing the future" (p. 211).

Increasing sensitivity to the long-term maladaptive properties of crime and delinquency may explain why most offenders do not persist in their offending beyond late adolescence or early adulthood (Moffitt 1993). Nonetheless, a small percentage of offenders maintain high levels of anti-social conduct into adulthood. The relevant literature contains accounts of offenders who, despite their failure at crime, "sustained a pattern of petty hustles or long-term drunkeness," and "resorted to desperate, high-risk crimes with apparent disregard for the potential consequences" (Shover 1983, 215). Representing the most perplexing cases, these offenders have been variously described as "sociopaths," "psychopaths," or "life-course-persistent" offenders (Lykken 1995; Moffitt 1993).

The self-defeating behavior of these offenders is likely to be a product of inadequate socialization and/or traits that interfere with effective socialization such as impulsiveness and irritability (Lykken 1995; Moffitt 1993; Patterson, DeBaryshe, and Ramsey 1989). Furthermore, because of these problems, life-course-persistent antisocial individuals are at risk for failure in a variety of developmental domains. As children they are exposed to parental maltreatment, fail at school, and are rejected by prosocial peers (Patterson, DeBaryshe, and Ramsey 1989). They are thus "robbed of chances" to practice prosocial behavior and consequently develop a "restricted behavioral repertoire" (Moffitt 1993, 683–684). Perhaps as a result, persistent offenders fail to substitute self-defeating behavior with conventional alternatives and also adopt a fatalistic attitude toward the possibility of behavioral change. The persistent offenders studied by Shover (1983), for example, saw their behavior as self-defeating but maintained the belief that it was "too late for them to accomplish anything in life" (p. 215).

DISCUSSION AND CONCLUSION

Data on the personal consequences of criminal and delinquent involvement provide abundant support for a rational choice interpretation. These data point to a number of immediate benefits of offending behavior, including the experience of positive emotional sensations (e.g., excitement, power, and sense of accomplishment), self-enhancement, pain-avoidance, the alleviation of negative affective states, and the maintenance of real or perceived control over the social environment. These data are important for several reasons. They point to the actual utility and possible adaptive value of offending behavior, supplement existing data on the expected utility of offending, and help to explain the appeal of criminal and delinquent involvement for many individuals.

Nevertheless, a complete assessment of the rationality of offending behavior must also consider its self-defeating aspects, which tend to surface in its more serious and persistent forms. While crime and delinquency may offer short-term gains, relevant data indicate that severe and chronic offending tends to be associated with a host of negative outcomes, including alienation from family and friends, low levels of educational and occupational status, incarceration and loss of freedom, poor health, victimization, accidents, and the prospect of an early demise. Thus, while criminal and delinquent behavior may be rational in the near term (at least in certain environmental contexts), in the long run it tends to be self-defeating and, hence, has the appearance of irrationality.

To be sure, the pursuit of risky behavior by itself is not a sufficient criterion for the attribution of irrationality (see Richters and Cicchetti 1993). But the combination of risk and certain other features of persistent criminality, documented in a number of cases, arguably points in this direction;

namely, persistence in offending behavior despite recognition of its self-defeating consequences (Shover 1983; see also Khantzian 1985).

This assessment does not exclude the possibility of "successful" criminal careers, although it should be noted that the success of such careers is often narrowly defined in terms of the ability to avoid arrest and incarceration. Nor does this assessment imply that chronic offenders necessarily reach a point when they no longer reap benefits from criminal involvement. In all likelihood, even the more serious and persistent offenders reap meaningful short-term benefits from crime and delinquency, despite the prospect of negative consequences in the long run. Among addicts, for example, Khantzian (1985) observes a stubborn reliance on powerful drugs to provide immediate relief from painful affective states, even as this coping strategy ultimately contributes to further psychic pain and other troubles.

In this sense, serious and chronic offending appears to resemble a form of irrationality referred to as "akrasia," or weakness of the will. As described by Elster (1986), akratic behavior involves the intentional pursuit of immediate gratification despite awareness of more reasonable options. Taking another drink "against one's own better judgement is a familiar example" (Elster 1986, 15; see also Trasler 1993).

Occasional akratic decision-making is understandable from a psychological standpoint. While the immediate consequences of behavior are predictable, distal consequences tend to be vague, less certain, and less controllable (Carroll and Weaver 1986). Akratic decision-making of a persistent nature is more difficult to understand, especially when accumulated experience has shattered illusions of personal invulnerability to negative consequences (Cusson and Pinsonneault 1986). Presumably, such behavior can be attributed to individual-level traits that interfere with adjustment to changing circumstances, such as impulsivity or psychiatric disorder (Khantzian 1985; Moffitt 1993; but see Sampson and Laub 1997). Measures of impulsivity and self-control do, in fact, account for some of the observed variance in serious offending (Longshore 1998).

The above assessment, while tentative, happens to be consistent with Moffitt's (1993) developmental taxonomy, which makes a distinction between "adolescence-limited" and "life-course-persistent" offending (see also Lyken 1995; Patterson, DeBaryshe, and Ramsey 1989; Raine 1993). According to Moffitt, most offenders can be classified as adolescence-limited offenders. Their offending behavior begins in adolescence as an adaptive response to the social world faced by teens (especially pressures to assert maturity and independence) and then declines as they move into adulthood, when such behavior is likely to interfere with social adjustment and life goals. The prevalence of adolescence-limited offending, in turn, is "so great that it is normal rather than abnormal" (Moffitt 1997, 39; see also Krueger et al. 1994; Shedler and Block 1990). In addition, the behavior of adolescence-limited offenders is flexible and responsive to changing circumstances. As such, the behavior of these short-term offenders cannot be described as psychopathology.

In contrast, the problem behavior of a much smaller subgroup of offenders begins early in life, resulting from a combination of neurological deficits and family adversity. These life-course-persistent offenders maintain high levels of antisocial involvement beyond childhood and adolescence. Their behavior contributes to additional problems, proves to be self-defeating, is unresponsive to changing circumstances, and is said to reflect a time-stable propensity to offend. The behavior of life-course-persistent offenders (believed to constitute approximately five percent of the male population), then, suggests psychopathology (Moffitt 1993).

In terms of the debate between rational choice and pathological interpretations, the above assessment suggests a compromise. Given the apparent short-term utility of criminal and delinquent adaptations, rational choice interpretations of offending behavior are highly credible. However, criminal and delinquent involvement appears to be rational in a limited and mainly "local" sense (what Niggli [1997] refers to as "instrumental rationality"). The predominant focus of the rational choice perspective is on the influence of situational factors surrounding the criminal event, and thus an emphasis on local or instrumental rationality is justified. Yet, in the interest of highlighting the "rational and adaptive aspects of offending" (Cornish and Clarke 1986, vi), it would be wise to stress that the focus here is on the instrumental rationality of immediate behavior—and not necessarily the rationality of criminal lifestyles or careers.

The negative consequences associated with life-course-persistent offending, on the other hand, lend a measure of plausibility to pathological interpretations. Yet pathological accounts appear to underestimate the short-term utility of offending behavior, perhaps because advocates of this approach tend to equate rationality with that which is reasonable, good, and is a contributor to long-term stability (what Niggli [1997] refers to as "value rationality"). This fact may explain the pervasive influence of pathological accounts (Conrad and Schneider 1992; Peele 1995; Richters and Cicchetti 1993) despite a growing body of evidence documenting the short-term utility of criminal and delinquent behavior.

The above assessment also has noteworthy implications for crime and delinquency control. Research on the short-term utility of crime and delinquency points to the self-reinforcing potential of deviant adaptations. This may help to explain not only the appeal of crime and delinquency for many individuals, but also the limited ability of formal punishment to deter offending behavior (Paternoster 1989; Foglia 1997). The short-term benefits of crime, delinquency, and drug use appear to be relatively certain and immediate (see Wood et al. 1997), whereas official punishment for such behaviors, although potentially severe, is rare and delayed (Felson 1998; see also Moffitt 1983).

Yet despite their self-reinforcing potential, criminal and delinquent adaptations are not universally appealing or reinforcing. Reinforcement of this kind is likely to be a "variable phenomenon," which is influenced by the characteristics of individuals "and their life situations" (Simons, Conger, and Whitbeck 1988, 303). The short-term benefits of criminal and delinquent involvement may be relatively unattractive and, in fact, *experienced* as less rewarding to individuals who possess significant stakes in conformity (see Wood et al. 1997). An important task for future research will be to identify the characteristics and life situations that are relevant in this regard (e.g., factors related to strain, social learning, and self and social control), with the hope of developing interventions that ultimately reduce the real or perceived utility and reinforcement value of criminal and delinquent adaptations (Brezina 2000a).

REFERENCES

Agnew, Robert. 1984. "Autonomy and Delinquency." *Sociological Perspectives* 27: 219–40.

———. 1990. "The Origins of Delinquent Events: An Examination of Offender Accounts." *Journal of Research in Crime and Delinquency* 27: 267–94.

———. 1992. "Foundation for a General Strain Theory of Crime and Delinquency." *Criminology* 30: 47–87.

———. 1997. "Stability and Change in Crime over the Life Course: A Strain Theory Explanation." In *Advances in Criminological Theory, Volume 7: Developmental Theories of Crime and Delinquency,* edited by Terence P. Thornberry, 101–32. New Brunswick, NJ: Transaction.

American Psychiatric Association. 1994. *Diagnostic and Statistical Manual of Mental Disorders,* (4th edition). Washington, D.C.: American Psychiatric Association.

Anderson, Elijah. 1994. "The Code of the Streets." *Atlantic Monthly* 5: 81–94.

Bardone, Anna M., Terrie Moffitt, Avshalom Caspi, and Nigel Dickson. 1996. "Adult Mental Health and Social Outcomes of Adolescent Girls with Depression and Conduct Disorder." *Development and Psychopathology* 8: 811–829.

Bennett, Trevor. 1986. "A Decision-Making Approach to Opioid Addiction." In *The Reasoning Criminal: Rational Choice Perspectives on Offending,* edited by Derek B. Cornish and Ronald V. Clarke, 83–102. New York: Springer-Verlag.

Brezina, Timothy. 1996. "Adapting to Strain: An Examination of Delinquent Coping Responses." *Criminology* 34: 39–60.

———. 1999. "Teenage Violence Toward Parents as an Adaptation to Family Strain: Evidence from a National Survey of Male Adolescents." *Youth & Society* 30: 416–44.

———. 2000a. "Delinquent Problem-Solving: An Interpretive Framework for Criminological Theory and Research." *Journal of Research in Crime and Delinquency* 37: 3–30.

———. 2000b. "Delinquency, Control Maintenance, and the Negation of Fatalism." *Justice Quarterly* 17: 779–807.

Carroll, John, and Frances Weaver. 1986. "Shoplifters' Perceptions of Crime Opportunities: A Process-Tracing Study." In *The Reasoning Criminal: Rational Choice Perspectives on Offending,* edited by Derek B. Cornish and Ronald V. Clarke, 19–38. New York: Springer-Verlag.

Caspi, Avshalom, Daryl J. Bem, and Glen H. Elder. 1989. "Continuities and Consequences of Interactional Styles Across the Life Course." *Journal of Personality* 57: 375–406.

Conrad, Peter, and Joseph W. Schneider. 1992. *Deviance and Medicalization* (expanded edition). Philadelphia, PA: Temple University.

Cornish, Derek B. 1993. "Theories of Action in Criminology: Learning Theory and Rational Choice Approaches." In *Advances in Criminological Theory, Volume 5: Routine Activity and Rational Choice,* edited by Ronald V. Clarke and Marcus Felson, 351–82. New Brunswick, NJ: Transaction.

Cornish, Derek B. and Ronald V. Clarke. 1986. *The Reasoning Criminal: Rational Choice Perspectives on Offending.* New York: Springer-Verlag.

Cusson, Maurice and Pierre Pinsonneault. 1986. "The Decision to Give Up Crime." In *The Reasoning Criminal: Rational Choice Perspectives on Offending,* edited by Derek B. Cornish and Ronald V. Clarke, 72–82. New York: Springer-Verlag.

Elster, Jon, ed. 1986. *Rational Choice.* Oxford: Blackwell.

Fagan, Jeffrey, and Deanna L. Wilkinson. 1998. "Social Contexts and Functions of Adolescent Violence." In *Violence in American Schools,* edited by Delbert S. Elliott, Beatrix A. Hamburg, and Kirk R. Williams, 55–93. New York: Cambridge University.

Feeney, Floyd. 1986. "Robbers as Decision-Makers." In *The Reasoning Criminal: Rational Choice Perspectives on Offending,* edited by Derek B. Cornish and Ronald V. Clarke, 53–71. New York: Springer-Verlag.

Felson, Marcus. 1998. *Crime and Everyday Life* (2nd Edition). Thousand Oaks, CA: Pine Forge.

Foglia, Wanda D. 1997. "Perceptual Deterrence and the Mediating Effect of Internalized Norms Among Inner-City Teenagers." *Journal of Research in Crime and Delinquency* 34: 414–42.

Hagan, John. 1991. "Destiny and Drift: Subcultural Preferences, Status Attainments, and the Risks and Rewards of Youth." *American Sociological Review* 56: 567–82.

———. 1994. *Crime and Disrepute*. Thousand Oaks, CA: Pine Forge.

———. 1997. "Defiance and Despair: Subcultural and Structural Linkages between Delinquency and Despair in the Life Course." *Social Forces* 76: 119–34.

Jacobs, Bruce A. 1999. *Dealing Crack: The Social World of Street Corner Selling*. Boston, MA: Northeastern University Press.

Jacobs, Bruce A. and Richard Wright. 1999. "Stick-up, Street Culture, and Offender Motivation." *Criminology* 37: 149–173.

Jencks, Christopher. 1992. *Rethinking Social Policy: Race, Poverty, and the Underclass*. Cambridge, MA: Harvard University Press.

Johnson, Bruce D., Mangai Natarajan, and Harry Sanabria. 1993. "'Successful' Criminal Careers: Toward an Ethnography within the Rational Choice Perspective." In *Advances in Criminological Theory, Volume 5: Routine Activity and Rational Choice*, edited by Ronald V. Clarke and Marcus Felson, 201–21. New Brunswick, NJ: Transaction.

Johnson, Eric, and John Payne. 1986. "The Decision to Commit a Crime: An Information Processing Analysis." In *The Reasoning Criminal: Rational Choice Perspectives on Offending*, edited by Derek B. Cornish and Ronald V. Clarke, 170–185. New York: Springer-Verlag.

Kaplan, Howard B. 1978. "Deviant Behavior and Self-enhancement in Adolescence." *Journal Of Youth and Adolescence* 7: 253–77.

———. 1980. *Deviant Behavior in Defense of Self*. New York: Academic Press.

Katz, Jack. 1988. *Seductions of Crime*. New York: Basic Books.

Khantzian, Edward J. 1985. "The Self-Medication Hypothesis of Addictive Disorders: Focus on Heroin and Cocaine Dependence." *American Journal of Psychiatry* 142: 1259–64.

Krueger, Robert F., Pamela S. Schmutte, Avshalom Caspi, Terrie E. Moffitt, Kathleen Campbell, and Phil A. Silva. 1994. "Personality Traits are Linked to Crime Among Men and Women: Evidence from a Birth Cohort." *Journal of Abnormal Psychology* 103: 328–38.

Labouvie, Erich. 1996. "Maturing Out of Substance Use: Selection and Self-Correction." *Journal of Drug Issues* 26: 457–76.

Longshore, Douglas. 1998. "Self-Control and Criminal Opportunity: A Prospective Test of the General Theory of Crime." *Social Problems* 45: 102–13.

Lykken, David T. 1995. *The Antisocial Personalities*. Hillsdale, NJ: Lawrence Erlbaum.

Marwell, Gerald. 1966. "Adolescent Powerlessness and Delinquent Behavior." *Social Forces* 14: 35–47.

Matza, David. 1964. *Delinquency and Drift*. New York: John Wiley & Sons.

Moffitt, Terrie E. 1983. "The Learning Theory Model of Punishment: Implications for Delinquency Deterrence." *Criminal Justice and Behavior* 10: 131–58.

———. 1993. "Adolescence-Limited and Life-Course Persistent Antisocial Behavior: A Developmental Taxonomy." *Psychological Review* 100: 674–701.

———. 1997. "Adolescence-Limited and Life-Course Persistent Offending: A Complementary Pair of Developmental Theories." In *Advances in Criminological Theory, Volume 7: Developmental Theories of Crime and Delinquency*, edited by Terence P. Thornberry, 11–54. New Brunswick, NJ: Transaction.

Mueller, Dennis C. 1986. "Rational Egoism versus Adaptive Egoism as Fundamental Postulate for a Descriptive Theory of Human Behavior." *Public Choice* 51: 3–23.

Mulvey, Edward P. and John F. LaRosa. 1986. "Delinquency Cessation and Adolescent Development: Preliminary Data." *American Journal of Orthopsychiatry* 56: 212–24.

Nagin, Daniel S., and Raymond Paternoster. 1993. "Enduring Individual Differences and Rational Choice Theories of Crime." *Law and Society Review* 27: 467–96.

Newcomb, Michael D. and L.L. Harlow. 1986. "Life Events and Substance Use Among Adolescents: Mediating Effects of Perceived Loss of Control and Meaninglessness in Life." *Journal of Personality and Social Psychology* 51: 564–77.

Niggli, Marcel A. 1997. "Rational Choice and the Legal Model of the Criminal." In *Rational Choice and Situational Crime Prevention*, edited by Graeme Newman, Ronald V. Clarke, and S. Giora Shoham, 25–45. Brookfield, VT: Ashgate.

Novacek, Jill, Robert Raskin, and Robert Hogan. 1991. "Why Do Adolescents Use Drugs?" *Journal of Youth and Adolescence* 20: 475–92.

Opp, Karl-Dieter. 1997. "Limited Rationality and Crime." In *Rational Choice and Situational Crime Prevention*, edited by Graeme Newman, Ronald V. Clarke, and S. Giora Shoham, 47–63. Brookfield, VT: Ashgate.

Paternoster, Raymond. 1989. "Decisions to Participate in and Desist from Four Types of Common Delinquency: Deterrence and the Rational Choice Perspective." *Law and Society Review* 23: 7–40.

Patterson, Gerald R. 1982. *A Social Learning Approach, Volume 3: Coercive Family Process*. Eugene, OR: Castalia Publishing.

Patterson, Gerald R., Barbara D. DeBaryche, and Elizabeth Ramsey. 1989. "A Developmental Perspective on Antisocial Behavior." *American Psychologist* 44: 329–35.

Peele, Stanton. 1995. *Diseasing of America* (2nd edition). New York: Lexington Books.

Piquero, Alex R., and Matthew Hickman. 1999. "An Empirical Test of Tittle's Control Balance Theory." *Criminology* 37: 319–41.

Piquero, Alex and George F. Rengert. 1999. "Studying Deterrence with Active Residential Burglars." *Justice Quarterly* 16: 451–71.

Raine, Adrian. 1993. *The Psychopathology of Crime: Criminal Behavior as a Clinical Disorder.* New York: Academic Press.

Richters, John E. and Dante Cicchetti. 1993. "Mark Twain Meets the DSM-III-R: Conduct Disorder, Development, and the Concept of Harmful Dysfunction." *Development and Psychopathology* 5: 5–29.

Robins, Lee N. 1966. *Deviant Children Grown Up.* Baltimore, MD: Williams and Wilkins.

Rosenberg, Morris, Carmi Schooler, and Carrie Schoenbach. 1989. "Self-esteem and Adolescent Problems: Modeling Reciprocal Effects." *American Sociological Review* 54: 1004–18.

Sampson, Robert J., and John H. Laub. 1993. *Crime in the Making.* Cambridge, MA: Harvard University Press.

———. 1997. "A Life-Course Theory of Cumulative Disadvantage and the Stability of Delinquency." In *Advances in Criminological Theory, Volume 7: Developmental Theories of Crime and Delinquency,* edited by Terence P. Thornberry, 133–61. New Brunswick, NJ: Transaction.

Shedler, Jonathan and Jack Block. 1990. "Adolescent Drug Use and Psychological Health: A Longitudinal Inquiry." *American Psychologist* 45: 612–30.

Shover, Neal. 1983. "The Later Stages of Ordinary Property Offender Careers." *Social Problems* 31: 208–18.

Simons, Ronald L., Rand D. Conger, and Leslie B. Whitbeck. 1988. "A Multistage Social Learning Model of the Influences of Family and Peers Upon Adolescent Substance Abuse." *Journal of Drug Issues* 18: 293–315.

Stafford, Mark C., and Mark Warr. 1993. "A Reconceptualization of General and Specific Deterrence." *Journal of Research in Crime and Delinquency* 30: 123–35.

Sykes, Charles J. 1992. *A Nation of Victims.* New York: St. Martin's Press.

Tanner, Julian, Scott Davies, and Bill O'Grady. 1999. "Whatever Happened to Yesterday's Rebels? Longitudinal Effects of Youth Delinquency on Education and Employment." *Social Problems* 46: 250–74.

Tittle, Charles R. 1995. *Control Balance: Toward a General Theory of Deviance.* Boulder, CO: Westview Press.

Trasler, Gordon. 1993. "Conscience, Opportunity, Rational Choice, and Crime." In *Advances in Criminological Theory, Volume 5: Routine Activity and Rational Choice,* edited by Ronald V. Clarke and Marcus Felson, 305–22. New Brunswick, NJ: Transaction.

Waldorf, Dan. 1983. "Natural Recovery from Opiate Addiction: Some Social-Psychological Processes of Untreated Recovery." *Journal of Drug Issues* 237–80.

Walsh, Dermot. 1986. "Victim Selection Procedures among Economic Criminals: The Rational Choice Perspective." In *The Reasoning Criminal: Rational Choice Perspectives on Offending,* edited by Derek B. Cornish and Ronald V. Clarke, 39–52. New York: Springer-Verlag.

Wells, L. Edward. 1989. "Self-enhancement through Delinquency: A Conditional Test of Self-Derogation Theory." *Journal of Research in Crime and Delinquency* 26: 226–52.

Wood, Peter B., Walter R. Gove, James A. Wilson, and John K. Cochran. 1997. "Nonsocial Reinforcement and Habitual Criminal Conduct: An Extension of Learning Theory." *Criminology* 35: 355–66.

Wright, Richard T., and Scott H. Decker. 1997. *Armed Robbers in Action.* Boston, MA: Northeastern University Press.

Chapter 12

The Impulsiveness and Routinization of Decision-Making

Kenneth D. Tunnell

INTRODUCTION

Rational choice theory and research, and public policies based on their assumptions, propose that decision-making is a problem-solving process of deliberative calculation. Recent theoretical revision includes the recognition that decision problems often are shaped within and solved through situational settings and with limited rather than full knowledge—a position that seemingly considers variables of both foreground and background of choosing and committing crime. Yet, as argued in this chapter, the dynamics and symbolic interactionism of the foreground remain largely ignored by rational choice theory. Furthermore, rational choice has typically paid little attention to those key variables of sociologies of the background, particularly social class and (sub)culture. Attention is given to decisions and actions that seemingly occur impulsively and routinely among both law violators and enforcers by highlighting moments when thought and action appear inseparable rather than as distinct processes. Relying on interactionism, issues of social class and subcultural entrenchment, this chapter questions the explanatory power of rational choice theory and suggests that a more holistic understanding of decisions is made possible through an integration with symbolic interactionism, realizing though, that through such a synthesis, rational choice theory may fade away.

THE LIMITS OF RATIONAL CHOICE THEORY

The majority of writing to date of rational choice theory and research based on its premises has described decision-making in simulated and hypothetical situations. In the criminological literature, rational choice is primarily limited to retrospective accounts of decision-making among street criminals and delinquent populations. In the main, studies using criminally active populations have not examined decision-making per se but rather target selections and commitments to crime as a way of life (e.g., Bennett and Wright 1984; Wright and Decker 1997; 1994). Across the board, research findings are mixed raising questions central to theoretical decision-making processes. In many respects the limited populations used in decision-making research likely contribute to the empirical obscurity and the theory's limited explanatory power. For example, within the rational choice theory and research tradition, little attention has been given to those decisions that are a part of everyday routine activities by such diverse groups as corporate executives, those authorized with enforcing the law (both domestically and internationally), and elected representatives entrusted with crafting legislation (i.e., those possessing rational-legal authority) (Weber 1922/1978). But, it is hardly surprising that these populations and their decision-making have not been central to rational choice theory and research. Were their behaviors subject to the application of rational choice theory with the same intensity and scrutiny as those usually studied within this tradition (e.g., street criminals), we likely would discover contradictory results. For example, we might find relatively high degrees of rationality among corporate executives, yet little evidence of such among street criminals and those entrusted with legitimate power and authority. Consider the following.

In February 1998, an Air Force crew flying through the Italian Alps sever a gondola cable, killing twenty people. The flight crew, according to some, was "hot dogging it." Others blamed the pilot for flying too low and too fast through the valley. The crew itself claimed ignorance of newly implemented flight standards and the location of the gondola cable; errors also occurred within the chain of command. If indeed, the flight crew was engaged in "hot dogging," was the decision to do so a rational one? If their claim that they did not know the cable was there is an accurate one, the information required for making a rational decision was less than optimal which raises questions about the rationality of their behavior. What of after the accident when the pilot (who later was convicted of obstructing justice) and the navigator (who pled guilty to conduct unbecoming of an officer) participated in destroying the video tape? What evidence supports an assumption that their decision-making was rational? Had they carefully considered the consequences of their behavior? Alternative behaviors? Their risks of detection? The pilot's statement that "I don't believe myself or the crew had a criminal mind" was echoed by his lawyer who claimed the pilot had "no criminal intent but had exercised poor judgement" (CNN May 7, 1999). In other words the pilot and crew engaged in poor or less than rational decision-making. Perhaps subcultural values, as much as methodical decision-making, set these tragic events into motion.

New York City policemen brutally beat and sodomized Abner Louima, a Haitian immigrant, during the night of August 9, 1997. Although for a time they denied everything and their lawyers distributed misinformation about Louima's sex life and injuries, one officer eventually confessed and was sentenced to prison. In those moments when fists met flesh, when Louima was dragged screaming, when he was held down by one and sodomized by another in a Brooklyn precinct restroom, can we really say that rational thinking was occurring? Did rational choice set into motion those decisions and actions to engage in such perverse and nearly universally condemned behaviors? Racist driven rage and brutality within a subculture that likely values and reproduces such behavioral traits may have precluded sound, reasoned, and dispassionate decision-making.

In New York City in February 1999, West African immigrant Amadou Diallo, who was unarmed, was shot nineteen times in his Bronx apartment building vestibule by four NYPD officers who fired a total of forty-one shots. Although charged with second-degree murder, they ultimately were acquitted by an Albany jury. Nonetheless, at what moment did the officers engage in rational decision-making? At what moment did they consider the alternatives to squeezing the trigger? What can rational choice theory inform us of the moment when adrenalin and sound logic come together in a swirl of panic, hate, fear and Dirty Harry policing? Can it offer much more than it has to date about such complex phenomena as human decision-making? Did those officers exercise equal degrees of rational thought? Why is it that no "cooler" heads prevailed? What kind of thinking process resulted in those officers believing they were in imminent danger? Is it a process capable of explanation within the rational choice paradigm?

Harvard biologist Richard Wrangham (1999) presents evidence that military leaders consistently overestimate their own army's abilities and power while consistently underestimating their enemy's. This type of thinking clearly can lead to devastating consequences. What components of their thoughts and actions reflect rational decision-making?

Lawmakers consistently support and allocate billions of dollars to fund the ongoing war on (some) drugs, although evidence suggests that few inroads have been made in restricting the supply or impacting the demand for currently illegal drugs. The voices of disparate individuals who suggest, at the least, considering decriminalizing certain drugs are drowned out by legislators who label them as irrational. Where is the rational debate on this issue? How is it that empirical research is ignored by allegedly well-meaning lawmakers? What part of this debate, and of the war on drugs itself, resembles rational choices, strategies and objective and dispassionate public policies?

Each of these vignettes raises fundamental issues about the decision-making of individuals entrusted with rational legal power and suggests that their rationality may be little different from street criminals operating within distinct subcultures and who impulsively and hedonistically act with little thought of alternatives or consequences (Tunnell 1992). Indeed, if one were to examine non-human animals, we likely might discover similar behavior patterns as those highlighted in the above examples. For in each case, decision-making (or at least how we theoretically define it) evidently is far different than theoretical explications. Perhaps the behaviors illustrated above are more similar to non-human pack behavior, including such universal responses as collective panic, fear, and defensive posturing, rather than something reflecting decision-problem resolution as elaborated in rational choice theory. Also, the above likely reflects impulsivity and routinization.

Beyond the forgoing examples that raise critical questions, in its current state rational choice theory is unable to adequately explain even the most everyday, instinctive or automatic social responses in, for example, the following human activities: (1) making love and decisions of when to do what, in which position, for what duration, in what order, or even during those times when one makes the most unusual kinds of requests of one's partner, (2) playing guitar when thinking is suspended as fingers meet ebony and steel in configurations that produce and reproduce sounds that the musician's hands, as much as head, have composed hundreds perhaps thousands of times and slip naturally into position, (3) building a fire when one knows to first use fuel with a low kindling temperature and slowly add fuel, occasionally adjusting air flow to reduce smoke, and knowing by feel as much as cognitive ability whether a piece of pine is too wet or oak too dense to burn in given conditions; and typically more complex than the previous three, (4) performing heart by-pass surgery, which currently is considered "routine procedure" as participants take their places and perform duties with little conversation among them and, as if moving in synchronicity, of one mind having performed the procedure nearly as often as the guitarist's fingers have slipped into a G chord. The point in each of these scenarios is that choices (if we can call them that) represent something other than rational calculation of potential outcome, alternatives, advantages, and disadvantages. For in these cases, the behavior involves little thought, let alone, theoretical rational thought as actions are routinized at the unconscious level. Yet, decisions clearly are being made as actions result from the mind and body working together.

Such behavior resulting from choices reflecting little rational calculation is not limited to those above scenarios. It also is indicative of individuals committed to careers in property crime and who engage in criminal exploits nearly daily. Likewise, it may be apropos to cops as they engage in repetitious daily activities fueled by fear, cynicism, distrust, and anger on the streets of America. Furthermore, lawmakers, as they approach potential legislation armed with ideologies, distrust of the opposition, and a determination to be re-elected, debate and often decide with seemingly little rational calculation taking place. Among lawmakers, lawbreakers, and law enforcers who daily engage in their profession's activities, we can say, with some degree of confidence, that their minds are made up; decisions have long been made and are manifest in particular worldviews that often preclude specific rational calculations about specific decision problems. Worldviews, values, and such routinized and predetermined decisions are typically shaped and reproduced within specific subcultures of law making, lawbreaking and law enforcing that, for the most part, receives little treatment in rational choice literature.

Given the often irrational and less than rational decisions among law violators and law enforcers, we are left with more questions than answers about rational choice theory's empirical validity. Consider for example the following questions. What exactly makes a decision a rational one? Is it an optimum outcome or is it a theoretically and logically sound process? If the process itself is carefully conducted with consideration of even the most inconsequential exigencies, yet the outcome disastrous, can we define the decision as rational? Or the converse; if the process represents nothing like theoretical decision-making but rather is a spontaneous, opportunistic cognitive leap into behavior whose outcome, as it turns out, could not have been more rewarding, is the decision rational?

The latter question describes examples iterated earlier of decisions that are the focus of this paper. Furthermore, this paper suggests a rational choice theory that is more inclusive of central sociological components and one that is theoretically integrated (e.g., Barak 1998, Chapter 8). More specifically, it suggests the development of a rational choice theory with a broader vision and one that links rational choice to symbolic interactionism and its attention to the foreground of crime, to background issues such as social class, subculture affiliation and consciousness, and inclusive of race, gender, and biography. In other words, this paper argues that for rational choice theory to adequately explain behaviors among lawmakers, law enforcers and lawbreakers, it must value theories and concepts that explore both the background and foreground of decisions and events and the strictures on which they operate, rather than simply offering explanations that reduce human behavior to events absent such powerful decision-shaping factors.

THE RELEVANCE OF THE BACKGROUND AND FOREGROUND TO CHOICE

Although rational choice theory's primary focus is on the foreground of crime, its explanations remain largely cognitive. Nonetheless, rational choice theory has undergone considerable revision; it treats decision-problem resolution as a situationally bounded act and recognizes that choice is based as much on perception as empirical reality. Yet, even with such theoretical revision, to date, situational decision-making has disregarded the rich, textured explanations that emerge from symbolic interactionist traditions. This is especially pertinent to those decisions made within subcultures which generate specific and culturally reproduced definitions. Rational choice theory tends to reduce the social and interactionist behaviors to minute, compartmentalized, and specific choice, which limits the rich explanations of something as complex as decision-making to emerge. For rational choice theory to transcend such limitations, it must embrace both the background and symbolic interactionism of the foreground of criminal events (as well as events specific to lawmaking and enforcing decisions). As it currently functions, rational choice is a theory that relies on explanations further removed from those central-most variables in sociology—class, gender, race, subculture, and biography. By passing over such fundamental background variables to focus on cognition, it also mostly ignores the foreground and how such is negotiated through symbolic interaction. It makes little use of the determinism of social variables, the significance of social structure, the meanings given to decisions and action, and the unpredictability of human agency. Indeed, some observers have made critical commentary on this epistemological shift. For example:

> Nowadays, prominent criminologists are losing interest in criminological depth, and indeed, in criminological truth. Pragmatic considerations prompt a return to surface phenomena—to choices and opportunities and rational calculations. . . . The fact that such policies do not address the 'root causes' or deep-lying problems is not perceived as a failing. (Garland 1995, 194)

In the main, rational choice theory explains criminal behavior as hedonistic. This undoubtedly is the case. Yet, it seems a safe assumption that the bulk of human behavior and decisions, at least within market societies, is hedonistic. Thus, it seems the issue for explanation is the *type* of behavior rather than the impetus to behave hedonistically. While most individuals may opt for behaviors that result in pleasure, most choose something other than crime. Rational choice theory treats crime as hedonistic behavior that is to some extent shaped by specific background factors. Background factors undoubtedly contribute to differences in offending and in choices generally. Class and culture remain important dimensions for understanding choice among hedonistic individuals who opt for crime (Tunnell 2000). The challenge for rational choice theory is to locate those background variables that are central to decisions; in other words, linking background to the immediacy of the foreground remains a central issue for any sociology of lawbreaking (and lawmaking and enforcing) (Williams and McShane 1999, 235; Tibbetts and Gibson, this volume).

THE CENTRALITY OF AGENCY

As a unit theory, rational choice is difficult to test and at times seemingly ignores the obvious evidence about human decisions. As an explanation, it has difficulty maintaining the rich face validity that we have come to expect from social theory. Rational choice is a theory in desperate need of revision, but revision of a particular nature. Its persistence may depend on its integration with more widely accepted social theories such as symbolic interactionism, a theory that offers greater explanation for human agency than the tenets of rational choice.

Symbolic interactionism, in all its vagaries, has as its central organizing motif the notion that social life is constructed by individuals in interaction with others. Social life is not a result of structure; nor does it exist beyond social interaction. It is produced through the rich, textured interactions and communications among people as they live their lives and as they come to give definitions to phenomena. Early symbolic interactionists, breaking from dominant ideas about human behavior as conditioned responses to external stimuli, emphasized the subjective experiences of social interaction (e.g., Mead 1967). Several points from early explications are useful for explaining human decision-making.

First, decision-problems, their solutions, their associated benefits and costs, and alternative actions are not necessarily objective social facts; they are, whether empirically accurate or inaccurate, subjective perceptions. Thus decisions are reached by one's understanding and knowledge filtered through their own personal subjective definitions of such.

Second, such perceptions of the decision-problem, are produced within interactive communication with others, not in isolation. Thus, it is a mutually shared and constructed decision problem rather than an individual psychological one that emerges within the interactionist tradition.

Third, as people construct decision-problems and give them meaning, they do this not because they are simply reacting to stimuli but because they have minds and selves, which unfortunately for our efforts of teasing out decision-making further complicates and at times masks our understanding of human decisions (excepting, of course, those most simple and concrete ones). Thus, individuals think through problems, but their resolutions are dependent on their own subjective understanding, relationships, intimates, life history, and social setting. In other words, their decisions are based on the meanings given to choices. The issue of meaning and its effect on human behavior is the cornerstone of symbolic interactionism.

This is especially the case with Blumer (1969) whose work emphasizes three aspects of the concept—*meaning*. First, individuals respond to things based on the meanings that those things have for them. These meanings may be qualitatively different for them than for others or for society generally. These things may be physical objects (e.g., guns, drugs, cash) or social situations (e.g., church service, a courtroom trial, legislative assembly, criminal subcultures). Social behavior and action (or inaction) are understood then based on the meanings that objects and situations hold for the individual. Thus committing crime, obeying the law, using drugs, and engaging in hedonistic behavior all have meanings that differ across individuals and groups (especially across subcultures). Meaning, therefore, is treated as ambiguous and as something that constantly is worked out rather than something that is concretely and universally defined (e.g., Garfinkel 1967).

Second, symbolic interactionism emphasizes that meaning arises from social interaction rather than from some objective qualities possessed by the thing or the social situation. The meaning of crime then, is not located in the act itself but in the beliefs about it generated within the dynamics of social interaction. The meaning, whatever it may be, also likely is not the first notion that one holds of an object or ceremony, for meanings arise and change shape through interaction and across time. Regarding active property criminals, for example, crime had a qualitatively different meaning for them as adolescents than it does as fortysomething-year-old adults. It also has a different meaning for them than it does for cops and legislators. The act is the same. The meaning is not. Constructed through interactions within subcultures, the act takes on different meanings. Thus, the evaluation of a decision problem for engaging in crime is different across groups; it is dynamic rather than static, as inferred by rational choice theory.

Third, meaning is revised through an interpretative process. This suggests that meaning changes through the give and take of interaction and shifting definitions of objects and social situations; it is not static as it changes with individuals' and groups' flexibility and individuals associated with them (e.g., Layder 1994, Chapter 4). For example, drug use often holds various meanings for individual users across their lives. When first exposed to drugs, often one's reaction is not entirely positive. But, when one comes to recognize the effects of drugs and, through social interaction, defines them as pleasurable, one develops more positive definitions about them (e.g., Becker 1963). Later in life, as individuals typically take on greater responsibilities than they had in their youth (e.g., careers, child rearing), different meanings about drugs are often developed. They may be defined as no longer relevant for stable, suburban, upwardly mobile parents, for example. These meanings shift through interpretation and social settings and across space and time; social interaction is the impetus for such flux.

The issue of why or how individuals first become involved in criminal behavior, for example, is considered only tangential to symbolic interactionism. Motivation to engage in crime is largely treated as a psychological issue. Rather, symbolic interactionism focuses on the processes by which individuals become committed to particular courses of action through social involvements, subcultures, socialization, and interaction (e.g., Becker 1970). The decision to commit or not commit a crime is understood within the context of shared ways of life, prior experiences, entrenchment in criminal subcultures, and definitions (constructed through social interaction) of doing or not doing a particular crime.

Thus, the decision, as inferred from symbolic interactionism, is much more compounded than that described within rational choice literature. The latter treats each decision problem as unique and as if it stands alone; the former treats it as behavior within the rich and processual life history shaped by interaction and communication with others. This interpretation recognizes that crime as a way of life, for example, may be regarded as instrumentally and expressively rewarding. It also recognizes that crime as a way of life becomes routinized as individuals become entrenched within that particular lifestyle given the strictures of legitimate lifestyles, for example, on their abilities to earn a living, remain autonomous, participate in street culture, and to continue using expensive and illegal drugs. Thus, crime becomes a commitment within which decision-problems rarely are confronted as rational choice theory describes. The decision (if one can call it that) is whether to remain in a criminal subculture. If the decision is made to remain, then deciding to commit a specific crime is a rote one that is far different from the procedures elaborated in rational choice theory. Consider the words of an individual fully entrenched within a criminal and drug subculture about his decision to commit a particular crime:

> With drugs you don't rationalize. It's just a decision you make. You don't weigh the consequences, the pros, the cons. You just do it (Tunnell 1992, 118).

Consider, too, the following words from a conversation with a repeat property offender who was physically addicted to pharmaceutical drugs and who engaged in drug use and crime on a daily basis:

> A. [I did burglaries] simply for the drug money. I drifted with that crowd and they either shoplifted or did home burglaries or some kind of violation of the law every day. Whatever it is, you violate the law every single day on end.

Q. How did you mentally handle thinking that at any time you were going to be arrested?

A. The drugs led the way. They made me think I could walk on water. I didn't judge anything at all. If I had just thought for a split second, but there wasn't no looking back, there wasn't no worries at the time (Tunnell 1992, 134–135).

Although there are various types of rationality, rational choice theory, as decision-making explanation, hinges on certain key components, without which rational choice theory fades from view. These components include: one's empirical knowledge of the benefits and costs of a given choice; knowledge of alternative actions and of benefits and costs associated with each; and a rational calculation between costs and benefits of a given choice compared to those of alternative choices.

More recently, rational choice theories have recognized that individuals often operate with limited rationality; that their knowledge of particular courses of actions and of their associated benefits and costs may be less than optimal. Nonetheless, rational choice theory's primary explandum is decision-making resulting from some semblance of rational calculation. This is its central thesis. Without this plank in its theoretical platform, rational choice theory becomes something else altogether. Yet, rational choice theory's explanations, when applied to real rather than hypothetical or retrospective decisions, yield far less than we have come to expect from social science theories. The explanations, however limited, evidently are further restricted by the theory's central components. Perhaps, once the empirical evidence compared to the theory's propositions are considered in totality, rational choice theory may be regarded to ultimately hold only marginal significance to sociologies of crime and deviance.

Rational choice theory, in and of itself, ignores such processes and the rich symbolic interactionist tradition; it tends to reify calculative decision-problem resolution. As a result, its explanatory power is limited far greater than it would be if integrated with symbolic interactionism. Yet, if rational choice theory were to be integrated with symbolic interactionism, it would no longer be rational choice theory. Rational choice would be lost in the new hybrid. For without the elements of rational calculation, such as costs and benefits, alternatives, and an evaluation of such, rational choice theory, as such, no longer exists and instead becomes subsumed into other theoretical explanations. Yet, rational choice, as a unit theory, and stated in its pure and unintegrated form, offers an inadequate account of criminal behavior. Indeed, with the exception of psychoanalytic and some biological theories "all other criminological theories assume no more or no less rationality in crime than do most rational choice models" (Akers 1994, 60). The danger with integrating rational choice theory with other theoretical explanations is that "the level of rationality it assumes is indistinguishable from that expected in other theories. . . . When the modifications reach this point, it is no longer appropriate to call the result rational choice theory" (Akers 1994, 60).

RATIONAL CHOICE AND POLICY

Rational choice theory clearly recognizes that differences in individuals' life chances and situations affect choice. Such factors also impact perceptions of decision options (i.e., alternatives), risks and rewards. Although policy makers are concerned with identifying situations which may trigger criminal acts, that evidently is the extent of any investigation into the background of crime. Lost in this myopic treatment are the pervasive issues of class, culture and consciousness and their often resulting trajectory of criminal events and careers (Tunnell 2000).

Rational choices are themselves event-specific decisions. As a result, public policies generally are aimed at specific prevention strategies rather than preventing crime in general (Williams and McShane 1999: 238). For example, nearly all public application of rational choice theory remains in the area of target hardening—efforts aimed at manipulating situations and opportunities for crime and victimization. Such measures typically disallow thorough examinations of the back and foreground of crime. Furthermore, they reflect and reproduce dominant ideologies of crime and victimization by implicating, first, that offenders *choose* to commit crime and, second, that physical changes, such as tweaking design strategies or walling off a few more communities are reasonable solutions to the crime problem. This approach places responsibility directly with individuals who choose to engage in crime and with potential victims who possess the wherewithal to offset their chances of victimization. Absent from this conceptualization is an appreciation of social forces, a public commitment to humanely reduce crime and victimization, and government responsibility to intelligently accept a lead role in progressive social change. Such dominant, yet simplistic, ideas were exemplified in Minnesota Governor Jesse Ventura's much propagated remark that it's not his (and thus the state's) problem that a young woman *chose* to become a single parent. Such off-hand remarks assign only personal blame and abdicate any public responsibility. The same logic and desperate short-sightedness applies to public understandings of crime and victimization in the United States.

Almost all applications of rational choice theory have been applied solely to street criminals with little regard to those far more harmful crimes—those of the powerful. Indeed, evidence suggests that some rational thought is part of corporate crimes. Indeed, if one were to examine activities mentioned in this paper (i.e., lawmaking, lawbreaking, and social responses), we might find that willful law violations within the capitalist class and within corporate organizations most closely resemble rational choice models. Yet, little attention is given to criminogenic structure in both street and suite crimes (e.g., Lanier and Henry 1998). Also, little attention is given to the importance of subcultures and one's commitment to and entrenchment within them. Organization and subculture also may be those most central elements for understanding choice among agents who possess rational-legal authority (e.g., Vaughan 1996).

CONCLUSION

Rational choice theory and research have made laudable efforts at adequately describing and measuring decisions. Yet, how much more precise can our methods and measurements become for understanding something as elusive, personal, cognitive, and perceptual as decisions? Given its difficulties at accounting for crime and the meanings that it holds for lawbreakers, rational choice theory also may be unlikely to explain "excitement and meaningless dissent" as well as activities that generate expressive or intangible pleasures such as that derived from both legal and illegal edgework (Presdee 1994, 187; Lyng 1990; Tunnell 2000, Chapter 3).

Sutherland (1947) claimed, and indeed academics continue to echo his position in their writing and teaching, that theory is supposed to explain lawmaking, lawbreaking, and the social response to both. Although most rational choice research has examined lawbreaking, with mixed findings as iterated in this paper, little attention has been given to the law enforcing arena and almost no attention to lawmaking processes. Even pedestrian observations of lawmaking suggest that legislators and congress are less than rational in their decisions as evidenced in some laws that are passed and by some that are not. As much as lawbreaking and law enforcing evidently are less than rational, punishment, too, is far from rational. If we consider the state's most extreme punishment—death—then we recognize that public and political support for it is hardly driven by rational thought. After all, both the public and politicians express confidence in the deterrent effect of capital punishment, although research does not support their misplaced and uninformed hopes. Perhaps the public and politicians recognize that vengeance—the only sensible explanation for our continued use of capital punishment—is not a rational or well-informed logic for state killing, thus leaving proponents with the embarrassing position of claiming a deterrent rather than a retributive motivation. Those making decisions to continue using this punishment type are engaging in less than rational choice. Something else is to explain for this punishment mode as well the activities of criminals—something other than rational calculative decisions and something other than that explained by rational choice theory.

Routine and impulsive decisions occur when thought and action appear inseparable and when structure crashes headlong into (among others) immediacy, rage, and hustle within subcultures. The daily decisions made within criminal, legislative, and policing subcultures, likely reflect culturally-based routinization rather than theoretically modeled decision-making. Rational choice theory, by recognizing its own limitations, can save itself from itself. After all, actors within the matrix of crime—criminals, politicians, publics, and enforcers—daily engage in decisions and behaviors that are shaped and explained by something far greater than the limited explanations espoused by rational choice theory. A holistic understanding of these decisions is far more likely to emerge by widening the theoretical net and fostering explanations of the subtleties and nuances of social life and choice.

REFERENCES

Akers, Ronald L. 1994. *Criminological Theories*. Los Angeles: Roxbury.

Barak, Gregg. 1998. *Integrating Criminologies*. Boston: Allyn and Bacon.

Becker, Howard. 1970. *Sociological Work*. Chicago: Aldine.

Becker, Howard. 1963. *Outsiders*. New York: Free Press.

Bennett, Trevor and Richard Wright. 1984. *Burglars on Burglary*. Hampshire, UK: Gower.

Blumer, Herbert. 1969. *Symbolic Interactionism: Perspective and Method*. Englewood Cliffs, New Jersey: Prentice-Hall.

Garfinkel, Harold. 1967. *Studies in Ethnomethodology*. Englewood Cliffs, New Jersey: Prentice-Hall.

Garland, David. 1995. "Penal Modernism and Postmodernism." In *Punishment and Social Control*, edited by Thomas G. Blomberg and Stanley Cohen, 181–213. New York: Aldine de Gruyter.

Lanier, Mark M. and Stuart Henry. 1998. *Essential Criminology*. Boulder: Westview.

Layder, Derek. 1994. *Understanding Social Theory*. London: Sage.

Lyng, Stephen. 1990. "Edgework: A Social Psychological Analysis of Voluntary Risk Taking." *American Journal of Sociology*. 95: 851–886.

Mead, George H. 1967. *Mind, Self and Society*. Chicago: University of Chicago Press.

Presdee, Mike. 1994. "Young People, Culture, and the Construction of Crime: Doing Wrong verus Doing Crime." In *Varieties of Criminology*, edited by Gregg Barak, 179–187. Westport, CT: Praeger.

Sutherland, Edwin H. 1947. *Principles of Criminology* (4th ed.). Philadelphia: J.B. Lippincott.

Tunnell, Kenneth D. 2000. *Living Off Crime*. Chicago: Burnham.

Tunnell, Kenneth D. 1992. *Choosing Crime*. Chicago: Nelson Hall.

Vaughan, Diane. 1996. *The Challenger Launch Decision: Risky Technology, Culture and Deviance*. Chicago: University of Chicago Press.

Williams, Frank and Marilyn McShane. 1999. *Criminological Theory* (3rd edition). Englewood Cliffs, New Jersey: Prentice-Hall.

Wrangham, Richard 1999. Unpublished paper presented at Origins Conference, Emory University, Atlanta, January 16.

Wright, Richard T. and Scott Decker. 1997. *Armed Robbers in Action*. Boston: Northeastern University Press.

Wright, Richard T. and Scott Decker. 1994. *Burglars on the Job*. Boston: Northeastern University Press.

Chapter 13

Dangerous Liaison? Rational Choice Theory as the Basis for Correctional Intervention

Francis T. Cullen, Travis C. Pratt, Sharon Levrant Miceli, and Melissa M. Moon

Rational choice theory has shaken up traditional criminology in important ways. It has questioned the image of offenders as mere vessels for criminogenic variables that propel them to break the law—as people who have, in a way, no mind of their own. It has shown the limits of theories that assume, implicitly if not explicitly, that offenders are fully unmindful of the consequences that might befall them. It has created a salient research agenda exploring how offenders make the decision to transform a criminal orientation into an actual criminal event. And it has led to fruitful insights into how structuring physical environments and sur-veillance strategies can undermine or enhance situational crime prevention (see, e.g., Clarke 1992; Clarke and Felson 1993; Cornish and Clarke 1986).

Despite these worthwhile contributions, we argue that rational choice theory provides, at best, a restricted basis on which to develop correction-al interventions. This limitation emerges because rational choice theory ignores many empirically established predictors of recidivism and, in turn, does not target these criminogenic factors for change (Andrews and Bonta 1998). At worst, rational choice theory and corrections make for a "dan-gerous liaison" because this theory tends to encourage policies and pro-grams that are *cost* oriented and thus unduly favorable to *punishment* and *deterrence*.

Not all rational choice theorists—a group in which we include econo-mists—embrace this view (see, e.g., Evans 1980; Orsagh and Marsden 1985; Williams and Fish 1971), and some provide insights into why repres-sive policies can have the unanticipated result of increasing crime (Cook 1980, 1986). Still, advocates of this perspective are generally hostile to correctional rehabilitation. Despite evidence to the contrary (Andrews et al. 1990; Cullen and Gendreau 2000; Gendreau and Ross 1979, 1987), they have boldly claimed that treatment programs "have little or no effect" (Cook 1986, 206) and that the "neglect of the offender's perspective probably underlies the catastrophic failure of rehabilitation" (Cornish and Clarke 1986, 202). They worry, as Votey and Phillips (1980, 298) note, that rehabilitation may boost offending because "such activities may not raise the cost to potential criminals of their criminal acts and in the extreme could even lower such costs."

Their rejection of rehabilitation also rests on two interrelated views (Luksetich and White 1982). First, by embracing the premise of rational choice, they "assume that offenders do not commit crimes because they are abnormal. They commit crimes because their expected benefits and costs— not their behavior—differ from non-offenders" (Luksetich and White 1982, 164–165). Because offenders are not different, there is nothing in them to fix. "Efforts at rehabilitating offenders are therefore wasted" (p. 165). Second, even if people differ in the propensities to offend, "the problem runs much deeper. Rehabilitation essentially involves altering a person's values. . . . This is extremely difficult" (p. 71). In contrast, *manipulating costs—that is, legal punishments—is assumed to be an easier task* and thus a more pragmatic approach to crime control. Thus, "one reason why economists stress altering the expected costs and benefits so heavily is a belief that these can be altered much more easily than the individual's basic value system" (p. 71).

The danger in this way of thinking about corrections can be seen in the work of Morgan Reynolds (1996, 3), who unhesitatingly proclaims: "Punishment works. Incarceration works." He argues that fluctuations in Texas's crime rate in the 1980s and 1990s vary directly with the amount of "expected punishment" handed out in the state, with expected punishment defined as "the amount of prison time criminals can expect to serve when they commit crimes, given the probabilities of being apprehended, convicted and sent to prison and given the median sentence served per crime" (p. i). Not surprisingly, he proclaims that the record of "rehabilitation . . . for repairing souls has been abysmal" (p. 7). Instead, the challenge is to build more prisons so that more offenders can be locked up for longer periods of time. "Get tough" juvenile codes that hold adolescents "accountable for their behavior" are also to be encouraged as a way of reducing youthful violence. Why is this so?

The answer, of course, is that offenders exercise rational choice. "Most crimes are not irrational acts," claims Reynolds (1996, 7). "Instead, they are committed by people who at least implicitly compare the expected benefits with the expected costs, including the costs of being caught and punished." In turn, "if the (objectively measured) expected cost of crime to criminals declines, crime increases and vice versa" (p. 7). The overriding purpose of corrections, then, is to be an instrument for raising the price of making illegal choices. Reynolds does allow, however, that while incarcerated, inmates should be put to work, because such employment "benefits nearly everyone" (p. 21). Prisoners' lives will be less tedious, they will acquire marketable skills and learn individual responsibility, and they can compensate victims and support their families. "For businesses," Reynolds adds, prison work "can provide access to a new pool of labor (both pre- and post-release), a new market for their goods and services, and a new source of goods and services to buy" (p. 21).

Reynolds's analysis can be criticized on a host of grounds. For example, he cites research selectively (e.g., he ignores all studies favorable to rehabilitation); he assesses his premises by conducting bivariate analysis of expected punishment and crime rates, thus creating the likely possibility that his model is misspecified; and he ignores data from other states that would be counter to those he cites from Texas (Clear 1994; Currie 1998; Petersilia 1992; Stolzenberg and D'Alessio 1997). We do not need to suggest that Reynolds's embrace of deterrence and position on "expected punishment" is fully in error, especially in terms of general deterrence; we will leave that to others to debate (see, e.g., Akers 2000; Nagin 1998a, 1998b; see also, Marvell and Moody 1999). Rather, his analysis is cited because, as noted, it shows how the logic of rational choice theory can readily constrain thinking about correctional policy. Predictably, Reynolds must start with a rejection of rehabilitation. His defense of raising the costs of crime by increasing incarceration—with apparently no limit to how extensive he wishes the prison binge to be—is unqualified. His blueprint for what should be done in prisons is vacant, with the exception that inmates should be engaged in economic activities—labor. No thought is given to what should be done with the four million offenders now under community supervision, other than to put more of them behind bars. His views might be dismissed as the odd ruminations of an obscure Texas economist, but such a judgment would be mistaken. As Clear (1994, 99) points out, Reynolds's research—and other studies like it—have been "distributed among state elected officials, immediately translated into legislative interest and calls for tougher sentencing" (see also, Currie 1998, 43–53). This research also finds its way into the media, including newspaper editorials written by conservative commentators who wish to depict the criminal justice system as overly lenient (Ridenour 1999).

What value, then, does rational choice theory have for developing effective strategies for intervening with offenders? Our answer comes in three parts. First, we contend that *punishment- or cost-oriented correctional programs* are largely ineffective in reducing recidivism. Second, we argue that *benefit- or incentive-oriented interventions* have some potential for reducing recidivism, but that they are, at best, a limited strategy for diverting offenders from criminal involvement. Third, we show that rehabilitation programs that are *not based on rational choice theory* have the greatest promise for achieving meaningful reductions in offender recidivism.

GETTING TOUGH IN CORRECTIONS: THE LIMITS OF SPECIFIC DETERRENCE PROGRAMS

There is considerable debate over whether the criminal justice system in general and the greater use of imprisonment in particular has a deterrent effect (see Kleiman 1999; Lynch 1999; Nagin 1998a, 1998b; Von Hirsch et al. 1999). This controversy is related to, but ultimately beyond, our narrower concern, which is to assess whether correctional programs should be based on rational choice theory. As will be discussed later, rational choice theory has the potential to justify correctional interventions that *invest* resources in offenders and that attempt to increase the *benefits* of making choices other than continued criminal involvement. Even so, as suggested above, the danger in rational choice theory is that it more readily suggests increasing the *costs* suffered by offenders ensnared in the correctional system.

The attractiveness of a cost-oriented approach to corrections is that, at first glance, costs or punishments seem so much more amenable to manipulation than the benefit side of the calculus. Again, actually dealing with and trying to change offenders is tough work, and typically the rational choice theorists have no stomach for this kind of enterprise. Instead, it is easier to contemplate how we might deter offenders simply by giving them longer sentences, by making their lives more painful while in prison or bothersome while on probation/parole, and by watching them more closely in the community so as to detect and punish their transgressions. A cost approach has another latent appeal: It is difficult to falsify. If recidivism is not prevented, then the claim can always be made that the costs of crime simply were not high enough (Clear 1994; Currie 1998).

We must admit that it is *theoretically possible* to design correctional interventions that help to deter crime by increasing the threat and/or application of costs to offenders. Laboratory experiments have shown that punishment, if applied in accordance with the principles of behavioral psychology, can diminish undesired behavior (Moffitt 1983). Achieving such optimal conditions in real-world correctional settings, however, is problematic (Moffitt 1983). In a modest, pragmatic approach, it might possible to achieve some deterrence by tinkering with how costs are exacted from offenders—for example, subjecting every probationer who fails a drug test to a short, but certain, stay in jail (Kleiman 1999). But even here such claims may be little more than wishful thinking. It is equally plausible that efforts to inflict more discomfort and pain on offenders will backfire (Braithwaite 1989, 1997; Sherman 1993; see also, Colvin 2000). Attempts to "up the ante" on offenders, especially if done in a stigmatizing and intentionally hurtful way, may generate "reactance" or defiance; they also may trigger differential responses contingent on the varying social circumstances and individual differences of offenders (Braithwaite 1997; Gendreau 1996; Moffitt 1983; Sherman 1993; more generally, see Brehm and Brehm 1981; Eagley and Chaiken 1993).

But we need not rely on theory or speculation to assess whether cost- or punishment-oriented corrections programs specifically deter offenders. The sea change in American corrections, which began in the 1970s and continues to this day, ushered in numerous correctional programs—implicitly, if not explicitly, based on rational choice/deterrence theory—whose intention was to increase the costs of offending (Clear, 1994; Cullen, Wright, and Applegate 1996; Currie 1998). Many of these programs fell under the rubric of "intermediate punishments"—intensive supervision, home confinement/electronic monitoring, shock incarceration, drug testing—and were subject to experimental and quasi-experimental evaluations. The results of these evaluations are clear. Borrowing phrasing that Robert Martinson (1974, 25) used in his indictment of rehabilitation, we can conclude, with some measure of confidence, that *with few and isolated exceptions, the punishment-oriented correctional interventions that have been reported thus far have had no appreciable effect on recidivism.*

Petersilia and Turner's (1993) classic evaluation of intensive supervision probation programs (ISPs), conducted for RAND, is particularly instructive. Using a randomized experimental design, they examined the impact of ISPs on recidivism in fourteen programs located in nine states. Importantly, these programs were control-oriented in that their goal was not to deliver treatment services but to increase the surveillance over offenders, with the cost of probation revocation looming overhead. In nearly all sites, offenders did, in fact, receive more contacts from parole agents. Despite this fact, there was no evidence that such scrutiny reduced offending. "At no site," observed Petersilia and Turner (1993, 310–311), "did ISP participants experience arrest less often, have a longer time to failure, or experience arrests for less serious offenses." These results are hardly idiosyncratic. Reviews of existing research reveal similar findings across a range of evaluations (Byrne and Pattavina 1992; Cullen, Wright, and Applegate 1996; Fulton et al. 1997; Gendreau, Cullen, and Bonta 1994; MacKenzie 1997).

The findings on other cost-increasing intermediate sanctions are no more promising. Glimmers of a deterrence effect pop up once in a while, but the effects are isolated and do not stick, usually decaying after a short period of time. More commonly, the research shows that home confinement, electronic monitoring, shock incarceration or "boot camps," and, to a lesser extent, drug testing have little impact on offender criminal behavior (see, e.g., Bonta, Wallace-Capretta, and Rooney 2000; Cullen, Wright, and Applegate 1996). Notably, a recent meta-analysis of these programs showed that these cost-oriented intermediate punishment programs either had no effect on, or were associated with *increases* in, recidivism (Gendreau et al. 2000; Gendreau, Goggin, and Fulton 2000).

In a similar vein, Lipsey (1992) and Lipsey and Wilson (1998) have used meta-analysis to explore the impact of a range of intervention programs with juvenile offenders, including serious juvenile offenders. Their research is noteworthy because of its methodological rigor and sensitivity to how treatment effects can vary by the type of intervention employed. Thus, their research revealed that "deterrence programs" (e.g., shock incarceration, scared straight programs) had no effect on recidivism. In fact, exposing youthful offenders to these punishment-oriented interventions was associated with an increase in recidivism of 12 percentage points for delinquent offenders generally and of 3 percentage points for serious, violent youths (see also, Andrews and Bonta 1998; Andrews, Dowden, and Gendreau 1999; Andrews et al. 1990).

For rational choice theorists, this research, which consistently shows the ineffectiveness of cost- or punishment-oriented programs, should prompt a measure of modesty, if not the outright admission that the theory has some explaining to do. One response may be that once offenders are in the correctional system, the key to deterrence is not subjecting them to more inconveniences or constraints in the community (such as through intensive supervision) but to more severe prison terms. That is, being locked up—not being watched and "hassled" by a probation or parole officer while free in society—is the cost that stings sufficiently to make continued criminality an unattractive option. The specific deterrence research on this topic is surprisingly slim, which might offer some temporary relief to beleaguered rational choice theorists. But they should not rest too comfortably. Although the research is limited, nonetheless, it is not favorable to the deterrence position (Von Hirsch et al. 1999). Thus, a recent meta-analysis by Gendreau, Goggin, and Cullen (1999) reports that even when the risk level of offenders is taken into account, offenders sent to prison have a *higher* recidivism rate than those given "less costly" community sentences. Further, when the authors compared offenders who received longer sentences versus those who received shorter sentences, those in the "more imprisonment" group had a recidivism rate that was 3 percentage points *higher* (see also, Gendreau et al. 2000).

INCREASING THE BENEFITS OF CONFORMITY

Although rational choice theory easily justifies cost-oriented, get tough correctional interventions, the theory is *not* inherently punitive. Saying that crime is "chosen" implies that an alternative option is available to offenders: engaging in conduct other than crime—conformity. If this prosocial option were made more attractive than crime, then the theory would predict that the choice to pursue crime would be forfeited. Most often, rational choice theorists assume that although other factors may affect offenders' calculations, the key choice facing offenders is whether to accrue income through illegal means or through employment. In turn, this leads to the assumption that if offenders' legitimate work opportunities are increased—either directly by providing employment or indirectly by equipping them with the "human capital" (e.g., occupational skills, education) needed to secure more lucrative jobs—then their risk of recidivating would plummet. Within corrections, this approach thus suggests that programs that build human capital in offenders should be particularly effective in reducing further criminal involvement.

This line of thinking is evident, for example, in Orsagh and Marsden's (1985) articulation of a "rational-choice theory of offender rehabilitation." They begin with the observation that "income is attainable through legitimate and illegitimate activity" (p. 272). Offenders are not destined to keep choosing criminal endeavors if the cost-benefit ratio of their choices is altered. Thus, "if income earned per unit of time spent on legitimate activity increases relative to income per unit of time spent on illegitimate activity, illegitimate activity will decrease" (p. 272). "Rehabilitation programs," conclude Orsagh and Marsden, "can work if they increase income or increase the desire to [or 'taste' for] work" (p. 272).

This approach largely hinges on the assumption that employment—its presence or its absence—is the main predictor of criminal behavior. Micro-level studies tend to be favorable to the premise that working—especially in quality jobs—reduces illegal conduct (see, e.g., Sampson and Laub 1993), but the research is far from unanimous in finding that employment is an elixir for criminal propensities (for reviews, see Bushway and Reuter 1997; Fagan and Freeman 1999; Freeman 1995; Piehl 1998; Williams, Cullen, and Wright 1996). Moreover, crime and work are intertwined in complex ways. Thus, as Piehl (1998, 302) notes, "while it is true that crime rates are higher in poorer communities, and incarceration and arrest rates are higher for people with lower earnings potential, it is also true that most people who commit crimes also work in the legal sector and most people with low earnings are not involved in the criminal justice system." Complicating matters still further, there is a growing body of research revealing that, at least for youths of school age, extensive involvement in the workplace may increase the risk of delinquent involvement (see, e.g., Cullen, Williams, and Wright 1997; Wright and Cullen 2000; Wright, Cullen, and Williams 1997).

Given the complex, if not ambiguous, relationship between employment and crime, it is not surprising that correctional programs aimed at increasing offenders' human capital tend to have modest, though not inconsequential, effects on recidivism. Reaching firm conclusions about the rehabilitative efficacy of employment programs and of vocational and academic educational programs is hampered by the methodologically weak evaluation research on these interventions (Bushway and Reuter 1997; Wilson, Gallagher, and MacKenzie 2000). In particular, many studies lack experimental designs and cannot rule out selection bias that might account for ostensible reductions in recidivism for the "treatment" group. Still, reviews of the extant research, although varying in their assessment, suggest that at least some "benefit-oriented" correctional interventions work at least some of the time.

In this regard, Gerber and Fritsch (1995) have reviewed studies evaluating the effectiveness of adult academic and vocational correctional programs. They conclude that there is "a fair amount of support for the hypothesis" that these programs "lead to fewer disciplinary violations during incarceration, reductions in recidivism, to increases in employment opportunities, and to increases in participation in education upon release" (pp. 136–137). In contrast, Bushway and Reuter (1997) are more reserved, if not at times pessimistic, about the prospects for denting recidivism through work and vocational correctional programs. They argue, for example, that many programs have not been found to be effective, such as summer jobs or subsidized work programs for youths at risk for crime, short-term non-residential training programs for such at-risk youngsters, and court-based diversion of offenders of varying ages into job training. Nonetheless, they also contend that "short-term vocational training programs for older male ex-offenders no longer involved in the criminal justice system" do "work" to decrease criminal conduct (Chapter 6, p. 35). They further suggest that other interventions, though not definitively effective, are "promising." These include intensive residential training programs for youths (e.g., Job Corps) and vocational education for adult prisoners (see also, Sherman et al. 1998).

Perhaps the most useful summary of benefit-oriented, human capital programs has been undertaken by Wilson, Gallagher, and MacKenzie (2000). They conducted a meta-analysis of thirty-three corrections-based education, vocational, and work programs. Each study had a comparison group and used an experimental or quasi-experimental design. Overall, they found that program participants had a recidivism rate that was 11 percentage points lower than the control group (based on the standard assumption that non-participants in the program had a recidivism rate of 50 percent). In their sample of studies, education programs reduced recidivism more than work programs. Despite these positive findings, Wilson and his colleagues hesitated offering the firm conclusion that these programs "work" because most studies were not rigorous enough to rule out selection bias. Still, the overall pattern of results is promising and unlikely to be fully accounted for by methodological factors.

The research in this area leads us to offer three conclusions. First, although the positive effects of benefit-oriented programs remain to be confirmed, it is clear that these correctional interventions are more effective than cost-oriented correctional programs, whose record in reducing recidivism is dismal. A challenge for rational choice theory is to explain why correctional interventions that attempt to boost the costs of reoffending are ineffective while those that seek to increase the benefits of conformity are, in the least, promising.

Second, one plausible answer to the challenge just posed is that rational choice theory is of limited value in explaining the effectiveness of correctional interventions. Thus far, we have assumed that rational choice theory is perhaps half right: wrong on the cost side, correct on the benefit side. But this perspective may be wrong about benefit-boosting programs as well. The distinct possibility exists that the effectiveness of work and education programs is not because they prompt offenders to "rationally calculate" that employment is more lucrative than crime. Instead, these programs may "work"—to the extent that they do—because they are conduits for prosocial learning, build social bonds, reduce exposure to strains caused by blocked opportunities, and so on. That is, they may help to decrease the impact on program participants of the kinds of criminogenic factors that other criminological theories link to continuing involvement in crime.

Third, rational choice theory provides little insight into what the next step should be in developing effective correctional interventions. In the end, its limited view of crime causation—ignoring or underplaying the multiple factors that place offenders at risk of recidivating—restricts its vision on how correctional programs should be designed so as to have the best chance at reducing offender recidivism. Tied to the confining cost-benefit framework—and ignoring the findings of scientific criminology (Andrews and Bonta 1998)—rational choice theory can offer no guidance other than to repeat its mantra that, once again, we should somehow try to use correctional interventions to increase the costs of crime or, though less often voiced, to increase the benefits of conformity.

THE COST OF RATIONAL CHOICE THEORY: IGNORING
EFFECTIVE CORRECTIONAL INTERVENTIONS

The most significant danger of rational choice theory is that it will justify, if not lend an aura of scholarly legitimacy to, correctional interventions that promise to reduce crime by inflicting greater costs on offenders. The language of "costs" is comforting, because it sanitizes what is really at stake: As Clear (1994) illuminates, the real issue is the wisdom of trying to make offenders less criminogenic by *harming* them. We have suggested that there is little evidence that attempts to specifically deter offenders through punishment-oriented correctional interventions have proven effective.

But if the legitimation of get tough interventions is a "sin of commission," then rational choice theory is also guilty of a "sin of omission." As noted right above, rational choice theory can be read as suggesting that crime might be mitigated by equipping offenders with human capital and thus making work more profitable than criminal ventures. This approach has some merit, but it has its own dangers: It conceptualizes offenders largely as economic actors and thus ignores most other aspects about them—whether that pertains to their individual psychological traits or their current social relationships (for exceptions, see Nagin and Paternoster 1993; Piquero and Tibbetts 1996). Phrased differently, by ignoring the psychology and sociology of offending, rational choice theory is reductionistic and blinds us to the full range of factors that might be targeted for change by treatment interventions.

Indeed, the almost knee-jerk rejection of rehabilitation by rational choice theorists—a rejection in which anti-treatment research is selectively cited—is predictable and often seems dictated by the mindless adherence to a theoretical paradigm that is useful but limited. To "assume rationality" can have its heuristic value, but it does not obviate the mounting empirical evidence documenting the factors that predict recidivism, including, for example, antisocial attitudes and cognitions, procriminal associations, low self-control/impulsive temperament, and a dysfunctional family life (Andrews 1995; Andrews and Bonta 1998). In the end, rational choice theory is silent on what should be done, *within the context of corrections*, to address these criminogenic risk factors that lurk around and inside offenders on a daily basis. Advocates of the rational choice perspective can theoretically consign them to the amorphous category of a "taste for crime"—a set of variables that disinterest them and that they choose to "hold constant" in their analyses—but this is hardly the basis for developing effective correctional programs that will inhibit the capacity of these criminogenic factors to foster recidivism.

As Van Voorhis (1987) notes, there is ultimately a "high cost" of ignoring the "success" of rehabilitation. Although more than a quarter century old, Martinson's research (1974; see also Lipton, Martinson and Wilks 1975)—ostensibly showing that "nothing works" in correctional intervention—continues to be cited as the "final word" in many commentaries on rehabilitation (see, e.g., Reynolds 1996, 24). But much has changed since Martinson identified the possibility that many treatment programs were ineffective in "appreciably" reducing recidivism. A revisionist movement, rooted in positivist criminology, has emerged that has built a persuasive empirical case demonstrating the effectiveness of correctional rehabilitation. Relying on meta-analyses—the quantitative syntheses of evaluation studies—to furnish a systematic assessment of the impact of treatment interventions on crime, they have reached three interrelated conclusions (Cullen and Gendreau 2000).

First, a wide variety of problematic human behavior, including criminal conduct, is amenable to change through planned interventions (Lipsey and Wilson 1993). Second, across all correctional interventions, treatment programs reduce recidivism approximately 10 percentage points (e.g., if the control group had a 55 percent recidivism rate, the treatment group would have a 45 percent rate) (Losel 1995; Redondo, Sanchez-Meca, and Garrido 1999). Third and most important, they have shown that there is considerable *heterogeneity* in treatment effects: While some programs have a modest or weak influence on recidivism, other interventions achieve substantial reductions in recidivism (e.g., upward of 25 percentage points over control groups) (Andrews et al. 1990; Lipsey and Wilson 1993).

The key, of course, is to disentangle the factors that differentiate programs that work from those that don't. Toward this end, Andrews, Bonta, Gendreau, and their colleagues have made considerable strides in demarcating and testing successfully a "theory of effective correctional intervention" (Andrews 1995; Andrews and Bonta 1998; Andrews et al. 1990; Dowden and Andrews 1999; Gendreau 1996). Programs that achieve the largest reductions in recidivism thus share certain features. First, they are not cost- or deterrence-oriented. Second, they target for change the "known" (or empirically established) predictors of recidivism. Third, they avoid unstructured and psychodynamic treatment modalities, and instead use programs that are "cognitive-behavioural, skill-oriented, and multimodal" (Losel 1995, 91). Fourth, they focus on high-risk rather than low-risk offenders. Fifth, when possible, they take into account offenders' individual differences (e.g., IQ, learning styles) in the delivery of treatment services.

Again, programs based on these principles achieve substantial reductions in recidivism (Cullen and Gendreau 2000). Ignoring these successes and the related strategy for building effective correctional interventions strikes us as inexcusable. To do so is to jeopardize public safety and to relegate offenders, especially serious offenders, to an unattractive life in crime.

Unfortunately, rational choice theory moves us away from this approach to constructing knowledge about "what works" with offenders. Instead, it clings to a narrow understanding of crime causation that sponsors correctional interventions that are replete with failure (cost-oriented programs) and, at best, with limited success (benefit-oriented programs).

CONCLUSION: THE FUTURE OF CORRECTIONAL INTERVENTION

Let us hasten to reiterate that we make no claim that rational choice theory is fully incorrect—especially in its more sophisticated statements (Cornish and Clark 1986, 1–16)—and neither do we contend that the perspective is devoid of useful *crime control* insights (e.g., on situational crime prevention). In the realm of *corrections*, however, we are less enamored with the prospects for this theory to direct the development of effective interventions. As noted, the infusion of rational choice ideas into corrections is a potentially "dangerous liaison." Admittedly, this perspective is not inherently repressive; it can logically suggest that crime can be reduced by investing resources in offenders so as to make the decision to conform more beneficial than illegal choices. Even so, rational choice theory most easily and most often lends itself to the view that: (1) the costs of crime influence offender recidivism, (2) these costs are easy to manipulate, and (3) correctional programs are a medium through which costs can be exacted and offenders can be prompted to recalculate the rationality of reoffending.

We have suggested that such an approach is doomed to failure. Cost-oriented interventions have not proven capable of decreasing recidivism, in large part, we suspect, because punishment leaves untouched the factors that truly underlie the return of offenders to crime. In the end, rational choice theory has something to learn from "traditional" criminology: (1) crime is not merely a rational choice but a reflection of a range of causal variables that make offenders different from non-offenders, (2) unless correctional interventions target these criminogenic factors for change, the risk of recidivism will not be affected, and (3) rehabilitation programs rooted in theoretically valid and empirically substantiated principles are our "best bet" for effective correctional programming.

REFERENCES

Akers, Ronald L. 2000. *Criminological Theories: Introduction, Evaluation, and Application*, 3rd ed. Los Angeles: Roxbury.

Andrews, D. A. 1995. "The Psychology of Criminal Conduct and Effective Treatment." In *What Works: Reducing Reoffending*, edited by James McGuire, 35–62. West Sussex, England: John Wiley.

Andrews, D. A. and James Bonta. 1998. *Psychology of Criminal Conduct*, 2nd ed. Cincinnati: Anderson.

Andrews, D. A., Craig Dowden, and Paul Gendreau. 1999. "Clinically Relevant and Psychologically Informed Approaches to Reduced Re-Offending: A Meta-Analytic Study of Human Service, Risk, Need, Responsivity, and Other Concerns in Justice Contexts." Unpublished manuscript, Carleton University.

Andrews. D. A., Ivan Zinger, R. D. Hoge, James Bonta, Paul Gendreau, and Francis T. Cullen. 1990. "Does Correctional Treatment Work? A Clinically Relevant and Psychologically Informed Meta-Analysis." *Criminology* 28: 369–404.

Bonta, James, Suzanne Wallace-Capretta, and Jennifer Rooney. 2000. "Can Electronic Monitoring Make a Difference? An Evaluation of Three Canadian Programs." *Crime and Delinquency* 46:61–75.

Braithwaite, John. 1989. *Crime, Shame and Reintegration*. Cambridge, England: Cambridge University Press.

———. 1997. "On Speaking Softly and Carrying Big Sticks: Neglected Dimensions of a Republication Separation of Powers." *University of Toronto Law Journal* 47: 305–362.

Brehm, Sharon S. and Jack W. Brehm. 1981. *Psychological Reactance: A Theory of Freedom and Control*. New York: Academic Press.

Bushway, Shawn and Peter Reuter. 1997. "Labor Markets and Crime Risk Factors." In *Preventing Crime: What Works, What Doesn't, What's Promising—A Report to the United States Congress*, edited by Lawrence W. Sherman, Denise Gottfredson, Doris MacKenzie, John Eck, Peter Reuter, and Shawn Bushway, Chapter 6. Unpublished report, University of Maryland.

Byrne, James and April Pattavina. 1992. "The Effectiveness Issue: Assessing What Works in the Adult Community Corrections System." In *Smart Sentencing: The Emergence of Intermediate Sanctions*, edited by James Byrne, Arthur Lurigio, and Joan Petersilia, 281–303. Newbury Park, CA: Sage.

Clarke, Ronald V., ed. 1992. *Situational Crime Prevention: Successful Case Studies*. New York: Harrow and Heston.

Clarke, Ronald V. and Marcus Felson, eds. *Routine Activity and Rational Choice—Advances in Criminological Theory*, vol. 5. New Brunswick, NJ: Transaction.

Clear, Todd R. 1994. *Harm in American Penology: Offenders, Victims, and Their Communities*. Albany: State University of New York Press.

Colvin, Mark. 2000. *Crime and Coercion: An Integrated Theory of Chronic Criminality*. New York: St. Martin's Press.

Cook, Philip J. 1980. "Punishment and Crime: A Critique of Current Findings Concerning the Preventative Effects of Punishment." In *The*

Economics of Crime, edited by Ralph Andreano and John J. Siegfried, 137–179. New York: John Wiley.

————. 1986. "Criminal Incapacitation Effects Considered in an Adaptive Choice Framework." In *The Reasoning Criminal: Rational Choice Perspectives on Offending,* edited by Derek B. Cornish and Ronald V. Clarke, 202–216. New York: Springer-Verlag.

Cornish, Derek B. and Ronald V. Clarke, eds. 1986. *The Reasoning Criminal: Rational Choice Perspectives on Offending.* New York: Springer-Verlag.

Cullen, Francis T. and Paul Gendreau. 2000. "Assessing Correctional Rehabilitation: Policy, Practice, and Prospects." In *Criminal Justice 2000: Volume 3—Policies, Processes, and Decisions of the Criminal Justice System,* edited by Julie Horney, 109–175. Washington, D.C.: U.S. Department of Justice, National Institute of Justice.

Cullen, Francis T., Nicolas Williams, and John Paul Wright. 1997. "Work Conditions and Juvenile Delinquency: Is Youth Employment Criminogenic?" *Criminal Justice Policy Review* 8: 119–143.

Cullen, Francis T., John Paul Wright, and Brandon K. Applegate. 1996. "Control in the Community: The Limits of Reform?" In *Choosing Correctional Interventions That Work: Defining the Demand and Evaluating the Supply,* edited by Alan T. Harland, 69–116. Thousand Oaks, CA: Sage.

Currie, Elliott. 1998. *Crime and Punishment in America.* New York: Metropolitan Books.

Dowden, Craig and D. A. Andrews. 1999. "What Works for Female Offenders: A Meta-Analytic Review." *Crime and Delinquency* 45: 438–452.

Eagly, Alice H. and Shelly Chaiken. 1993. *The Psychology of Attitudes.* Fort Worth, TX.: Harcourt, Brace, Jovanovich.

Evans, Robert, Jr. 1980. "The Labor Market and Parole Success." In *The Economics of Crime,* edited by Ralph Andreano and John J. Siegfried, 325–335. New York: John Wiley.

Fagan, Jeffrey and Richard B. Freeman. 1999. "Crime and Work." In *Crime and Justice: A Review of Research,* vol. 25, edited by Michael Tonry, 225–290. Chicago: University of Chicago Press.

Freeman, Richard B. 1995. "The Labor Market." In *Crime,* edited by James Q. Wilson and Joan Petersilia, 171–191. San Francisco: ICS Press.

Fulton, Besy, Edward J. Latessa, Amy Stichman, and Lawrence F. Travis III. 1997. "The State of ISP: Research and Policy Implications." *Federal Probation* 61 (December): 65–75.

Gendreau, Paul. 1996. "The Principles of Effective Intervention with Offenders." In *Choosing Correctional Options That Work: Defining the*

Demand and Evaluating the Supply, edited by Alan T. Harland, 117–130. Newbury Park, CA: Sage.

Gendreau, Paul, Francis T. Cullen, and James Bonta. 1994. "Intensive Rehabilitation Supervision: The Next Generation in Community Corrections?" *Federal Probation* 58 (March): 72–78.

Gendreau, Paul, Claire Goggin, and Francis T. Cullen. 1999. *The Effects of Prison Sentences on Recidivism.* Ottawa, Canada: Public Works and Government Services Canada.

Gendreau, Paul, Claire Goggin, Francis T. Cullen, and D. A. Andrews. 2000. "The Effects of Community Sanctions and Incarceration on Recidivism." *Forum on Corrections Research* 12 (May): 10–13.

Gendreau, Paul, Claire Goggin, and Betsy Fulton. 2000. "Intensive Supervision in Probation and Parole." In *Handbook of Offender Assessment and Treatment*, edited by Clive R. Hollin, 195–204. London, England: John Wiley.

Gendreau, Paul and Robert R. Ross. 1979. "Effective Correctional Treatment: Bibliotherapy for Cynics." *Crime and Delinquency* 25: 463–489.

———. 1987. "Revivification of Rehabilitation: Evidence from the 1980s." *Justice Quarterly* 4: 349–407.

Gerber, Jurg and Eric J. Fritsch. 1995. "Adult Academic and Vocational Correctional Education Programs: A Review of Recent Research." *Journal of Offender Rehabilitation* 22: 119–142.

Kleiman, Mark A. R. 1999. "Getting Deterrence Right: Applying Tipping Models and Behavioral Economics to the Problems of Crime Control." In *Perspectives on Crime and Justice: 1998–1999 Lecture Series*, vol. 3, 1–29. Washington, D.C.: National Institute of Justice.

Lipsey, Mark W. 1992. "Juvenile Delinquency Treatment: A Meta-Analytic Inquiry into the Variability of Effects." In *Meta-Analysis for Explanation: A Casebook*, edited by Thomas D. Cook, Harris Cooper, David S. Cordray, Heidi Hartmann, Larry V. Hedges, Richard J. Light, Thomas A. Louis, and Frederick Mosteller, 83–127. New York: Russell Sage.

Lipsey, Mark W. and David B. Wilson. 1993. "The Efficacy of Psychological, Educational, and Behavioral Treatment." *American Psychologist* 48: 1181–1209.

———. 1998. "Effective Intervention for Serious Juvenile Offenders." In *Serious and Violent Juvenile Offenders: Risk Factors and Successful Interventions*, edited by Rolf Loeber and David P. Farrington, 313–345. Thousand Oaks, CA: Sage.

Lipton, Douglas, Robert Martinson, and Judith Wilks. 1975. *The Effectiveness of Correctional Treatment: A Survey of Treatment Evaluation Studies.* New York: Praeger.

Losel, Frederich. 1995. "The Efficacy of Correctional Treatment: A Review and Synthesis of Meta-Evaluations." In *What Works: Reducing Reoffending*, edited by James McGuire, 79–111. West Sussex, England: John Wiley.

Luksetich, William A. and Michael D. White. 1982. *Crime and Public Policy: An Economic Approach*. Boston: Little, Brown.

Lynch, Michael J. 1999. "Beating a Dead Horse: Is There Any Basic Empirical Evidence for the Deterrent Effect of Imprisonment?" *Crime, Law and Social Change* 31: 347–362.

MacKenzie, Doris Layton. 1997. "Criminal Justice and Crime Prevention." In *Preventing Crime: What Works, What Doesn't, What's Promising— A Report to the United States Congress*, edited by Lawrence W. Sherman, Denise Gottfredson, Doris Layton MacKenzie, John Eck, Peter Reuter, and Shawn Bushway. Unpublished report, University of Maryland.

Martinson, Robert. 1974. "What Works?—Questions and Answers About Prison Reform." *The Public Interest* 35 (Spring): 22–54.

Marvell, Thomas B. and Carlisle E. Moody. 1999. "Female and Male Homicide Victimization Rates: Comparing Trends and Regressors." *Criminology* 37: 879–902.

Moffitt, Terrie E. 1983. "The Learning Theory Model of Punishment: Implications for Deterrence." *Criminal Justice and Behavior* 10: 131–158.

Nagin, Daniel S. 1998a. "Criminal Deterrence Research at the Outset of the Twenty-First Century." In *Crime and Justice: A Review of Research*, vol. 23, edited by Michael Tonry, 1–42. Chicago: University of Chicago Press.

―――――. 1998b. "Deterrence and Incapacitation." In *The Handbook of Crime and Punishment*, edited by Michael Tonry, 345–368. New York: Oxford University Press.

Nagin, Daniel S. and Raymond Paternoster. 1993. "Enduring Individual Differences and Rational Choice Theories of Crime." *Law and Society Review* 27: 467–496.

Orsagh, Thomas and Mary Ellen Marsden. 1985. "What Works When: Rational Choice Theory and Offender Rehabilitation." *Journal of Criminal Justice* 13: 269–277.

Petersilia, Joan. 1992. "California's Prison Policy: Causes, Costs, and Consequences." *The Prison Journal* 72: 8–36.

Petersilia, Joan and Susan Turner. 1993. "Intensive Probation and Parole." In *Crime and Justice: A Review of Research*, vol. 17, edited by Michael Tonry, 281–335. Chicago: University of Chicago Press.

Piehl, Ann Morrison. 1998. "Economic Conditions, Work, and Crime." In *The Handbook of Crime and Punishment*, edited by Michael Tonry, 302–319. New York: Oxford University Press.

Piquero, Alex and Stephen Tibbetts. 1996. "Specifying the Direct and Indirect Effects of Low Self-Control and Situational Factors in Offenders' Decision Making: Toward a More Complete Model of Rational Offending." *Justice Quarterly* 13:481–510.

Redondo, Santiago, Julio Sanchez-Meca, and Vincente Garrido. 1999. "The Influence of Treatment Programs on the Recidivism of Juveniles and Adult Offenders: An European Meta-Analytic Review." *Psychology, Crime, and Law* 5: 251–278.

Ridenour, Amy. 1999. "Context of Silliest Lawsuits Ever." *Cincinnati Enquirer*, July 20, p. A6.

Reynolds, Morgan O. 1996. *Crime and Punishment in Texas: An Update*. Dallas, TX: National Center for Policy Analysis.

Sampson, Robert J. and John H. Laub. 1993. *Crime in the Making: Pathways and Turning Points Through Life*. Cambridge, Mass.: Harvard University Press.

Sherman, Lawrence W. 1993. "Defiance, Deterrence, and Irrelevance: A Theory of the Criminal Sanction." *Journal of Research in Crime and Delinquency* 30: 445–473.

Sherman, Lawrence W., Denise Gottfredson, Doris L. MacKenzie, John Eck, Peter Reuter, and Shawn D. Bushway, eds. 1998. *Preventing Crime: What Works, What Doesn't, What's Promising*, National Institute of Justice Research in Brief. Washington, D.C.: U.S. Department of Justice, National Institute of Justice.

Stolzenberg, Lisa, and Stewart J. DAlessio. 1997. "'Three Strikes and You're Out': The Impact of California's New Mandatory Sentencing Law on Serious Crime Rates." *Crime and Delinquency* 43: 457–469.

Van Voorhis, Patricia. 1987. "Correctional Effectiveness: The High Cost of Ignoring Success." *Federal Probation* 51 (March): 59–62.

Von Hirsch, Andrew, Anthony E. Bottoms, Elizabeth Burney, and P. O. Wikstrom. 1999. *Criminal Deterrence and Sentence Severity: An Analysis of Recent Research*. Oxford, UK: Hart Publishing.

Votey, Harold J., Jr. and Llad Phillips. 1980. "Social goals and Appropriate Policy for Corrections: An Economic Appraisal." In *The Economics of Crime*, edited by Ralph Andreano and John J. Siegfried, 297–324. New York: John Wiley.

Williams, Nicolas, Francis T. Cullen, and John Paul Wright. 1996. "Labor Market Participation and Youth Crime: The Neglect of 'Working' in Delinquency Research." *Social Pathology* 2: 195–217.

Williams, Vergil L. and Mary Fish. 1971. "Rehabilitation and Economic Self-Interest," *Crime and Delinquency*, 17: 408–413.

Wilson, David B., Catherine A. Gallagher, and Doris Layton MacKenzie. 1999. "A Meta-Analysis of Corrections-Based Education, Vocation, and Work Programs for Adult Offenders." *Journal of Research in Crime and Delinquency* 37: 347–368.

Wright, John Paul and Francis T. Cullen. 2000. "Juvenile Involvement in Occupational Delinquency." *Criminology* 38: 863–892.

Wright, John Paul, Francis T. Cullen, and Nicolas Williams. 1997. "Working While in School and Delinquent Involvement: Implications for Social Policy." *Crime and Delinquency* 43: 203–221.

Chapter 14

The Impact of Lambda Skewness on Criminology: A Contingent Analysis

Thomas B. Marvell

INTRODUCTION

Criminals' individual crime rates (lambdas) have a distribution that is highly skewed, and the skewness is "to the right" such that a few criminals commit many more crimes than others and these few are responsible for most crimes. The extent of this skewness, however, is far from settled. The thesis here is that the skewness might be much greater than commonly assumed, and that this has important implications for rational choice theory in criminology and for criminal justice policy. Currently they both assume that the skewness is at the low end of the feasible range. If skewness is at the high end—and there is substantial evidence that it is—then theory and policy should be reconsidered.

The study traditionally cited for the extent of skewness is Wolfgang, Figlio, and Sellin (1972, 89), which studied a cohort of Philadelphia boys from ten to eighteen years old. They estimated that 18 percent of offenders account for 62 percent of all offenses committed by the sample. This finding has been replicated several times for (e.g., Shannon 1991; see generally the literature review in Piquero, 2000), and this degree of skewness is now commonly accepted in criminology (e.g., Auerhahn 1999; Weiss 1987, 27). Several concerns, however, raise suspicions. The studies are limited to juveniles and might not apply to adults. Criminality is determined by arrests, which might be for crimes not committed and which vastly underestimate crimes actually committed. Finally, the findings are based on the uncertain assumption that frequent criminals are as likely to be arrested for each crime as infrequent criminals.

A second source of information about skewness comes from criminals' accounts of their activities. The major study is the 1979 Rand Corporation survey of samples of newly admitted prisoners in California, Michigan, and Texas (Chaiken and Chaiken 1982). Among the criminals who said they committed non-drug crimes[1] when on the street (80 percent of the sample) the median criminal committed crimes at an annualized rate of fifteen, and the ninetieth percentile figure is 605 (Chaiken and Chaiken 1982, 44). The Chaikens illustrate the extreme skewness of the distribution by showing that if the distribution were symmetric, such as a normal distribution, then the ninetieth percentile would be only about twice the median, rather than the actual forty times.

The Chaikens did not calculate percentages, such as Wolfgang did, for the portion of crimes committed by the high-end criminals, but these figures can be estimated from Chaiken and Chaiken (1982, 222). On an annualized basis, the top 10 percent of criminals commit approximately 80 percent of the crimes, and the top 5 percent commit approximately 65 percent.[2] Henceforth in this paper, for the sake of simplicity, the top 10 percent of criminals are called "active criminals," and the others are called "ordinary criminals."

Thus, a crude comparison is that the Rand survey suggests roughly four times more crime concentration at the high end than Wolfgang et al. found. Even this is probably an understatement because the Rand sample of criminals consists of adults who had been convicted of crimes serious enough, or convicted of enough crimes, to result in a sentences of incarceration. The 5 percent and 10 percent figures use a base of relatively serious criminals.

The mean annual crime rate is approximately 2,000 for the top five percentile, and 1,400 for the top ten percentile.[3] As for the types of crimes committed, the best indicator available for active criminals is crimes committed by what the Chaikens call "violent predators," the most active of their ten categories of criminals. On average, 14 percent of their non-drug crimes are robberies, 32 percent burglaries, 32 percent larcenies, 8 percent auto thefts, 7 percent forgery, and 8 percent fraud (calculated from Chaiken and Chaiken 1982, 219–221).

It takes relatively few active criminals committing 1,400 crimes a year to account for most crime in the United States. After adjusting for underreporting, there are roughly 50 million Uniform Crime Report (UCR) crimes a year. Thirty thousand active criminals would account for more than 80 percent of these. Of course, this assumes that the active criminals remain on the street—that is, that they continue committing crime at a high pace for some time before being arrested and convicted. Our knowledge is scanty on this topic. Marvell and Moody (1984, 114) estimated that the chances of arrest per robbery declines greatly and continuously as criminals' individual robbery rates rise, such that on average chances of arrest of active criminals for any one robbery are very small.[4] As a result, the average chance of arrest over the course of a year is actually greater for occasional robbers (approximately 20 percent) than for active robbers (approximately 12 percent). (Criminals' overall chances of arrest during a year are higher than these figures suggest because most commit crimes other than robbery, for which they might also be arrested.) Some active criminals, one can surmise, are inept and are apprehended soon after they hit the streets. At the other end, as Chaiken and Chaiken (1985) stress, there may well be some active criminals who manage to evade arrest and conviction altogether. All things considered, the typical active criminal is at least as likely to be on the street as the typical ordinary criminal, even though the former commits far more crimes.

All the calculations so far, including the chances of arrest, are derived from the Rand surveys and depend on the assumption that respondents who report very large crime rates give reasonably accurate answers to questions concerning how many crimes they commit. Perhaps these prisoners did not understand the survey instruments, but two research projects designed to test the sensitivity of prisoner estimates of crime activity to variations in the survey procedure found little impact (English and Mande 1992; Horney and Marshall 1992). Perhaps the prisoners who report very high crime rates are not telling the truth, "amusing themselves at the expense of the researchers by giving outrageous reports" (Marvell and Moody 1994, 113). One would assume that convicted criminals are less truthful than ordinary citizens. Perhaps the respondents do not remember how many crimes they committed. Wright and Decker (1997, 13–14) conducted informal interviews with active robbers and gave up trying to calculate their lambdas because the respondents had only a hazy idea about how often they had robbed during their careers. However, the prison surveys went to considerable lengths to mitigate this problem; the lambdas are based on criminal activity reported for the past year or two, not the total career, and most studies contain internal tests to locate prisoners with poor memories. Also, the difference between ordinary and active criminals are so extreme that it cannot be due to memory differences.

Spelman (1994) and Simon (1999) argue that the criminals reporting high lamdas give inaccurate answers generally, but their reasoning is clearly false. They compared the actual arrest records with the prisoners' accounts of the number of times they were arrested, and found that prisoners who reported high lambdas generally reported more arrests than the official records show. This is meaningless because the arrest records outside the state were not included, and as discussed below, active criminals are more likely to be mobile than ordinary criminals. In general, many criminals have arrest records in more than one state, and those with the most arrests are more likely to be arrested in more than one state (Orsagh 1992). Also, juvenile records were not included in the official count. And it is likely that the Rand researchers missed many prior arrests due to incomplete and confusing records, especially in Michigan.

The strongest argument for the accuracy of the extreme lambda estimates is that they have been replicated in prisoner surveys in a sizable number of jurisdictions. In the Rand study, the extent of skewness occurred in samples of inmates in California and Michigan jails, and California, Michigan, and Texas prisons. Subsequently similar results were found in three new studies in New Orleans jails (Miranne and Geerken 1991, 508–510), Nebraska prisons (Horney and Marshall 1991), and Colorado prisons (English and Mande 1992, 73).

Graphs provided by English and Mande, for example, indicate that 10 percent of the robbers (i.e., prisoners who said they committed at least one robbery) account for 80 percent of the robberies estimated on an annualized basis, 10 percent of the burglars accounted for almost 80 percent of the burglaries, 10 percent of the thieves accounted for 70 percent of the larcenies, and 10 percent of the auto thieves accounted for 75 percent of auto thefts. The percentages for assault are a little lower, and those for fraud and forgery are a little larger. These figures are clearly consistent with the estimate from the Rand study that 10 percent of criminals are responsible for 80 percent of the non-drug crimes on an annualized basis.

Table 1. Indications of Skewness in Three Studies

	Lambdas			Ratios of	
	Median	Mean	90th Percentile	Mean to Median	90th to Median
Rand total	15	220	605	15	40
California prison	42	258	989	6	24
California jail	17	221	735	13	43
Michigan prison	17	222	645	13	38
Michigan jail	9	147	438	16	49
Texas prison	9	107	338	12	38
New Orleans	4.4	66	166	15	38
Nebraska	4.2	172	483	33	115

Notes: These lambda distributions are for non-drug crimes, and pertain only to prisoners who said they committed at least one non-drug crime in the sample time frame (66% to 85% of the subjects). Data are from Chaiken and Chaiken (1982: 215,222), Miranne and Geerkin (1991), and Horney and Marshall (1991).

Similar estimates are not given in, nor can they be estimated from, the Nebraska and New Orleans studies and the five subsamples in the Rand study. Here the extent of skewness is suggested by the ratio of the mean to the median and the ratio of the ninetieth percentile to the median.[5] As can be seen in Table 1, the studies usually do not depart far from the total Rand sample; the major exceptions are the lesser skewness for the California prison sample and the greater skewness in the Nebraska prison sample. In other words, if the extreme skewness described above with respect to the overall Rand survey results is due to a few subjects who misunderstand the survey instrument or who are exaggerating, there must be similar misunderstanding and exaggerating at all sites, and it must be done by roughly the same portion of subjects. That would be an unlikely coincidence.

There is very little research that sheds light on what active criminals are like. Perhaps the best source is biographies (e.g., Comwell and Sutherland 1956; Jackson 1969 and 1972; King and Chambliss 1984; Malcolm X and Haley 1964; Martin 1970). These criminals view crime as an enterprise in which intelligence, skill, experience, and flexibility are important. They are probably more intelligent, and certainly more skilled than ordinary criminals. Their income comes almost exclusively from crime. They work in small groups, and they take pains to plan their crimes. They are very mobile, moving away from a town as soon as they fear the police have noticed them or when skipping bail. Their mobility means that they do not accumulate crime records in any one state. The active criminals are far from upright citizens; their lifestyles are marked by drinking, drugs, gambling, and use of prostitutes (but they are probably less likely to be drug addicts or alcoholics than ordinary criminals). They seldom have wives or long-term partners.

Besides being able to escape arrest, active criminals are adept at escaping conviction if apprehended. Most biographies listed above discuss the same procedure by which active criminals manage to have charges dismissed. When arrested, they hire a lawyer known to be a fixer. The lawyer contacts the victim and offers reimbursement for the loss, perhaps with a bonus, if the complaint is not pressed. The victim generally agrees, probably stimulated in part by the desire to avoid court appearances. The lawyer then persuades the arresting police officer not to press the case. It is not clear whether these procedures are still common, however, since the biographical information is decades old.

The case for the active criminal is not ironclad. Again, there is a chance that reports by a few prisoners of enormous crime volume are mistaken or fabricated. Perhaps these criminals are more vulnerable to arrest than calculated above, such that they spend little time on the street before they are incarcerated again. Unfortunately, research on these topics has nearly stopped, leaving these issues hanging. The findings run counter to the experiences of researchers and other criminal justice practitioners. They face severe selection bias: the vast bulk of criminals they encounter are ordinary criminals, and the few criminals who are active have every incentive to hide that fact from the police and courts.

In all, the evidence available suggests that it is probably more likely than not that the active criminals exist and that they account for the great majority of UCR crimes. The rest of the paper explores the consequences on criminology theory and practice if one assumes that this is the actual situation. For stylistic reasons, the language used assumes that these facts are certain; left out are numerous qualifications, such as "assuming that active criminals account for the great majority of crimes." The reader, however, must keep in mind that the analysis is contingent upon this assumption. It is not intended as an absolute argument.

The discussion is broad and touches many areas of criminology. The order of topics is the implications for individual-level research, rational choice theory, incapacitation research, sentencing, and structural correlates of crime.

IMPLICATIONS FOR INDIVIDUAL-LEVEL RESEARCH

Lambda skewness affects individual-level criminology research because few subjects are active criminals and each subject is counted as one unit. Findings pertain only to ordinary criminals, who contribute little to the crime rates. This is true whether the studies are based on general samples or on samples of criminals, and whether criminality is determined by official records or self-reported crime. Therefore, unless there is little difference between active and ordinary criminals, findings from individual-level studies have limited importance for crime reduction efforts. In illustrating this point, the discussion below is divided into four topics: criminal personality, criminal career description, regression research, and policy implications.

Criminal Personalities

Perhaps the two most important contemporary theories of criminal personality are by Gottfredson and Hirschi (1990) and Caspi and Moffitt (e.g., Caspi et al. 1996; Moffitt et al. 1996). The two are similar in that many elements overlap. Also, both are based on studies of ordinary criminals, and there is good reason to believe that they do not apply to active criminals. The central trait of criminals, according to Gottfredson and Hirschi (1990), is low self control. They are typically risk-seeking, impulsive, hot tempered, self-centered, and favoring physical rather than mental activities. Caspi et al. argue that criminals tend to be (1) low on constraint, (2) high on negative emotionality, and (3) low on positive emotionality. The first trait is that they seek thrills, contest social norms, and act impetuously. The second is that they have low thresholds for anxiety and anger, and they perceive the world as threatening. In the third, they view life generally as an unpleasant experience and are reluctant to have close relationships with others.

Whatever the merits of these descriptions, they do not apply to active criminals, who comprise at most a very small part of the samples of citizens or criminals used to develop the personality traits. The traits are nearly the exact opposite of traits posited earlier for the active criminals—that is, of criminals who are skilled at committing crimes and escaping apprehension. The Gottfredson/Hirschi and Caspi/Moffitt traits are of criminals who are most likely to be labeled as criminals, either in official records or self-reports, and not necessarily of persons who engage in the most criminal activity. The personality traits are probably at least partly artifacts of the procedures for identifying criminals. Determining criminality through official records almost always means counting local arrests or convictions. Persons with putative criminal personalities are particularly likely to be arrested and convicted. Their risk-seeking nature suggests that they are more likely to commit crimes when chances of apprehension are relatively high. Their impulsiveness, their tempers, and their aversion to mental activity suggest that they make little effort to plan crimes, again increasing the chance of arrest. Also, once arrested, these criminals are probably more likely than others to be convicted because they are less able to navigate the criminal justice system.

Studies based on self-reports of criminality encounter similar problems. The act of admitting to crimes is itself a risk-taking act—a criminal has nothing to gain from such admissions, apart from the thrill of talking about the crimes. From the respondents' viewpoint, there is an uncertain possibility that the admissions will become known to the authorities. It is even possible that thrill-seeking respondents fabricate or exaggerate criminal activity. A rational criminal who has committed many crimes and who is risk-aversive would not wish to admit to the crimes.

Another reason why persons with putative criminal personalities might report more crime in surveys—are less reluctant to admit to criminal activity—is that they are less likely to believe that criminal activity is wrong. Respondents are more likely to remember and admit to criminal behavior if such behavior is consistent with their values and beliefs (Weiss 1987, 29–31). Especially under the Caspi/Moffitt theory, the criminal personality includes an angry world view, in which the person is alone and the surrounding society is adverse. Hence, they are likely to believe that criminal activity is a justifiable adaptation to their situations.

Descriptions of Criminals' Careers

The large body of research on criminal careers is not likely to apply to active criminals, who comprise at best a small portion of the samples studied. The common finding is that most criminals terminate criminal activity at a fairly young age. The data used to describe criminal careers usually come from arrest records, and it is likely that arrests taper off simply because criminals learn through experience to improve their modus operandi. The curves describing the terminations of criminal careers might in reality be the inverse of learning curves. This problem probably applies mainly to active criminals, who are adept at escaping arrest.

Another use of arrest records to determine the shape of criminals' careers is the estimates of lambda by Blumstein and Cohen (1979) and Cohen (1986). They estimated the mean crime rate for a sample of criminals by counting the number of arrests in local records and dividing by the probability of arrest for each crime. The resulting estimate is approximately ten UCR crimes per criminal per year, an order of magnitude lower than the mean lambda obtained from prisoner surveys. Their calculations, however, assume that there is no correlation between a criminal's crime rate and chances of arrest, which is clearly wrong (Blumstein, Cohen, and Visher 1988).

Researchers routinely find that ordinary criminals specialize little (see the summary in Kempf 1987; also Wolfgang, Figlio, and Sellin 1972). Gottfredson and Hirschi (1990, 91) cite lack of specialization as a corollary to their theory of criminal personality: Criminals have general criminal propensities, and the particular crime they commit is influenced by the setting and opportunities presented. An unstated assumption is that the criminals are unskilled, because in any endeavor skill typically presupposes specialization. Many of the personality traits posited by Gottfredson and Hirschi, impulsiveness and adverseness to complex tasks and mental activities, suggest lack of skill. However, the findings of lack of specialization are not based on active criminals, who are more skilled than ordinary criminals, and it is likely that the active criminals do specialize in the same manner as other skilled workers.

Regression Research

Most individual-level research that attempts to determine causes of criminal behavior is regression research. The findings are largely irrelevant from a crime-control perspective because, again, the samples contain few active criminals, who are different from ordinary criminals and who are responsible for the great majority of crimes.

This problem does not affect research with aggregate data. Whenever results differ between individual- and aggregate-level studies, macro-level research is more useful from a crime-control prospective. The obvious reason is that aggregated crime rates include crimes by active criminals, in essence weighting them according to how many crimes they commit. The active criminals contribute to the results of aggregate-level research in proportion to the amount of crime they commit.[6] This is an example of disaggregation bias, which can occur when the disaggregated research violates the assumption required for regression analysis that the coefficients are the same for each observation. That is, individual-level crime regressions assume that each subject's criminality is related to each regressor in the same way, which again means that they make the unjustified assumption that ordinary and active criminals are affected the same way by the factors studied. Aggregation mitigates, but does not eliminate, this problem because the coefficients are essentially weighted averages of the coefficients for individual criminals, weighted according to the amount of crime each commits.[7]

Effectiveness of Treatment Programs

The huge body of research that attempts to evaluate treatment programs designed to reduce criminal behavior suffers from similar problems and, thus, cannot be used to establish crime-reduction policy. Because nearly all delinquents and criminals placed in a program evaluated are ordinary criminals (because, of course, nearly all criminals are ordinary criminals), and the program's effectiveness is determined by its impact on ordinary criminals. To my knowledge, this research never evaluates the impact of the programs on active criminals. Such an evaluation is probably not feasible, even with the most sophisticated controlled experiment designs, because the researcher cannot easily identify the active criminals in their sample and cannot easily gather a sample of active criminals large enough for analysis. Thus, optimistic views concerning the ability of criminal justice programs to reduce crime and the ability of researchers to determine that such programs work (e.g., Catalano, Arthur, Hawkins, Berglund, and Olson 1998) are mistaken.

Especially objectionable are studies such as Donohue and Siegelman (1998) and Greenwood, Model, Rydell, and Chiesa (1998) that make cost-benefit comparisons of various programs that are believed to reduce crime, for example imprisonment versus giving child-rearing aid. These either ignore active criminals altogether or are based on mixtures of evaluations that take account of active criminals (e.g., by using aggregate data) and those that ignore them, which renders any comparison invalid.

Another problem with these evaluations is the use of arrest records to determine whether a program has succeeded concerning a particular subject. Typically "recidivism" is determined by whether the subject is arrested. These research procedures are questionable because of the low chances of arrest generally and the much lower chances for active criminals. An arrest is probably a better indicator of ineptness than of criminality.

Policy Implications

In sum, unless individual-level research can distinguish between ordinary and active criminals, it has little direct applicability to crime control policy. A top priority for research should be to develop the tools needed to identify active criminals. This would enable courts to give longer sentences to active criminals, the topic of a later section.

Obviously, also, individual-level research has policy importance in many areas other than crime control. Racial discrimination is an obvious example. The criminal personality models discussed above suggest that ordinary criminals lead anguished lives, which individual-level research should attempt to alleviate. Individual-level research is best viewed as a tool to reduce the number of criminals—that is criminal-reduction rather than crime-reduction. Understanding why individuals engage in criminal behavior might eventually reduce the number of persons subjected to the criminal justice system, a humanitarian effort to spare petty criminals from the discomforts involved.

RATIONAL CHOICE THEORY AND ACTIVE CRIMINALS

The difference between active criminals and the criminal personality types discussed above is largely the degree of rationality criminals use. A rough approximation is that active criminals use something close to "normative rationality" and ordinary criminals use "limited rationality" or no obvious rationality at all. The notion of limited rationality, with uncertain goals and crude measures to reach them, is a difficult foundation for theory formation or hypothesis testing. Focusing on active criminals might provide a firmer foundation for linking rational choice theory and crime rates.

Ordinary criminals with the criminal personalities described above have a strong streak of irrationality—recklessness, thrill seeking, and hot tempers. Katz (1988) argues, on the basis of secondary sources, that assumptions of rationality usually do not apply to criminals, largely because thrill seeking is a major goal. Wright and Decker (1994, 1997) argue, on the basis of interviews with working robbers and burglars, that although economic concerns dominate, thrill seeking is often a major goal; and although there is some utilitarian concern in the selection of targets, most crimes are not rationally planned. These arguments pertain to ordinary criminals, and to my knowledge no rational choice analysis has dealt with active criminals.

Although not much is known about active criminals, it is safe to conclude that they are considerably more rational than ordinary criminals in the sense that they calculate their chances of success and plan their crimes. Their ability to escape arrest is strong evidence of this. Chaiken and Chaiken (1985) studied a subgroup in the Rand survey who had relatively high lambdas and very small chances of arrest, and found that they plan crimes especially thoroughly. They are also less likely to be heroin addicts.

Thus, the fact that active criminals dominate crime rates strengthens rational choice theory in the sense that there is some justification for assuming that crime rates are dominated by actors who plan their crimes with an eye toward the most gain for the least risk to maximize their income. On the other hand, active criminals complicate rational choice theory because researchers and criminal justice officials might not be able to anticipate the strategies and tactics these criminals use. Active criminals are probably more knowledgeable about the criminal enterprise than criminologists, and they may be as intelligent. It is also questionable whether police or other criminal justice personnel have the ability to determine what calculations active criminals might make to evade crime-reduction efforts.

As a general rule, criminologists, when using rational choice theory, develop vague theory because it is difficult to forecast the outcome of partly rational thought processes, whereas economists develop simple rational choice theory, with simple hypotheses, because they assume that criminals have a rational thought process that is simple and clear cut.

These problems with rational choice theory are best explained with examples, but I warn the reader that explication of the complexities is tedious. The first example is the argument by the economists Lott and Mustard (1997) that right-to-carry laws, which facilitate concealed weapon use by citizens, reduce crime because criminals fear that victims might defend themselves with guns. The theory, in their view, applies only to violent crime, where criminals face their victims. This is arm-chair speculation by cloistered academics. Lott and Mustard give only slight, mostly anecdotal, evidence concerning how criminals think in relation to concealed handguns. Since only a small percent of the citizens apply for and get gun permits, it is uncertain whether a savvy criminal is frightened by an extremely small chance that a victim might carry and use a gun as a result of the laws. Perhaps the greater availability of guns increases violent crime by turning innocuous altercations into shootings. In spite of Lott and Mustard's contentions, the deterrence argument probably applies to property crimes as much as to violent crimes, because burglars and thieves also fear being discovered by armed citizens. On the other hand, the right-to-carry laws might increase crimes, including property crimes, because criminals are more likely to carry firearms. Active criminals might be able to obtain permits because, as discussed above, they are adept at escaping convictions (which would bar a permit). Also, they feel safer carrying guns illegally; after the right-to-carry law, a person noticing someone carrying a gun would have less cause to question its legality. Rational criminals carrying guns are likely to increase property, as well as violent, crimes because the guns reduce the risk of apprehension and retaliation.

A second example is substitution. It is well known that crime control attempts might prompt criminals to substitute other crimes—either other types of crime or crimes at different locations (e.g., Barr and Pease 1990). That knowledge, however, has little practical use unless one can predict where the deflection will appear. Researchers studying crime deflection assume the ability to determine a priori the specific other crimes and other places to which criminals might move. Typically they find no evidence of deflection and then concluded that there is no deflection (see the research summarized in Eck 1997; see also Ayres and Levitt 1996). As a practical matter, it is not feasible to prove the absence of substitution, and any evidence that it does take place can only be interpreted as the minimum extent. Examples of problems that rational choice theory encounters because it cannot adequately deal with substitution are found in Cook's (1979) analysis of how criminals might react to an increase in arrest rates. If they move on to crimes that are less risky and have less chance of arrest, Cook argues, more arrests can lead to more crimes because the substituted crimes are less lucrative on average, and criminals seeking to maintain their criminal income must commit more crimes. This in turn would lower arrest rates, making it appear that lower arrest rates caused more crime. Cook (1986) gives a similar analysis concerning criminals' likely reactions to policies to increase sentencing.

The economic model of crime (e.g., Becker 1968; Ehrlich 1973), one variety of rational choice theory, has little robustness in the face of the distinction between ordinary and active criminals. That theory starts with the assumption that people choose between legitimate and illegitimate activities, and that they do so by balancing the relative rewards and risks. This has little applicability to active criminals. Active criminals differ from ordinary criminals in that they tend to be full-time professionals. The economic theory might apply to ordinary criminals, who commonly engage in legitimate work and do not have the ability to derive substantial gain from illegitimate work. But active criminals are not likely to leave their professions for the legitimate sector, where their employment possibilities would provide far less income and status than does crime. The skills needed for successful criminals are seldom useful in legitimate jobs. When faced with enhanced law enforcement activities, active criminals probably modify, rather than limit, criminal activity.

Researchers applying the economic model tend to emphasize arrests and convictions; they are costs of crime, which criminals weigh against the illegal income. However, the argument that higher arrest rates deter criminals might not apply to active criminals because the additional arrests are of ordinary criminals, who dominate the arrest statistics. Active criminals, who dominate the crime statistics, might not interpret rising arrest rates as applying to them. The same goes for increasing convictions, especially since active criminals are better able to have charges dismissed.

These examples only begin to illustrate the complexity of rational choice theory once researchers take into account the fact that active criminals are responsible for most crime and, thus, it is *their* rational thought that researchers must consider when researching crime rates. Knowledgeable and reasonably intelligent criminals have available a wide variety of responses to any crime-reduction effort. With active criminals, the possible paths of action become more complex and involve more advance planning, just as the choices become more complex in a chess game between experts than one between novices. Rational choice theories developed with respect to ordinary criminals cannot be used for active criminals. The net result is that rational choice and economic theories of crime are virtually unbounded. With a little imagination, one can conjure rational reasons for numerous possible reactions to specific situations. Researchers are presented with a cafeteria line of many tempting lines of theory, and they typically feel free to choose which to apply to the research task at hand and which to ignore. In practice, researchers do not make explicit the process of choice, and the selection often seems arbitrary. Also, in practice, if a researcher is eclectic and refuses to ignore applicable theory, the usual consequence is that there are theoretical reasons for a wide variety of responses and for feedback mechanisms, such that rational choice theory cannot be used to forecast criminal activity or even to formulate hypotheses.

In summary, rational choice theory becomes hopelessly complex when one focuses on active criminals. It essentially boils down into a battle of wits between the criminals, on the one hand, and the criminal justice researchers and practitioners, on the other. The latter might win the battle with ordinary criminals, but it takes considerable hubris to believe they can win against active criminals. Rational choice theory, especially the economic version, implodes when faced with the complexity needed to deal with active criminals. Because economic theory is mainly limited to study designs that use aggregate crime rates (which are dominated by active criminals), it is unlikely to be realistic or to have predictive power.

INCAPACITATION

Incapacitation, of course, is the process by which criminals are rendered less able to commit crimes because they are restrained. The restraint is primarily incarceration in prison or jail, although there are many forms of limited incapacitation, such as probation and hospitalization. Incapacitation is best viewed as a continuum between total incapacitation, execution, and the rather slight incapacitation with lightly supervised probation. Imprisonment is at the high end, although prisoners do commit crimes in prison and do sometimes escape and commit crimes on the street.

The crime-reduction impact of incapacitation is commonly believed to be outside rational choice theory. One could argue otherwise by claiming that it reduces crime by increasing the costs of committing crimes. The major costs are greater sanctions (e.g., more rigorous confinement, lower chances of early release, and additional prison terms) if caught escaping, and the substantial government forces devoted to capturing escapees. In any event, advocates of rational choice theory tend to de-emphasize incapacitation. Economists often simply ignore it and only consider deterrence when discussing the crime-reduction impact of imprisonment rates (e.g., Block 1997). Kessler and Levitt (1999) go so far as to exaggerate the importance of deterrence over incapacitation by conducting an analysis based on questionable assumptions that seem calculated to produce that result (an example is the assumption that all criminals convicted of major crimes were sentenced to prison before sentence enhancement laws).

Studies of the impact of prison populations on crime can be divided into two strategies, (1) extrapolating from criminals' individual crime rates and (2) regression studies. Both have produced widely varying results. The major reason for the difference is that studies finding little or moderate impacts downplay the importance of active criminals. Because they are responsible for the bulk of crime, active criminals account for nearly all of the incapacitation and deterence impact.

The first strategy calculates the incapacitation impact by estimating how much crime prisoners would commit if on the street, usually using lambdas derived in ways discussed in the introduction. If one simply assumes that imprisonment eliminates these crimes, the resulting calculation suggests a very large impact, almost two hundred non-drug crimes (as defined above) averted per prisoner per year (Zedlweski 1987; Cavanagh and Kleinman 1990). These results are dominated by the active criminals, who report the great bulk of the crime.

Many researchers question this procedure and adjust the estimates downward, to between ten and twenty crimes averted per prisoner. The major adjustment is to reduce greatly the average lambda of prisoners by eliminating the criminals who report the most crimes or by truncating their lambdas. That is, researchers decide (without presenting any evidence)[8] that active criminals do not exist, and adjust the data accordingly (see the literature summary in Marvell and Moody 1994; see also Spelman 1994; Zimring and Hawkins 1995; Canela-Cacho, Blumstein, and Cohen 1997). Similarly some researchers (e.g., Auerhahn 1999; Levitt 1996) advocate a similar tactic, using median figures for crimes reported, rather than means, to estimate the number of crimes averted. This eliminates not only active criminals from the analysis, but in effect limits it to minor criminals. It is equivalent to asserting that auto accidents are not a problem because the median accident is only a fender bender.

These researchers make several other adjustments to criminals' average crime rates in order to lower incapacitation estimates, all of which are based on the assumption that active criminals do not exist. There are three adjustments that are most important: First, they claim that many prisoners would not commit crime if on the street because they would terminate their criminal careers. As discussed earlier, claims of career termination are based on ordinary criminals and probably do not apply to active criminals. The claims are also based on arrest statistics, and criminals probably learn to evade arrest as they gain experience.

Second, these researchers assume that other criminals would substitute for imprisoned criminals, especially when there is co-offending. This might be true for ordinary criminals, but not active criminals. The latter prefer to work with other active (i.e., skilled) criminals, and since they are few in number, the more who are imprisoned the less likely those on the street are to find co-workers. As a consequence, active criminals might reduce their criminal activity; in which case the crime-reduction impact due to incapacitation can have a magnifying effect, reducing crimes by criminals on the street as well as those imprisoned. In this regard, Glaeser, Sacerdote, and Scheinkman (1996) found that crime rates decline substantially as the number of potential criminal partners decline. If active criminals still on the street continue to commit crime either alone or by joining with less skilled criminals, they are more likely to be apprehended.

Third, some researchers argue that when prisons are expanding, the additional prisoners have much lower lambdas than inmates already in prison. The reason is that as prisons expand, the criteria for imprisonment must be lowered. However, they give no evidence that lowered criteria are responsible for prison population increases, as opposed to longer prison terms or an expanding criminal population. More important, this reasoning assumes that criminals' personal crime rates and personal arrest rates are not negatively correlated (see especially Canela-Cacho, Blumstein, and Cohen 1997), but as discussed above, this is not the case.

Another common procedure for estimating the crime-reduction impact of imprisonment is to regress crime rates on prison populations. Several studies of USA national crime trends find large negative relationships between crimes and prison populations in the same year. Devine, Sheley and Smith (1988), with a 1948–85 time series analyses, find that for each 10 percent more prisoners, homicides decline by 15 percent to 19 percent, robberies by 26 percent to 31 percent, and burglaries by 19 percent to 20 percent. Marvell and Moody (1997, 1999) also find associations almost as large for homicide with time series analysis over 1931–94: roughly 10 percent to 15 percent fewer homicides for each 10 percent increase in prison populations. They also estimate a 25 percent decline for robberies and 5 percent for assault, using a 1948–94 time series analysis.

Two state-level, as opposed to national-level, regression studies reach considerably weaker results (Marvell and Moody 1994; Levitt 1996). They find that crime reduction is significantly related to prison population growth, but the size of the association is moderate. For example, Levitt concludes that 10 percent more prisoners reduces homicides by 2 percent, rapes by 3 percent, robberies by 7 percent, assaults and burglaries by 4 percent, and larcenies and vehicle thefts by 3 percent.

Marvell and Moody (1998) argue that the difference between state and national time series results is due to the fact that criminals cross state lines. State-level studies focus on state imprisonment and state crime and, thus, miss the incapacitation impact of a state's prison population on crime elsewhere. Also, imprisoning criminals does not reduce crime in the state though incapacitation if they would have moved elsewhere if on the street. Marvell and Moody (1998) conducted separate state homicide regression over 1930–92 with prison populations in and outside the state as independent variables. Homicide has a much larger (negative) relationship with prison populations outside the state than those in the state. A 10 percent increase in prison populations outside the state leads to, on average, 8 percent fewer homicides; while a 10 percent increase in a state prisoners leads to only 2 percent fewer homicides. Similar results were found for rape, robbery, assault, burglary, larceny, and motor vehicle theft over 1960–96. This implies that crime rates are dominated by criminals who move from state to state. To my knowledge, there is no research concerning how often criminals move, but the biographical literature discussed above suggests that active criminals are constantly on the move, largely so that they do not come to the attention of local criminal justice officials and so that they do not build up conviction records in any one jurisdiction.

In summary, incapacitation works to reduce crime because a few inmates are active criminals. Failure to realize this fact has caused many studies to underestimate the impact of incapacitation. Luckily, the states have ignored this research and have continued to expand prison populations, which rose at a rate of about 8 percent a year over the past two decades and caused crime rates to decline, except when interrupted by the crack epidemic. Since the incapacitation impact is due to active criminals, imprisonment of most ordinary criminals cannot be justified from a cost-benefit point of view. Unfortunately, courts and prisons do not have the ability to determine whether particular defendants and prisoners are active or ordinary criminals; so a policy to limit imprisonment to minor criminals would result in more active criminals on the street as well, thus causing more crime.

IMPLICATIONS FOR SENTENCING

Likewise, because the incapacitation impact is due to active criminals, courts should seek to sentence them to substantial prison terms. The problem is locating them. There are no good tools. It is clear that present sentencing criteria are ineffective because they are based on the assumption that all criminals are ordinary criminals with similar chances of arrest.

Typically the two most important sentencing criteria are the severity of the crime convicted of and the defendant's past record of convictions. This is most clearly shown in sentencing guidelines (e.g., Tonry 1993). In practice, past convictions listed in a pre-sentence report often determine whether the defendant is sentenced to prison. As noted earlier, however, active criminals may not have records of past convictions. They are adept at avoiding arrest; if they are arrested, they are adept at getting their cases dismissed; and if they have been convicted, the sentencing court might not know about prior convictions because the convictions are in other states. Judges are probably more likely to sentence ordinary criminals to prison than active criminals. This ensures that prisons are filled with stumble-bums, inept criminals who would do relatively little harm outside prisons. Jackson (1969, 32), who closely studied prisoners so described prison inmates, adding that a very few are "competent working criminals who had a run of bad luck or a moment of carelessness." In conclusion, judges and legislators should view past convictions as indicators of ineptness rather than of the number and types of crimes committed; and past record of convictions should have little, if any, role in sentencing.

Three-strikes laws, which mandate very long sentences for certain criminals convicted of a third felony (usually a violent felony) are particularly ill advised. Their primary result is to fill prisons with stumblebums, who are caught over and over again, but who contribute little to the crime rates. The laws might even increase crime if three-strike criminals fill the prisons to the extent that terms for other criminals are reduced. Marvell and Moody (2001) found that the twenty-four state three-strikes laws had no discernable impact on crime, except that they produced a large increase in homicides, as criminals eliminated witnesses in order to escape the three-strike penalties.

Unfortunately, too little is known about active criminals to identify them, and one can only speculate concerning what sentencing criteria should be used. The crime-reduction value of sentencing and incapacitation, results from the fact that, by luck, a few of those sentenced to prison happen to be active criminals. Therefore, from the point of view of reducing crime by incapacitation, all convicted criminals should be sent to prison, and a few active criminals will be caught in the net. Otherwise, for the purposes of crime control, there is probably no system better than a lottery for determining which convicted criminals are sent to prison. Neither strategy is possible, of course, because crime reduction is not the only consideration. Cost to the state would prohibit sentencing all to prison; sentencing by lottery would give the impression that the criminal justice system is unfair and arbitrary. For all practical purposes, virtually the only information that is reliable and relevant for sentencing is the crime of which convicted. Therefore, the fairest way to ration prison space is on the basis of the severity of that crime.

It would be far better, of course, to find criteria that enable judges to give more and longer prison terms to active criminals. There is a great need for more research to help identify active criminals. Such an obvious need has not been ignored, but prior efforts failed and, apparently, made researchers and funding agencies reluctant to re-enter the area. The earlier research, which mainly grew out of the prisoner interview studies, goes under the rubric of "selective incapacitation." Greenwood and Abrahamse (1982) listed prisoner characteristics associated with self-reported crime rates and suggested that they be used as sentencing criteria (for example, prior conviction for the same offense, in prison or jail for most of the time in the last two years, first conviction before sixteen years old, drug addiction, and employed less then half the time in the last two years). Greenwood and Abrahamse claimed that these factors produce modestly strong associations with crime rates. However, when other researchers tested the scale, sometimes using other data sets, they found that the criteria predicted criminality poorly (e.g., see the summary in Miranne and Geerken 1991; Auerhahn 1999). Also, because Greenwood and Abrahamse truncated the lambdas, in practice they did not attempt to locate the active criminals.

What is needed is research specifically tailored to find characteristics of active criminals. It must start with theory concerning why and where ordinary and active criminals differ, and it must test hypotheses derived from these theories. As suggested earlier, tentative hypotheses might be that active criminals less often hold legitimate jobs than other criminals, are usually older, are less often drug addicts, more often work with one or two other criminals (as opposed to alone or in gangs), are much more likely to travel, are more likely to have been arrested in many different jurisdictions, and are less likely to have strong roots in the community (e.g., less likely to have lived long with a member of the opposite sex and to have relatives and close friends there).

It is possible that courts could now use some of these factors in sentencing, even though the theory and empirical support are very incomplete. The factors have more justification than past criminal convictions. Some are now occasionally used as secondary criteria in sentencing, especially employment and ties to the community. Judges give weight to out-of-state convictions, as they do to in-state convictions, but they should consider them as evidence of movement rather than of the amount of prior criminal behavior. For the same reason, judges should consider out-of-state arrests that do not result in convictions; at present, it is rare for judges to consider any arrest not followed by conviction. Finally, although courts have made substantial progress in finding records in other states, the process is still spotty (Geerken 1994), and enough resources should be devoted to ensure that all the defendant's arrests and convictions throughout the nation are known to the sentencing court.

STRUCTURAL CORRELATES OF CRIME

A vast body of criminology research regresses crime rates on various features of society that are theorized to be related to crime. These theories are almost always based on ordinary criminals, and the research does not discuss active criminals, or even lambda skewness in general. Given that active criminals account for the bulk of crime rates and differ from ordinary criminals, these theories are likely to provide weak explanations of crime rates. In fact, anyone familiar with the literature knows that inconsistent and weak results are the norm.

A frequent topic, which was discussed earlier, is the impact of economic conditions on crime rates. The theory that crime, particularly property crime, rises with worsening conditions is based on the assumption that some people turn to crime when they cannot earn what they desire legitimately. Again, one can imagine many ordinary criminals reacting that way, but most active criminals are unlikely to even consider legitimate employment. Although most research on the topic does find a negative association between economic conditions, usually measured by employment, and crimes (e.g., Chiricos 1987), the association is seldom strong, and many studies find positive associations.

Because criminals arrested are usually in their late teens or early twenties, many argue that crime rates rise and fall with the size of this age group (e.g., Steffensmeier, Streifel, and Harer 1987). Arrests occur in less than 5 percent of crimes, however, and one should not assume that this is a representative sample. A likely explanation for the pattern of arrest ages is that younger criminals are less able to escape arrest. They are less experienced criminals. More important, active criminals, who are good at escaping arrest, are vastly under-represented in arrest data in relation to the amount of crime they commit. Although direct evidence concerning the ages of active criminals is lacking, they are probably older than ordinary criminals because, as noted earlier, they probably continue their careers longer. If this is the case, than the high-arrest age group is younger than the age groups responsible for most crime, and trends in the size of the high-arrest age group are weakly related to changes in crime rate trends. Indeed, in a review of the literature that regresses crime rates on age group size, Marvell and Moody (1991) found no consistent evidence that the latter has an impact.

Similar arguments can be used to suggest that putative associations between crime and such factors as divorce rates, alcohol consumption, education levels, population density, and poverty rates are likely to be slight because they are based on ordinary criminals. The same is true for some current trends in law enforcement, community policing and emphasizing the reduction of minor crimes.

CONCLUSION

Again, the arguments in the five preceding sections are conditional upon the existence of active criminals. The arguments apply in full force if the active criminals have lambdas as high as those found in the prisoner surveys, and the top 10 percent of criminals commit on average roughly 1,400 non-drug crimes (as defined above) a year when on the street and account for roughly 80 percent of all these crimes. If this is true, the study of crime rates is the study of active criminals. The arguments also apply to a substantial degree if the skewness is not this great, such as that found in juvenile arrest studies. Researchers, I fear, will continue to ignore the evidence of lambda skewness. The generally accepted picture of criminals appears to be that of impetuous, unskilled, often bumbling young men. This results from selection bias; these are the sort of criminals with whom researchers, as well as criminal justice officials, are most likely to deal (they are more numerous and more easily located). It is also the sort generally portrayed in fiction and the news. When looking at analogous legitimate activities, the generally accepted picture of criminals is similar to that of manual laborers, who have moderate differences in skill, income, and prestige. If instead criminal activity is viewed as an enterprise where skills—especially the ability to evade capture—are important, than a better analogy is athletics. There the distribution is skewed in a manner similar to that found in the prison surveys; a very small percentage are successful professionals and have incomes many times larger than those of ordinary athletes, amateurs and semi-professionals, who rely mainly on unrelated jobs for their livelihoods.

Another reason for the temptation to dismiss the evidence of extreme lambda skewness is that proof is not ironclad. However, this is one of the few areas in criminology where research has been replicated several times with the same result reached. If one were to conclude that the prisoner respondents exaggerated, one would have to advance the unlikely coincidence that they exaggerated in approximately the same proportion and to approximately the same amount in all the sites studied. Given this evidence, the burden of proof is now with researchers to show that the assumptions upon which their work rests are correct. Researchers should give convincing evidence that skewness is slight or moderate whenever their results might be affected by skewness. I fear that long-held beliefs will prompt researchers to advance weak and spurious arguments against the skewness found in prison studies, such as that by Spelman (1994) discussed earlier, and then continue with business as usual. At the least, when reporting research results, researchers should include caveats specifying the assumptions made pertaining to skewness. For example, a common assumption is that skewness is not related to other variables studied, which implies that active criminals are the same as ordinary criminals.

Given the practical realities of the social science process, it is unlikely that the impact of skewness will be considered unless editors and reviewers require it, and they cannot easily do so if they do not address the issue in their own work. In this way, a discipline can overlook an annoying problem indefinitely.

NOTES

1. The Chaikens' category of non-drug crime consists of robbery, assault, burglary, larceny, auto theft, forgery, and fraud. That is the definition used throughout the present paper.

2. The figure for the top five is calculated by assuming that they are the top 10 percent in the six categories of criminals (who are about half the criminals) who commit the most crimes. The total crimes committed by the bottom 90 percent are estimated from the table on page 222 and subtracted from the total crimes committed by these six categories. This figure is then divided by the total crimes committed by the full sample. The 10 percent estimate is done the same way, except the top 25 percentile is used for the three highest criminal categories (along with the top 10 percentile for the highest fourth through sixth categories).

3. As will be discussed, some researchers who have analyzed the Rand data truncate at the ninetieth percentile—that is, they assumes that all who say they commit more than 605 crimes a year only commit that many. This results in an estimate that the top 10 percent of criminals commit approximately 50 percent of the crimes.

4. These calculations are based on a reanalysis of a study Blumstein, Cohen, and Visher (1988), which in turn is based on arrest data and self-reported crime data in the Rand prison survey. The reanalysis removed adjustments that Blumstein et al. made to the self-reported crime data (they truncated at the ninetieth percentile level).

5. Two additional prisoner surveys were conducted in Wisconsin and New Jersey by DiIulio and Piehl (1991) and Piehl and DiIulio (1995), but the reports of these studies only give enough information to present the mean/median ratios; the median for non-drug crimes is twelve in both studies, and the mean for Wisconsin is given as 141. The mean for New Jersey is not given, but its likely value can be estimated from figures presented (Piehl and DiIulio 1995:25) at about 300. The mean/median ratios are thus twelve and twenty-five, similar to the ratios in Table 1.

6. Macro-level research encounters a similar problem, heteroscedasticity, in that different units (e.g., cities) have uneven influences on overall crime rates. Also, small units often have as much or more influence on regression results as large units. These problems can be handled by using weighted regressions. Individual level studies could use weighted regressions, weighting by the amount of crime each subject commits, but this would be difficult because crime rates for the active criminals are understated for reasons given above.

7. Violations of the assumption that coefficients are the same for each unit are a threat to aggregate-level studies because of differences between coefficients in units. There are, however, procedures to deal with this by using pooled time series data where separate variables can be constructed for each unit.

8. As discussed earlier, there exists a specious argument by Spelman (1994), discussed above, based on the fact that criminals reporting high lambdas report more arrests than researchers found in the criminal records. The criminal records are incomplete, largely because out-of-state arrests are not included.

REFERENCES

Allen, John. 1977. *Assault With a Deadly Weapon: The Autobiography of a Street Criminal*. New York: McGraw-Hill.

Auerhahn, Kathleen. 1999. "Selective Incapacitation and the Problem of Prediction." *Criminology* 37:703–743.

Ayres, Iam, and Steven D. Levitt. 1998. "Measuring Positive Externalities for Unobservable Victim Precautions." *Quarterly Journal of Economics* 113:43–78.

Barr, Robert, and Ken Pease. 1990. "Crime Placement, Displacement and Deflection." In *Crime and Justice: An Annual Review of Research. Vol. 12.* Edited by Michael Tonry and Norval Morris. Chicago: University of Chicago Press.

Becker, Gary S. "Crime and Punishment: An Economic Approach." *Journal of Political Economy* 78:493–517.

Block, Michael K. 1997. "Supply Side Imprisonment Policy, in National Institute of Justice," *Two Views of Imprisonment Policies*. Washington, D.C.: U.S. Department of Justice.

Blumstein, Alfred, Jacqueline Cohen, and Christy Visher. 1988. *Linking the Crime and Arrest Process to Measure of Individual Crime Rates: Variations in Individual Arrest Risk per Crime*. Pittsburgh, PA: Urban Systems Institute.

Blumstein, Alfred and Jacqueline Cohen. 1979. "Estimation of Individual Crime Rates from Arrest Records." *Journal of Criminal Law and Criminology* 70:561–585.

Canela-Cacho, Jose A., Alfred Blumstein, and Jacqueline Cohen. 1997. "Relationship Between the Offending Frequency of Imprisoned and Free Offenders." *Criminology* 35:133–176.

Caspi, Avshalom, Terrie E. Moffitt, Phil A. Silva, Magda Stouthamer-Loeber, Robert F. Krueger, and Pamela S. Schmutte. 1994. "Are Some People Crime Prone? Replications of Personality-Crime Relationships Across Countries, Genders, Races, and Methods." *Criminology* 32:163–196.

Cavanagh, David P. and Mark A. R. Kleinman. 1990. *A Cost-Benefit Analysis of Prison Cell Construction and Alternative Sanctions*. Cambridge, MA: BOTEC Analysis Corporation.

Chaiken, Jan M. and Marcia R. Chaiken. 1982. *Varieties of Criminal Behavior*. Santa Monica, CA: Rand Corporation.

Chaiken, Marcia R. and Chaiken, Jan M. 1985. *Who Gets Caught Doing Crime?* Washington, D.C.: Bureau of Justice Statistics.

Chiricos, Theodore G. 1987. "Rates of Crime and Unemployment: An Analysis of Aggregate Research Evidence." *Social Problems* 34:187–222.

Cohen, Jacqueline. 1986. "Research on Criminal Careers: Individual Frequency Rates and Offense Seriousness." In *Criminal Careers and "Career Criminals,"* Vol. I. Edited by Alfred Blumstein, Jacqueline Cohen, Jeffrey A. Roth, Jeffrey A., and Christy Visher. Washington, D.C.: National Academy Press.

Catalano, Richard F., Michael W. Arthur, J. David Hawkins, Lisa Berglund, and Jeffrey J. Olson. 1998. "Comprehensive Community- and School-Based Intereventions to Prevent Antisocal Behavior. In *Serious and Violent Juvenile Ofenders: Risk Factors and Successful Interventions*. Edited by Rolf Loeber and David P. Farrington. Thousand Oaks, CA: Sage.

Comwell, Chic, and Edwin H. Sunderland. 1956. *Professional Thief*. Chicago: Phoenix Books.

Cook, Philip J. 1979. "The Clearance Rate as a Measure of Criminal Justice System Effectiveness." *Journal of Public Economics* 11:135–142.

Cook, Philip J. 1986. Criminal Incapacitation Effects Considered in an Adaptive Choice Framework. In *The Reasoning Criminal: Rational Choice Perspectives and Offending*. Edited by Derek B. Cornish and Ronald V. Clarke. New York: Springer-Verlag.

DiIulio, John J. and Anne Morrison Piehl. 1991. "Does Prison Pay? The Stormy National Debate Over the Cost-Effectiveness of Imprisonment." *The Brookings Review* 1991:28–35.

Devine, Joel A., Joseph F. Sheley, and M. Dwayne Smith. 1988. "Macroeconomic and Social-Control Policy Influences on Crime Rate Changes, 1948–1985." *American Sociological Review* 53:407–420.

Donohue, John J. and Peter Siegelman. 1998. "Allocating Resources Among Prisons and Social Programs in the Battle Against Crime. *Journal of Legal Studies* 27:1–43.

Eck, John. 1997. "Preventing Crime in Places." In *Preventing Crime: What Works, What Doesn't, What's Promising*. Edited by Lawrence W. Sherman, Denise Gottfredson, Doris McKenzie, John Eck, Peter Reuter, and Shawn Bushway. Washington, D.C.: Office of Justice Programs.

Ehrlich, Issac. 1973. "Participation in Illegal Activities: A Theoretical and Empirical Investigation." *Journal of Political Economy* 81:521–567.

English, Kim and Mary J. Mande. 1992. *Measuring Crime Rates of Prisoners*. Denver: Colorado Department of Public Safety.

Geerken, Michael R. 1994. "Rap Sheets in Criminology Research: Considerations and Caveats." *Journal of Quantitative Criminology* 10:3–21.

Glaeser, E. L., B. Sacerdote, and J.A. Scheinkman. 1996. "Crime and Social Interaction." *Quarterly Journal of Economics* 111:507–548.

Gottfredson, Michael R. and Travis Hirschi. 1990. *A General Theory of Crime*. Stanford, CA: Stanford University Press.

Greenwood, Peter W. and Allen Abrahamse. 1982. *Selective Incapacitation*. Santa Monica, CA: Rand Corporation.

Greenwood, Peter W., Karyn E. Model, C. Peter Rydell, and James Chiesa. 1998. *Diverting Children from Life of Crime: Measuring Costs and Benefits*. Santa Monica, CA: Rand Corporation.

Horney, Julie and Ineke H. Marshall. 1992. "An Experimental Comparison of Two Self-Reported Methods for Measuring Lambda." *Journal of Research in Crime and Delinquency* 29:102–121.

Jackson, Bruce. 1969. *A Thief's Primer*. Toronto: Macmillian.

Jackson, Bruce. 1972. *In the Life: Versions of the Criminal Experience*. New York: Holt, Rinehard and Winston.

Katz, Jack. 1988. *Seductions of Crime: Moral and Sensual Attractions in Doing Evil*. New York: Basic Books.

Kempf, Kimberly L. 1987. "Specialization and the Criminal Career." *Criminology* 25:399–421.

Kessler, Daniel and Steven D. Levitt. 1999. "Using Sentencing Enhancements to Distinguish Between Deterrence and Incapacitation." *Journal of Law and Economics* 42:343–364.

King, Harry and William J. Chambliss. 1984. *Harry King: A Professional Chief's Journey.* New York: John Wiley and Sons.

Levitt, Steven D. 1996. "The Effect of Prison Population Size on Crime Rates: Evidence From Prison Overcrowding Litigation." *Quarterly Journal of Economics* 111:319–351.

Lott, John R. and David B. Mustard. 1997. "Crime, Deterrence, and the Right-to-Carry Concealed Handguns." *Journal of Legal Studies* 24:1–68.

Malcolm X and Alex Haley. 1964. *The Autobiography of Malcolm X.* New York: Grove Press.

Martin, John. 1970. *My Life in Crime: The Autobiography of a Professional Criminal.* Westport, CT: Greenwood Press.

Marvell, Thomas B. and Carlisle E. Moody. 1991. "Age Structure and Crime Rates: The Conflicting Evidence." *Journal of Quantitative Criminology* 7:737–273.

Marvell, Thomas B. and Carlisle E. Moody. 1994. "Prison Population and Crime Reduction." *Journal of Quantitative Criminology* 10:109–139.

Marvell, Thomas B. and Carlisle E. Moody. 1997. "The Impact of Prison Growth on Homicide." *Homicide Studies* 1:205–233.

Marvell, Thomas B. and Carlisle E. Moody. 1998. "The Impact of Out-of-state Prison Population on State Homicide Rates: Displacement and Free-rider Effects." *Criminology* 36:513–535.

Marvell, Thomas B. and Carlisle E. Moody. 1999. "Female and male Homicide Victimization Rates: Comparing Trends and Regressors." *Criminology* 37:879–902.

Marvell, Thomas B. and Carlisle E. Moody. 2001. "The Lethal Effects of Three-Strikes Laws." *Journal of Legal Studies* 30:89–106

Miranne, Alfred C. and Michael R.Geerken. 1991. "The New Orleans Inmate Survey: A Test of Greenwood's Predictive Scale." *Criminology*, 29:497–518.

Orsagh, Thomas. 1992. *The Multi-State Offender: A Report on State Prisoners Who were Criminally Active in More than One State.* Washington, D.C.: Bureau of Justice Statistics.

Piehl, Ann Morrison and John J. DiIulio. 1995. "'Does Prison Pay?' Revisited." *The Brookings Review* 1995(Winter):21–25.

Piquero, Alex R. 2000. "Assessing the Relationship Between Gender, Chronicity, Seriousness, and Offense Skewness in Criminal Offending." *Journal of Criminal Justice* 28:103–115.

Shannon, Lyle W. 1991. *Changing Patterns of Delinquency and Crime: A Longitudinal Study in Racine.* Boulder, CO: Westview Press.

Shaw, Clifford R., Henry D. McKay, and James F. McDonald. 1938. *Brothers in Crime*. Chicago: University of Chicago Press.

Simon, Leonore M. J. 1999. "Are the Worst Offenders the Least Reliable?" *Studies on Crime and Crime Prevention*, 8:210–224.

Spelman, William. 1994. *Criminal Incapacitation*. New York: Plenum.

Steffensmeier, Darrell, Cathy Streifel, and Miles D. Harer. 1987. "Relative Cohort Size and Youth Crime in the United States, 1953–1984." *American Sociological Review* 52:702–710.

Tonry, Michael. 1993. "Sentencing Commissions and Their Guidelines." In *Crime and Justice: A Review of Research, Vol. 17*. Edited by Michael Tonry. Chicago: University of Chicago Press.

Weiss, Joseph G. 1986. "Issues in the Measurement of criminal careers." In *Criminal Careers and "Career Criminals," Vol. 2*. Edited by Alfred Blumstein, Jacqueline Cohen, Jeffrey A. Roth, and Christy Visher, 1–51. Washington, D.C.: National Academy Press.

Wolfgang, Marvin E., Robert M. Figlio, and Thorsten Sellin. 1972. *Delinquency in a Birth Cohort*. Chicago: University of Chicago Press.

Wright, Richard and Scott Decker. 1994. *Burglars on the Job: Streetlife and Residential Break-ins*. Boston: Northeastern University Press.

Wright, Richard and Scott Decker. 1994. *Armed Robbers in Action*. Boston: Northeastern University Press.

Zedlweski, Edwin W. 1987. *Making Confinement Decisions*. Washington: National Institute of Justice.

Zimring, Franklin E. and Gordon Hawkins. 1995. *Incapacitation: Penal Confinement and the Restraint of Crime*. New York: Oxford University Press.

Chapter 15

Deterrence, Rational Choice, and Criminal Offending: A Consideration of Legal Subjectivity

Michael Massoglia and Ross Macmillan

A rational choice perspective posits a relatively simple algorithm for crime: the probability of crime increases as the potential benefits of a crime outweigh the potential costs of a crime (Becker 1968). From this perspective, crime is explained in terms of a balance between the "costs" and "rewards" of offending. When the perceived benefits of engaging in crime outweigh its costs, offending is more likely. Yet, while the rewards of crime are often seen as self-evident or intrinsic to the act of crime itself (Gottfredson and Hirschi 1990), understanding and articulating the costs of criminal activity has been the subject of considerably more controversy. Typically, the costs of crime are linked to notions of deterrence in which various sanctions, both formal and informal, are seen as the key to preventing and controlling crime. As a consequence, identifying the nature and role of deterrence in criminal offending is central to criminological theory and reflects an on-going belief in the rational choice model of offending.

While ideas of deterrence and the rational choice model continue to organize understandings of offending, empirical evidence of the role of deterrence and rational choice model in general have been mixed. Some research suggest effects of perceived rewards, yet little effects for the deterrence elements of rational choice models (Pilivian et al. 1986; Gibbs 1986). Others conclude that only the certainty of punishment, and not the severity of punishment, influences offending decisions (Paternoster 1989; Tittle 1980). Still others suggest that perceived deterrence has variable effects on offending depending on a host of social and individual factors (Braithwaite 1989; Keane et al. 1986; Nagin and Paternoster 1993; Sherman and Smith

1992; Tittle 1980). In perhaps one of the most authoritative statements on the topic, Tittle (1980:241) concluded that:

> Social control as a process seems almost completely in informal sanctioning. Perceptions of formal sanction probabilities or severity do not appear to have an effect, and those that do have an effect that are evident turn out to be dependent upon perceptions of informal sanction.

Ultimately, the variable effects of the deterrence aspects of the rational choice equation have led some to question its overall utility in explaining crime (Gottfredson and Hirschi 1990; Wilson and Herrnstein 1985).

In this chapter, we argue that ambiguity in the role of deterrence in criminal offending may stem from a failure to fully consider the social structure of criminal justice activity and the degree to which this influences the internalization of formal controls by individuals. In elaborating this problem, we integrate classic work on deterrence with recent work in the sociology of law to articulate a theory of "legal subjectivity." Legal subjectivity refers to the degree to which people see themselves as differentially subject to criminal justice control. The notion of legal subjectivity has important implications for deterrence and the rational choice model by highlighting the social structure around perceptions of criminal justice sanctions and by providing a starting point for identifying for whom criminal justice sanctions are a salient aspect of everyday cognition.

To develop a theory of legal subjectivity, this chapter has two objectives. First, we examine the theoretical underpinnings of legal subjectivity by considering notions of deterrence in classical criminology and the social structure of criminal justice activity in contemporary work in the sociology of law and social control. Second, we examine legal subjectivity as a psychometric construct. We do so by assessing the degree to which perceptions of risks of criminal justice intervention are consistent with perceptions of criminal justice sanctions across a range of possible offenses, and the degree to which such perceptions are stable over time. These analyses speak to issues of deterrence and rational choice processes by assessing the degree to which adolescents and early adults have generalized perceptions of their vulnerability to criminal justice control that are relatively fixed. As such they provide an indication of "legal subjectivity" that are unlikely to be rooted solely or even largely in experiences with the criminal justice system and should have important consequences of criminal offending.

DETERRENCE AND THE CLASSICAL PERSPECTIVE IN CRIMINOLOGY

The origins of formal deterrence are typically traced to the classic work of Cesare Beccaria (1992) [1775]. While the specific philosophy underlying

Beccaria's arguments on crime and justice are the subject of some debate, a central tenet of Beccaria's work was the idea that the state, through a system of criminal justice, plays a central role in deterring crime. For Beccaria, one of the central functions of the government was the allocation of punishments to deter not only individuals from offending again, but also potential offenders in the larger society who may contemplate criminal acts. Specifically, he argued that *the degree of the punishment, and the consequences of the crime, ought to be contrived to have the greatest possible effect on others while causing the least possible pain to the delinquent* (Beccaria 1992 [1775]: 36). In this respect, the state's use of punishment served societal needs for both specific and general deterrence.

Importantly, punishment was not simply retribution. Indeed, Beccaria was deeply skeptical of the effectiveness of a state that was overly punitive. Instead, he proposed a formula for punishment in which punishment would be most effective when it was a certain outcome of crime, a swift consequence to crime, and severe. Through immediate, certain, and severe punishments, the state can instill a sense of the "costs" of crime among its citizens by showing punishment to be the necessary consequence of crime.

Notions of deterrence and rational choice are also traced to Jeremy Bentham largely because of his principle of utility. Bentham proposed that every person acts in view of his (her) self-interest (Mack 1969). Similar to his predecessor Beccaria, he emphasized the role of the state in curbing self-interest among the masses. In his classic treatise *Introduction to the Constitutional Code*, Bentham argued that the right and proper end of government is the greatest happiness to the greatest number. Thus, the ultimate role of government including the actions of the criminal justice system is to make the interests of the individual and the community congruent. In such a situation people can act in ways that serve *both* the interests of the community and the interests of the individual.

Thus, Bentham argues that formal mechanisms of control serve to address behavior deemed not in the interests of greater society. Bentham's work advances the notion that laws must be devised and used such that antisocial activities become unprofitable. In particular he emphasized the role of the state, particularly through incarceration in his discussion of punishment. The key to deterring crime in Bentham's framework is to recognize that punishment is the infliction of pain, and thus capitalizes on individuals desire to avoid pain. Therefore, punishments make some activities seem less profitable than other activities that do not bring about the imposition of sanctions. Punishments thus serve to deter people from a specific course of actions that might serve self-interest at the expense of community interests.

While it may seem obvious, the key feature of Beccaria and Bentham's work is their emphasis on the state and state sanctions in the control of criminal activity. In this respect, they emphasized punishments that deprive offenders of various liberties. Fines place economic constraints on individuals. Incarceration removes a wide variety of freedoms. Other punishments characteristic of various eras involved physical punishment and immediate pain to the offender. As the application of such sanctions would be seen as obvious consequences of criminal offending, the rational actor should refrain from offending or re-offending so as to avoid the resulting pain and deprivations.

The work of Beccaria and Bentham has served to organize considerable empirical research. In particular, it has led to "economic" models of sanctions and offending in which the perceived "costs" of criminal justice sanctions should deter future offending. In other words, by increasing the costs of offending through criminal justice sanctions, the overall utility of offending will be diminished. By extension, those who perceive the costs of offending to be significant should be less likely to offend than others. Empirically, measuring perceived costs of offending has involved a number of different strategies. For some the study of costs incorporate both risks of criminal justice intervention, risks of criminal justice sanctions and risks of social sanctions that may result from criminal justice interventions (Piliavin et al. 1986; Williams and Hawkins 1992). Others have thought even more broadly about costs and incorporated non-criminal justice exposure (Bachman et al. 1992; Nagin and Paternoster 1993). Still, other research simply measures costs by personal perceptions of the degree to which criminal justice sanctions would undermine the quality of their lives (Nagin and Paternoster 1993; Piquero and Paternoster 1998; Tittle 1980). Regardless of the measurement specifics, the legacy of Bentham and Beccaria has been a research tradition based on "economic" models of sanctions and offending that emphasize perceived "costs" of criminal justice sanctions.

Yet, one dimension of deterrence that has received considerably less empirical attention is the source of such perceptions of the criminal justice system. It is clear that perceptions of criminal justice sanctions should extend beyond individuals who are directly subject to them. The notion of "general deterrence" by which individuals who may contemplate offending are restrained due to the punishment of others is a direct reflection of this idea. Yet, the specific mechanisms by which individuals develop perceptions of their own risk of criminal justice sanctions are largely unarticulated in the early works. In contemporary work, such perceptions are typically seen as developing from specific involvement with the criminal justice system (Bridges and Stone 1986; Horney and Marshall 1992; Piliavin et al. 1986; Paternoster and Piquero 1995; Piquero and Paternoster 1998; Stafford and Warr 1993). Yet recognizing that perceptions of the criminal justice system extend beyond sanctioned offenders but are still located in the activities of the criminal justice system leads to important questions concerning the social structure of criminal justice activity and the ways in which people are socialized to see themselves as potential objects of criminal justice control. It is here where sociological research on the stratification of social controls provides some important insights.

THE STRATIFICATION OF SOCIAL CONTROLS

Sociologists who study social control have long recognized that controls are not applied equally across all social groups. Instead, some groups are more likely to be the objects of social control in general, and specific types of social controls are more likely to be directed at certain types of individuals (Gibbs 1986). The work of Donald Black (1976, 1979 1984) on the behavior of law provides an important starting point.

Black argues that systems of social control interact in intricate ways when reacting to deviant behavior. Black partitions social control into law (government authority) and informal social control, and describes a complex process in which higher or lower amounts of law are brought to bear upon a person or group. Emphasizing "variation in the quantity of law," Black illuminates a process by which formal sanctions are differentially applied across social groups in society. In particular, he uses the notion of "adversary effects" to refer to the tendency of the law to be applied downward. In the contexts of disputing parties, the law is more likely to be applied to a party occupying a lower status. This refers to both the actual determination of responsibility and the application of sanctions. Just by virtue of probability, lower status individuals will more often be the objects of criminal justice sanctions. In providing examples, Black places particular emphasis on issues of race and class in the allocation of formal social controls. Thus, Black's argument suggests a distinctive social structure to law and by extension deterrence.

While Black focuses almost exclusively on the application of law, recent work in the stratification of informal controls illuminates the psychological manifestation of control processes within individuals. Hirschi (1969), for example, argues that individual's experiences with social control cause them to internalize control structures. More specifically, the attachment of individual to others in society, particularly family members, forms the foundation for socialization and is "the essence of internalization" (p.18). Building upon such work, Hagan and colleagues (1989) argue that this internalization process is influenced by larger systems of stratification. In particular, they argue that family class position combined with historical patterns of gender socialization structure the application of social controls. In particular, socialization that allocate females to private spheres and males to more public spheres have the consequence that males are simply more likely to be objects of formal mechanisms of control, while females are more likely to be objects of informal controls. Consistent with Hirschi (1969), Hagan and colleagues focus largely on informal or family based controls and argue that children internalize (informal) control structures and this internalization regulates future behavior.

TOWARD A CONSIDERATION OF LEGAL SUBJECTIVITY

The stratification of social controls has important implications for theory and research on deterrence and rational choice as it suggests a social structure to formal sanctions, particularly the criminal law. Importantly, the same process by which informal controls are differentially applied and internalized should also apply to formal controls. Although previous work has focused largely on informal controls, it still anticipates a psychological construct that reflects general perceptions of one's vulnerability to criminal justice sanctions that is rooted in childhood socialization and early experience. In this respect, research on the stratification and internalization of informal controls suggests the idea of "legal subjectivity." By this, we mean that people will differ in the degree to which they are socialized to see themselves as objects of criminal justice control, will differ in the degree to which they internalize a general sense of vulnerability to criminal justice sanctions, and will differ in the degree to which they incorporate such beliefs in their everyday cognitions. In the same manner by which informal controls associated with the family are differentially internalized by individuals, we would expect that formal controls, more specifically personal perceptions of vulnerability to criminal justice sanctions, would also be internalized. In the language of deterrence theorists, general deterrence should be a uniform outcome. We use the term legal subjectivity to refer to the differential degree to which individuals perceive themselves as potential objects of criminal justice control.

With its origins in socialization and experience, legal subjectivity should have three basic qualities. First, perceptions of their vulnerability to criminal justice control should be relatively consistent. In other words, individuals should have general sensibilities concerning their risks of criminal justice sanctions that should extend across a range of offense types. Second, we would expect consistency in perceptions of both risk of criminal justice sanctions and severity of sanctions. Both of these reflect the broader issue of vulnerability to criminal justice control and should be similar manifestations of socialization processes. Finally, we would expect that legal subjectivity should be relatively stable over the life course. By this we mean that legal subjectivity should develop in childhood and early adolescence and then are a relatively stable over the remainder of the life course.

AN EMPIRICAL ASSESSMENT OF LEGAL SUBJECTIVITY

To assess these expectations, we use data from the National Youth Survey, a national probability sample of households in the continental United States (Elliott, Huizinga, and Ageton 1985). The initial sample contained 1,725 with a response rate of 73%. Comparisons with census data show the NYS mirrors the youth population in the United States reasonably well. While the full data cover a period from 1976 to 1986, our analysis is confined to waves six (1983) and seven (1986) when respondents were asked about perceptions of the criminal justice system. Sample attrition over waves is not dramatically affected by key variables such as age, class, ethnicity, place of residence, or reported delinquency (Elliott, Huizinga, and Menard 1989).

Our legal subjectivity construct has two primary dimensions: perceptions of risk of criminal justice involvement and perceptions of what sanction would likely incur. Perceived risk of criminal justice involvement is measured in terms of perceived risk of arrest. Respondents reported the probability (ranging from 0 to 100 in 10 unit increments) they would be arrested for specific types of offenses. We focus on arrest as it typically represents the initiation of criminal justice intervention (Reiss 1971). Perceptions of sanctions are measured in terms of a cumulative scale indicating what type sanction is expected if one were to offend. Responses include: (1) no punishment, (2) released without charges, (3) dismissed at court, (4) fined and released, (5) probation/suspended sentence, (6) short time in jail, and (7) long time in jail. To assess the generalizability of such perceptions, we assess perceptions of arrest and perceptions of sanctions in reference to four different types of offending: (1) stealing something worth more than 50 dollars, (2) breaking into a building, (3) strong-arming someone, and (4) attacking someone. As these questions were asked in both the 1983 and 1986 waves of data, we make further use of these items to assess stability in perceptions over time. While bearing some consistency with classical notions of "certainty" and "severity" of punishment, together these dimensions indicate individual perceptions of general vulnerability to criminal justice control. In other words, they assess variation in the degree to which people see themselves and their actions as subject to criminal laws. Descriptions of these variables are seen in Table 1.

Table 1: Inventory of variables (N=1336)

Variable	Description	Mean* (1986/1983)	SD (1986/1983)
Perceptions of Arrest	*"What are the chances you would be arrested if you committed the following crimes?"*		
Steal something more than $50	0=0%chance to 9=90% chance	.00/.00	2.93/2.84
Break into a building	0=0%chance to 9=90% chance	.00/.01	2.84/2.79
Strongarm others	0=0%chance to 9=90% chance	.01/.01	2.89/2.75
Attack someone	0=0%chance to 9=90% chance	.00/.00	2.71/2.56
Perceptions of Sanctions	*"What are the likely punishments if arrested for the following crimes?"*		
Steal something more than $50	1=released without charges, 2=dismissed at court, 3=fined and released, 4=probation/suspended sentence, 5=short time in jail, 6=long time in jail	-.01/.00	.89/.87
Break into a building	1=released without charges, 2=dismissed at court, 3=fined and released, 4=probation/suspended sentence, 5=short time in jail, 6=long time in jail	.00/.00	.92/.91
Strongarm others	1=released without charges, 2=dismissed at court, 3=fined and released, 4=probation/suspended sentence, 5=short time in jail, 6=long time in jail	.00/-.02	1.04/1.01
Attack someone	1=released without charges, 2=dismissed at court, 3=fined and released, 4=probation/suspended sentence, 5=short time in jail, 6=long time in jail	.00/.00	.97/.96

*All variables were centered at the mean.

Before moving to the analytic results, we briefly differentiate the measures that we employ from those used in other deterrence research. First, our measures explicitly reflect the perception that one is *personally* vulnerable to criminal justice control. Considerable research on deterrence has focused on the perception that generalized others are vulnerable to criminal justice control (Bridges and Stone 1986; Erickson et al. 1977; Jensen et al. 1978; Paternoster and Piquero 1995). Second, we explicitly measure perceptions of criminal justice sanctions. Contemporary work often combines criminal justice and non-criminal justice sanctions into summary measures of sanction costs (Bachman et al. 1992; Piliavin et al. 1986; Nagin and Paternoster 1993; Williams and Hawkins 1992). Third, we measure perceptions of the criminal justice system across a wide range of offending. Much previous work has focused on a single or small number of offenses (Bachman et al. 1992; Nagin and Paternoster 1993; Piliavin et al. 1986; Piquero and Paternoster 1998; Williams and Hawkins 1992). Our use of multiple measures allows us to assess the generality of perceptions of criminal justice sanctions beyond that considered in earlier work. Finally, the measured used directly reference common criminal behaviors that the respondent might engage in rather than using a scenario approach characteristic of some earlier work (Bachman et al. 1992; Nagin and Paternoster 1993).

To empirically assess legal subjectivity, we use confirmatory factor analysis to specify a measurement model using the eight perceptions of arrest probability and perceptions of sanction items. Our assessment is guided by theoretical ideas concerning legal subjectivity and deterrence, while the validity of our construct is based on assessment of factor loadings and standard goodness of fit indicators. (For a comprehensive discussion, see Bollen 1989). Assessments of goodness of fit make use of traditional chi-square statistics, goodness of fit indices that adjust for degrees of freedom (AGFI), and Bentler and Bonnett's (1980) related normed fit index (NFI). This latter statistic assesses model fit by the degree to which the model accounts for sample covariances relative to a more restricted, nested model (often the null model), essentially setting a baseline for model fit assessment.

We begin by modeling legal subjectivity in early adulthood, using data from the 1986 wave. An initial model consisted of all eight items loading on a single latent variable. This model does not fit the data well, the χ^2 to degrees of freedom is over eighty and the good of fit indices are well below conventional levels ($\chi^2=1690$, df=20, AGFI=0.52, NFI=0.65). Furthermore, many of the manifest variables have poor loadings on the latent variable. Given the overall poor model fit, we next considered a model with two latent variables that differentiates perceptions of arrest risk from perceptions of sanctions. This model corresponds to most contemporary research that differentiates perceptions of arrest or "certainty" from perceptions of punishment or "severity." While this model is a significant improvement in fit over the one factor model, it still does not provide a good fit to the data. The ratio of χ^2 to degrees of freedom is high at 28:1 and the goodness of fit indicators are well below conventional standards (χ^2=532, df=19, AGFI=0.80, NFI=.89).

Importantly, this model also included a parameter to assess the covariance between the two latent variables. Importantly, the correlation between the factors was sufficiently high (.61) to suggest a general consistency between perceptions of arrest risk and severity of sanctions. In terms of a measurement model, this consistency suggests a higher order construct in which both latent variables load on a higher order factor. In this model, the higher factor can be seen to represent legal subjectivity by indicating the general perception that one's actions are more or less subject to formal criminal justice sanctions. In such a model the gamma parameters demonstrate the degree to which the lower order factors are manifestations of the higher order construct. In this case, the gamma loadings are more than reasonable at .64 for the arrest risk latent variable and .65 for the perceptions of sanctions latent variable. This modification from the two factor model with correlated factors is consistent with our theoretical notions of legal subjectivity and with the addition of several sets of correlated errors provides a good fit to the data (χ^2=24.178, df=11, AGFI=.985; NFI=.96). Specific parameters of this model are shown in Figure 1. Importantly, this model supports our arguments concerning legal subjectivity by showing a general construct in which the observed variables are manifestations of first order latent variables of perceptions of arrest and perceptions of sanctions in reference to several types of criminal offending and the first order latent variables are manifestations of the second order construct of legal subjectivity.

Having demonstrated the empirical dimensions of legal subjectivity, we next examine its stability and reliability over time. If legal subjectivity is a psychological trait that has its origins in early socialization and experience, we expect considerable stability in late adolescence and early adulthood. To assess this, we use similar measures of perceptions of arrest and perceptions of sanctions from the 1983 wave of the NYS. While the length of time between periods is not overly long, the time frame does correspond to our theoretical ideas about the development of legal subjectivity over the life course and considers stability during the transition to adulthood, a pivotal stage of life course development. To assess stability we combined the wave six and seven models and include a parameter to assess correlation between both second order factors over time. This model is shown in Figure 2.

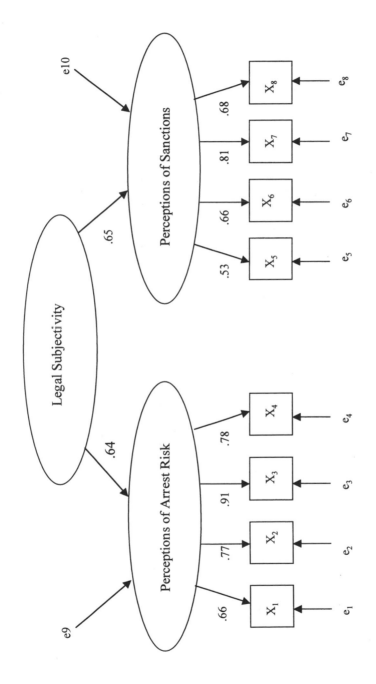

Fig. 1: Second-order Factor Model of Perceived Subjectivity to Legal Sanction

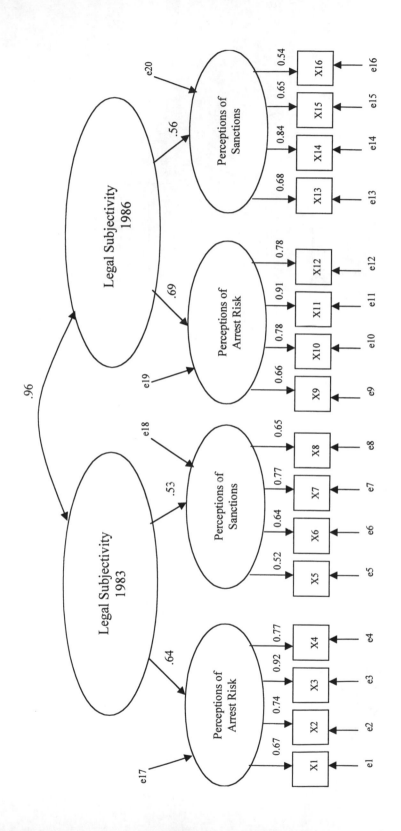

Fig. 2: A Second-order Factor Model of Perceived Subjectivity to Legal Sanction: An Assessment of Stability over Time

Adopting a similar strategy as before, we estimated second-order factor models in 1983 and 1986 and assessed covariance over time. Our final model fit the data reasonably well (χ^2 =750, df=87, AGFI=.89 NFI=0.93). In this model model, the manifest variables all load reasonably well on the perceptions of arrest latent variable (ranging from a low of .65 to a high of .92) and the perceptions of sanctions latent variable (ranging from .84 to .51). Furthermore, the first order latent variables have reasonably strong loadings on the higher-order legal subjectivity latent variable (ranging from .54 to .69). We acknowledge the fit indices do not provide unconditional support for our measurement model, however it appears to represent the data well. Given the sample size and design of our model, we appear to have sufficient statistical power to detect measurement error correlations that are trivial or substantially unimportant. (See a discussion in Matsueda and Bielby 1986). More importantly, the correlation assessing the stability of legal subjectivity demonstrated over time is extremely high at .96, indicating that legal subjectivity is extremely stable, at least from late adolescence to early adulthood.

Taken as a whole, the model parameters indicate that our latent measures of legal subjectivity are reasonably reliable over time and highly stable. This is consistent with our view that legal subjectivity is developed in the early part of the life course through childhood socialization and experience and then likely remains part of one's psychological toolkit for the remainder of the life course.

DISCUSSION

In the last two decades, efforts to understand the role of the state in deterring crime have been organized around economic rather than sociological ideas. This has shifted the focus of deterrence research toward utilitarian equations in which simply raising criminal justice intervention should deter crime and away from more sociological issues such as social differentiation and its implications for the application of social controls. Importantly, this has separated the role of the state in deterring crime from considerations of the social structure of law. As a result, recent criminological research has given little attention to how people see themselves differentially subject to criminal justice control and what implications this may have for offending.

To further understand issues of deterrence, rational choice and offending, this chapter links together classic work on deterrence and its emphasis on state centered sanctions with sociological research on the stratification of formal control. To this end, we have suggested that understanding the links between perceptions of criminal justice activity and criminal offending might be served by a consideration of differences in the degree to which people see themselves and their actions as subject to criminal justice activity. Contenporary research typically differentiates certainty of arrest from severity of sanction and focuses on the "costs" of sanctions personally defined. Combined with the fact that research often focuses on such perceptions with respect to a single type of crime, the general issue of perceived subjectivity to criminal justice intervention is relatively unexplored.

To examine this issue, this research used confirmatory factor analysis to examine a theoretical construct of "legal-subjectivity." Specifically, we demonstrate a general, higher order construct that reflects both perceptions of arrest and perceptions of sanctions. This higher order construct reflects perceptions of arrest risk and perceptions of sanctions across a range of behaviors, both violent and non-violent, common and rare. Finally, this construct is very stable over time. While this latter analysis did not involve a particularly long time period, it did encompass a period from late adolescence to early adulthood when much of the sample made the transition to adulthood. Taken in sum, these models demonstrate a general construct that indicates the degree to which people see themselves and their actions as subject to legal control and which we have called "legal subjectivity."

The notion of legal subjectivity has several implications for understanding deterrence, rational choice, and criminal offending. First, it draws attention to the social structure of criminal justice sanctions. While considerable work argues that perceptions of arrest risk and sanctions are rooted in experiences with the criminal justice system, both personal and vicarious (Stafford and Warr 1993), such experiences are driven by factors beyond involvement in crime. Systematic attention needs to be paid to the social structure around criminal justice experiences to understand how perceived deterrence is formulated.

In this regard, the notion of legal subjectivity draws attention to socialization within and beyond the family as a source of perceptions of the criminal justice system. Research on the stratification of social control suggests that socialization is the basis of psychological processes by which individuals internalize control structures (Hagan et al. 1989; Hirschi 1969). In the same way in which family socialization may make informal controls salient for individuals, it may also influence the internalization of formal controls. While contemporary research is only beginning to tease out the complex intersection of different systems of stratification and the ways in which class, race, gender, and age shape the application and internalization of social controls, we would expect considerable structural differentiation in legal subjectivity.

Second, while the analyses presented in this chapter focused exclusively on the levels of the perceived risk of arrest and perceived sanction variables, a full understanding of legal subjectivity would also investigate variation in the importance of such perceptions for individual action. If such perceptions are rooted in larger processes of socialization, we would expect perceptions of the criminal justice system to vary across social groups in their salience for potential offending. Considerations of criminal justice sanctions should be most important for those who are the most likely objects of criminal justice activity and thus most likely to perceive themselves as potential objects of criminal justice activity. Thus, perceived vulnerability to criminal justice sanction may be most consequential for offending for young, African-American males and least consequential for older white females. For those who are most likely to see themselves and their behavior as subject to criminal law, perceptions of the criminal justice system are likely a more important part of the psychological toolkits that are used to govern their everyday conduct.

Third, the notion of legal subjectivity with its basis in general processes of social control suggests links between systems of formal and informal control beyond those considered in prior work (cf. Tittle 1980). In particular, Black's (1976) work on the behavior of law suggests that legal controls are typically present when more informal controls are absent. Drawing from this same reasoning, we might expected that perceived vulnerability to criminal justice sanctions might be most effective among individuals with low social bonds. More specifically, perceptions of the criminal justice system might be most consequential for those with low levels of attachment, commitment, and involvement with conventional social institutions like work, education, and family. Note that this expectation is the opposite of what might be anticipated from a more economic approach. From the latter perspective, the salience of criminal justice sanction would be most consequential for those *with* strong social bonds as the such ties would increases the "costs" of criminal justice penalties (Nagin and Paternoster 1994).

The notion of legal subjectivity further suggests a ground for synthesis between economic and sociological perspectives on offending and between theories of social control and theories of rational choice. Specifically, it highlights the important yet typically neglected *social* basis of perceptions of the criminal justice system. While much previous work has suggested variation in perceptions of criminal justice sanctions and variation in the salience of such perceptions, the overall findings have been mixed. Moreover, much of this work is unguided by any specific theory that would serve to organize issues of why some people perceive themselves as being more likely objects of criminal justice sanctions and for whom such considerations are important in decisions to offend. To initiate such a theory, we have integrated classic work on deterrence, rational choice, and offending with contemporary work on the stratification of legal controls. In further demonstrating the psychometric structure of legal subjectivity, we provide an initial step in what we hope will be work that further accounts for the role of perceptions in deterrence processes and the more general rational choice structure of offending. Ultimately, such work should further theoretical development of the individual and structural contingencies that shape offending over the life course.

REFERENCES

Bachman, Ronet, Raymond Paternoster, and Sally Ward. 1992. "The Rationality of Sexual Offending: Testing a Deterrence/Rational Choice Conception of Sexual Assault." *Law and Society Review.* 26: 343–372.

Beccaria, Cesare. 1992 [1775]. *An Essay on Crimes and Punishment.* Boston: Branden. Publishing Company.

Becker, Gary. 1968. "Crime and Punishment: An Economic Approach." *Journal of Political Economy* 78:189–217

Bentler, Peter and Douglas Bonett. 1980. "Significance Test and Goodness of Fit in the Analysis of Covariance Structures." *Psychological Bulletin* 88: 588–606.

Berk, Richard, Alec Campbell, Ruth Klap, and Bruce Western. 1992. "The Deterrent Effect of Arrest in Incidents of Domestic Violence: A Bayesian Analysis of Four Field Experiments." *American Sociological Review* 57: 698–708.

Black, Donald. 1976. *The Behavior of Law.* New York: Academic Press.

———. 1989. *Sociological Justice.* New York: Oxford University Press

———. ed. 1984. *Toward a General Theory of Social Control.* New York: Academic Press.

Bollen, Kenneth. 1989. *Structural Equations with Latent Variables.* New York: Wiley.

Braithwaite, John. 1989. *Crime Shame, and Reintegration.* New York: Cambridge University Press.

Bridges, George and James Stone. 1986. "Effects of Criminal Punishment on Perceived Threat of Punishment: Toward an Understanding of Specific Deterrence." *Journal of Research in Crime and Delinquency* 23: 207–239.

Durkheim, Emile. 1984 [1893]. *The Division of Labor.* New York: Free Press.

Elliott, Delbert, David Huizinga, and Susan Ageton. 1985. *Explaining Delinquency and Drug Use.* Beverly Hills: Sage Publications.

Elliott, Delbert, David Huizinga, and Scott Menard. 1989. *Multiple Problem Youth: Delinquency, Substance Abuse, and Mental Health Problems.* New York: Springer-Verlag.

Erickson, Maynard, Jack Gibbs, and Gary Jensen. 1977. "The Deterrence Doctrine and the Perceived Certainty of Legal Punishments." *American Sociological Review.* 42: 305–317.

Gibbs, Jack. 1986. In *Deterrence theory and research: The law as a behavioral instrument: Nebraska Symposium on Motivation.* edited by Gary Melton. Lincoln: University of Nebraska Press

Gottfredson, Michael and Travis Hirschi. 1990. *A General Theory of Crime.* Stanford: Stanford University Press

Hagan, John. 1989. *Structural Criminology.* New Brunswick: Rutgers University Press.

Hecter, Michael and Satoshi Kanazawa. 1997. "Sociological Rational Choice Theory." *Annual Review of Sociology* 23: 191–214.

Hindelang, Michael, Travis Hirschi, and Joe Weis. 1981. *Measuring Delinquency.* Beverly Hills: Sage Publications.

Hirschi, Travis. 1969. *Causes of Delinquency. Berkeley.* University of California Press.

Horney, Julie and Ineke Marshall. 1992. "Risk Perceptions Among Serious Offenders: The Role of Crime and Punishment." *Criminology* 30: 575–594.

Jensen, Gary, Maynard Erickson, and Jack Gibbs. 1978. "Perceived Risk of Punishment and Self-reported Delinquency." *Social Forces.* 57: 57–78.

Keeton, George and George Swarzenberger. 1948. *Jeremy Bentham and the Law.* London: Stevens & Sons Limited.

Mack, Peter. 1969. edt. *A Bentham Reader.* New York: Pegasus.

Matsueda, Ross and William Bielby. 1986. "Statistical power in covariance structure modeling." in *Sociological Methodology,* 16:120–58.

Nagin, Daniel and Raymond Paternoster. 1993. "Enduring Individual Differences and Rational Choice Theories of Crime." *Law and Society Review* 27: 467–496.

———. 1994. "Personal Capital and Social Control: The Deterrence Implications of a Theory of Individual Differences in Criminal Offending." *Criminology* 32: 581–603.

Paternoster, Raymond and Alex Piquero. 1995. "Reconceptualizing Deterrence: An Empirical Test of Personal and Vicarious Experiences." *Journal of Research in Crime and Delinquency* 32: 251–286.

Pillavin, Irving, Rosemary Gartner, Craig Thorton, and Ross Matsueda. 1986. "Crime, Deterrence, and Rational Choice." *American Sociological Review* 51: 101–119.

Piquero, Alex and Raymond Paternoster. 1998. "An Application of Stafford and Warr's Reconceptualization of Deterrence to Drinking and Driving." *Journal of Research in Crime and Delinquency.* 35: 3–39.

Reiss, Albert. 1971. *The Police and the Public.* New Haven: Yale.

Sherman, Lawrence and Doug Smith. 1992. "Crime, Punishment, and Stake in Conformity: Legal and Informal Control of Domestic Violence." *American Sociological Review* 57: 680–690.

Stafford, Mark and Mark Warr. 1993. "A Reconceptualization of General and Specific Deterrence." *Journal of Research in Crime and Delinquency* 30: 123–135.

Tittle. Charles. 1980. *Sanctions and Social Deviance: The Question of Deterrence.* New York: Praeger.

Williams, Kirk and Richard Hawkins. 1992. "Wife Assault, Costs of Arrest, and the Deterrence Process." *Journal of Research in Crime and Delinquency* 29: 292–310.

Wilson James and Richard Herrnstein. 1985. *Crime and Human Nature.* New York: Simon and Schuster.

Contributors

Jean-Marc Assaad is a Doctoral Student, Department of Psychology, McGill University.

Brenda Sims Blackwell is Assistant Professor of Criminal Justice at Georgia State University.

Timothy Brezina is Assistant Professor of Sociology at Tulane University.

Ronald V. Clarke is Professor of Criminal Justice at Rutgers University.

Derek B. Cornish is Professor of Social Policy at the London School of Economics.

Francis T. Cullen is Professor of Criminal Justice at the University of Cincinnati.

G. David Curry is Professor of Criminology and Criminal Justice at the University of Missouri at St. Louis.

Scott H. Decker is Professor of Criminology and Criminal Justice at the University of Missouri at St. Louis.

Sarah Eschholz is Assistant Professor of Criminal Justice at Georgia State University.

M. Lyn Exum is Assistant Professor of Criminal Justice at the University of North Carolina at Charlotte.

Chris L. Gibson is a Doctoral student, Department of Criminal Justice, University of Nebraska, Omaha.

Matthew Hickman is a Doctoral Student, Department of Criminal Justice, Temple University.

Ross Macmillan is Assistant Professor of Sociology at the University of Minnesota.

Michael Massoglia is a Doctoral Student, Department of Sociology, the University of Minnesota.

Thomas B. Marvell, is Director, Justec Research Center in Williamsburg, Virginia.

Sharon Levrant Miceli is a Doctoral Student, Division of Criminal Justice, University of Cincinnati.

Jody Miller is Assistant Professor of Criminology and Criminal Justice at the University of Missouri at St. Louis.

Melissa M. Moon is Assistant Professor of Criminal Justice at Northern Kentucky University.

Raymond Paternoster is Professor of Criminology and Criminal Justice at the University of Maryland.

Alex R. Piquero is Associate Professor of Criminology and Sociology at the University of Florida.

Nicole Leeper Piquero is Assistant Professor of Criminology and Sociology at the University of Florida.

Travis C. Pratt is Assistant Professor of Criminal Justice at Rutgers University.

Sally S. Simpson is Associate Professor of Criminology and Criminal Justice at the University of Maryland.

Stephen G. Tibbetts is Assistant Professor of Criminal Justice at California State University, San Bernardino.

Kenneth D. Tunnell is Professor of Criminal Justice, Eastern Kentucky University.

Deanna L. Wilkinson is Assistant Professor of Criminal Justice at Temple University.

John Paul Wright is Assistant Professor of Criminal Justice at the University of Cincinnati.

Index